MANAGING CORPORATE SOCIAL RESPONSIBILITY IN ACTION

Corporate Social Responsibility Series

Series Editor:
Professor David Crowther, De Montfort University, Leicester, UK

This series aims to provide high quality research books on all aspects of corporate social responsibility including: business ethics, corporate governance and accountability, globalization, civil protests, regulation, responsible marketing and social reporting.

The series is interdisciplinary in scope and global in application and is an essential forum for everyone with an interest in this area.

Also in the series

The Employment Contract and the Changed World of Work
Stella Vettori
ISBN 978-0-7546-4754-4

The Cooperative Movement
Globalization from Below
Richard C. Williams
ISBN 978-0-7546-7038-4

Capitalist Networks and Social Power in Australia and New Zealand
Georgina Murray
ISBN 0 7546 4708 0

Stories, Visions and Values in Voluntary Organisations
Christina Schwabenland
ISBN 0 7546 4462 6

Whistleblowing and Organizational Social Responsibility
A Global Assessment
Wim Vandekerckhove
ISBN 0 7546 4750 1

Repoliticizing Management
A Theory of Corporate Legitimacy
Conor Cradden
ISBN 0 7546 4497 9

Managing Corporate Social Responsibility in Action
Talking, Doing and Measuring

Edited by

FRANK DEN HOND
Vrije Universiteit, The Netherlands

FRANK G.A. DE BAKKER
Vrije Universiteit, The Netherlands

PETER NEERGAARD
Copenhagen Business School, Denmark

ASHGATE

© Frank den Hond, Frank G.A. de Bakker and Peter Neergaard 2007

All rights reserved. No part of this publication may be reproduced, stored in a retrieval system or transmitted in any form or by any means, electronic, mechanical, photocopying, recording or otherwise without the prior permission of the publisher.

Frank den Hond, Frank G.A. de Bakker and Peter Neergaard have asserted their moral right under the Copyright, Designs and Patents Act, 1988, to be identified as the editors of this work.

Published by
Ashgate Publishing Limited
Gower House
Croft Road
Aldershot
Hampshire GU11 3HR
England

Ashgate Publishing Company
Suite 420
101 Cherry Street
Burlington, VT 05401-4405
USA

Ashgate website: http://www.ashgate.com

British Library Cataloguing in Publication Data
Managing corporate social responsibility in action :
    talking, doing and measuring. - (Corporate social
    responsibility series)
    1. Social responsibility of business
    I. Hond, Frank den II. Bakker, Frank G. A. III. Neergaard,
    Peter
    658.4'08

Library of Congress Cataloging-in-Publication Data
Managing corporate social responsibility in action : talking, doing and measuring / edited by Frank den Hond, Frank G.A. de Bakker and Peter Neergaard.
        p. cm. -- (Corporate social responsibility series)
    Includes index.
    ISBN 978-0-7546-4721-8
    1. Social responsibility of business. 2. Industrial management. I. Hond, Frank den. II. Bakker, Frank G.A. de. III. Neergaard, Peter.

    HD60.M3645 2007
    658.4'08--dc22
                                                                                2006039300

ISBN 978-0-7546-4721-8

Printed and bound in Great Britain by Antony Rowe Ltd, Chippenham, Wiltshire.

Contents

List of Figures	*vii*
List of Tables	*viii*
Notes on Contributors	*ix*
Foreword	*xi*
Acknowledgements	*xii*
List of Abbreviations	*xiii*

1 Introduction to Managing Corporate Social Responsibility in Action: Talking, Doing and Measuring
Frank den Hond, Frank G.A. de Bakker and Peter Neergaard   1

PART 1: TALKING: CSR IN DISCOURSE

2 The Making of Meaning in the Media: The Case of Corporate Social Responsibility in the *Financial Times*
Helena Buhr and Maria Grafström   15

3 The Commercialization of CSR: Consultants Selling Responsibility
Karolina Windell   33

4 Tracing the Evolution of Corporate Discourse on Corporate Social Responsibility: A Longitudinal, Lexicological Study
Frank G.A. de Bakker, Claes Ohlsson, Frank den Hond, Stefan Tengblad and Marie-France B. Turcotte   53

PART 2: DOING: CSR IN PRAXIS

5 The Bottom Line of CSR: A Different View
Esben Rahbek Pedersen and Peter Neergaard   77

6 Lost in Translation: The Case of Skandia's 'Ideas for Life'
Pauline Göthberg   93

7 'What about me?' The Importance of Understanding the Perspective of Non–Managerial Employees in Research on Corporate Citizenship
Elliot Wood   111

8   Exporting Knowledge and Values: A Discussion of Managerial
     Challenges when Attempting to Diffuse CSR across Company and
     National Borders
     Eirik J. Irgens and Harald Ness   127

PART 3: MEASURING: CSR IN SCALES

9   The Development of a CSR Industry: Legitimacy and Feasibility as the
     Two Pillars of the Institutionalization Process
     Aurélien Acquier and Franck Aggeri   149

10   Marketing Corporate Social Responsibility in a National Context:
     The Case of Social Rating Agencies in France
     Philippe Zarlowski   167

11   Superimposition or Continuity? Corporate Social Responsibility in
     Non–Profit Organizations
     Paolo Rossi   187

CONCLUSION

12   Managing Corporate Social Responsibility in Action: Reconciling
     Rhetorical Harmony and Practical Dissonance
     *Frank den Hond, Frank G.A. de Bakker, Peter Neergaard and
     Jean–Pascal Gond*   205

Bibliography   *227*
Index   *259*

List of Figures

2.1	Number of Articles in the *Financial Times* Containing the Term 'Corporate Social Responsibility', per year, 1984–2003	16
3.1	Categories of Consultants Selling CSR Services	38
3.2	Visual Accounts of CSR and Coexisting Labels	41
3.3	Sociogram of Consultants in Sweden, 2002–2003	47
5.1	The Bottom Line of Environmental Labelling	88
5.2	Environmental Labelling and Goal Achievement	89
6.1	The Development of Ideas for Life (IfL) Chronologically	106
7.1	A Framework for Analyzing CSR	122
9.1	Market Interdependencies in the CSR Field	155
9.2	A Typology of Standardization Initiatives	160
10.1	The Field of Social Rating Agencies in France	172

List of Tables

2.1	Themes and Terminology Associated with CSR in the Financial Times, 1999–2003	23
2.2	The Meaning of CSR as Conveyed in the *Financial Times*, 1999–2003	28
3.1	Rhetorical Strategies	43
4.1	Description of Dataset per Industry	60
4.2	Description of Dataset	61
4.3	Occurrence of CSR Discourse	63
4.4	Occurrence of Geographical Perspectives	67
4.5	Occurrence of Various Stakeholders	69
5.1	Motives for Addressing CSR	81
5.2	Companies' Motives for Adopting Environmental Labelling	83
5.3	Direct Costs and Organizational Barriers	84
5.4	Benefits of CSR	86
5.5	Benefits Achieved from Environmentally Labelled Products	87
8.1	The Export and Editing of CSR: Mapping from the Headquarter's Point of View	142
10.1	Corporate Governance Models	170
10.2	CSR in Discourses and Activities: Two Competing Views	182
11.1	Summary of the Main Motives, Strengths and Weaknesses Encountered by the Organizations in the MOSES Project	197

Notes on Contributors

Aurélien Acquier is an Associate Professor of Strategic Management at ESCP–EAP and an associate researcher at the Center for Organization and Management Science (CGS) of Ecole des Mines, Paris, France.

Franck Aggeri is an Assistant Professor of Management at the Center for Organization and Management Science (CGS) of Ecole des Mines de Paris, Paris, France.

Frank G.A. de Bakker is an Assistant Professor of Strategic Management at the Department of Public Administration and Organization Science and a research affiliate of the Centre for Innovation and Sustainable Entrepreneurship (CIMO), both at Vrije Universiteit, Amsterdam, the Netherlands.

Helena Buhr is a PhD student at the Department of Sociology, University of Michigan, United States of America.

Jean–Pascal Gond is a Lecturer at the International Centre for Corporate Social Responsibility, Nottingham University, Nottingham, United Kingdom.

Pauline Göthberg is a PhD student at the Department of Business Studies, Södertörns Högskola/Uppsala University, Huddinge, Sweden.

Maria Grafström is a PhD student at the Department of Business Studies, Uppsala University, Uppsala, Sweden.

Frank den Hond, is an Associate Professor of Strategic Management at the Department of Public Administration and Organization Science and a research affiliate of the Centre for Innovation and Sustainable Entrepreneurship (CIMO), both at Vrije Universiteit, Amsterdam, the Netherlands.

Eirik J. Irgens is an Associate Professor of Organizational Sociology at the Program for Management Studies, Nord–Trøndelag University College (HINT), Levanger, Norway, and an affiliated researcher at Learning Lab Denmark, The Danish University of Education, Copenhagen, Denmark.

Peter Neergaard is a Professor of Quality and Environmental Management at the Department of Operations Management, Copenhagen Business School, Frederiksberg, Denmark.

Harald Ness is an Associate Professor of Organizational Sociology at the Program for Management Studies, Nord–Trondelag University College (HINT), Levanger, Norway.

Claes Ohlsson is a PhD candidate at the Gothenburg Research Institute and the Departement of Swedish Language, Göteborg University, Göteborg, Sweden.

Esben Rahbek Pedersen is a post–doc at the Department of Operations Management, Copenhagen Business School, Frederiksberg, Denmark.

Paolo Rossi is a research fellow in Information Systems and Organizations at the Department of Sociology and Social Research, University of Trento, Trento, Italy.

Stefan Tengblad is an Associate Professor of Business Administration at the School of Business, Economics and Law, Göteborg University, Göteborg, Sweden.

Marie–France B. Turcotte is a Professor of Strategic Management at the École des Sciences de la Gestion, Université du Québec à Montréal, Montréal, Canada.

Karolina Windell is a PhD candidate at the Department of Business Studies, Uppsala University, Uppsala, Sweden.

Elliot Wood is a Lecturer in Organizational Psychology at the School of Psychology, The University of Western Australia, Perth, Australia.

Philippe Zarlowski is an Associate Professor at ESSEC Business School, Cergy–Pontoise, France.

Foreword

It's time to move the idea of CSR into the business mainstream. This can only happen when a broad range of business school faculty take on the task of showing how their disciplines can contribute to a better understanding of CSR. Corporate Social Responsibility (CSR), or even better, Corporate Stakeholder Responsibility (CSR), is about the practice of business. It is about how we create value and trade with each other. And, it is about the kinds of societies that we want to create and live in. In recent years, national governments, the European Commission, the United Nations, a number of NGOs, many business schools, and thousands of corporate executives have begun to turn their attention to this idea that capitalism is a vital part of civil society. Business is not now, and never has been inconsistent with thinking about how we remake our world to live better.

This is a very timely book by a distinguished set of interdisciplinary authors. Their broad range of backgrounds and experiences make this collection of essays especially timely. They represent an approach to CSR, while European in flavour, many can learn from it around the world. In particular their emphasis on "talking, doing, and measuring" grounds CSR in the world of practice. And, it is an approach that will work across societies, industries, and companies.

Amidst the global scandals in business, we have a moment that is worth seizing. We can be the generation that makes business and capitalism better, if we so choose. The scholars who have written the essays in this volume are committed to putting business, ethics, and society together into a conceptual whole that makes for better businesses and better civil societies.

R. Edward Freeman
The Darden School
University of Virginia
Charlottesville, VA. USA
6 November 2006

Acknowledgements

The editors would like to thank the following people for their assistance in reviewing book chapters:

Bastiaan van Apeldoorn, Vrije Universiteit, Amsterdam, the Netherlands
Ariane Berthoin–Antal, Social Science Research Centre, Berlin, Germany
Hervé Corvellec, Lund University, Helsingborg, Sweden
Peter Dobers, Mälardalen University, Västerås, Sweden
Fernanda Duarte, University of Western Sydney, Sydney, Australia
Carolyn Egri, Simon Fraser University, Burnaby, Canada
Dick de Gilder, Vrije Universiteit, Amsterdam, the Netherlands
Jean–Pascal Gond, Nottingham University, Nottingham, United Kingdom
Tobias Hahn, Institute for Futures Studies and Technology Assessment, Berlin, Germany
Heledd Jenkins, University of Cardiff, Cardiff, United Kingdom
Joanne Lawrence, INSEAD, Fontainebleau, France
Peter Malkjaer, Copenhagen Business School, Copenhagen, Denmark
Enno Masurel, Vrije Universiteit, Amsterdam, the Netherlands
Esben Rahbek Pedersen, Copenhagen Business School, Copenhagen, Denmark
Hanna Pesonen, University of Jyväskylä, Jyväskylä, Finland
Anton Plesner, Copenhagen Business School, Copenhagen, Denmark
Michael Jay Polonsky, University of Victoria, Melbourne, Australia
Annette Risberg, Copenhagen Business School, Copenhagen, Denmark
André Sobczak, Audencia Nantes École de Management, Nantes, France
Laura Spencer, Brunel Business School, Uxbridge, United Kingdom
Peter Stanwick, Auburn University, Auburn, USA
Klaasjan Visscher, University of Twente, Enschede, the Netherlands

List of Abbreviations

B2B	Business to Business
B2C	Business to Consumer
BITC	Business in the Community
BPR	Business Process Reengineering
CEO	Chief Executive Officer
CFP	Corporate Financial Performance
CSP	Corporate Social Performance
CSR	Corporate Social Responsibility
DJSI	Dow Jones Sustainability Index
DM	Diversity Management
EC	European Commission
EMS	Environmental Management System
FRR	Fonds de Réserve des Retraites
GRI	Global Reporting Initiative
ILO	International Labour Organization
MBO	Management by Objectives
MNC	Multinational Company
NGO	Non–Governmental Organization
NHO	Confederation of Norwegian Business and Industry
NPM	New Public Management
NPO	Non–Profit Organization
QC	Quality Circle
SEC	Securities and Exchange Commission
SME	Small and Medium–sized Enterprises
SRI	Socially Responsible Investment
TQM	Total Quality Management
UN	United Nations
USD	US dollars
WBCSD	World Business Council for Sustainable Development

Chapter 1

Introduction to Managing Corporate Social Responsibility in Action: Talking, Doing and Measuring

Frank den Hond, Frank G.A. de Bakker and Peter Neergaard

Introduction

As early as in the 18th century, companies have acted in socially responsible manners by building houses and schools for their employees and their children (Cannon 1994, Carroll and Buchholtz 1999). Michell (1989) traced the emergence of corporate social responsibility as a concept back to the 1920s. He sees the discussion as an ideological movement to legitimize the power of large corporations. However, since the mid 1990s, political and public debates about the social responsibilities of firms have gained renewed force. Increasing numbers of companies are beginning to realize that they can no longer ignore the moral expectations society places on them. Many firms are working to deal with a variety of often inconsistent and conflicting norms and demands placed upon them. They struggle with the question of how to define their role as good corporate citizens. They respond to societal demands by endorsing standards, adopting a code of conduct, or reporting on social or environmental performance according to norms proposed by the Global Reporting Initiative (GRI) or the AA 1000 framework.

Various types of actors have assumed increasingly important roles in influencing the demands and norms that define socially acceptable corporate behaviour: not only national governments, but also supra–national bodies such as the United Nations and the European Union, and various non–corporate actors in the civil society. They stimulate firms to increase transparency on social issues, require them to disband detested practices, push them to adopt other practices that are more 'socially beneficial', and urge national governments to define and enforce minimum standards of corporate social responsibility (CSR). CSR has thus become an important concept on the public agenda and continues to be a topic of interest in different spheres of society. In parallel, the concept has also gained a prominent position in academic work, both by theory–oriented scholars, such as in business ethics (Carroll 1999; Joyner and Payne 2002; Zadek 1998) and management (Lockett, Moon and Visser 2006; Whetten, Rands and Godfrey 2002), as well as by practice–oriented scholars, as shown for instance by the many studies on different 'business and society' initiatives (Austin 2000; Selsky and Parker 2005).

This development reflects a broader trend to see business and society as being interwoven. It is increasingly argued that firms need to manage their social responsibilities to remain legitimate. The CSR literature contains a broad array of suggestions on how to organize CSR (for example De Bakker, Groenewegen and Den Hond 2005; Epstein and Roy 2001; Lockett, Moon and Visser 2006). However, the question of how to manage CSR in specific situations remains quite poorly addressed, as different firms face different problems and opt for different solutions. Although sometimes the CSR concept seems to be a well-defined, unequivocal concept, in its diverse applications the concept loses much of its definitional pertinence. 'The term is a brilliant one; it means something, but not always the same thing, to everybody' (Votaw 1973: 11).

How could such a popular and seemingly well–received concept cause so much confusion, and what could firms learn from insights in different management practices? In the opening volume of this series on CSR, Crowther and Rayman-Bacchus (2004b: 14) stated that their aim was 'to present a spectrum of approaches from a variety of scholars from different countries and from different disciplines in order to show the diversity of the debate and the diversity of contributors.' In this volume, we build on this diversity in practices. The contributions in this volume focus on different aspects of managing CSR *in action* to capture differences in discourses and practices around CSR. What are firms *talking* about when they mention CSR? What are they *doing*? And what is the role of *measuring*? Before introducing the chapters in the three main parts of this volume, we briefly review the debate on CSR and discuss its current popularity.

The Changing Popularity of CSR

A wide variety of corporate practices has been developed under the vignette of CSR, most often in reference to acts of responsibility. Etymologically, to be responsible is to be answerable (Lucas 1993), to be able and willing to answer. As a matter of moral principle, being or acting 'responsible' is good. But things change once the principle is turned into practice. Immediately, many questions rise, for example regarding the realm for which responsibility is to be assumed, and the manners by which it is to be expressed. And things get worse once multiple responsibilities towards different stakeholders have to be addressed, all the more so if these responsibilities are incompatible or conflicting. Indeed, various corporate audiences express different expectations regarding how firms should assume their social responsibilities. The differences between principle and praxis are all the more visible once the CSR debate is examined at different levels of abstraction. If the CSR debate is examined at a high level of abstraction, there are two different positions. These are (1) firms do not *and* should not have any social responsibilities beyond maximizing shareholder value (Friedman 1962; Jensen 2002), versus, (2) firms do have such responsibilities and should act accordingly (Quazi and O'Brien 2000; Roberts 2003).

According to the first position 'the social responsibility of business is to increase profits' (Friedman 2001: 29). 'The business of business is business' is an often used quote from Friedman. Jensen further elaborates this viewpoint by stating that

'200 years' worth of work in economics and finance indicate that social welfare is maximized when all firms in an economy maximize total firm value' (2002: 239). In this perspective any investments in CSR will be theft of shareholders' money. The position is firmly based in contractual theory. The argument is often repeated in the business press that a particular company is striving to maximize shareholder return.

The second position states that companies, because of the impact they have, should act socially responsible. Although within this position there is some variety in concepts, definitions, and interpretations (Carroll 1999; van Marrewijk 2003), fundamentally, concepts such as corporate social responsibility, corporate social performance, stakeholder management, corporate citizenship, business virtue, business ethics, or corporate sustainability all are manifestations of one and the same underlying position, namely that corporate decisions have moral consequences and that therefore corporate decision makers should consider the moral consequences of their decisions (Freeman 1994).

However, the two positions are less conflicting if the former is reformulated to stress the firm's obligation to act socially responsible if doing so maximizes shareholder value, and if the latter is believed, as many observers have suggested, to result in outcomes beneficial to the firm, if not in the short term, then at least in the long term. The claim has often been made that firms practicing CSR are more successful than others, for instance in terms of financial performance (Orlitzky, Schmidt and Rynes 2003; Waddock and Graves 1997). Companies that meet the expectations of stakeholders and society at large are expected to gain a competitive advantage over other firms (Sinding 2000). If this is the case, there would not be a conflict between the practice of CSR and maximizing shareholder value. Because creating value for shareholders seems to be dominant for management today, 'many contemporary advocates of CSR have implicitly accepted Friedman's position that the primary responsibility of companies is to create wealth for their shareholders' (Vogel 2005: 27). For that reason, business is turning to the research community to provide the 'business case' for CSR. However, attempts to provide evidence for a positive correlation between CSR and financial performance have not been that successful up till now (Margolis and Walsh 2003).

Expressions of the position that companies should act responsible are plentiful: the overview in Appendix 1.1 displays an apparent consensus among governments, leading firms, and NGOs about the abstract principle that firms should behave responsibly towards their social, economic, and physical environments.

If it is the case that indeed greater responsiveness to stakeholder demands leads to increased financial performance and competitive advantage, at least for some firms in some situations, then it is understandable that firms would like to retain control over how and to what extent they invest in CSR. Thus, it has been suggested that self-regulation in CSR may provide win-win-win solutions for both companies, regulatory authorities and society at large (Elkington 1994; Porter and Van der Linde 1995; Neergaard and Pedersen 2003):

- *firms* see advantage in self–regulation because it prevents them from public regulation and outside pressure from various stakeholders;

- *regulatory authorities* see advantage in self–regulation because it reduces the need to implement unpopular and costly command and control policies;

- *society* sees advantage in self–regulation through CSR because it results in social and environmental standards that exceed the requirements of government regulation.

Nevertheless, there is debate and struggle once it comes to the implementation of this broad consensus in specific situations. For example, in the UN *Global Compact*, policymakers, businesses and some NGOs signed a set of principles concerning environmental protection, labour rights and human rights (Kell 2003), but this initiative also was met with criticism from other NGOs (Hoedeman 2002), as is the entire concept of CSR (Christian Aid 2004; Corporate Watch 2006). Apparently, consensus exists regarding the fact that principles of responsibility are important in a business setting, but disagreement arises once it comes to practicing such a principle. For instance, as Fauset (2006, II) of Corporate Watch argued: 'Ultimately, CSR is not a step towards a more fundamental reform of the corporate structure but a distraction from it. Exposing and rejecting CSR is a step towards addressing corporate power.'

From a historical perspective, there are striking parallels between the current and earlier debates. Publications on CSR have been around since at least the 1950s (Carroll 1999). At that time, the debate was centred on the same two positions identified above. Authors such as Bowen (1953) and Davis (1960) held a pro–social responsibility position, whereas Levitt (1958) and especially Friedman (1962) are still cited today for the strong stance they took to defend the opposite position. Since then, much research has been done to provide support for the moral superiority of the pro–responsibility position, as well as to prove its instrumental value in creating long–term economic profits to firms. The proliferation of concepts that Carroll (1999) refers to can be interpreted as a consequence of the ongoing attempts to increase the plausibility of the moral legitimacy and the instrumental value of this pro–responsibility position (de Bakker et al. 2005; Rowley and Berman 2000).

These developments leave the CSR debate in a curious position. On the one hand, at a general and abstract level of discourse, consensus seems to have been established regarding the relevance of addressing issues of corporate responsibility. Some criticisms have been raised at this level, both from neo–liberals – if CSR is not hypocrisy, it is at best nothing more than a reconfirmation of the benefits of self–regulation in a free market context – and anti–capitalists – if CSR is not hypocrisy, it is at its worst nothing more than the empty promise of the illusory benefits of self–regulation in a free market context. On the other hand, at the more concrete level of implementing CSR in a specific context, many different interpretations of CSR seem to be around. Once it is put into practice, the seemingly single–faced concept of CSR breaks down into a concept that is variegated, sundry, and fragmented.

The overall question that we seek to address in this volume therefore can be formulated as how we can make sense of this difference. By presenting a collection of studies, we want to come to terms with this remarkable difference by scrutinizing in three subsequent parts: the abstract discourse in which CSR is given a broad and general meaning, a number of contexts in which CSR is actually implemented and thus obtains a locally circumscribed meaning, and finally the way that measuring and measures of CSR form a connection between the general and the specific, the global and the local meanings of CSR. As there is both a broadly shared understanding of the overall concept of CSR, as well as a range of contextual differences that emerges upon the implementation of the concept in particular contexts, the question rises how the two observations are connected. We address this question by comparing and contrasting the meaning of CSR, or of what is presented in its name, in various contexts, thereby subscribing to a form of discourse analysis, which is based on 'the structured and systematic study of collections of interrelated texts and processes of their production, dissemination, and consumption' (Phillips 2002: 24). Applying such a discursive approach allows us to gain an understanding of how the CSR concept is given meaning in interaction. How do interrelating actors together shape and modify a sense of what could be regarded as socially responsible corporate behaviour? The first two parts of this volume address such questions, but at different levels of analysis. The third part of the volume concerns elements of CSR measurement, as measuring CSR, and making CSR measurable, play critical roles in any attempts to reconcile the gap between the abstract discourse and its meaning in praxis. After all, it is through measurement that definitions and practices are reinforced and legitimated. The overall analysis in these three parts thus delivers a rich understanding of the mixed endorsement of CSR among firms, governments and NGOs, and the ways in which different actors are involved in shaping CSR, and thereby provides a better understanding of the actual implementation of this important concept.

Part 1 – Talking: CSR in Discourse

From observing the CSR debate, one gets the impression that representations of CSR are highly similar (see also Appendix 1.1). Whether one considers policy documents, corporate statements, or some NGO claims; they all use similar language, make similar claims and express similar ideas. In that sense, CSR has characteristics of a popular management concept, such as 'total quality management', 'business process re–engineering' or 'new public management'. They all address some general concern to management (such as: quality, cost control, or in the case of CSR, social legitimacy) in a combined problem–solution package, with general relevance for many firms across a wide range of industries and countries, and whose adoption by managers adds to their reputation of being 'good', that is modern and rational, managers (Abrahamson 1991). New concepts and catchy abbreviations provide consultants with new services to sell to companies. As Peters recently claimed: 'Social responsibility is good capitalism. Or, put the other way, good capitalism is socially responsible' (2004: 215). Although anti-capitalist critics maintain that 'CSR enables business to propose ineffective, voluntary, market-based solutions to social and environmental crises under guise of being responsible' (Fauset 2006: II), the concept has become quite popular. How did this apparent conceptual homogeneity come about, how is it reinforced and can it be observed across different national settings? The first part of this volume focuses on the CSR discourse at a broad, general level of analysis. Three chapters discuss how CSR is represented in different contexts by analysing CSR–related discourses in the business press and in corporate annual reports, as well as the role of consultants in the construction and diffusion of CSR.

Buhr and Grafström ask how the CSR concept spread and gained legitimacy. Their take is original in considering the role of print media in legitimating the CSR discourse. They analyze how CSR is represented in the *Financial Times*. Buhr and Grafström subscribe to the view that the business press is an important arena for the development and diffusion of CSR. Within this arena, management models, including CSR, are shaped, edited and translated. By assessing how the content of CSR was constructed within and by this influential newspaper, they contribute to understanding the process of agenda–setting of CSR in a business context.

Windell discusses how consultants in Sweden contributed to the construction and spread of CSR and how they created a market for CSR services. Central in her chapter is a distinction between two types of consultants, the so-called world–saviours and the money–makers, reflecting both the ethical and instrumental motive to CSR. Both types of consultants have very different ideas about what CSR encompasses. By viewing consultants as agenda–setters and institutional entrepreneurs, Windell discusses how different societal expectations and demands are put forward by different actors and packaged under a new label, CSR, by consultants. Yet, the worldviews of the two types of consultants influences what exactly gets packaged under the label, depending on whether the consultants seek to promote other interests than commercial ones alone.

De Bakker et al. conclude the first part of this volume. Through a longitudinal, lexicological study they analyze how major stock–listed companies in Sweden, the Netherlands, and Canada represent the relationship of their firms with the social, economic and natural environments in their annual reports over time. The analysis of De Bakker et al. is based on ten–year intervals to track changes. The chapter makes clear that dramatic changes occurred in representations in annual reports, as is testified by the joint emergence of terms such as 'sustainability' and 'environment' as examples of a developing CSR discourse, by the increased use of a term like 'globalization', and by the simultaneous decrease in terms referring to a national political and economic discourse, such as national authorities or trade unions.

Although some variation is visible, at the discourse level, the suggestion of homogeneity of the CSR concept thus can be confirmed, as is the tenet of the first part of this volume. However, the same level of homogeneity is not to be expected once CSR is actually implemented in specific contexts of place and time. Once talking shifts to doing, different contexts in which firms operate therefore become more influential. CSR as a management concept to effectively deal with different pressures is thus likely to result in varying outcomes. This is the topic of the second part of this volume.

Part 2 – Doing: CSR in Praxis

The second part of this volume addresses the contexts in which CSR is advanced and developed in praxis. There are several reasons why one would expect CSR in practice to differ from the abstract discourse. For example, when viewed as a management concept, the diffusion thereof into local praxis requires a process of translation, which usually includes subtle modifications that render the concept suitable to a specific context by taking in or leaving out some details (Czarniawska and Sevón 1996; Sahlin-Andersson and Engwall 2002a). Specifically, firms have different stakeholders and face diverging social and environmental challenges, depending for instance on the nature and location of their operations. They are hence likely to experience different stakeholder pressures (Wood 1991). The context of the companies plays a central role in explaining the actual behaviour of firms regarding CSR. Not only the discursive struggle is important to grasp how companies consider CSR, but also the specific context in which CSR is implemented can shape or modify the concept. In implementing CSR, different social and environmental strategies are available to companies but the options are likely to differ among countries, industries and companies. Although institutional settings have shown to affect firms' interaction with government and other stakeholders at the macro level, the four chapters in this part suggest that there are even more dimensions along which companies differ in making operational CSR.

Pedersen and Neergaard argue that the notorious measurement problems and the heterogeneous nature of CSR make it highly unlikely that academics and practitioners will ever be able to give a definitive answer to the question of why companies engage in CSR practices. However, it might be possible to reach some kind of consensus on some of the typical costs and benefits associated with CSR. Companies then have to make their own judgments as to whether the perceived benefits from implementing CSR are likely to exceed the costs, keeping in mind that economic benefits are not the only issue relevant for companies. The chapter presents some of the most frequently raised motives, costs, benefits and barriers that companies face when they plan and implement social and environmental improvements.

When addressing issues related to CSR in practice, the focus often is on the role of management. Wood shifts this focus to consider the non-managerial employee. Building on role theory, he views a firm's engagement in CSR practices as acts of corporate redefinition, and then explores the personal understanding of such a corporate redefinition by individual employees. More specifically, he poses the question of what might be the individual consequences of voluntary work as a form of CSR. He suggests that the way voluntary work is presented to employees makes a significant difference in how they perceive such work. Consequently, divergence in the efficacy of CSR programs among firms may partly be explained by differences in (internal) representations as non-managerial employees are highly influential in the day-to-day implementation of CSR.

Another example of the variation in practices might be found within multinational firms. Irgens and Ness studied a Norwegian firm that observed a spectacular growth from being a small, nationally operating firm in 1962 to a transnational company with many subsidiaries today. The focus of their chapter is to what extent, during this expansion process, the CSR policies and practices of the Norwegian operations were transferred to the firm's international operations. These authors turn to institutional theory and organizational learning perspectives to seek for explanations for the challenges encountered in creating a corporate-wide standard for CSR and thus in exporting knowledge and values across a wide variety of subsidiaries.

Variation in practices can also develop over time. In the final chapter of this part, Göthberg presents a longitudinal study of a special department within the Swedish insurance company Skandia. In recent years, the department has been presented as the corporate department for CSR activities, but in earlier stages of its existence the department has fulfilled different roles. Apparently, the department is a very versatile tool for the company's management in offering a tailored solution to the different stakeholder demands in different periods in time, a situation that the author compares to Cohen, March and Olson's (1972) 'garbage can' model. This chapter therefore provides an insight in how a company is able to relate, or even re-label, its practices to new societal demands such as CSR. In a sense, re-labelling could also be seen as a matter of discourse rather than practice. We chose to include this chapter in this part of the volume as the re-labelling seems to go beyond selling old wine in new bottles. As for all these practices, the proof of the pudding is in the eating. To determine whether these practices achieve any of their objectives, some form of measurement is required. It is the topic for the third part of the volume.

Part 3 – Measuring: CSR in Scales

Talking about CSR and practicing the concept in one form or another increasingly is supplemented with reporting on any CSR–related activities and the progress therein. In fact, the measurement of CSR might well play a mediating role between the *talking* and *doing* as conceptual definitions are contrasted with practices. It is in the measurement of CSR and rating of CSR performance that ex ante expectations are confronted with actual practices. The final set of chapters therefore addresses social reporting practices and standards. By presenting insights in how such reporting and rating practices have developed, some ways of reconciling talking and doing are highlighted.

Acquier and Aggeri argue that the broad consensus on the need for companies to report on non–financial performance has created new markets in which a number of 'prescribers' – organizations that offer services to assist firms in reporting their non–financial performance – compete for market share. This competition in what the authors call the 'CSR reporting industry' is a strong driver in the development of the CSR concept, convincing potential clients of the need to use the services they provide. In developing their argument, Acquier and Aggeri combine insights from two streams of literature, neo-institutional theory and collective learning theory, which allows them to address the gap between rhetoric and reality.

Zarlowski focuses on the situation in one country, addressing the emergence of CSR rating agencies in France. Such agencies are intermediaries between companies expected to disclose information on their social responsibilities and, on the other hand, investors and other stakeholders such as customers and the general public. The role of such agencies is to collect, analyze, interpret, synthesize and diffuse information about the social performance of companies. In the transformation from discourse to practical implementation, such agencies thus play an important role in defining CSR, acting as information gatekeepers and as standard setters, hence influencing the actual shaping of CSR. Understanding the role of these agencies thus is instrumental in understanding the different forms of CSR in action. Moreover, this chapter also illustrates that a concept such as CSR needs to be framed to fit with its specific institutional context. Some translation from a universal concept to a specific application is required in accordance with the arguments in second part of the volume.

Finally, many rating agencies in the CSR reporting industry focus on larger firms as potential clients. Rossi therefore takes on the question how social reporting in small not–for–profit organizations differs from that in for–profit organizations. The way these organizations organize their reporting and accounting practices reflects a variety of approaches and interpretations concerning CSR. Partly through participatory research, Rossi investigated how several social reporting initiatives in small organizations were developed and implemented. From his observations, he developed a taxonomy to understand the differences encountered. This taxonomy is based on two dimensions: the level of stakeholder engagement and the type of data applied in reporting (that is, data generated ad hoc versus existing data).

Concluding Remarks

The collection of chapters gathered in this volume offers new insights and plenty ideas and leads for further research, highlighting differences between talking, doing and measuring CSR and related concepts, but also providing suggestions to overcome the difficulties that arise around CSR in action. It would be too early to make any detailed inferences on the findings presented in the chapters in this introductory chapter; we encourage you to read the rich accounts we brought together in this volume. However, in the final chapter, we will indeed provide an analysis of the collected findings.

To give you a 'sneak preview' of that chapter, we will suggest that the first set of chapters (Part 1) does indeed confirm homogeneity in the CSR concept, at least in the various examples drawn from a European context. The set also demonstrates a high level of correspondence with the much older American debate on CSR. The set of praxis chapters (Part 2) shows that differences do exist in CSR in action. Heterogeneity is observed, for instance along a larger number of dimensions than currently found in most of the literature. Reasons for this observation could be found in the translation of CSR as somewhere in the late 1980s, the CSR concept may well have been imported into Europe from the United States. This happened, not only because CSR was seen as a part of a solution to country–specific problems, but also as a corollary to the advent of economic globalization. It can also be seen as the downsizing of the public sector and deregulation, spreading from the USA to Europe (Neergaard and Pedersen 2003). 'Translation' did not so much occur at the level of the abstract yet programmatic concept, but all the more so in its adoption in specific contexts (Part 2), as well as in the development of different scales to measure and compare organizations' levels of CSR (Part 3). Our argument will be completed by suggesting how measuring CSR is a connection between these two levels, not as an instrument of translation, but as a post hoc attempt to reconcile the diversity found in praxis with the overall abstract concept. We conclude the final chapter by advancing the proposition that, because of all this, it is very unlikely that any attempt to homogenize CSR at the practical level will be successful, and we point out some of the problems that might emerge if such attempts are nevertheless pursued.

Appendix 1.1 Selected CSR Definitions

Amnesty International (Amnesty International, 'What is Corporate Social Responsibility (CSR)?', <http://www.amnesty.ie/user/content/view/full/770/>, accessed 19 September 2006)

'Transnational corporations have a massive scope of influence – from business executives in Dublin to assembly line workers in Jakarta to shoppers along the Champs Elysee, millions of people are daily effected by the practices, dealings, and guiding philosophies of transnational corporations.

With such a wide sphere of influence comes a significant amount of responsibility, especially when it comes to human rights. Corporations can impact human rights in a plethora of ways – by operating in areas of conflict, financially supporting oppressive regimes, by not adhering to international labour standards, and by using subcontractors that abuse human rights. "Corporate Social Responsibility" is a philosophy of ethical business whereby all corporate decisions are made with the utmost respect and concern for human rights.'

Christian Aid (Christian Aid 2004: 5)

'Christian Aid defines Corporate Social Responsibility – CSR – as an entirely voluntary, corporate-led initiative to promote self-regulation as a substitute for regulation at either national or international level. CSR is a catch-all term increasingly used by business, which encompasses the voluntary codes, principles and initiatives companies adopt in their general desire to confine corporate responsibility to self-regulation. Increasingly, corporate self–regulation in the form of CSR is also being embraced beyond the business world by, among others, governments, and multilateral institutions such as the World Bank and UN.'

CSR Europe (CSR Europe, 'Corporate Social Responsibility', <http://www.valuebasedmanagement.net/organizations_csr.html>, accessed 19 September 2006)

'By sharing experience and enhancing the capacity of current and future managers, CSR Europe member companies are committed to promote the following principles as part of achieving business success:

- Conduct business responsibly by contributing to the economic health and sustainable development of the communities in which we operate.

- Offer its employees healthy and safe working conditions, ensure fair compensation, good communication as well as equal opportunity for employment and development.
- Offer quality, safe products and services at competitive prices, meet customers' needs promptly and accurately and work responsibly with our business partners.
- Minimise the negative impacts our activities can have on the environment and its resources, while striving to provide our customers with products and services that take sustainable consumption into account.
- Be accountable to key stakeholders through dialogue and transparency regarding the economic, social and environmental impacts of our business activities.
- Operate a good governance structure and upholds the highest standards in business ethics.
- Provide a fair return to our shareholders while fulfilling the above principles.'

European Commission (EC 2001: 5)

'Corporate social responsibility is essentially a concept whereby companies decide voluntarily to contribute to a better society and a cleaner environment.'

International Finance Corporation (IFC, member of the World Bank Group, <http://www.ifc.org/ifcext/economics.nsf/Content/CSR-IntroPage>, accessed 10 October 2005)

'Corporate social responsibility is the commitment of businesses to contribute to sustainable economic development by working with employees, their families, the local community and society at large to improve their lives in ways that are good for business and for development.'

International Standards Organization (ISO 2004: 27–28)

'OSR [Organizational Social Responsibility] is taken to mean a balanced approach for organizations to address economic, social and environmental issues in a way that aims to benefit people, communities and society.'

MVO Platform (Dutch Platform on CSR: 'CSR frame of reference', July 2003, <http://www.mvo-platform.nl/>, accessed 29 March 2006)

'CSR is much more than a mere involvement in social affairs (for example through neighbourhood improvement projects) and charity – no matter how praiseworthy such causes may be. Such actions cannot be seen as an alternative for responsible economic, social and ecological behaviour in a company's core business. Corporations should do everything within their power to enable and promote CSR throughout the value-creation chain that they are part of. CSR is a process in which corporations take responsibility for the social, ecological and economic consequences of their actions – throughout their product and service delivery chains – making themselves accountable, and engaging in a dialogue with all those involved.'

United Nations Conference on Trade and Development (UNCTAD 1999: 1)

'Corporate social responsibility concerns how business enterprises relate to, and impact upon, a society's needs and goals. All societal groups are expected to perform certain roles and functions that can change over time with a society's own evolution. Expectations related to business enterprises, and particularly TNCs [transnational corporations], are undergoing unusually rapid change due to the expanded role these enterprises play in a globalizing society. Discussions relating to TNC social responsibility standards and performance therefore comprises an important component of efforts to develop a stable, prosperous and just global society.'

UN Global Compact (Global Compact, 'About the Global Compact', <http://www.unglobalcompact.org/AboutTheGC/index.html, accessed 9 March 2007)

'Through the power of collective action, the Global Compact seeks to advance responsible corporate citizenship so that business can be part of the solution to the challenges of globalization. In this way, the private sector – in partnership with other social actors – can help realize the Secretary-General's vision: a more sustainable and inclusive global economy.'

World Business Council on Sustainable Development (WBCSD, <http://www.wbcsd.ch/templates/TemplateWBCSD1/layout.asp?type=p&MenuId=MzI3&doOpen=1&ClickMenu=LeftMenu>, accessed 8 October 2004)

'The commitment of business to contribute to sustainable economic development, working with employees, their families, the local community and society at large to improve their quality of life.'

PART 1
Talking: CSR in Discourse

Chapter 2

The Making of Meaning in the Media: The Case of Corporate Social Responsibility in the *Financial Times*

Helena Buhr and Maria Grafström[1]

Introduction

Recent studies of organizational and institutional theory have stressed the impact of business media on managerial trends and fashions (Alvarez, Mazza and Strandgaard Pedersen 2005; Sahlin-Andersson and Engwall 2002a). In our chapter, we add to this discussion by analyzing how the business press ascribes meaning to the concept of corporate social responsibility (CSR). Since the late 1990s, interest in CSR has expanded rapidly and CSR is increasingly regarded as a natural component of good management (Margolis and Walsh 2003). Several studies have stressed how the meaning of CSR has been shaped by various individuals and organizations, such as non-governmental organizations (NGOs) (Henriques 2001; Ruggie 2004), consumers (Micheletti 2003), investors (Schueth 2003), governments and international governmental organizations (Kell 2003), consultants (Windell this volume), and firms themselves (de Bakker, Ohlsson, den Hond, Tengblad and Turcotte this volume). Conspicuously absent from the literature, however, is consideration of the role of the business media in shaping the meaning of CSR.

In this chapter we address this gap by exploring how business media texts ascribe meaning to CSR. Building on earlier institutional studies of the impact of texts and rhetorical patterns on managerial and organizational trends (Abrahamson and Fairchild 1999; Lawrence and Phillips 2004; Phillips, Lawrence and Hardy 2004; Suddaby and Greenwood 2005), we demonstrate how articles in the business press contribute to shaping the meaning of a new management concept. Specifically, we investigate how the British newspaper, the *Financial Times*, one of the most widely distributed and influential business media organizations in Europe, ascribes meaning to the CSR concept. Our analysis covers articles from 1988 to 2003; in particular, we focus on the years 1999–2003, the period when the *Financial Times*' interest in CSR mounted and debate about the concept was intense (see Figure 2.1). Until

---

1 The authors are grateful for comments and challenging questions from the editors, from Kerstin Sahlin-Andersson, Stefan Jonsson and the other participants in the GEMS project; and from the participants in track 18 at the 2004 EGOS conference in Ljubljana, Slovenia.

1998, the newspaper rarely referred to the term 'corporate social responsibility' or its abbreviation, 'CSR'. A few years later, in year 2002, interest in CSR peaked and the *Financial Times* published over 100 articles per year about the topic.

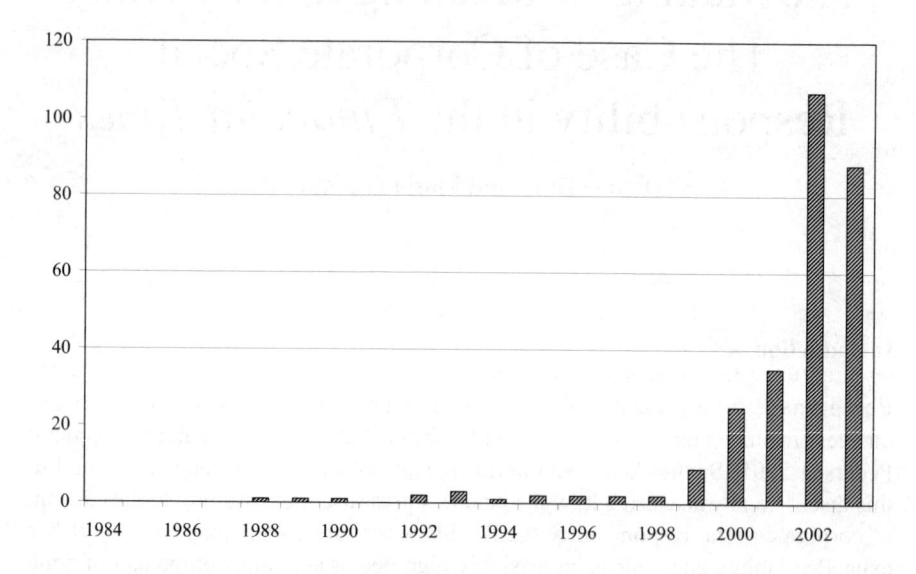

Figure 2.1 Number of Articles in the *Financial Times* Containing the Term 'Corporate Social Responsibility', per year, 1984–2003

In the first part of our chapter, we briefly review the literature concerning managerial trends and meaning, with a particular focus on the impact of the business press. In the second part, we describe the data and research method, while in the third, we analyze our empirical findings concerning the meaning of CSR as conveyed in the *Financial Times*. Finally, we present the conclusions and discuss the implications of our study for broader concerns about the business press and the meaning of managerial concepts.

Managerial Trends and Meaning

The question of how the meaning of CSR is created and shaped in the business press relates to a broader debate about the socially constructed nature of management. The theoretical foundation of this chapter is grounded in the institutional research tradition and the argument that management represents a response, not only to an organization's technical requirements, but also to more general historical and cultural processes. Scholars in the field of institutional analysis have devoted extensive attention to how the definition of 'management' has varied over time. In particular, several studies have examined the emergence and spread of management models, such as Total Quality Management (TQM) (Zbaracki 1998), quality circles

(Abrahamson 1996; Abrahamson and Fairchild 1999), and New Public Management (NPM) (Christensen and Laegreid 2002). CSR – a concept which gained in prominence in the 1960s, declined in the 1980s, but has recently boomed in the late 1990s – is an interesting example of a managerial trend (see the chapters by den Hond, de Bakker and Neergaard, and Göthberg in this volume).

Understanding management as historically contingent has raised challenging questions as to why the definition of management changes over time and how emerging management trends gain legitimacy. Earlier studies of management trends have singled out various factors that drive the diffusion of management ideas and force organizations to adopt similar structures. Particularly well-known is the framework of DiMaggio and Powell (1983), which stresses coercive, normative, and mimetic mechanisms as explanations for why managerial ideas diffuse.

Yet, despite the attention paid to how and why management concepts are disseminated, we know little of the process by which the *meaning* of a new trend forms. Recent studies have stressed the importance of devoting more attention to this research topic (Abrahamson and Fairchild 1999). 'Meaning' refers to a collective belief system consisting of definitions, categories, symbols, and means–ends relationships. Meaning underlies all social practices and is particularly important in explaining macro structures, such as the organization of markets and industries (Mohr forthcoming). Moreover, meaning is constitutive, so in this context is closely related to the mechanisms that explain why certain management ideas become widely diffused and institutionalized. Managerial concepts gain meaning through theorization processes; they are de-contextualized from their original setting and rationalized as universal ideas (Czarniawska and Sevón 1996, 2005a; Greenwood, Suddaby and Hinings 2002; Røvik 2002; Sahlin-Andersson 1996; Strang and Meyer 1993). In particular, management concepts associated with rationality and progressiveness have often become widely diffused (Abrahamson 1996).

The Business Press and Managerial Trends

To capture the meaning of social phenomena, several researchers have turned to media texts. Texts mediate between broader social belief systems and applied practices (Fiss and Hirsch 2005; Wodak and Busch 2004). In particular, scholars in the field of political communication have a long tradition of studying how media organizations shape perceptions and set the agenda regarding what is important (McCombs and Shaw 1972; Muraskin 1988). More recently, Carroll and McCombs (2003) have suggested that the insights of political communication studies can be extended to the analysis of the business community. Yet, despite the expansion of the business press since the 1960s and the development of business news into a specialized news genre (Grafström 2005; Kjaer and Langer 2005; Tienari, Vaara and Ainamo 2002), surprisingly little attention has been paid to the role of the business press in shaping the meaning of managerial concepts.

Earlier studies have mainly focused on how the business press shapes public opinion regarding individual corporations. Media attention influences both the public's general awareness of companies, and the specific attributes associated with a particular firm. For example, Pollock and Rindova (2003) stress that media visibility shapes the perceived legitimacy of companies, and the effect can be positive or negative depending on how the media frames a given firm. Closely related to this argument are studies that relate visibility in the business press to perceptions of corporate reputation (e.g. Deephouse 2000).

Shifting the level of analysis from individual organizations to broader managerial trends, media attention has been regarded as an indicator of the legitimacy of a management concept. Legitimacy refers to the degree of collective acceptance, in other words, the popularity of a concept. For example, Abrahamson (1996) refers to the annual number of print media articles as an indicator of the popularity of management ideas, such as quality circles or employee stock ownership programmes. A similar understanding of media attention is found in the population ecology literature. There, media visibility is used as an indicator of the legitimacy of organizational forms (Baum and Powell 1995).

More recent studies have added to the literature view that media attention does more than merely reflect managerial trends. Media organizations are also critical sources of information through which managers learn about new management concepts. Burns and Wholey (1993), for instance, show how information about matrix management presented in the professional media had a significant impact on organizations' adoption of matrix management. In this sense, the media is an important carrier of management knowledge (Sahlin-Andersson and Engwall 2002a).

The 'carrier' concept provides a bridge between the business media and meaning creation. As a carrier of managerial concepts, the business media imbues concepts with meaning. Business media organizations do not only echo or copy what they see and hear, but rather continuously shape and reshape meaning systems through linguistic framing and interpretations of existing practices and ideals. In this process of translation, a mixture of existing practices and added insights emerges, and is spread further (Czarniawska and Sevón 1996; Sahlin-Andersson 1996). For example, Hirsch (1986) shows how the institutionalization of hostile takeovers was influenced by the linguistic framing in the business press. Through the newspaper articles, new management practices were justified and gained legitimacy. Hence, media organizations function as 'sensemakers' and 'sensegivers' in promoting certain images and understandings of reality, while excluding others (Risberg, Tienari and Vaara 2003: 134).

Our study draws on this recent interest in understanding how the business press shapes managerial trends. Yet more than merely studying the level of media attention, we are interested in how texts ascribe meaning to a management concept. This chapter investigates this matter by considering how the meaning of CSR has been formed and conveyed in the *Financial Times*.

Data and Research Method

Our work builds on the recent interest in textual analysis in organizational and institutional studies (Grant, Hardy, Oswick and Putnam 2004; Suddaby and Greenwood 2005; Ventresca and Mohr 2002). Whereas scholars of media studies have a long tradition of regarding media texts as either the output of journalistic efforts or messages in the relationship between sender and receiver, we consider the texts themselves as our primary data source. Texts are considered as carriers of values and meaning (Colyvas and Powell 2005; Mohr 1998). To trace broad patterns of social and cultural meaning, various media genres are particularly useful sources of data (Bell and Garrett 1998; Wodak and Busch 2004).

The empirical study is based on a content analysis of articles about CSR published in the British newspaper the *Financial Times*. The *Financial Times* is the most popular European business daily with a circulation of over 450,000 per day (as of 2002) and approximately 1,600,000 readers worldwide. The European Business Readership Survey of 2002 found that European business people rate the *Financial Times* as the most popular international business daily (EBRS 2002 in: Media Live 2006). Moreover, the *Financial Times*, together with the magazine *The Economist*, is among the printed media that provide the most extensive coverage of CSR (Vogel 2005).

The articles analyzed were found by searching the Factiva database. We started broadly, searching for all articles in the *Financial Times* (all editions) that contained the term 'corporate social responsibility' or the abbreviation 'CSR'. Thereafter, we qualitatively screened to exclude articles that contained the abbreviation CSR, but where the term clearly had another meaning.[2] Moreover, we excluded articles in which corporate social responsibility or CSR were mentioned only in passing in the article but not further discussed. The final dataset contained 268 articles from the years 1988–2003.[3] In order to capture how the meaning of the concept developed over time, we divided the articles into groups covering two periods. In the first period, 1988–1998, CSR was rarely mentioned in the *Financial Times* and only 16 articles were published about the topic. The articles averaged 775 words in length; authorship of eleven of the articles was unattributed, and the other five articles from this period were written by different authors. In the second period, 1999–2003, discussion of CSR intensified, with 252 articles about CSR being published. The articles appearing in the second period averaged 724 words in length and were written by 123 different authors (19 articles were unattributed). In the second period, 6.0% of the articles were editorials, 18.7% external comments, 69.4% news articles, and 6.0% brief notes.

---

2   In the *Financial Times*, CSR was also used as an abbreviation for the China Securities Regulatory Commission, the Comprehensive Spending Review, and the Cambridge Silicon Radio. In addition, CSR is the name of an Australian conglomerate that produces building products and sugar.

3   The database used in our study covers the *Financial Times* from 1980 and onwards. From other longitudinal studies (see for example the analysis of academic articles by de Bakker, Groenewegen and den Hond 2005), we know that CSR was also a topic in the 1960s and 1970s. Consequently, CSR might have been discussed in earlier articles appearing in the *Financial Times*.

Data Analysis

The data analysis was based on quantitative and qualitative text analysis, a method proved strong for understanding processes of meaning creation and institutionalization (e.g. Suddaby and Greenwood 2005). Due to the small number of articles in the first period, 1988–1998, the textual analysis of this subset of data was based on a qualitative approach. The texts were coded and analyzed using NVivo 2.0, a software package for qualitative data analysis (Richards 1999). The programme allows for an iterative research process, alternating between the data and the coding scheme and letting categories emerge and change as the research proceeds. In the analysis, we identified themes of content associated with CSR.

The larger number of articles from the second period, 1999–2003, allowed for a combination of qualitative and quantitative textual analysis. In an initial exploratory stage, we conducted a corpus analysis of the articles in this subset of data. A corpus analysis is an established linguistic method for analysing the vocabulary of a text and discerning discursive patterns. Frequency counts showed how many times particular words were mentioned in the articles. To capture the special characteristics of our dataset, we excluded high-frequency words that appear in all newspaper articles, words such as 'a', 'the', and the various prepositions and pronouns. In addition, we excluded low-frequency words, by us defined as mentioned fewer than 100 times in the total dataset, in order to focus on the words that carry most meaning and give the texts their special internal character. The remaining words were sorted, with help of the qualitative coding, into different themes that reflected the CSR discussion in the *Financial Times*.

In order to get a more comprehensive understanding of how the business press imbues CSR with meaning, we subsequently performed a more detailed content analysis of the articles from the 1999–2003 period. Again the coding was conducted using the NVivo software. Keeping in mind our research question about the meaning of CSR, we organized the data into two main categories for the final analysis. The first category built on our corpus analysis and focused on discursive themes associated with CSR. The second category focused on rhetoric related to the concept.

In the next section, we present our empirical findings regarding how the texts in the *Financial Times* convey the meaning of the CSR concept. We start with an overview of the early articles about CSR published in the 1988–1998 period; thereafter, we turn to a deeper analysis of articles from 1999–2003, a time when the attention devoted to CSR expanded rapidly.

The Nascent Meaning of CSR in the *Financial Times*, 1988–1998

Although our database covers all the issues of the *Financial Times* back to 1980, the first article on 'corporate social responsibility' was published in May 1988. It was a short article entitled, 'Business leaders from the US and UK yesterday pledged themselves to much more active involvement in the public and social issues and problems than at any time since the 19th century'. The article presented a summary of the British–American Conference on Private Sector Initiatives, which had been attended by the British Prime Minister, Margaret Thatcher, and Prince Charles, and which was addressed on videotape by the president of the United States, Ronald Reagan. During the conference, the core argument was that corporate social responsibility had to become central to business practices:

> corporate social responsibility is a central part of business practice – the challenges to our fellow corporate leaders in both countries are to set higher goals for private sector initiatives, communicate our achievements more widely, and set a climate supportive of the efforts of our employees and the communities in which we do business. (*Financial Times*, 4 May 1988)

This article from 1988 is typical of the early discussion of CSR in the *Financial Times*. CSR was mainly linked to issues such as job creation and charitable donations. In other early articles, CSR was associated with topics such as city development and the integration of minority groups. CSR was presented as a new idea for the British business community. The inspiration for how to become socially responsible and a good 'corporate citizen' was drawn mainly from American firms and business schools.

In the mid 1990s, CSR also started to be associated with marketing. Firms were asked to be ethically sound when creating advertising campaigns. Other articles highlighted the idea of 'social cause marketing', suggesting that companies can gain competitive advantage from being associated with socially responsible values.

The 1988–1998 period was a time when the meaning of CSR was nascent in the British and European contexts. From having been almost non-existing phenomenon in the *Financial Times* in the early 1980s, some articles started to pay attention to CSR. In this way, these articles can be seen paving the way for the coming development of the concept. At this time, the term 'corporate social responsibility' was used interchangeably with other terms, such as 'corporate citizenship' and 'corporate ethics'. The abbreviation CSR was still not used in the articles. Moreover, the small number of articles indicates that the meaning of the concept was nascent.

The Meaning of CSR Develops Further, 1999–2003

By the turn of the millennium, discussion of CSR in the *Financial Times* had intensified, reflecting an increased interest in social responsibility on the part of the British business community. In this period, this London-based newspaper reported on a number of events and processes in UK, linking several new policies and practices to the CSR concept. In the UK, pension funds were now required to disclose policies concerning social and environmental issues, which made CSR a matter of public concern. Concurrently, companies started to report on social and environmental issues. In April 2000, the British prime minister appointed a minister of corporate social responsibility, and simultaneously the British government, in particular the Department of Trade and Industry, started a number of initiatives to support CSR. Moreover, several organizations, such as Business in the Community (BITC) and the Prince of Wales International Business Leaders Forum, adopted the concept of CSR and started to promote it. The relevant articles in the *Financial Times* reflected the

CSR-related activities that had been mobilized. For example, attention was directed toward BITC's annual award for leaders committed to CSR, the appointment of the new CSR minister, and the launch of various CSR initiatives. Moreover, a number of articles paid attention to companies that adopted new social and ethical policies.

In the 1999–2003 period, CSR became disconnected from the US context. In contrast to the 1988–1998 period, CSR was no longer driven by imitation of US firms. Although some articles in the *Financial Times* still described US firms as models of CSR development, leading in the implementation of measures such as codes of conduct (the *Financial Times*, 5 August 1999) and the appointment of special ethics officers (the *Financial Times*, 19 August 1999), these articles were exceptions. Instead, the *Financial Times* focused on the emerging British approach to CSR, which had been developed with support from the government and various NGOs.

In addition to the *Financial Times*' focus on CSR in the UK, in this period CSR also began to attract international attention, with organizations such as the European Union and the United Nations entering the discussion. CSR was associated with the globalization debate and discussion of the role of capitalism in a globalized world. For example, the launch of the UN initiative Global Compact in January 1999 and the demonstrations during the WTO meeting in Seattle in late 1999 set the scene for the discussion in the *Financial Times*. Moreover, this discussion was influenced by various international initiatives in support of CSR, such as the European Commission's Green Paper on CSR in 2001 and the development of international guidelines and reporting principles for CSR. In the *Financial Times*, articles about CSR were no longer included only in the national news section, but also in sections such as 'world news' and 'international economy'.

Themes and Vocabulary Associated with CSR, 1999–2003

In contrast to the 1988–1998 period, in the years 1999–2003 the term 'corporate social responsibility' gained prominence. The term began to be used in a more distinct way, and no longer simply as a synonym for other terms, such as business ethics. Parallel to this, the acronym 'CSR' started to be used in the articles, which can be interpreted as a sign of increased public awareness of the concept. By the end of the period, some articles even referred to CSR without spelling out what the abbreviation stood for.

When the discussion of CSR intensified in the years 1999–2003, the concept obtained multiple meanings. In addition to the initial focus on job creation and charitable donations, the debate concerning CSR expanded and the concept came to be associated in the *Financial Times* with several discursive themes. In Table 2.1, we identify five core themes and the vocabulary related to them.[4]

---

[4] The corpus analysis program counts words based on their exact spellings, which results in different word counts for the same word in its singular and plural forms. Also related words, such as 'sustainable' and 'sustainability', are counted separately. In Table 2.1, the word counts for related words are added together.

Table 2.1 Themes and Terminology Associated with CSR in the Financial Times, 1999–2003 (word counts are presented in parentheses)

Social and Environmental Concerns	Moral and Ethical Concerns
CSR is a commitment to social and environmental issues.	*CSR emphasizes the moral and ethical dimensions of business.*
Social (1048); environmental/ environment (558); sustainable/ sustainability (260); human (126)	Responsibility/ responsible (888); ethical (186); need (168); rights (135); good (206); value (107)
Spatial Embeddedness	**Stakeholders Relations**
The corporation is a transnational entity and CSR can be practiced at different geographical levels.	*CSR is about the relationship between business and society. The firm as a nexus of stakeholder relations.*
World (288); UK (276); European/Europe (269); global (251); international (213); countries (162); local (137); London (108)	Government/governments (327); people (277); public (257); community (255); employees (152); organization (150); society (143); investors (133); labor (124); staff (116); school/schools (284)
Relationship between CSR and Business	**Other Issues Related to CSR**
CSR represents corporate practices and is, in many cases, closely related to the core business of the firm.	
Company/ companies/ company's (1955); business/businesses (1263); corporate (981); executive/ executives (304); management (232); investment (204); financial (192); industry (182); director (173); chief (161); managers (148); market (140); governance (123); economic (118); trade (108), leaders (103)	Report/ reports/ reporting (563); new (363); issues (287); programme/ programmes (238); standards (159); performance (155); impact (155); survey (138); reputation (135); research (135); pressure (133); oil (132); risk (129); change (128); policy (128); approach (118); fund (109); support (107); action (100)

Self-evident in the discussion of CSR was a strong emphasis on social and environmental issues. In contrast to the 1988–1998 period, the meaning of the term 'social' expanded in the years 1999–2003 and came to include issues such as working conditions, human rights, poverty, and health problems in developing countries. Ecological concerns, such as climate change and oil spills, were also discussed in the articles. The vocabulary reflected this development, and words such as 'social', 'environment', 'human', and 'sustainability' were frequently referred to in the texts.[5]

---

5 The high frequency of the words 'social' and 'responsibility' is partly explained by the fact that the selection criteria used in our study was that the article should contain the term

Second, discussion of CSR was associated with concerns about morality and ethics, and the articles used words such as 'responsible', 'good', 'ethical', and 'value'. Moreover, the ethical roots of the CSR discussion were demonstrated through the close connection between CSR and the term 'business ethics'.

A third theme that became associated with CSR at this time was the transnational nature of corporations. As described above, the spatial scope of CSR expanded over time. In 1988–1998, CSR was mainly cited in discussions of social concerns at a local or national level. In the 1999–2003 period, however, CSR was also associated with the globalization debate and the concept now referred to firms' behaviours at a global scale in addition to local issues in the companies' home countries. Hence, important in the CSR vocabulary were geographical terms, such as 'global', 'world', 'countries', 'national', and 'local'.

Fourth, CSR became closely connected to an image of the firm as a nexus of stakeholders. Many articles claimed that firms needed to adopt a broader outlook on their environment, encompassing more than just the shareholders. As a result, there was talk about corporate relations with employees, customers, NGOs, governments, and the general public. In many articles, such stakeholders were not only described, but were also allowed to voice their ideas concerning what business ought to be about. Quotations from government representatives and NGOs were particularly prevalent. Many articles began to include alternative perspectives on what the firm ought to be striving for, through references to stakeholder groups with divergent interests.

A fifth theme that was salient in the CSR debate was the relationship between CSR and business. In the articles, words such as 'managers' and 'executive' were frequently used. Other business terms such as 'investment' and 'market' also frequently occurred in the *Financial Times*' articles about CSR. As discussed later in this chapter, the proponents and opponents of CSR each took different stands on the relationship between CSR and business, making this theme critical in our analysis of rhetorical patterns. The opponents argued that CSR would distract firms' attention from profit generation, whereas the proponents emphasized CSR as a *business* concern, drawing attention to the connection between high ethical and moral standards and long–term success.

An Emerging Debate about the Role of Business in Society

Our analysis shows how the attention paid to CSR in the *Financial Times* was linked to a broader debate about the role of business in society. As the interest in CSR increased, it became evident that the idea challenged traditional norms and ideals of the appropriate role of business. In the first period, 1988–1998, before interest in CSR mounted, none of the articles questioned the appropriateness of the concept. However, in the 1999–2003 period, when CSR had gained more attention, the concept became the subject of debate. In the *Financial Times*, CSR was not only discussed in news articles, but also in editorials, external comments, and analytical articles. These articles highlighted the blurred boundaries between social and commercial activities.

'corporate social responsibility' or the abbreviation CSR.

For example, one article asked the following: 'if an organisation's objectives are social, can it really conform to the norms of a business enterprise?' (*Financial Times*, 5 July 2001).

The opponents of CSR supported the argument that 'the business of business is business'. In articles advocating this view, in which CSR was questioned or presented negatively, the authors argued that the appropriate role of a commercial enterprise is to generate profits for its shareholders and not to engage in social and environmental initiatives. They claimed that CSR would distract the firms' attention from profit generation, and as a result markets would become distorted. The quotation below exemplifies such criticism of CSR. The article from which it is extracted was published in the 'Comments and Analysis' section, and the author elaborated on the potential consequences of CSR and why the concept could be dangerous not only for the firms themselves, but also for the economic and democratic development of society as a whole:

> [...] powerful objections can be made to such a radical redefinition of corporate objectives: it accepts a false critique of the market economy; it endorses an equally mistaken view of the powers of multinational businesses; it risks spreading costly regulations worldwide; it is more likely to slow the reduction of global poverty than to accelerate it; it requires companies to make highly debatable political judgments; and it threatens a form of global neo-corporatism, in which unaccountable power is shared between companies, activist groups, some international organisations and a few governments. (*Financial Times*, 15 May 2001)

The author of the article supported the view that the market and firms are profit maximizing organizations. In the same vein, other articles in which CSR was questioned invoke the idea of a free-market economy. In particular, the opponents of CSR attacked the idea of developing new government policies concerning CSR, as well as the increased costs that such policies would impose.

In the *Financial Times*, however, positive attitudes to CSR overshadowed the criticism. The opponents of CSR also admitted the difficulty in arguing against CSR: 'Nobody would wish to defend corporate irresponsibility or suggest that business should behave antisocially. It is little wonder therefore that corporate social responsibility is a popular notion. To attack it is like assailing motherhood' (*Financial Times*, 16 May 2001). In the 1999–2003 period, 80 per cent of the articles are in support of CSR, 17 per cent are neutral, and only three per cent oppose the concept.

The Enron Collapse as a Watershed

In the *Financial Times* articles, proponents of CSR rallied around a shared rhetoric, which combined examples of unethical and irresponsible behaviours with justifications as to why CSR efforts were needed. In this section, we show how negative exemplars were central to forging the meaning of CSR in the *Financial Times*.

Protests, scandals, and crises set the scene for many *Financial Times* articles about CSR. By referring to earlier, troublesome situations, the articles called for the readers' attention. Controversies concerning the oil, pharmaceutical, and clothing industries were frequently cited to illustrate what could happen if companies ignored CSR. Examples were also drawn from lawsuits and fines against corporations. In particular, the operations of multinational corporations were scrutinized.

The collapse of Enron in the autumn of 2001 marked a watershed in the discussion of CSR. After the Enron scandal, discussion of CSR was intense and in 2002 over 100 articles about CSR were published in the *Financial Times*. The Enron case became a point of reference for irresponsible behaviour and low ethical standards. Moreover, the scandal prompted debate in the *Financial Times* about good corporate governance, transparency, and accountability. Several articles put forward the argument that corporate scandals must be taken seriously: scandals were not only ruining the reputation of individual companies, but were also damaging public trust in the entire corporate sector. To rebuild trust in the corporate world, something had to change:

> Post-Enron, the pressure is on to present all relevant information to shareholders, including non-financial information such as risks and issues of reputation. We have seen what happens when companies are less than open [...]. (*Financial Times*, 26 September 2002)

In the *Financial Times*, the post-Enron period was described as one in which the existing ethical and moral standards of managers were questioned. Working according to formal regulations was no longer enough with respect to risk management and principles of 'good' management. Along with calls for improved corporate governance, CSR attracted increased attention as a model of best practice. Anita Roddick, founder and co-chair of the Body Shop, claimed in a letter to the editor of the *Financial Times* that, 'People are no longer prepared to accept that one powerful section of society is somehow immune from the same moral constraints as the rest of us' (*Financial Times*, 15 October 2001).

The Rationale for CSR

In addition to references to bad exemplars, the meaning of CSR in the *Financial Times* was constructed through the use of positive reasoning. Embedded in many of the texts was a belief that CSR constituted a moral obligation. The texts stressed the economic power of the corporate sector and its duty to assume an active role in social welfare and development efforts. Problems such as poverty, famine, human rights, health issues, and poor education were claimed to belong the corporate sphere of influence. Several articles pointed out certain firms that had successfully fulfilled their social responsibilities, for example, through supporting local schools or helping combat disease and poverty.

Yet, such moral- and value-based argumentation in many cases did not stand by itself, but rather was buttressed by economic rationales as to why CSR was important. As outlined above, many *Financial Times* articles about CSR were rooted in the broader debate concerning the appropriate role of business in society and potential tensions between social objectives and profit generation. Whereas the opponents of CSR pointed out the risk that CSR could distract firms from their primary function as profit generating entities, most articles displayed the opposite viewpoint. For example, in the following quotation the chief executive of a multinational bank reported on the company's CSR work. The quotation presents both moral and economic arguments as to why a firm should adopt CSR as part of its practices:

> Companies that operate in developing countries have a moral and a business obligation to help counter the disease [HIV/AIDS]. [...] While the cost of Aids and HIV in terms of human life has been given much-deserved attention, there are signs that businesses are at long last beginning to recognise the economic threat they face. (*Financial Times*, 29 November 2002)

In various articles, CEOs, consultants, and researchers all raised voices in favour of CSR. For example, one article presented the results of a survey, concluding that 'Corporate social responsibility is the coming vogue and a certain winner for companies that practice it' (*Financial Times*, 7 March 2001). Another article, which also presented the results of a survey, presented an equally positive view of CSR. The survey, conducted by Business in the Community (BITC), summarized the views of 200 chief executives, chairmen, and directors in ten European countries:

> They give strong backing to the idea that responsible social and environmental behaviour pays dividends, especially if it is a mainstream part of business activities. Nearly 80 per cent agree that companies that integrate responsible practices will be more competitive; and 73 per cent accept that 'sustained social and environmental engagement can significantly improve profitability'. (*Financial Times*, 18 June 2002)

Besides general statements supporting CSR, the texts in the *Financial Times* contained many examples of companies that proudly talked about their CSR work as a critical success factor. CSR was referred to as a business policy that would create new market opportunities, competitive advantage, and customer satisfaction. Through working actively with CSR, companies would also build goodwill, improve their reputations, and strengthen their brand names; internally, CSR would help companies attract and motivate employees. All these arguments supported the understanding of CSR as compatible with profit maximization.

A variant of the economic argumentation used by CSR proponents cited the reduction of risks. Several articles argued that CSR could be used as a risk-management strategy, associating CSR with corporate reputation. CSR was described as a tool for preventing negative news and remaining untainted by scandal. This argument also concluded that CSR is a *business* issue and that good ethics would pay off.

To summarize, the articles in the *Financial Times* dealing with CSR revealed an overwhelmingly positive attitude to the concept. Our textual analysis indicates that the rhetoric used was based on a rationalized means–ends logic. CSR was suggested to be a solution to various problems. The construction of a positive meaning of CSR in the *Financial Times* can be summarized as three text components defined by different logics of argumentation (see Table 2.2).

Table 2.2 The Meaning of CSR as Conveyed in the *Financial Times*, 1999–2003

Rhetorical Strategy	Logic of Argumentation	Typical Words	Narrative Time
Citing themes associated with CSR	Defines what CSR is about	See results in Table 2.1	Present
Describing problems that can occur if CSR is neglected	Bad ethics equals bad business Not paying attention to CSR can have unanticipated consequences, i.e., scandals such as Enron	Unethical Crises Scandal	The "old" way of doing business (history)
Presenting CSR as a solution	CSR as a success story Good ethics equals good business	Profit Competitiveness Innovative Risk management	The "new" way of doing business (present and future)

The meaning of CSR evolved through three rhetorical strategies. First, the articles specified what CSR was about by associating the concept with different discursive themes. As shown in this chapter, the scope of CSR broadened with time, and came to include new issues and topics for discussion. Second, the articles ascribed meaning to CSR by citing negative exemplars, such as the Enron case. Such texts illustrated how unethical behaviour could result in poor business. Third, CSR was justified as a means to achieve success. Articles adopting this strategy contained many examples and presented rationales as to why managers need to work with CSR. The rhetoric was future oriented and presented CSR as the 'new way' of doing business. This rationalized combination of problems and solutions presented CSR as an attractive model.

The News Value of CSR: From an Oxymoron to an Imperative

In the *Financial Times*, CSR was presented as business news. In line with journalistic norms, the articles dealing with it focused on the unexpected, controversial, and deviating elements of CSR. The early articles paid considerable attention to the idea of CSR in and of itself: as we have seen in this chapter, the potential tension between commercial and social objectives gave CSR news value. CSR was presented as an oxymoron that challenged the fundamental understanding of what business ought to be about.

Given the extraordinary character of CSR in the context of markets and profit maximization, the early articles reported on the newness of CSR in the British and European contexts. Around the turn of the millennium, a number of new CSR practices were highlighted in the *Financial Times*, practices such as the first CSR reports, the establishment of CSR indices, and the creation of new CSR think tanks. Special attention was devoted to how companies previously embroiled in controversy started to work with CSR. CSR dilemmas in, for example, the oil, pharmaceutical, and tobacco industries were frequently discussed in the articles in the *Financial Times*. For example, British American Tobacco's decision to donate money for the establishment of an international CSR research centre resulted in an article discussing potential conflicts of interest when private companies donate funds to CSR research.

Over time, CSR coverage changed its character. In contrast to the early articles, in later articles the reader was expected to be familiar with the concept of CSR and its meaning. As a result, discussion of the existence or non-existence of CSR faded away, and instead the articles directed reader attention to the development of more specific CSR guidelines. For example, some articles described the new AA1000 standard and the UN-supported Global Reporting Initiative (GRI). The articles no longer bothered informing the reader of the existence of CSR, but rather kept the reader up to date with the latest tool and trends in the CSR field. One article concluded that 'new standards, guidelines or indices on CSR appear[ed] almost weekly' (*Financial Times*, 12 May 2003). By the end of 2003, discussion of CSR had matured and the concept was no longer thought of as odd or provocative; now, the *Financial Times* described CSR as a natural part of management.

Conclusions

While previous studies of management trends have focused on how new concepts are diffused and adopted by organizations, our analysis emphasizes the importance of understanding how the meaning of managerial concepts is formed. The study integrates insights into the socially constructed nature of management and the role of the business press as a carrier of meaning. In particular, we explore how the *Financial Times*, in the years 1988–2003, ascribed meaning to the CSR concept. In the beginning of the studied period, CSR was perceived as a relatively new concept and it was generally assumed that reader familiarity could not be taken for granted. Even though discussion of the role of business in society has historical roots (den Hond, de Bakker and Neergaard this volume), CSR was a malleable idea around the turn of the millennium and the debate about CSR imbued the concept with meaning.

One conclusion of our study is that the meaning of CSR as conveyed in the *Financial Times* reflected the general development of the concept around the turn of the millennium. This conclusion is related to the role of the media as information mediators in the business community. The *Financial Times* associated several themes with CSR: social and environmental concerns, the transnational characteristics of corporations, CSR's relationship to business, moral and ethical concerns, and stakeholder relations.

These themes are also known from other discussions of CSR – for example, in academia (de Bakker, Groenewegen and den Hond 2005), by consultants (see Windell this volume), and in the involved firms themselves (see Olsen *et al.* this volume). Moreover, these other participants in the CSR field are referred to in the articles in the *Financial Times*. In this sense, the business media texts were related to the broader debate in society concerning CSR.

Our analysis shows also how CSR became business news. In the typical media manner, *Financial Times* articles about CSR stressed successful examples and problematic situations. The articles typified the journalistic focus on large corporations, unexpected events, and deviating practices. In this way, CSR was a fruitful basis for creating media stories with clear 'heroes' and 'villains'. For example, great attention was paid to key events in the business community, such as the collapse of Enron, how controversial industries handle CSR, and examples of companies that successfully implement CSR. We have also shown that *Financial Times* coverage of CSR was strikingly positive. Even if opponents claimed in some articles that CSR was in conflict with the logic of the private sector, most texts expressed a positive attitude to CSR. Some texts even explicitly argued that corporations should direct more attention to CSR. In other articles, a positive image of CSR was supported by references to companies that had successfully implemented CSR.

Whereas our study is limited to examining a single key newspaper, the *Financial Times*, other business media organizations potentially play a similar role in shaping the meaning of managerial ideas. Besides other influential newspapers, such as the *Wall Street Journal*, *Les Echos*, and *Handelsblatt*, relevant business media also include periodicals, television, radio, and the Internet. Comparative and longitudinal studies of media organizations would contribute to a more comprehensive understanding of how the media ascribes meaning to management concepts through the use of various rhetorical patterns and linguistic framing. Moreover, future research needs to address the broader processes by which the business media shapes managerial trends. For example, in addition to editing and determining whose voices will be heard and in what way, the *Financial Times* has ascribed meaning to CSR through arranging conferences and publishing books. Furthermore, the *Financial Times* is a co-founder of the FTSE Group, which produces the FTSE4Good, one of the world's leading financial market CSR indices. This suggests that media can indeed shape the meaning of management trends through a variety of channels.

To conclude, the results presented in this chapter indicate the importance of paying increased attention to how the meaning of management trends, such as CSR, is formed in the business press. Textual analysis of business news articles is a compelling method for better understanding the ongoing construction of management concepts. In contrast to earlier studies, which have used media attention as an indicator of the legitimacy of a managerial concept, our analysis exposes how the business press also ascribes meaning to management trends. Whereas examining the concept of legitimacy focuses on the collective acceptance of a managerial practice, studying *meaning* can build insight into the issues associated with a new management concept, who needs to pay attention to the concept, and why the concept is needed in the first place. This chapter presents one example of such a study, through analyzing how the *Financial Times* has ascribed meaning to the CSR concept.

Chapter 3

The Commercialization of CSR: Consultants Selling Responsibility

Karolina Windell

Introduction

At the end of the 1990s Corporate Social Responsibility (CSR) was not a widely spread idea among Swedish corporations. However in 2005, 77 percent of the 31 corporations listed on the Stockholm Stock Exchange (A–list) had WebPages communicating their view on social responsibility under the headings of 'CSR', 'Sustainability', or 'Environment & CSR'. Organizations and individuals contributing to the circulation of CSR have increasingly paid attention to CSR over the last decade, and CSR has become a widely spread management idea within the business community. Just as other management ideas, CSR is a vague and rather unclear concept, being referred to by an acronym and mobilized by fashion–setters in the business community (Røvik 2002). Nevertheless, CSR differs from other management ideas. It is not primarily an idea about improving management to increase corporate efficiency. It is an idea about responsibility, implying that corporations should expand the scope of their responsibility. There is no set definition of CSR today – and there was none yesterday. In earlier as well as in contemporary times researchers, practitioners, politicians, and representatives of civil society have been searching for clarifications and definitions of the idea (cf. Carroll 1979, 1999; Garriga and Melé 2004). CSR is also a contested idea. Critics have argued that it hinders corporations in performing well, as it takes resources away from the core business (Friedman 1962; Henderson 2001), whereas other have sought to provide evidence for the correlation between CSR and financial performance (Margolis and Walsh 2003). Although there are different and conflicting definitions and interpretations of CSR, it has become a popular management idea.

Simultaneously with the proliferation of CSR, academic attention for the topic has increased. CSR is being studied within different disciplines and with different perspectives. In particular, it is striking to note that CSR is related to diverse parts of the corporation, and that it addresses different types of corporate activities. For example, several studies examine the relationship between CSR and financial performance and seek to find evidence for a positive correlation (Margolis and Walsh 2003; Schnietz and Epstein 2005; Waddock and Graves 1997). Another strand of literature has focused on CSR in relation to management, including decisions and actions related to how to implement or organize CSR activities, and how to integrate different frameworks for CSR into business operations (Leipziger 2003; Waddock

2004; Zadek 1998, 2004). A third strand of literature addresses CSR in relation to different aspects of marketing, such as branding and differentiation (Cerne 2003; Kotler and Lee 2005; Maignan and Ferrell 2004), or to political consumption (Klein et al. 2004; Micheletti and Stolle 2004; Sen and Bhattacharya 2001). Yet other researchers are interested in examining the spread and adoption of CSR in different geographical contexts (Chapple and Moon 2005; Fukukawa and Moon 2004; Maignan and Ralston 2002; Matten and Moon 2004).

Despite the significant rise in the number of CSR studies over the last few years, limited attention has been given to the proliferation and popularization of CSR. Specifically, questions of how and why CSR has developed as a management idea in recent decades have been scarcely examined. However, early contributions to this area of research include studies on the role of NGOs in promoting CSR (Segerlund 2005), the increase of professionals in the area of CSR, such as CSR educational institutions (Matten and Moon 2004) and the growth of socially responsible investment firms (for example Louche 2004; Sjöström 2004; Waddock and Graves 1997; Zarlowski this volume). Buhr and Grafström (this volume) contribute to this issue by examining how media organizations such as the *Financial Times* ascribe meaning to CSR. Likewise, Göthberg (this volume) and de Bakker et al. (this volume) provide insight into how corporations themselves contribute to the development of CSR.

In this chapter, I add to research on CSR by examining the role of consultants in the commercialization of CSR. Previous studies have shown that consultants are important fashion–setters in the business community, and are critical for the creation and dissemination of management ideas (Kipping and Engwall 2002; Meyer 1996; Sahlin–Andersson and Engwall 2002b; Suddaby and Greenwood 2001). Therefore, addressing their work is a suitable starting point for an exploration of the expansion of CSR. Drawing from literature on the spread of management ideas and institutional entrepreneurs, this chapter addresses how and why consultants turn the ideas about the social responsibility of business into a management idea, known as Corporate Social Responsibility, often presented under the acronym CSR. Empirically, the chapter focuses on a group of consultants selling CSR services in Sweden in 2002–2003.

The remainder of this chapter consists of four parts. First, I outline the theoretical framework. The chapter builds on new–institutional literature about the flow of ideas and construction of management fashions. Further, 'institutional entrepreneurs', as a vital actor group in transforming institutionalized ideas, are accounted for. Second, the research design and the empirical data are outlined. In the third section, the empirical results are presented. Hereby, the questions of how and why consultants work with CSR are explored. The rhetorical strategies used by consultants in order to mobilize CSR receive particular attention. Finally, I present the conclusions that can be drawn from the empirical results.

The Flow of Management Ideas

The spread and popularization of management ideas, such as Total Quality Management (TQM), Management by Objectives (MBO), Quality Circles (QC), Business Process Re–engineering (BPR), and New Public Management (NPM) have been addressed by several scholars (Abrahamson 1996; Abrahamson and Fairchild 1999; Mueller, Sillince, Harvey and Howorth 2003; Røvik 2002; Walgenbach and Beck 2002; Westphal, Gulati and Shortell 1997; Zbaracki 1998). Popular management ideas constantly change, they come and they go. Thus, just like other actors in society, managers are guided by fashion (Czarniawska and Sevón 2005b). The reason why certain ideas achieve a breakthrough, while others do not, is a question that several researchers have tried to answer. It is argued that fashionable, popular ideas tend to be simplistic, vague and conform to dominating norms about progress and efficiency (cf. Meyer 1996; Røvik 2002). In the corporate world this means that ideas need to be presented as rational, that is, they need to promise corporate progress, to become attractive. Or as Meyer (1996, 252) puts it: 'to properly develop and travel, an idea must be organized in terms of great abstract truths, not mundane realities'. In other words, popular management ideas do not necessarily lead to corporate success but to gain legitimacy and become widely spread, ideas do need to be presented as contributing to increased success.

The legitimization of ideas has partly been described in terms of theoretization (Greenwood, Suddaby and Hinings 2002; Strang and Meyer 1993). Theoretization has been introduced as one stage in the process of institutionalization, in which vague concepts are connected to concrete problems and presented as a rational solution to these problems (cf. Hwang and Powell 2005). Similarly, Czarniawska and Sevón (2005b) argue that ideas need to be translated and objectified in order to travel, which means that they are turned into objects such as books, labels and models. In the process of transforming new ideas into legitimate ideas, discourse, rhetorical strategies and persuasive language play significant roles (Czarniawska–Joerges 1988; Fiss and Hirsch 2005; Mueller et al. 2003; Suddaby and Greenwood 2005; Zbaracki 1998). Hence, rhetoric and discourse are means of presenting ideas in a convincing way. Through rhetoric the content of ideas is created. Moreover, rhetorical strategies contribute to mobilizing and spreading the ideas. Therefore, persuasive argumentation may help or hinder the establishment of new ideas, by connecting them to already established norms (Suddaby and Greenwood 2005).

However, rhetoric does not develop by itself and ideas do not travel by themselves. Rhetorical strategies are constructed and used by actors. And ideas are carried, circulated and mediated by actors in a broader environment. Previous research has highlighted the construction and circulation of management ideas in the interplay between several actors such as business media, business schools and consultants (Sahlin–Andersson and Engwall 2002c). Researchers in new–institutional theory have recently drawn attention to how, partly through discursive means, institutional entrepreneurs contribute to the flow of new organizational models and practices (Hwang and Powell 2005; Lawrence and Phillips 2004; Maguire, Hardy and Lawrence 2004). Thereby, it is argued that institutional entrepreneurs are actors or groups of actors that purposively seek to influence the outcome of new practices in accordance with their own interests. Hence, institutional entrepreneurs shape the conditions in the business community by reconstructing institutionalized practices (Hwang and Powell 2005).

Consultants as Fashion–Setters

The number of consultants has expanded and in concert with this, their role in the business community has changed (Kipping and Engwall 2002; Sahlin–Andersson and Engwall 2002b). Consultants are fashion–setters in the business community in several ways: they carry new ideas into corporations; they transform ideas into management knowledge; and they develop management techniques. Thereby, they are important designers of management ideas, by timely taking hold of new ideas and turning them into saleable services (Ernst and Kieser 2002; Kipping and Engwall 2002; Scarbrough 2003).

Since the turn of the last century, the world market for consultancy services has increased between ten to fifteen percent per year (Armbüster and Kipping 2003). They have not only expanded in scale, but also in scope. Established accounting firms such as the 'big five' have transformed themselves from accountancies into consulting firms and lately into multidisciplinary business service providers (Suddaby and Greenwood 2001). Hence, they have incorporated new areas of work such as advertising, public relations, lobbying and investment banking. This development is described as a process of colonizing new areas of work to dominate the field of management (Suddaby and Greenwood 2001).

Consultants have thus become legitimate experts and 'problem–solvers' within firms, for example by focusing on cutting costs and improving productivity and long–term profitability (cf. Meyer 1996; Wright 2002). By improving their services they uphold their image as experts and retain the demand for their services (Abrahamson 1996; Kieser 2002; Wright 2002). Hence, in this growing literature consultants are highlighted as establishers of management knowledge that develop ideas about business into commercial products and create a demand for these ideas. Thereby, consultants are a pervasive force in the business community by carrying and mediating management trends. Kieser (2002) even goes as far as claiming that managers might become their marionettes, given their dependence on consultancy expertise.

Drawing on these previous studies, we can conclude that consultants both create and diffuse ideas. Several studies have demonstrated how consultants carry new ideas and create a demand for their services. Against this backdrop, this chapter analyzes how consultants have commercialized CSR into saleable services. Hence, in order to contribute to explanations why and how CSR has proliferated during the last decade, this chapter addresses the role of consultants in this development. Three empirical questions are addressed: (1) Who are the consultants involved in shaping and proliferating CSR? (2) How do they go about packaging CSR into an attractive and legitimate management idea? (3) What are their motives for commercializing CSR?

By answering these questions this study aims to shed light on the recent popularization of CSR and to develop insights into consultants' means and motives in furthering new management practices and creating new legitimate management ideas.

Research Design and Method

Whereas consultants selling CSR services have been established in several European countries, the Swedish situation is used as an illustration in this chapter. The chapter examines a group of consultants in Sweden as they established CSR consulting. The chapter builds on 23 in–depth interviews with consultants operating in the field of CSR in Sweden. The respondents were CEOs, directors of CSR departments, or owners of smaller consultancy firms. In some cases two consultants working at the same consultancy took part in the interview. All interviews were conducted face–to–face (with the exception of one interview that was conducted over the phone). They lasted between 1 to 1½ hours and were taped and carefully transcribed. The chapter also builds on observations at seminars arranged by consultants, where the issue of CSR was debated with other interested parties, such as consultants, corporate representatives, NGOs and politicians.

At the time of the interviews 2002–2003, CSR consulting was a new and growing market in most European countries, including Sweden. Thus, one methodological difficulty was to identify consultants working with CSR. Several of them used labels that were intertwined with the label of CSR. The sampling was considered to be an empirical question and was developed using a snowball technique. Hence, I contacted one consultancy firm that addressed CSR on its webpage, and thereafter the respondent was asked to mention the names of the firm's strongest competitors. When the competitors were interviewed they were asked the same question at the end of the interview. Finally, it was no longer possible to find new consultants that were mentioned as strong competitors in the area of CSR. However, two of the consultants that were mentioned as competitors did not want take part in the study. By searching the Internet for consultants offering CSR services one additional consultancy was found. It would have been possible to contact a number of other consultancies in Sweden asking them whether they were selling CSR services. However, consultants constantly tend to search for new services and to offer what the customers ask for. Therefore, there would have been a possibility that some of those asked would have stated that they were selling CSR service, even though this might not have been the case. Therefore it was decided to only contact the consultancies that explicitly offered CSR services.

The consultancies in the study differed in terms of size and where they operated. Some consultancies were larger firms operating on a global level, whereas others were smaller firms, mostly operating on a national level. At the time of the study, it was a methodological challenge to keep track of CSR consultants and to encircle the actual population. Several of the consultants worked in different organizations at different times; in their own consultancy, in larger consultancy firms and in corporations. Some of them also carried the concept of CSR into new consultancies as they switched their working places. Moreover, some of the small and middle-sized consultancies merged and some of them closed down.

Even though the study explores consultants working in Sweden, it is worth mentioning that they had both formal and informal contacts with other international consultancies and international networks in the area of CSR. Thereby, it might be assumed that consultants in Sweden are developing and spreading CSR partly based on the experience of consultants in other countries.

In the following section, the empirical results are presented. First, the background and the emergence of CSR consultants in Sweden will be accounted for. Then, the chapter turns to the means used by the consultants to commercialize CSR. The process of commercializing CSR is discussed in terms of packaging and mobilizing CSR through rhetorical strategies. Finally, the consultants' motives for selling CSR are described.

```
Categories of CSR consultants
    ├── Accounting Consultants
    ├── Management Consultants
    ├── Communication Consultants
    ├── Ethical Investment Analysis Consultants
    ├── Business Ethics Consultants
    └── Environmental-Sustainability Consultants
```

Figure 3.1 Categories of Consultants Selling CSR Services

The Emergence of CSR Consultants in Sweden

In the early 1990s, the first consultancies addressing social responsibility were established in Sweden. There were few consultants explicitly acknowledging social responsibility as a new potential area of work. At this point in time these consultants used widely different labels to express the ideas about the social responsibility of business, which made it a heterogeneous area of work. Several of the consultants that early on took notice of these ideas had previously been working with environmental issues or business ethics. Even though the first consultancies were initially working with environmental issues or business ethics, this changed as time went by. At the end of the 1990s the number of consultants selling CSR had increased. Those selling CSR services in 2002–2003 had rather different backgrounds and represented diverse areas of the consulting field. Based on the interviews I identified six categories of consultants working with CSR within the field of consulting (see Figure 3.1).

Hence, the consultants represented a wide range or areas within the consultancy field, which also meant that they addressed CSR differently. The business ethics, ethical–investment analysts and the environmental–sustainability consultants can be considered to be the early movers, whereas the accounting, communication and management consultants were the groups that entered the area of CSR later. The early movers argued that their attention had been drawn towards social responsibility because of different governmental initiatives. The UN/WCED report, *Our common future*, presented by the Brundtland Commission in 1987, where the concept of sustainability was launched, and the 1992 *UNCED Conference* in Rio de Janeiro were mentioned in particular as an inspiration for combining environmental issues with social issues. The later movers were encouraged by the *UN Global Compact* and the Swedish governmental counterpart *Globalt Ansvar.*

As the first consultancies, which often consisted of one or two persons, started to sell CSR services, corporations and investors were rather indifferent to the concept of CSR. The consultants argued that they had to convince corporations of the benefits to be gained from attending to social responsibility and to understanding the content of the coexisting labels. They wrote books about CSR, made comments on CSR or gave advice on how to become a socially responsible corporation in different newspapers and magazines. Also, open seminars and debates were arranged in cooperation with, for example, consultants, corporations, universities and NGOs. These activities were important to increase awareness of CSR and to expand market demand. During the end of the 1990s and the beginning of the 21st century several corporate scandals occurred in both the global and the Swedish business community, which many believed helped consultants to put CSR on the corporate agenda. In the next section, I describe how consultants went about conceptualizing ideas about the social responsibility of business and creating a new management idea, labelled CSR.

Packaging Ideas about the Social Responsibility of Business

As shown in other studies, it is easier to make ideas attractive and to make them flow if they are objectified into a label. However, as general ideas of the social responsibility of business were spreading among the consultants in Sweden, various coexisting labels were in use. Throughout the 1990s consulting that addressed the social responsibility of business was presented under various labels: sustainability, corporate citizenship, corporate philanthropy, business ethics, and to some extent CSR. This meant that consultants talked about social responsibility under different labels and these labels were used in different contexts. In other words, the consultants choose to use the label that their clients preferred, which implied that the same service could be marketed under different labels.

At the beginning of the 21st century several labels were, however, abandoned, and CSR became the most frequently used term. Consultants converted to use the CSR label as it was argued that it would become the most commonly used label by corporations and other actors. Corporate social responsibility, abbreviated to CSR, was at that time the label used both internationally by, for example, the UN and the European Commission, and nationally by the Swedish government as well as other organizations.

The coexistence of different, yet related, labels might have been helpful when consultancies first started to sell social responsibility to corporations. They could distinguish themselves and offer unique services under their own labels, and connect these services to labels that were familiar to their clients. However, the diversity of labels eventually became a problem, because it made corporations confused about what social responsibility actually meant. As the demand for social responsibility was still low, it was believed that a common label would increase the demand for social responsibility services and would help the consultants to establish a market. They argued that they had to cooperate to convince corporations about the value of social responsibility, which partly meant a change to using one common label, namely CSR.

In the 1990s, CSR was a vague idea without a set definition. In the general discourse CSR was ascribed different meanings. The underlying meaning was that being socially responsible meant profitable business. However, what a socially responsible corporation looked like was not agreed upon. A diversity of issues had been placed under the label of CSR and several templates, interpretations and conflicting regulative frameworks for CSR were circulating, for example Global Compact, GRI, SA 8000. According to the consultants the vagueness of CSR made it far too difficult a concept for corporations to handle. Corporations often contacted consultants claiming that they wanted to address CSR, however, they did not understand what CSR meant and how they should adopt it. The consultants therefore devoted much of their time to telling corporations about the content and meaning. However, they also stated that it was rather tricky to clarify what CSR actually meant. As one of the consultants expressed it:

> There are so many concepts that are circulating. [...] Today, there is confusion. What do we actually mean with social responsibility or CSR? Is that actually the same thing as Corporate Citizenship or Sustainability? Or what is it? (Consultant Ö, 10/10 2002).

All the consultants frequently made similar statements. Since they were in the business of CSR, one would expect them to be able to account for the content without difficulty. But that was not the case. Most of them had trouble to describe how they interpreted CSR. To answer the question of what CSR meant to them, the consultants often grabbed a pen and paper and started to draw intertwined circles. The numbers of circles were usually three or four. There was some variation among the words written in these circles and frequently words such as environment, economic and social factors, appeared. The circles were often encircled and named CSR. Sometimes CSR or Corporate Citizenship (CC) was written in the circle of social factors and then all three circles were enclosed in a circle called Sustainability. The circle of

Corporate Governance was often added to this overall picture. Figure 3.2 provides two examples of such drawings.

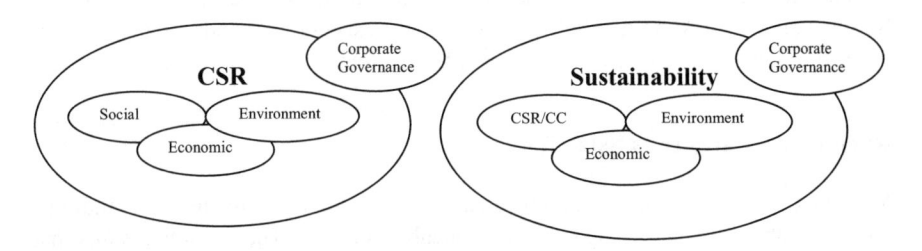

Figure 3.2 Visual Accounts of CSR and Coexisting Labels

During the process of defining CSR with pen and paper the consultants, explained that the area of CSR was under construction and that they themselves were in the process of learning and developing the area. One consultant stated:

> CSR, what is it? Some kind of philosophy? Something that everyone talks about, but no one can put his or her finger on. Is there an area or is it an attempt to create an area? Could you explain to me, what CSR is? [...] We are about to learn. It is a process of learning. So, we start with trial and error. (Consultant L, 30/10/2002)

One part of developing CSR into a saleable management idea was to find a common label and then to define its meaning and content. However, this did not mean that CSR had to be transformed into one precise or standardized definition, practice or model; several definitions of CSR were developed. Hence, the label of CSR became the most common used label although it did not mean the same to the consultants in practice. The multiplicity of definitions did not make CSR a difficult concept to market; its 'fluffiness' made it flexible and easy to adjust to several types of industries. CSR could thus be applied to a manufacturing industry with production in third world countries, as well as to a service industry operating nationally.

So, CSR was developed into a concept that addressed a diversity of corporate activities and corporate problems, such as child labour, safety at workplaces, abuse of alcohol among employees and discrimination at workplaces. Besides, the lack of a consistent definition of CSR gave consultants an opportunity to construct one and to fill it with a meaning that corresponded with their own visions and ideas about CSR. This often meant that they developed CSR into issues close to their traditional area of work. Even though most consultants did not wish to develop or subscribe to a standardized definition, some consultants argued that standardization would be the only way to evaluate corporate performance on social issues.

Just as important as finding a common label and defining its meaning, was the packaging of CSR into explicit services. The consultants turned CSR into services that related to their traditional area of work and thereby diverse CSR niches were developed. Thus, CSR was packaged into different types of practical work. For example, accountants specialized in social reporting, management consultants in developing CSR policies, communication consultants in communicating CSR, ethical investment analysts in socially responsible investment, et cetera. However, the consultants also offered other services. Often these extra services were similar. Services such as stakeholder dialogues, risk analyses, codes of conducts and different kinds of education were offered by most of consultants.

Rhetorical Strategies as Sales Tools

Making CSR into an attractive management idea did not only involve finding a common label and packaging CSR into saleable services. The consultants also had to successfully distribute and market the idea of CSR to corporations. To do so, they needed to convince their customers about the value of CSR. Several interviewees stated that CSR was met with scepticism within the business community. Several corporate representatives and managers considered the allocation of resources to social issues as a waste of resources. According to the consultants the dominating view among several managers was that 'the business of business is business', and thus the managers could not understand why they should pay attention to social issues, which were not directly related to their core business.

The consultants sought to convincingly introduce CSR to the corporate representatives. They often contacted corporations through the information manager, Investor Relations manager, the environmental manager, or sometimes even through the top management to inform them about CSR. However, it was not unusual that corporations contacted the consultancies in order to be helped with CSR issues. The corporate representatives were often sceptical about CSR when they first discussed the issue. The following quotes from two interviewees show how consultants sought to change the attitudes of the corporate representatives:

> And then the question is raised. Why should corporations be socially responsible? And there are two good arguments, whereas one is better than the other. First, otherwise the corporation will go bankrupt and the brand will be jeopardized. The second argument says, it is a business case and the corporation can earn cash. (Consultant L, 30/10/2002)

> Corporations need to recognize the correlation. What is the core of all this? How can this further business activity? Nevertheless, business shall maximize profit and it is harder to motivate a project like this, if it is expensive and if the corporations do not really see the necessity for it. (Consultant P, 14/10/2002)

In order to convince corporations about the value of CSR, different rhetorical strategies were used. CSR was wrapped up in economical arguments and linked to dominant values in the business environment. Moral arguments were downplayed and economical arguments were prominently advanced, as the consultants experienced that corporations would not listen to arguments other than those about increased profitability. Hence, they argued in favour of CSR in terms of progress and cost–benefit.

The consultants used a *proactive* and a *reactive* rhetorical strategy to convince corporations about the superiority of CSR. Both types of strategies drew on economical arguments. CSR was presented as a modern business strategy, indispensable for any corporation. CSR was argued to be a corporate imperative for tackling increased stakeholder demands. Hence, it was argued that customers, NGOs, investors, employees, governmental organizations and the media among others demanded social responsibility from corporations, and that they in fact had the power to influence corporations to a greater extent than before. The reactive rhetorical strategy thus presented CSR as a risk minimizing strategy. So, if corporations did not implement CSR, and thus did not meet stakeholder demands, it would lead to reputation damage and financial losses. The proactive rhetorical strategy, on the other hand, suggested that if a corporation implemented CSR, the corporation would handle the demands of the stakeholders in a successful way and gain from it, as this eventually would result in increased profits.

Table 3.1 Rhetorical Strategies

Reactive Argumentation	Proactive Argumentation
Keep license to operate	Increase license to operate
Protect reputation	Enhance reputation
Eroded band	Value added brand
Retain employees	Recruit the best employees
Maintain morale	Enhance morale
Maintain efficiency and profits	Increase efficiency and profits
Good business sense	Good business sense

The reactive rhetorical strategy thus framed CSR as the response to an increased societal criticism of corporations, fostered by non–governmental organizations (NGOs) and activist groups, whereas the proactive rhetorical strategy framed CSR, not only as a solution to existing corporate problems, but also as a great opportunity to improve the business. In the very beginning of the consultants' work with CSR, the reactive rhetorical strategy was primarily used. Thereby, changing conditions in the business world were highlighted and the consultants argued that corporations had to adjust to these changes by attending to social issues.

> In our job we often have to identify problems and risks for the corporations so that they avoid getting into trouble. Corporations can be caught in the hands of media. NGOs will attack them, if their business operations are unhealthy. Corporations can be sued, and they can get fines and all that. (Consultant SB, 17/10/2002)

There is an invisible forefinger out there, consisting of different NGOs. It is the global civil society against the corporations. Their forefinger has always been visible, but now their power is greater. (Consultant B, 17/10/2002)

According to the consultants, corporations generally adopted CSR because they feared being accused of bad behaviour by their stakeholders. The consultants stated that CSR first and foremost was a risk minimizing strategy and a listener's strategy for corporations. However, the consultants believed that this attitude would change within the coming years and that CSR would become a proactive business strategy. They considered it a victory to be able to present CSR as a business case and therefore, they gradually began to present CSR as a proactive business strategy. Using examples of 'the good' versus 'the bad' corporation, the consultants tried to convince corporations that CSR was in fact a proactive business strategy. Interestingly, all consultants used the same bad examples. They used the stories about the collapse and scandal of *Enron, WorldCom, Parmalat* and their Swedish counterparts, to demonstrate corporations that social responsibility is a vital part in all businesses. The good examples that were used to illustrate the advantages of CSR were more divergent. However, several consultants independently declared that Anita Roddick 'had done it' and they argued that the success of *The Body Shop* illustrates that CSR is a fruitful management strategy: these consultants argued that Anita Roddick had succeeded in creating a profitable but yet responsible corporation.

So, rhetorical strategies based on the language of economics were used as central sales tools. CSR was presented as a concept that would either increase profits or would prevent the loss of profits. Thereby, the consultants persuaded corporations that CSR was not about expenses, but about revenues. The ethical and moral dimension of CSR was only briefly mentioned, and when it was, it was argued that being good, makes good business sense.

World Saviours and Money–Makers

In the previous section the consultants' means of selling CSR were addressed. It was shown how the consultants used the same type of rhetorical strategies in order to mobilize CSR. Yet, the motives for commercializing CSR have not been explored. In this section this will be attended to.

In Table 3.1, six categories of consultants were identified. However, during the interviews, it soon became clear that the six categories of consultants could be condensed into two new categories. The consultants represented two fundamentally different groups, which I call: *world saviours* and *money–makers*. These two groups have radically divergent perspectives on the meaning and content of CSR, as well as different opinions about what role corporations should play in society. For several of the world–saviours, CSR was not only a question of marketing new services, but also a matter of beliefs and ideological conviction. The quote from consultant W illustrates this further:

> We have established our firm for a reason other than the one that you normally establish consultancies for. We founded our consultancy with the ambition of changing the world,

and that goes for all people working with us. We want to change the world with our costumers as tools. (Consultant W, 06/11/2002)

The attitude of consultant W was no exception. Several of the CSR–consultants were not primarily driven by market demand. Instead, they argued that they were motivated by their own political agendas and visions about how to change corporations and make them contribute to a better society. This group of consultants often referred to themselves as world–saviours. In the interviews they talked unreservedly and openheartedly about their visions and ideals in life, and how they wanted to change the world by influencing corporate behaviour. As stated by consultant B:

I believe that I have a kind of a world–salvation–soul. I want to make business nicer. (Consultant B, 05/11/2002)

The world–saviours can be found in all of the six previously mentioned categories. A similarity between these consultancies is that they often consisted of one or two persons whose dream and ambition was to change the world. The world–saviours argued that their intentions were more than just earning money or expanding an established business into new areas.

Our mission is to make small improvements every day – in investments, in business, in our own business, and of course, in the world. (Consultant F, 22/20/2002)

Their intentions were often reflected in the consultancy names, which sometimes contained words as sympathy, care, concern or respect. The world saviours considered it necessary to attain direct access to corporations in order to exert influence on corporate behaviour. They had noted the authority and legitimacy that consultants have in the business environment, which motivated them to join the profession. They stressed that, as consultants, they could successfully influence corporations, which would not be possible for NGOs. Some of them claimed that they had established a consultancy instead of an NGO, since it is 'easier to influence corporations if you are inside and not standing on the outside and banging on the door' (Consultant Ö, 10/10/2002).

When our consultancy was launched, the idea was to create help, to be a catalyst, a guide for transforming business into sustainable business. Initially, we wondered whether to create a NGO or to lobby for public opinion. We realized that this form, a profit–driven–consultancy, was the best way. (Consultant Ö, 10/10/2002)

The *money–makers*, as I label the consultants that did not make any claims about wanting to change the world, had often entered the area of CSR in the late 1990s. They argued that they were driven by the business opportunity of CSR. They considered CSR to be a business case both for themselves and for corporations. They argued that they had expanded their services in accordance with market demand and stated that CSR was highly profitable both for themselves and their clients.

The consultants that actively tried to market CSR in an early stage, I would say was a smaller consultancy that had some kind of commitment, an idealistic interest in these questions. I am not saying that we are uncommitted. [...] But here you have to see the introduction of CSR as a strict business decision. (Consultant, BJ, 14/10/2002)

However, these classifications of consultants into world–saviours and money–makers should not be understood as if world saviours did not take any interest in earning money or as if money–makers did not have any real commitment to the CSR issue. The classification illustrates that the consultants themselves claimed to have different motives for selling CSR.

Another obvious difference between the two groups was the attitude towards the meaning and regulation of CSR. Several of the world–saviours argued that a common or standardized definition for CSR was needed to prevent CSR from becoming corporate window-dressing. To avoid that, it was argued that CSR had to be formalized. Otherwise it would not be possible to measure and evaluate corporate social performance and CSR would easily become a concept without true implications. However the money–makers were sceptical to standardization as they argued that CSR had to be adjusted to each corporation. The world–saviours often had a critical attitude towards other consultants. They mainly criticized other consultants for turning CSR into a marketing strategy without any content or implications for corporate behaviour. World–saviours repeatedly stressed the importance of credibility and argued that CSR is not about market communication, but about 'walking the talk'. The money–makers on the other hand stressed that a common definition of CSR was in fact impossible, as CSR needed to be designed according to the conditions of each industry and to each corporation's level of ambition.

Relationships: Collaboration and Competition

Even though the interviewees had mixed ideas about how and why CSR should be transformed into practice, and even though they competed in a tough market where several consultants were driven out of business, collaboration was regarded as being of great importance to market CSR. Contradicting statements regarding the actual demand for CSR were made. On one hand it was claimed that there was an enormous interest for CSR issues among corporations. On the other hand, the consultants stated they had to make a lot of effort to get in touch with corporations, and that CSR services only represented a minor part of their total revenue (that is, for those consultants offering other services than CSR alone). Furthermore, several smaller consultancies specialized in CSR had gone out of business in recent years. Along with this, it was often indicated that the overall situation for consultants had become tough since the 'dotcom crash'.

The consultants claimed that it was a low priority for corporations to hire consultants to deal with social responsibility. Nevertheless, they believed in a future for CSR issues and they compared CSR with the environmental movement. It was expected that CSR would develop similar to the rise of environmental issues in the 1980s. However, it was also claimed that CSR had to be mobilized by several groups of actors for this to happen. Collaboration between consultants therefore was claimed to be of significant importance. The CSR consultants were very familiar with each other and in some cases even befriended. Several consultants hired each other for assignments where special expertise was needed. They also arranged seminars, wrote books or engaged in other activities together to spread the word about CSR.

The sociogram in Figure 3.3 illustrates the relationships between the CSR consultants in Sweden. Sociometry is the study of the structure of ties within a group (de Nooy, Mrvar and Batagelj 2005). The sociogram shows relationships between the consultants and the centrality of their position within the group. The sociogram – based on the interviews – depicts interviewees' perception of competitors in the area of CSR. They were asked to mention those consultants that they considered to be their competitors. The sociogram also shows the consultancies that were driven by ideological conviction and the ambition to change the world, and those that were not. The black circles represent *world–saviours* and the white circles represent *money–makers*.

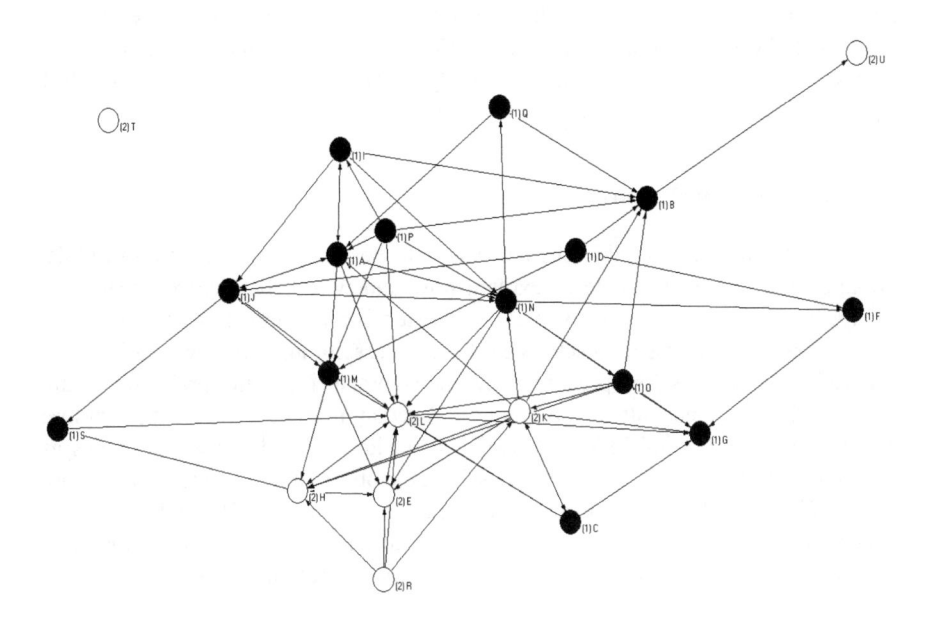

Figure 3.3 Sociogram of Consultants in Sweden, 2002–2003 (black circles represent world–saviours; white circles money–makers)

As shown in the sociogram, the world–saviours (black circles) are numerous. The sociogram also gives a picture of the relationship between world–saviours and money–makers. It depicts that world–saviours and money–makers to a large extent mention competitors within the same categories as they belong to. Hence, the money–makers often referred to other money–makers and vice versa. This could be explained by the fact that they did not consider consultants in the other category as being in the same business, even though they all were selling services under the label of CSR.

However, several world–saviours mentioned the central consultant L, which is a money–maker. Consultant L was one of the larger consultancies in Sweden, which had been an early mover in environmental consulting. This consultancy was described as a newcomer in the area of CSR. However, given its knowledge in environmental consulting and its expertise in reporting, it was believed to also become successful in CSR consulting, and was therefore mentioned as a competitor by several interviewees. Moreover, several world–saviours and one money–maker mentioned consultant B, at the top right hand corner, as a competitor. This consultant was one of the early movers in the area of CSR and was therefore well-known. However, consultant B only regarded consultant U to be a competitor, even though this consultancy was not known by any of the others. This can be explained by the fact that consultant B and consultant U represented a niche within CSR that the others did not serve. Furthermore, consultant T, in the top left hand corner, might need further explanation. This consultant was found on an Internet search. Consultant T was just entering the area of CSR and therefore had little knowledge about CSR consulting. This consultant clearly was a late mover in the area of CSR and was primarily driven by the increasing market demand.

Discussion and Conclusions

The point of departure for this chapter was that, despite the proliferation of CSR, few attempts have been made to explain how and why CSR has expanded as a management idea. Moreover, even though extensive research has addressed the role of consultants as fashion–setters in the business community, few studies have explored their motives for spreading new management ideas and practices. Using interview data from consultants operating in Sweden, this chapter sought to explore the commercialization of CSR as a management idea by addressing the means as well as the motives of those involved. Based on the observations two conclusions are drawn and further developed. First, the commercialization of CSR is a three–stage–process; and second, consultants operate as institutional entrepreneurs that mobilize normative claims as they commercialize CSR through rhetorical strategies.

The Commercialization of CSR in Three Stages

The empirical results illustrated that CSR is a fluffy label, based on ideas about the social responsibility of business that embrace a multitude of corporate activities. During its commercialization, CSR became popular while it also remained an ambiguous concept. The commercialization of CSR consisted of a three–stage–process. Consultants turned ideas about the social responsibility of business into a management idea in three sequential stages: (1) labelling, (2) packaging and (3) mobilizing.

Stage (1): Labelling Fluffy Ideas. In the early 1990s, ideas about the social responsibility of business were circulating in society. These ideas were rather unspecific and embraced almost all corporate activities. As it was unclear what these ideas actually meant and what the scope of social responsibility was, these ideas can be characterized as fluffy. The consultants that acknowledged ideas about the social responsibility of business at an early stage turned these ideas into diverse labels. These ideas thus were conceptualized into a variety of labels. In the first stage of the commercialization of CSR, these coexisting labels were reduced to a common label, as it was argued that a common label would facilitate the creation of market demand for consultants' services addressing social responsibility. Coexisting labels could have been an advantage to consultants, as this enabled them to differentiate themselves. However, when fluffy ideas were turned into fluffy labels, it became a drawback since the ideas were neither simplified nor clarified. Hence, labelling ideas about the social responsibility of business into one label could help consultants to raise awareness. This means that the consultants could draw attention to general ideas about the social responsibility of business by presenting them as a mangement idea labelled CSR.

Stage (2): Packaging a Fluffy Label. However, finding a common label was not sufficient, the label of CSR had to be filled with content and CSR had to be packaged into saleable services. The fluffiness of CSR made it possible for consultants to translate it into services in their own area of expertise. The consultants developed CSR services that were close to their traditional area of work; accountants sold services related to social reports, management consultants worked with CSR policies, et cetera. Hence, several different types of services that addressed different aspects of corporate behaviour and activities were developed. Subsequently the fluffy label of CSR was maintained fluffy since it was not put into one concrete form; rather it was turned into diverse services.

Stage (3): Mobilizing a Label. Finally, the label of CSR had to be mobilized to create a demand for CSR services. In the final stage of commercializing CSR the consultants had to convince the business community of the value of CSR. By using rhetorical strategies, built on economical arguments, they reduced CSR into more specific problems that were related to the business world. Thereby, consultants tried to convince corporations about the efficiency and utilization of their models and frameworks for CSR. Consequently, the evolving rhetoric addressed logical rationales in order to capture corporate interests. In other words, CSR was presented in a way that made sense to the business community. Linking CSR to dominant norms in the business world about progress and efficiency, that is, increasing profits, enabled the commercialization of CSR. Thereby, CSR was clarified and simplified, which turned it into a management idea that could be understood by corporations.

In conclusion, one could argue that abstract ideas that are turned into a fluffy label that takes on different forms, can become a popular management idea if the accompanying rhetoric is sufficiently convincing.

Institutional Entrepreneurs: Consultants Building Normative Claims

Consistent with previous studies of management ideas, we can conclude that CSR is packaged as an idea that is based on prevailing business norms. Hence, consultants support their promotion of CSR by arguing that it contributes to increased progress and profits in the business community. Moreover, the empirical results demonstrate that even though consultants shared the same means, they did not share the same motives for commercializing CSR. Hence, consultants as a group of actors are not to be understood as a homogenous group, rather as a heterogeneous group with similar means but dissimilar motives.

For some consultants selling CSR was about expanding their services and meeting market demands. For others the commercialization of CSR was not an end in itself, they had the ambition to change the world by spreading CSR. Hence, the findings demonstrate that one group of consultants purposively sought to promote other interests than commercial ones alone. For some individuals, becoming a consultant was a way of advocating CSR in order to change what they considered to be social injustice in the world. By presenting themselves as CSR consultants they gained authority to influence the construction of CSR according to their own agenda. In this particular case, these consultants in several ways resemble NGOs, which seek to fulfil an ideological conviction. Hence, the borders between different actor groups such as consultants and NGOs are blurred in this case, as both seek to fulfil similar ends.

The consultants argued that corporations had to adopt CSR to meet new stakeholder claims. However, they did not only mediate these claims, but also functioned as a pressure group constructing these normative claims themselves. Thereby, I argue the consultants can be characterized as institutional entrepreneurs that have potential opportunities to create and mobilize normative claims in corporations. Their authority to provide corporations with recipes on how to handle new issues makes them influential players in the business community. They have legitimacy as decision makers and transformers in the business world. For this reason, consultants can be understood as potential transformers of established business norms. Hence, consultants should not only be understood as mediators of ideas circulating in society, but also as actors that purposively shape these ideas on the basis of their own agenda. In some cases their agenda consist of just expanding their own area of expertise and to provide corporations with ideas that enhance their productivity. In other cases their agenda consists of shaping ideas that seek to transform corporations in terms of their role and position in society.

Rhetorical Strategies Commercializing CSR

No matter whether the consultants want to improve social justice or expand their area of expertise, they need to commercialize CSR into products that can be sold. Regardless of their motives, they put CSR on top of the corporate agenda by translating ideas about the social responsibility of business into a management idea through rhetoric built on economic rationales rather than on moral rationales. Hence, by using the language of economics and thus presenting CSR as a business case, they convince corporations about the necessity and advantages of adopting CSR.

Consultants promote CSR as a corporate imperative, not because of moral reasons but because of financial ones. The consultants expressed ambitions of changing corporations because of ideological and moral convictions. For this reason, one could argue that economical arguments function as Trojan horses. The economical arguments frame CSR as a management idea that improves corporate performance, even though these consultants primarily seek to improve society by changing corporate behaviour. Thereby, normative claims about corporations as socially responsible are incorporated into corporations on the pretence that CSR is about increased profits. In other words, the consultants could not provide evidence that CSR would lead to improved profitability, and their aim was not to improve corporate profitability either, rather to improve corporate behaviour. For some consultants the commercialization of CSR was a means to radically change corporate behaviour and to transform the role that corporations play in society. Still, they used a rhetoric that emphasised that CSR was a true business case.

Rhetorical strategies are important to build and mobilize new ideas as well as new normative claims. As argued by Suddaby and Greenwood (2005: 60): 'Rhetorical strategies are the ways in which the meaning systems that underpin institutions are manipulated'. Therefore, rhetoric should not be dismissed as mere rhetoric. Therefore, we can concede that rhetoric mobilizes CSR, and that rhetoric might disrupt the established and institutionalized view about what responsibilities corporations should assume in society.

Chapter 4

Tracing the Evolution of Corporate Discourse on Corporate Social Responsibility: A Longitudinal, Lexicological Study

Frank G.A. de Bakker, Claes Ohlsson, Frank den Hond, Stefan Tengblad and Marie-France B. Turcotte[1]

Introduction

One way of tracing the emergence of corporate social responsibility (CSR) as a central theme in the contemporary discussions about the relationship between firms and society is to analyze how companies communicate about their efforts regarding CSR. Among the many different ways by which companies may communicate about these efforts, how they do so in their annual reports stands out. The perceived credibility of information in annual reports is related to the external auditing process that at least the financial parts of the annual report must undergo before it can be published (Jenkins and Yakovleva 2006; Neu, Warsame and Pendwell 1998). This chapter is based on the idea that how firms write about issues of CSR in their annual reports provides insight in their position vis-à-vis these issues. It might be expected that there are significant differences between firms in this respect, as well as between firms from different industries and countries. Further, firms may take different positions at different moments in time. Although it has been suggested that the recent emergence of CSR is related to the advent of economic globalization (Jenkins 2005), it is unlikely that in earlier days, firms did not consider, and act on, their social responsibilities (den Hond, de Bakker and Neergaard this volume).

In order to explore such issues, we analyzed a sample of major stock-listed companies from three different countries on how these companies reported on issues relating to their social, economic and natural environments, at different moments in time. We studied either the letter from the CEO section or the entire annual report, comparing how textual representations of issues related to CSR in these reports have changed over time. Our study is based on a comparative design: taking CSR

---

1   The authors would like to acknowledge Lotte van der Bent and Miguel Rojas for their assistance in data collection and analysis. Parts of the research were kindly supported by the Vrije Universiteit, Centre for Innovation and Corporate Social Responsibility (CIMO) and by the program INÉ of the Social Sciences Research Council of Canada.

representations in annual reports as the units of analysis, the study design allows for comparison over time, across issues, and between firms, sectors and countries. It takes an initial Swedish study (Ohlsson and Tengblad 2004) as a point of departure and supplements that with data from two other countries, meanwhile refining the initial analysis in response to findings from the other countries. Doing so enables us to provide a descriptive, empirical study on similarities and differences between these countries and to develop a notion of how these differences and similarities might have come about. Such a description allows us to trace developments in how firms in different contexts talk about CSR and related issues in their annual reports.

This study therefore builds on a tradition within the management and accounting literatures of studying annual reports on CSR-related themes (for example Abbott and Monsen 1979; Bowman and Haire 1975; Gray, Kouhy and Lavers 1995; Tilt 2001), which is an important theme in studying corporate annual reports (Stanton and Stanton 2002). However, the study of CSR in corporate annual reports is often limited to content analysis on particular themes, using empirical data from companies rooted in one country (for example Campbell 2003; Day and Woodward 2004; Kolk 2003; Igalens 2004; Caron and Turcotte, in press). Other studies include Judd and Tims' (1991) investigation of how CEOs express their companies' customer orientation through their letter in the annual report, or Segars and Kohut's (2001) study on the effectiveness of CEO letters. Although Yuthas, Rogers and Dillard (2002) aimed to investigate several ethical characteristics of discourse found in annual reports, the use of lexicological techniques for a comparative analysis of corporate texts from different languages is relatively new.

Within language studies the study of business texts has only recently started. For instance, Thomas (1997) studied the linguistic structures of management messages in annual reports and how positive and negative messages are communicated differently, whereas Hyland (1998) focused on meta-discourse of CEOs and how a positive message is manifested in the annual report in order to influence the reader. Malavasi (2005) studied how evaluation is carried out in annual reports by the use of different categorizations in language, whereas another study focused on how visual devices are used as discursive strategies in annual reports (Ruiz-Carrado, Palmer-Silveira and Fortanet-Gómez 2005). Several readability studies are also available in this context (Courtis 1995; Sydserff and Weetman 1999). Specific lexicological approaches have not been applied frequently, nor have they been adapted for a multi-country, multi-language analysis. We expect that our lexicological approach is a useful alternative method to trace the development of social phenomena as they emerge in corporate texts.

In this chapter, we first discuss our choice to focus on annual reports as a source to trace firms' positions towards CSR. Then we provide a theoretical background to our specific lexicological approach and discuss our methodology and the three datasets. This section is followed by a detailed presentation of our empirical data: the 'Letter from the CEO'-section in the annual report or, in one country, the complete non-financial part of the annual report. In the analysis, we highlight the emergence of a CSR discourse, the apparent shift in geographical perspective and relationships with stakeholders, as themes that stand out in the comparison. Our main finding is that during the 1990s, the increase in voluntary CSR reporting is paralleled by a shift in the geographical focus of the firm from being predominantly 'national' to 'international' and 'global'. The chapter concludes with some notes on the implications of our findings, both concerning their content and the methods applied.

Annual Reports

Annual reports are a well-known means of communication between firms and their stakeholders. An annual report is, by definition, a tool for impression management because, as a written self-description, it helps creating a desired identity for the organization that publishes it (Arndt and Bigelow 2000; Stanton and Stanton 2002). Annual reports help managers to shape the impressions that observers of the firm hold (Neu et al. 1998; Tinker and Neimark 1987). They are intended to create confidence in the company and thus to gain external legitimacy for the firm (Preston and Post 1975). Important stakeholders in this respect are shareholders. Current shareholders are to be convinced to keep their shares, whereas prospective shareholders should be inclined to make an investment. In order to attract or retain shareholders, the messages communicated in the annual report need to respond to the values of shareholders.

The text that accompanies a firm's financial annual report aims to demonstrate how that firm's management is effective and efficient in securing the firm's economic and social viability (Hyland 1998; Segars and Kohut 2001). Particularly the accompanying letters of the CEO are intended to meet and influence the readers' expectations of what a competent top management team should be concerned about. To create an impression of competency, effectiveness and efficiency, CEOs 'frame their corporate facts and figures' (Rogers 2000: 427). Issues of CSR might fit in with this impression of competency, as both normative contributions and empirical research from the CSR literature have suggested that disclosures about CSR help to reinforce organizational legitimacy (Adams, Hill and Roberts 1998; Bowman 1978; Neu et al. 1998). Has this literature influenced what CEOs think what is expected from them in terms of corporate performance? And if so, how do these representations evolve over time?

Changes in the nature and amount of CSR representations in annual reports and CEO letters can be seen as a reflection of changes in how firms think to be able to reinforce their legitimacy with the users of the annual report. Looking at the messages within the annual financial reports as discursive practices therefore allows researchers to track the development of the CSR concept within firms. The international dimension in this tracking process is highly relevant. As firms operate in an increasingly internationalized context, for instance with respect to financial and product markets or supply chains, they need to gain legitimacy in this context too, next to maintaining legitimacy in the national contexts in which they are rooted. It has been suggested that, to some extent, something like a 'national' CSR culture exists (cf. Habisch, Jonker, Wegner and Schmidpeter 2005). However, as CSR is also being presented as a philosophy of self-regulation that is aimed to achieve capitalism with a human face in an epoch of globalization, it is to be expected that firms need to find legitimacy at a global level too. Firms' CSR representations would then have to be presented in a delocalized language, moving from a local-situational context to a macro-system context (Alvesson and Karreman 2000).

Triggered by Ohlsson and Tengblad's (2004) initial study from Sweden, in this chapter we explore how firms from different countries represent themselves in their annual reports as being socially responsible and whether these representations have changed over time. In the next section, we will discuss the lexicological approach we have taken, illustrated by some elements of our dataset. A more elaborate presentation of the dataset follows afterwards.

Texts, Genres and the Use of Corpora

Language can either be studied as a distinct, formal system, or in use as a social or psychological phenomenon. This chapter takes the latter approach where language is seen as a way of conveying information and also as a part in the creation of company images. Obviously, companies make extensive use of written language in many ways and documents and texts are widely used in for instance accounting, marketing and policy-making. This study focuses on texts in annual reports from selected companies in Sweden, Canada and the Netherlands. Annual reports are sets of texts that can be seen as a genre in which several subgenres can be identified. We consider this textual genre as a set of norms that determine what can be written and in what way (Swales 1990; Halliday and Matthiessen 2004). To some extent genres are stable, as they provide a framework for packaging meaning (such as information, values, etcetera) in the form of texts. However, genres are also unstable in the sense that the framework can change once the setting and use for the genre change. This study shows that, the genre of corporate annual reports has become more elaborate in most countries, as much more narrative texts have been incorporated. Meanwhile it can still be seen as relatively stable, as it continues to contain narrative sections that are similar in all three countries. These sections, or subgenres, are interesting to study since they are not standardized by legislation nor stipulated to be in an annual report. Nevertheless, they are part of the norms that make up the larger genre of annual reports: a proper annual report is expected to contain such sections.

The Canadian and Swedish samples in our study consist of narratives that belong to the subgenre 'Letter from the CEO' (or 'Letter from the Board of Directors'). The Dutch sample consists of the complete non-financial part of annual reports, as this subgenre is hardly found in annual reports of firms from this country. In both cases, the focus of our analysis is on words that carry meaning (content words), in contrast to words that mainly make texts coherent (functional words, see for example Halliday and Matthiessen 2004). In most languages, content words tend to be names, nouns, adjectives and verbs, and they can also be represented in larger units such as nominal phrases or compound words. By finding and categorizing such content words or units of content words, it is possible to pattern themes or discourses within texts (Stubbs 2002; Williams 1983).

Our analysis is a combination of two types of linguistic methods. The first step is to collect relevant texts into a corpus that enables sorting and mapping of words used in these texts. The second step is to observe how certain keywords are actually functioning in their context by a close reading of the texts and to group such words in themes or semantic fields (see below). A corpus can be described as a body of text or texts. It can be linguistically analyzed in several ways (Stubbs 1996, 2002). For our purpose, the selected letters of CEO and annual reports from the different time-periods were quantified with the help of computer software.[2] Quantification provides the possibility to sort all words in the texts, either by frequency or in alphabetical order, which enables a range of descriptions, per text and across all different texts from the selected periods. This quantification gives us a tool to compare texts from different years, but it also facilitates standardization of search processes among the researchers. The software can produce an index of all words and also 'concordances' of selected words. A concordance is a presentation of a selected word in its context, where the word searched for is centered; this makes it easier to quickly analyze a large body of text than through close reading alone.

Our method for selecting words has partly been initiated by 'buzz words' that can be found in broader CSR-vocabulary (such as documents from institutions like the European Commission or the UN but also from companies and media) and partly from the lists of word frequency and alphabetical word order derived from the material (for a similar methodology see Piper 2000). Making concordances enables the compilation of lists of salient words and clusters of words that constitute a semantic field (a group of semantically related words with a similar meaning, Lyons 1995). Because our texts were in four different languages, we used semantic fields to ensure that similar phenomena were studied. By using concordances, we were not only able to see how word patterns changed over time, but also to uncover how similar words received different meanings.

A highly standardized research protocol was developed in a pilot study on the 'Letter from the CEO'-sections of fifteen Swedish companies (Ohlsson and Tengblad 2004). This protocol was followed in data collection and analysis of the texts of companies from Canada and the Netherlands. Steps in the protocol consisted in making explicit criteria for which companies to include, the production of text files, the use of concordance software, and how to analyze the wordlists and concordances. During the process, we needed to adapt the initial list of words used to identify semantic fields, as in different countries and languages different aspects of CSR are highlighted, similar semantic fields around CSR aspects are denoted by different words. Further, compound words are frequently applied in Swedish and Dutch, but not in French and English. Thus, results from one country were input for subsequent additional analysis in the other two countries. In an iterative mode, we were eventually able to produce results that form a consistent base for the comparative analysis.[3]

---

[2] Different software packages were used (Concorder Pro in Sweden, WordSmith Tools 4.0 in Canada, and Concordance in the Netherlands), but they allow for similar procedures.

[3] Further details regarding our methodological choices can be obtained from the authors.

Data Selection

For our analysis of CEOs' messages, we selected annual reports from the years 1981, 1991 and 2001 from companies that are based in Sweden, Canada and the Netherlands. We compare developments in CSR discourses over space and time by means of a lexicological analysis and assess whether corporations have created a discursive space in their annual reports to show how they behave in a more socially responsible way, or whether the rise of a CSR discourse merely replaces or re-labels other topics that are related to stakeholder responsibility.

The logic of comparative case studies (Yin 2003) suggests that cases should be sufficiently homogeneous *and* different along relevant dimensions, in order enable making more general inferences about the influence of particular factors. Departing from the Swedish study, we therefore included countries with comparable characteristics: the Netherlands and Canada. First of all, the three countries can be characterized as highly developed welfare states, a context in which the national state traditionally has played an important role in socio-economic policy, as opposed to a context of self-regulation (Pasquero 1997). Moreover, each country scores high on the UN Human Development Index for 2004 (rankings 2, 4 and 5 for Sweden, Canada and the Netherlands).[4] We have made a study of three small or medium-sized, relatively post-modern countries (Inglehart 1997), heavily dependent on foreign trade. In these respects, the choice of these three countries is based on a 'most similar' research design (Pasquero 1988). It is to be expected, however, that these countries will also differ on many other dimensions influential to CSR representations but relating to national characteristics, including geography (closeness to the USA, relative importance of secondary and tertiary industries), types of traditions and institutions (cf. regarding development of socio-economic policies), and adherence to competing economic unions or trade agreements (EU, NAFTA). Given this mixture of differences and similarities, comparing these three countries is more indicative than predictive.

Annual reports have been collected for the years 1981, 1991 and 2001. The selection of years was made in the Swedish pilot study and applied in the other two studies as well. First, this choice was made to ensure each of the three decades was represented at a 10-year interval, and secondly for the economic conditions to be about the same. Of course, selecting shorter intervals between the sampling years would have created more continuity in the data, but we faced a trade-off between the length of time that we could look back and the amount of practical work related to quantifying text. The three years selected were all downturn years. 1981 was a year plagued by the effects of the second oil-crisis. In Sweden this year preceded the large Swedish devaluation that took place in the autumn of 1982; in Canada and the Netherlands this was a period of economic depression as well. 1991 was a very problematic year for the Swedish economy with unemployment reaching very high levels. The Canadian and Dutch economies also suffered from a recession in

---

4 Even though the 2005 version of the HDI places these countries on position 6, 5 and 12 respectively, this still are very high positions on the ranking. As the data were gathered in 2004 and early 2005, we decided to stick to the 2004 figures in this chapter.

1991. Finally, in all three countries 2001 was characterized by weakening market demand, severe problems in the IT sector and political instability in the wake of the terror attacks on 11 September 2001. Choosing downturn years limits the risk that our data are confounded by favourable economic circumstances; in such situations, slack resources might be an explanation for the interest in CSR (Hussain 1999). The initial Swedish selection of years thus appeared suitable for our purposes.

The main criterion for selecting companies is that they have been listed at the Stockholm Exchange, Amsterdam Stock Exchange/Euronext,[5] or the Toronto Stock Exchange throughout the entire period. We also wanted to include the largest of the listed companies in each country, measured by numbers of employees and by capital assets, as such companies receive large media attention and are more scrutinized by the general public than smaller companies (Adams et al. 1998). In addition, we also decided to select only firms that had been listed on the respective stock-markets as separate funds, thus ruling out large acquisitions or mergers.[6] For example, in the Dutch sample we did not include a major financial corporation such as ABN-Amro, as ABN and Amro merged only in 1991. Most of the selected firms are highly visible; a well-known company can be expected to adhere to external expectations to a larger extent than very small companies on the stock exchange. Meanwhile, given their size, these companies also can be expected to be able address issues of CSR in their business plans. The selected companies are based in different industries, as shown in Table 4.1. It appeared impossible to find companies that operate in similar industries in all three countries. For example, whereas in Sweden there is an independent automobile industry, there is not in Canada or the Netherlands. And while there still is some textile industry in the Netherlands, this industry is virtually non-existent in Sweden and Canada, at least at the major stock markets. In brackets we indicated whether the company was mainly oriented on a business-to-business (B2B) or business-to-consumer (B2C) market, as it could be expected that this dimension influences the amount and nature of a firm's involvement in, and reporting on, CSR (McWilliams and Siegel 2001).[7]

For Sweden and Canada, the sample for analysis consists of the 'Letter from the CEO'-sections that these annual reports contain. Several firms did not have a 'Letter from the CEO'-section, but rather a 'Letter from the Board'; in such cases we used the 'Letter from the Board', as both types of letters can be argued to belong to the same subgenre. In both countries, there are no legal requirements to include such a letter in the annual report. Nevertheless, there are strong expectations among the audience that the annual report of a major company does start with such a letter (Skulstad 2002). Its theme is always a reflection on the affairs of the company of the previous year from the firm's point of view and often also comprises an outlook into the near future. The structure and form of these letters is usually quite similar. In 1991 and 2001 all the selected annual reports contain CEO or Board letters, but

---

5   In 2000, the stock exchanges of Amsterdam, Brussels and Paris merged into Euronext.

6   Our reason for doing so was to be able to analyze trends of CSR representations at level of the individual firm. However, firm-level results are not presented here.

7   A description of the selected companies is available from the authors.

several annual reports in the 1981 sample lack such a letter. This can be seen as a part in the development towards more elaborate annual reports (Lee 1994).

Table 4.1 Description of Dataset per Industry (B2B – operates mainly in business-to-business markets, B2C – operates mainly in business-to-consumer markets)

	The Netherlands	Sweden	Canada
Airlines	KLM (B2C)		
Textiles	Blydenstein (B2C) Gamma (B2B)		
Media & entertainment	Telegraaf (B2C) VNU (B2C)		
Porcelain	De Porceleyne Fles (B2C)		
Food & Beverages	Heineken (B2C) Numico (B2C) Unilever (B2C)		Molson (B2C)
Engineering & machinery	Econosto (B2B) Stork (B2B) Ten Cate (B2B) Batenburg (B2B)	Atlas Copco (B2B) Sandvik (B2B) SKF (B2B) Trelleborg (B2B)	
Electronic & electrical equipment	Hagemeyer (B2B) Philips (B2C) Nedap (B2B)	Electrolux (B2C)	
Energy			Atco Group (B2B/B2C)
Retail	Ahold (B2C) Macintosh (B2C)	H&M (B2C)	Canadian Tire (B2C) Hudson Bay Company (B2C) Jean Coutu (B2C)
Finance		Handelsbanken (B2B/B2C) SEB (B2B/B2C) Skandia (B2B/B2C)	
Holding Companies		Industrivärden (B2B) Investor (B2B)	Power Corp. (B2B)
IT & Telecom		Ericsson (B2B)	
Paper & Pulp		SCA (B2B)	Abitibi-Consolidated (B2B) Domtar (B2C)
Building & Construction		Skanska (B2B)	
Automobile manufacturing		Volvo (B2B/B2C)	Magna (B2B) Bombardier (B2B)
Mining & Metallurgy			Acier Leroux (B2B) Alcan (B2B) Cambior (B2B) Placer Dome (B2B) IPSCO Inc. (B2B) Ivaco (B2B)

Table 4.2 Description of Dataset

	Sweden			Canada			the Netherlands		
	1981	1991	2001	1981	1991	2001	1981	1991	2001
Number of Letters or Director's reports analyzed	11	15	15	11	16	16	18	18	18
Average number of words per text analyzed	1,100	1,050	1,400	1,750	1,350	1,700	4,900	4,300	8,600
Index (1981=100)	100	95	127	100	74	97	100	88	176

The Dutch dataset is different. As CEO letters were not as generally available in Dutch reports, we conducted our analyses on the entire Director's report, that is the non-financial part of the annual report. After all, CEO letters are likely to emphasize certain aspects of the corporation's policy and affairs but these aspects need to be substantiated and explained in the full report. Using these full reports therefore is an appropriate way to trace similar developments; we expect the main issues addressed to be quite similar and therefore comparable.

To enhance comparability, the absolute figures in terms of word counts within the corpus will be recalculated into occurrences per 1,000 words. Table 4.2 provides a brief overview of our data set. Our sample of texts shows that from 1991 to 2001 the average length of text analyzed increases. This reflects a broader trend that annual reports get longer over time, as more additional information is voluntarily being added, in addition to the legally required (financial) information. In line with longer annual reports and the introduction of new types of information, the reports in 2001 have been stylized and printed in a manner that almost resembles glossy magazines.

Results

To trace the evolution of a corporate discourse on corporate social responsibility, we emphasize a comparison between the three datasets. Rather than presenting each dataset extensively, we present our findings under three common themes: the emergence of a CSR discourse; a shift in geographical perspective; and relationships with stakeholders.

Emergence of a CSR Discourse

After having analyzed the concordances derived from the annual reports, we distinguished four semantic fields in the CSR discourse: CSR as a distinct phenomenon, the ethics and moral values associated with CSR, environmental issues and sustainability. Developments over time in these four groups of semantically related words with a similar meaning (Lyons 1995), are presented in Table 4.3. To enhance the comparability among the datasets, the findings are presented both in absolute and in relative numbers (occurrences per 1,000 words).

Table 4.3 Occurrence of CSR Discourse (number of occurrences per 1,000 words in brackets)

	Sweden 1981	Sweden 1991	Sweden 2001	Canada 1981	Canada 1991	Canada 2001	the Netherlands 1981	the Netherlands 1991	the Netherlands 2001
CSR as a phenomenon	7 (6.4)	2 (1.9)	10 (7.1)	1 (0.6)	7 (5.2)	18 (10.6)	1 (0.2)	3 (0.7)	41 (4.8)
Ethics and moral values	0	0	7 (5.0)	1 (0.6)	2 (1.5)	3 (1.8)	0	0	55 (6.4)
Environment	0	13 (12.4)	8 (5.7)	2 (1.1)	15 (11.1)	10 (5.9)	11 (2.2)	84 (19.5)	119 (14.9)
Sustainability	0	0	19 (13.6)	4 (2.3)	1 (0.7)	3 (1.8)	0	1 (0.2)	34 (4.0)
Total	**7 (6.4)**	**15 (14.3)**	**44 (31.4)**	**8 (4.6)**	**25 (18.5)**	**34 (20.1)**	**12 (2.4)**	**88 (20.4)**	**258 (30.1)**

A first semantic field that stands out is CSR as a distinct phenomenon. In this semantic field, we counted wordings for corporate social responsibility or for responsible actions taken by the companies, assuming that an increase in attention for issues related to CSR should also be reflected in the texts we studied. The English expressions 'corporate social responsibility' or 'CSR' as such were not found in the Dutch or French language samples, but the Dutch and French equivalents for 'CSR' were found (respectively 'maatschappelijk verantwoord ondernemen/MVO' and 'responsabilité sociale d'entreprise/RSE', as well as various expressions that comprise words such as 'societal' and 'responsible'.[8] The concordance software allowed us to check the meaning of each of the three elements in their context; we recoded for CSR if that meaning was implied. Table 4.3 shows an increase in occurrences of CSR related vocabulary over time in the Canadian and Dutch samples.

The relative number of occurrences of CSR terminology in our sample is higher for the Canadian corpus. In an historical analysis, Pasquero (2005) described CSR as a concept having its origins in the United States. The proximity of Canada to the United States might explain that the diffusion of the concept started earlier in that country. Nevertheless, in the past years, European institutions have strongly adopted and adapted this concept (for example, Habisch et al. 2005). This is consistent with the increase of occurrences we observe in the Swedish and Dutch concept in 2001. The occurrences in the Swedish sample of 1981 are referring to the firms' responsibility for the Swedish economy and the acknowledgement of the close bonds between (mainly) the Swedish export industry and the Swedish state (cf. Ohlsson and Tengblad 2004).

Not only do our data suggest a quantitative increase in references to CSR-related issues; there also appears to be a qualitative change in the way these issues are presented over time. For instance, the only occurrence of CSR in the 1981 Canadian sample presents profits as being a superior obligation to CSR issues, a *conditio sine qua non*:

> Il ne faut pas oublier que l'amélioration de la qualité de notre vie, la modernisation de nos installations, nos obligations envers nos actionnaires et la société en général dépend de l'importance de nos profits [It should not be forgotten that the improvement of the quality of our life, our obligations towards our shareholders and the society in general depends on the importance of our profits] (Alcan 1981 – Canada).

Later references to CSR in Canada suggest that companies have taken a more positive stance toward CSR. It is associated with 'performance', 'excellence' and 'prestige'. Social responsibility is given a high priority and is something that is shared with other stakeholders.

> Dans la dernière partie de l'année 2001, le Conseil d'administration a adopté une nouvelle politique intégrée en matière d'environnement, de santé et de sécurité (ESS) qui fait de l'amélioration des résultats dans ces domaines cruciaux une responsabilité partagée par tous les employés, à tous les échelons de la Société. [In the last semester of 2001, the

---

8 Some examples from the Dutch sample include: 'gezond ondernemen', 'duurzaam ondernemen', 'maatschappelijke verantwoordelijkheid van de onderneming', and 'verantwoord ondernemen'.

Board of directors adopted a new integrated policy pertaining to the environment, health and security, which makes the improvement of results in this crucial domain a shared responsibility with employees, at all levels.] (Alcan 1981 – Canada).

In Sweden and the Netherlands, negative stances toward CSR cannot be found. Still, although there seems to be a quantitative development in addressing CSR issues in our samples, it is doubtful whether there also is any real qualitative evolution between 1981 and 2001. Vocabulary in 2001 certainly changed as annual reports and CEO letters are addressed at a wider (stakeholder) audience, but *what* companies' responsibilities towards society exactly are often remains unspecified in the texts. There are, however, few occasional counter-examples, such as:

Tot onze verantwoordelijkheid op sociaal gebied rekenen we ook het treffen van medische voorzieningen voor onze medewerkers in West Afrika [We consider it our social responsibility to cater for health care provisions for our employees in West Africa] (Gamma 2001 – Netherlands).

The fact that this quote is an exception supports Caron and Turcotte's (in press) findings that the presentation of financial performance as a preliminary condition to social and environmental performance, or presenting the two types of performance as convergent phenomena, is a strong trend in contemporary annual reports. CSR vocabulary is apparently used in such a way that it fits with 'traditional' financial language.

Regarding the second semantic field, ethics and moral values, it is shown in Table 4.3 that an increase is also found in the use of the words relating to 'ethics' and 'ethical'. To map this semantic field, we also included the mentioning of 'codes of conduct' and 'values' in a moral, as opposed to a financial, connotation. Furthermore, we noticed an increase in the discourse regarding moral issues related to the natural environment, even if the environmental discourse has been around significantly longer. An example of the ethics and values field is:

We owe it to our employees, our clients and our shareholders – and especially the public – to operate this business in a responsible and ethical way. That is what we try to do – every day, everywhere (original English version, Skanska 2001 – Sweden).

Again, as in the previous semantic field, the phrasing firms choose tends to be in fairly abstract language; although Skanska claims to operate 'in a responsible and ethical way', it remains implicit how the company does so.

This leads to the third field: environment. This is the biggest semantic field for the CSR-discourse in our dataset and in all three countries salient occurrences are found. The notions environment/environmental are the most common; they are also used in compound words for the Swedish and Dutch samples. We therefore focused on these terms only, not including more ambiguous issues such as waste, recycling or emissions. The increase in the prevalence of this semantic field reinforces earlier findings: not only do more companies report on environmental issues (Gray et al. 1995), but they also use more words in reporting. However, after peaking in the 1991 sample, the relative numbers of these environmental notions decreased. This might be a signal that reporting on environmental issues has become a normal practice and therefore no longer merits much separate attention (cf. Green 2004). Since the second half of the 1990s, a number of the larger companies has also started to publish separate, verified environmental or sustainability reports (cf. Kolk 2003; Skulstad 2002). The Dutch sample shows a different picture from the other two countries as even the relative figures are higher than in the other two countries. Several reasons for this strong occurrence of environmental references could be suggested. The growing environmental awareness at the end of the 1980s evoked strong responses in the Netherlands and companies were eager to show their concern and awareness. An additional explanation might be that the Dutch dataset is based on the entire non-financial report; these reports often also included extensive social and environmental sections that provided detailed explanations of a firms' environmental policy. Where in the other two countries environmental management might be mentioned in the CEO letter somewhat in the passing, the full reports provided enough discursive space for firms to elaborate on their activities.

In the final semantic field, we counted wordings for 'sustainability' and 'sustainable' as this field gradually emerged as a separate area of attention related to CSR. Not surprisingly, these wordings are mainly found in 1991 and 2001, which would a priori be signalling the increased momentum that the concept of sustainability has gained since the late 1980s. We notice however fairly low figures for Canada on sustainability, and in fact these numbers are lower when occurrences referring to sustainable competitive advantage and sustainable profits are eliminated. In comparison, occurrences referring to the environment are more numerous, suggesting that sustainable development is perceived as perhaps too complex a program to embrace. Although sustainability issues can be observed in all three countries, they are phrased in different ways. For instance, in Sweden the phrase 'long-term' is frequently applied in this context where it is not in Canada or the Netherlands. Of course, 'environment' and 'sustainability' are regularly used as synonyms as the sustainability debate is sometimes seen as a continuation or an extension of the environmental management debate. For reasons of completeness, however, we differentiated between the two. The semantic field 'sustainability' we identified only contains references to the terms 'sustainable' and 'sustainability' and became more prominent at a later moment in time.

Shift in Geographical Perspective

A second major theme is the shift in geographical perspectives found in our sample of reports. Table 4.4 exhibits that the firms in our samples increasingly present themselves as operating in a globalizing context. Overall, there is a significant reduction in the mentioning of any national context. The semantic field 'national' comprises words such as 'Dutch/Swedish/Canadian', 'domestic' and 'national'. The words 'foreign' and 'abroad', which stand in opposition to 'domestic' and 'national', appear less frequently, too. The geographical focus appears to be changing as references to the semantic field 'global' steeply increase over time. This increase might indicate a growing international orientation of companies in each of the three countries we studied.

Table 4.4 Occurrence of Geographical Perspectives (number of occurrences per 1,000 words in brackets)

	Sweden			Canada			the Netherlands		
	1981	1991	2001	1981	1991	2001	1981	1991	2001
Global, Globalization, the World	32 (29.0)	43 (41.0)	90 (64.3)	8 (4.6)	26 (19.3)	38 (22.4)	33 (6.7)	30 (7.0)	204 (23.7)
International	35 (31.8)	34 (32.4)	6 (4.3)	6 (3.4)	4 (3.0)	10 (5.9)	47 (9.6)	59 (13.7)	100 (11.6)
Foreign, Abroad	23 (20.9)	10 (9.5)	4 (2.9)	1 (0.6)	0	0	60 (12.2)	24 (5.6)	29 (3.4)
National	73 (66.3)	85 (81.0)	28 (20.0)	102 (58.3)	93 (68.9)	75 (44.1)	120 (24.5)	71 (16.5)	90 (10.5)
Total	163 (148.0)	172 (163.9)	128 (91.5)	117 (66.9)	123 (91.2)	133 (72.4)	260 (53.0)	184 (42.8)	423 (49.2)

To scrutinize these possible shifts in geographical perspective, we briefly investigated to where the attention is shifting. Different patterns stand out: for the Swedish and Canadian companies in our sample, references to North America and particularly the USA are becoming more important whereas for the Netherlands, both Europe and North America/USA gain significance. This emergence of 'Europe' in the latter sample is probably also related to the observed increase of references to 'international', as from a Dutch perspective 'Europe' is not necessarily 'global'. Discussions of the implication of extension of the European Union and later the introduction of the European currency – the Euro – are other reasons for this increase. Altogether, a shift in geographical focus can be observed in all three subsets of our sample.

Relationships with Stakeholders

Next to the content and scope of firms' discursive practices regarding CSR, tracing at whom these practices are targeted is a relevant approach to trace any potential development in the evolution of a corporate discourse on CSR. The final theme therefore regards the relationship with stakeholders. We traced the use of the word 'stakeholder' and the mentioning of different stakeholder groups such as employees, consumer/customers and distributors over time. Many stakeholder categories are mentioned across all years in all samples, as shown in Table 4.5. Yet, the distribution of frequencies across different categories of stakeholders clearly changes.

Meanwhile, references to the term 'shareholder' also increased. It seems that an increase in the variety of categories of stakeholders mentioned is matched by an increased use of the word 'shareholder'. As such, mentioning more categories of stakeholders might serve to suggest a discourse of reconciliation, or of no conflict between stakeholders and shareholders, but shareholders remain very central. The quote below expresses both reconciliation and shareholder focus:

> These principles also demonstrate, in tangible terms, our commitment to the Company's stakeholders and our recognition that they are partners in our success. I strongly believe our core principles will continue to provide our shareholders even greater growth and profitability in the years ahead (Magna 2001 – Canada).

Meanwhile, from this overview of stakeholders, one can note a decrease of references to national authorities and unions, which underlines again the shift in geographical perspective suggested before. National politics and those involved seem to become less central to the companies, or at least they are mentioned less in the annual reports/CEO letters. The fairly sudden rise in usage of the term stakeholder in the Dutch sample of 2001 can probably be attributed to the incorporation of the term in Dutch language.

Table 4.5 Occurrence of Various Stakeholders (number of occurrences per 1,000 words in brackets)

	Sweden 1981	Sweden 1991	Sweden 2001	Canada 1981	Canada 1991	Canada 2001	the Netherlands 1981	the Netherlands 1991	the Netherlands 2001
Stakeholder	2 (1.8)	0	2 (1.4)	0	1 (0.7)	3 (1.8)	0	0	13 (1.5)
Shareholder	13 (11.8)	15 (14.3)	31 (22.1)	11 (6.3)	14 (10.4)	37 (21.8)	10 (2.0)	17 (4.0)	67 (7.8)
Employee	40 (36.4)	31 (29.5)	54 (38.6)	0	1 (0.7)	1 (0.6)	176 (35.9)	172 (40.0)	300 (34.9)
Customer, Consumer	12 (10.9)	29 (27.6)	106 (75.7)	15 (8.6)	28 (20.7)	36 (21.2)	45 (9.2)	85 (19.8)	210 (24.4)
Distributor	1 (0.9)	0	10 (7.1)	10 (5.7)	10 (7.4)	23 (13.5)	0	4 (0.9)	18 (2.1)
Competitors	6 (5.5)	2 (1.9)	10 (7.1)	3 (1.7)	6 (4.4)	5 (2.9)	5 (1.0)	2 (0.5)	11 (1.3)
State, Government	15 (13.6)	6 (5.7)	0	2 (1.1)	4 (3.0)	2 (1.2)	67 (13.7)	30 (7.0)	20 (2.3)
Unions	5 (4.5)	0	0	4 (2.3)	3 (2.2)	0	97 (19.8)	46 (10.7)	63 (7.3)
NGOs, Charities	0	0	0	0	3 (2.2)	3 (1.8)	0	0	0
Total	94 (84.4)	83 (79.0)	213 (152.0)	45 (25.7)	64 (51.7)	110 (64.8)	400 (81.6)	356 (82.9)	702 (81.6)

One caveat however needs mentioning: we ran several statistical tests to investigate whether any significant differences could be found between different countries, different issues or different periods outlined above. Unfortunately, our small sample size and the potential bias introduced by looking at large firms only resulted in little statistical underpinning for our observations. As we think this is partly due to the sample size and as we can observe similar patterns across the three countries studied, we still think it is worth reporting these findings as an onset to more rigorous approaches to trace the evolution of corporate discourse on corporate social responsibility through using a longitudinal, lexicological study.

Discussion and Conclusion

This is not the first study to look at how CSR is addressed in corporate annual reports and in the introduction we already referred to several of these studies. For instance, using content analysis, Jenkins and Yakovleva (2006) provided a review of the development of social and environmental reports in one industry, the mining industry, over time. Another study looked at CSR reports of different companies across different industries in one country, the United Kingdom and found that companies are eager to report on their CSR activities as they anticipate benefit from doing so (Idowu and Towler 2004). However, in this chapter we have taken another approach, using a different methodology. Although our lexicological method certainly has its pitfalls, we think it provides a useful addition to research on the evolution of management concepts, bridging content analyses on particular themes and pure linguistic approaches. In this section we will first discuss our findings and make some inferences, then relate these briefly to outcomes of other research and finally address the main difficulties associated with our study and some ways to overcome them.

In this chapter, we set out to answer the question how CSR representations in annual reports from Swedish, Canadian and Dutch companies have changed over time. We applied a lexicological approach, mapping developments in semantic fields related to CSR because we believe this alternative approach has some advantages in comparability of results over time and space. Nevertheless, our analysis is to be understood as tentative. Given the varying sizes of the corpora that we analyzed, not only between 'Letter of CEO'-sections (Sweden, Canada) and 'Directors' reports' (the Netherlands), but also between annual reports of individual companies, they cannot be compared directly, only the trends that they exhibit. We therefore presented our findings in both absolute and relative numbers. We found a clear increase (both in relative and absolute numbers) on a number of topics that are linked to the general CSR-discourse in the 2001 sample, centered around three themes, along with a notable decrease in several other topics. Although there are differences in the three national samples, the overall patterns appear to be fairly similar and that is an important observation.

Our data suggest a gradual rise of the CSR discourse that occurs simultaneously with a decrease of other discourses on social, economic and political development in a company's home country, and with a rise of language use related to internationalization and globalization. These findings hold for all three countries studied. Based on our limited observations, we tentatively argue that the rise of the CSR discourse is related to the increasing globalization. To gain and maintain legitimacy – sometimes called a social license to operate – firms in all three countries need to demonstrate their engagement in CSR-related issues to maintain stakeholder approval. As the attention for an international or global dimension increases over time, the frame of reference firms have to keep in mind also changes. No longer do just national debates determine what is considered to be proper, legitimate corporate behavior or what firms should be reporting about. For instance, CSR guidelines from the UN or the OECD are developed to be applicable worldwide, as are reporting standards such as SA8000 or GRI (Global Reporting Initiative). The broadening international scope hence brings along certain requirements on both the type of issues and the mix of stakeholders that need to be addressed; our lexicological analysis shows this change in themes that is addressed in the corporate texts over time.

Meanwhile, as companies have become more international, their annual reports have become more 'global' in their content. There is an interesting twist to this 'global' connotation of CSR though. Not only does it refer to a wider geographical area of applicability, perhaps even suggesting universal relevance, it also seems to imply considerable vagueness and imprecision in its definition, as we were unable to find much content in our samples about what exactly firms consider to be their social responsibilities. This might well be another characteristic of the modern CSR discourse.

The comparison between the three countries thus shows some striking similarities. Still, it is difficult to attribute these similarities to any contextual factors, merely based on our lexicological analysis from annual reports. Other methods might bring more clarity here, such as critical discourse analysis (cf. Fairclough 1995) that highlights the context in which discourses are shaped. A possible extension of the lexicological approach and the use of corpora is to focus on phrases and how CSR-issues are addressed and purported on a composition level of the texts (cf. Stubbs 2002). However, really comparing national and international contexts across three countries at three different points in time will be a daunting task. Furthermore, to investigate whether the many references to CSR-related terminology are substantiated by any real activities from firms, communications research might also be useful. David (2001) for instance studied the interplay between visual and textual elements in annual report to create what she calls 'cultural myths'. These alternatives are beyond our scope; our lexicological approach therefore might serve as an initial alternative, providing a first, fairly descriptive cut at tracing CSR's diffusion outside the academic debates within the management communities.

Over the past decades, the CSR concept and related issues indeed seem to have become firmly rooted in firms' reporting vocabulary. Yet, this observation result must be tempered: while the reported concerns for stakeholders have increased through time, that increase remains marginal compared with the reported issues aimed specifically at shareholders. Our results also show the diffusion of the CSR concept outside the United States, and particularly its recent but strong adoption in Europe: this is in line with observations of other research (cf. Habisch et al. 2005; Maignan and Ralston 2002).

Although our chapter is descriptive in nature, we can make a few inferences, based on our observations. The increase of CSR-related topics seems to indicate an institutionalization process; CSR has gained a strong foothold in firms' reporting practices. The development of reporting standards underlines this observation, although the inverse argumentation need not hold. If attention to some topic significantly decreases this could either mean that topic has become less relevant, or that it has gained so much socio-cognitive legitimacy that it has become redundant to mention it (Green 2004) – it is taken for granted. Whereas the CSR discourse clearly takes a global perspective, it is difficult to tell which of these possible explanations really holds in explaining the decrease in importance of the national context. We would suggest, however, that the increase in CSR is related to a decline of more local discourses on responsibility. Firms need to please extending audiences that are increasingly beyond the borders of the nation-state.

One limitation of our study is the potential problem of comparability between the samples, as we combined lexicological analysis of the Directors' reports with that of 'Letter from the CEO'-sections. It might be the case, for example, that representations of CSR are underestimated when only analyzing the 'Letter of the CEO'-section. As we were not aware of the existence of such differences in national traditions of styling annual reports, we had little opportunity to correct for this difference in building the corpora for comparative analysis. Given such differences, it would be advisable for future research to analyze the entire Director's reports.

Another limitation of our study might be the choice of relatively long periods of time between the sampled years. Although this remains to be tested, we suggest that a choice of shorter time-intervals would not produce different results. CEOs, or more broadly top-management teams, can exert considerable influence on the CSR stance of a particular company (cf. Agle, Mitchell and Sonnenfeld 1999; Hemingway and Maclagan 2004), and consequently, changes of CEOs and in top-management teams may result in significant changes in a firm's CSR stance. Adding intermitting years to the analysis may exhibit that such changes have taken place. However, we consider it unlikely that such events have a considerable impact on the aggregate results over the entire sample. Further, we would argue that if such changes occur, they are more likely to go with the trend than against it: if there is normative or mimetic pressure on firms to represent themselves as CSR-prone, a new CEO or top-management team is quite likely to follow this trend.

Notwithstanding these problems, our three-country comparative study provides a useful onset to compare differences in CSR discourses as emerging in important corporate documents: annual reports, aimed at communicating the company's viewpoints to its relevant audiences. Our study has shown the applicability of linguistic methods in understanding the shaping of CSR in different contexts.

Following up on these findings, we provide some suggestions for further research. Our data could be presented in greater detail, which would allow us to refine our analysis. For example, differentiating among the firms in our samples (for example on level of internationalization of production, or type of industry) could reinforce the relation between the rise of the CSR discourse and the more international / global orientation. A natural follow up to this research would be to further explore the idea of national 'CSR cultures', as according to analysts in this tradition, companies from different institutional settings are likely to differ in their textual responses on this seemingly unifying global concept (on similar differences in research genres, Swales 2004). Our study, however, provides indications that despite different national traditions, firms might increasingly use similar words, phrasings and examples to show that and how the are socially responsible, or at least that such cultures might need to be defined at aggregation levels beyond that of the nation state. As argued, going from a mere descriptive study into critical discourse analysis would then be a related line of research as in such analysis, the context in which discourses are shaped is emphasized. The enthusiastic adoption of CSR by companies in many countries offers an interesting and relevant context for such discourse studies.

PART 2
Doing: CSR in Praxis

Chapter 5

The Bottom Line of CSR: A Different View

Esben Rahbek Pedersen and Peter Neergaard

Introduction

The first reports on social responsible behaviour date back to the 18th century, but contemporary CSR is often associated with the second half of the 20th century, where scholars and practitioners began to put CSR on the public agenda (Garriga and Melé 2004). In the beginning, the focus was primarily on social issues, but as the negative environmental impacts from production became harder and harder to ignore, pollution prevention also became an important issue in the CSR discourse. In the 1990s, CSR became increasingly associated with globalization and the growing societal expectations towards companies. In the same period, the CSR literature discussed a number of new issues such as child labour, slave labour, community interests, working conditions, etc. (Carroll and Buchholtz 1999; Kolk 2000).

Even though the meaning and content of CSR have changed over time, it has always been debated whether CSR is in accordance with or in conflict with good business practice, i.e. making profit. Proponents of CSR argue that CSR can improve staff morale, reduce costs and safeguard the company from negative press coverage, customer sanctions and public regulation. As such, there is no conflict between social/environmental and economic goals (Gallarotti 1995; Porter and Kramer 2002; Bonifant, Arnold and Long 1995; Waddock and Smith 2000b).

Opposite to this 'win-win' view, critics see CSR as a counterproductive initiative or even a theft of the shareholders' money. The statement that 'the social responsibility of business is to increase profits' (Friedman 1970: 32) is standard in most writing on CSR. In particular, contractarian theorists have criticised companies' CSR activities. Jensen states, '200 years' worth of work in economics and finance indicates that the social welfare is maximized when all firms in an economy maximize total firm value' (Jensen 2002: 239). In other words, if firms maximize shareholder wealth, they will advance social welfare in the long run by letting the 'invisible hand' operate freely.

'Many contemporary advocates of CSR have implicitly accepted Friedman's position that the primary responsibility of companies is to create wealth for their shareholders' (Vogel 2005: 27). As a consequence, a large number of researchers have attempted to measure the costs and benefits of social and environmental initiatives to uncover CSR's 'business case'. The research includes both numerous case studies and a large body of quantitative research on the relationship between Corporate Social Performance (CSP) and Corporate Financial Performance (CFP)

(Griffin and Mahon 1997; Utting 2000; Plesner and Neergaard 2005). Margolis and Walsh (2003) have reviewed 127 empirical studies conducted between 1972 and 2002 dealing with the relationship between CSP and CFP. Almost half of the studies pointed to a positive relationship between CSP and CFP (Margolis and Walsh 2003: 274). Only seven studies indicated a negative relationship, 28 studies revealed a non-significant relationship and the remaining studies presented a mixed set of findings. Margolis and Walsh conclude that the compilation of findings suggests a positive relationship between CSP and CFP and that very little evidence points to a negative relationship. Their conclusion is supported by a similar review of Orlitzky, Schmidt and Rynes (2003). Apparently, there is no conflict between CSR and maximizing shareholder value.

However, it may turn out that what appears to be a definite link between CSP and CFP is illusory due to a range of methodological problems associated with measuring the costs and benefits of CSR (Margolis and Walsh 2003). A number of reviewers see all kinds of theoretical and methodological issues in this research (Griffin and Mahon 1997; Margolis and Walsh 2001; Orlitzky et al. 2003). Some important problems are listed below:

- There are important differences between the various CSR initiatives (standards, reporting systems, labelling schemes, codes of conduct, etc.), and different initiatives are likely to generate different costs and benefits. Making general statements about the costs and benefits of CSR is therefore problematic.
- CSR has a different meaning to different people at different times.[1] The low-stringency in terminology implies a lack of generally accepted criteria for measuring CSR.
- The choice of financial performance (CFP) measure may have implications for the relationship. One study reports on a negative relationship between Corporate Social Performance (CSP) and stock return and a positive relationship between CSP and operating efficiency (ROA) (Plesner and Neergaard 2005).
- Costs and benefits differ among industries. Companies operate in different industrial contexts, which might affect their social, environmental and economic performance (Griffin and Mahon 1997; Plesner and Neergaard 2005).[2]
- The size of companies also has an impact on the cost and benefits that can be expected from CSR (Plesner and Neergaard 2005). In consequence, generalising experience from MNCs to SMEs (and vice versa) is not without problems.

---

1   In this chapter, we will define CSR in accordance with the European Commission (EC 2002: 5), who sees CSR as: 'a concept whereby companies integrate social and environmental concerns in their business operations and in their interaction with their stakeholders on a voluntary basis.'

2   Ironically, a socially irresponsible fund, the Vice Fund, investing in the alcohol, arms, gambling and tobacco industries was beating the S&P 500 and the Dow Jones average by a few points (*The Economist*, 30 October 2003).

- It is difficult to measure the costs and benefits of CSR, which is probably the reason why most companies never do it. For instance, an analysis of ISO14001 certified companies in Switzerland concluded that only 6% tried to measure the benefits (Hamschmidt and Dyllick 2001). Therefore, companies' knowledge about the actual costs and benefits is quite limited.
- The cost and benefits of CSR are separated in time. The costs are payable here and now, whereas the benefits tend to show up years after the original investment (Freiman and Walther 2001).
- The costs and benefits observed by companies in the CSR literature do not necessarily reflect the corporate landscape. For instance, in relation to environmental management, Kolk (2000: 6) argues that: 'existing research frequently concentrates on 'best cases', those firms in which environmental management is relatively advanced or has shown significant progress'. If conclusions about the costs and benefits of CSR are based on best cases, it is questionable whether the findings have any general validity.

Where some of the above-mentioned issues can be dealt with (for example size and industry) in a research design, others are of a more fundamental nature (for example the ambiguity of CSR and the difficulties with quantifying costs and benefits) and imply that we are unlikely to see – at least in the near future – a widespread consensus with regard to the net impact of CSR. Therefore, it might be fruitful to acknowledge the diversity of CSR and devote more time and energy to analyze the costs and benefits of specific CSR activities without making oversimplified conclusions about the 'business case' of CSR (Vogel 2005). In this spirit, we will analyze a specific CSR initiative – environmental or eco-labelling. During the last two decades, a large number of environmental labels have been lounged by industrial sectors, NGOs and national and international organizations (EPA 1998; Pedersen and Neergaard 2006). From a business perspective, the labels are expected to legitimate business practice and enhance the competitive edge (EPA 1998; Porter and Van Der Linde 1995). Environmental labels can be viewed as a response to increased stakeholder demands for more environmentally responsible business. Through eco-labelled products, companies indicate CSR awareness to a variety of stakeholders. However, realising the diverse nature of CSR, we do not claim that the experience from environmental labelling can be generalized across all types of CSR activities. Eco-labelling is in this context used as a proxy for CSR. This chapter will address the rationale for adopting eco-labelling by a number of Danish companies and the results achieved by these companies. The chapter falls in four parts:

- The companies' motives. The first section deals with the main drivers (motivations) for implementing CSR.
- Direct costs and organizational barriers. This section describes some of the frequent costs and organizational barriers associated with CSR initiatives.
- Benefits from implementing CSR. This section analyses the companies' perception of benefits achieved and discusses how the benefits relate to the original motives.

- Relationship between costs and benefits. This section does not try to uncover the business case of CSR or whether CSR pays off. However, the section will describe how companies perceive the net impacts of CSR.

Each section will present a brief literature review. The literature will draw on research on environmental management systems (EMS) and labelling as a great deal of empirical literature on CSR is still dominated by research on the implementation of EMS and eco-labelling, which is probably because the various CSR standards (AA1000, CERES, SA8000, Global compact, etc.) are less institutionalised than the environmental standards ISO14001 and EMAS. For each of the four topics, we will present the findings from a research project analysing Danish companies' perception of costs and benefits in relation to environmental labelling (Pedersen et al. 2004). A brief description of this project is presented below.

Methodology

In 2003, the Danish Environmental Protection Agency sponsored a project aiming at measuring the costs and benefits of environmental labelling in a Danish context. The labels in question were the Swan Label and the EU Flower.

- The Swan label is a Scandinavian label that was introduced by the Nordic Council of Ministers. The Swan label calls attention to the product's impact on the environment throughout the product's lifecycle, and the requirements are continuously raised to ensure that the Swan products are always at the cutting edge of environmentalism (Pedersen and Neergaard 2006). The label is available for nearly 60 different product groups.
- The EU Flower was launched by the European Parliament and the Council in 1992 and revised in 2000. The label is awarded to the most environmentally friendly products within a large number of non-food products. Flower labelled products are available throughout Europe. The requirements are similar to the Swan label.

In 2004 a web-based questionnaire was sent to all 154 Danish companies that are licensed to produce environmentally labelled goods in accordance with the requirements of the EU 'Flower' and/or the Nordic 'Swan' label. Before the survey was mailed each company was contacted by phone to locate the person responsible for eco-labelling. The survey was subsequently mailed to that person. Out of these 154 Danish companies, 74 (48%) filled in the questionnaire. The questionnaire consisted of twenty questions on objectives, cost, benefits, attitudes and effects of eco-labelling. Predefined categories were used for most questions and a 5-point scale was employed. More than 80 percent of the companies had less than 100 employees in Denmark. The participating companies represent the following industries: graphical production, chemicals, textiles and others. The results of the survey may therefore apply to SMEs. However, the Danish textile industry has a large production in other countries. Therefore, the number of employees in Denmark is not an accurate measure of company size. If, for example, total sales is used as a measure of size instead off these companies would be medium to large companies.

Table 5.1 Motives for Addressing CSR

Internal	External
• Increasing management and control of internal processes.	• Increasing control with the social and environmental performance in the supply chain.
• Identifying potential areas for improvement in the company.	• Customer requirement.
• Reducing costs of waste, energy, environmental pollution, work related diseases, etc.	• Ensuring compliance with existing regulation and preventing future governmental actions.
• Personal commitment to social and environmental improvement by management.	• Improving customer loyalty.
• Motivating employees and reducing staff turnover.	• Response to pressure from societal groups and individuals (NGOs, communities, insurance companies, etc.).
• Extending quality management system.	• Improving existing and potential investors' confidence in the company.
• Strengthening process and product innovation.	• Preventing negative social and environmental impacts on the external environment.
	• Gaining access to new markets.
	• Improving corporate image and community relations.
	• Preventing new social and environmental legislation.
	• Attracting new employees

Source: Compiled from: Bansal and Bogner (2002), Bansal and Hunter (2003), Biondi et al. (2000), del Brio et al. (2001), Gallarotti (1995), Fombrun et al. (2000), Hamschmidt and Dyllick (2001), Kolk (2000), Morrow and Rondinelli (2002), Poksinska et al. (2003), Rosen (2001), Smith (2003) and Zutshi and Sohal (2004).

Motives for Implementing CSR

According to the literature, companies have different motives for implementing CSR. Some want to improve the corporate image whereas others see CSR as a means to obtain costs reductions. In addition, some companies adopt CSR simply because they think it is the right thing to do. Table 5.1 lists some of the internal and external motives mentioned in the various studies of CSR. Internal motives refer to the company's internal processes and the relationship with inside stakeholders (employees, managers). The external motives concern the relationships with upstream and downstream business partners as well as the company's responses to societal demands formulated by outside stakeholders. However, the boundaries between internal and external benefits are blurred. Internal benefits might generate positive impacts on the external environment (and *vice versa*).

Empirical research, for instance on environmental management systems (EMS), indicates that companies are guided primarily by external motives. Biondi, Frey and Iraldo (2000: 61) concluded that the main drivers for adopting EMS were: '(...) the need to comply with increasing legal requirements; the desire for competitive advantage; and the need to satisfy customer requirements (...)'. Zutshi and Sohal (2004), Hamschmidt and Dyllick (2001), and Poksinska, Dahlgaard and Eklund (2003) also report that companies are primarily motivated by external motives.[3] Why do external motives dominate the research of CSR? An important reason might be that the CSR literature prioritises the external benefits from CSR. For instance, CSR is often legitimated by reference to the growing societal pressure on companies, e.g. from employees or NGOs (cf. Fombrun, Gardberg and Barnett 2000; Kaptein and Van Tulder 2003). If companies fail to meet these demands, they might be faced with public criticism, which could have a negative impact on sales, market shares, brand value and stock prices.

From our research on eco-labelling among Danish companies, we can also conclude that the companies have been guided primarily by external motives. Out of these, the most important motives include the present or future demand for eco-labelled products and the potential benefits from an improved corporate image – see Table 5.2. Two out of three companies mention customer demands as the prime driver for the labelling scheme. This response may be explained by the fact that most of the companies are small and engaged in B2B relationships. Other research has pointed to that the consumers are not the prime driver of eco-labelling (Pedersen and Neergaard 2006). Only one third of the companies have adopted environmental labelling primarily because they expect internal, environmental improvements in the production and less than half see the labelling as part of their strategy. When CSR often is seen as a response to external pressures in the literature, it is not surprising that companies expect external benefits from CSR.

---

3 For instance, Poksinska et al. (2003: 593) conclude that the: 'decision on whether or not to implement ISO14001 involves considerations outside of the company: commercial, governmental or public pressure. It is also concluded that considerations for the corporate image is the most important motive.'

Table 5.2 Companies' Motives for Adopting Environmental Labelling

Question: Please specify the company's objective for environmental labelling?		Primary Objective	Secondary Objective	Not Important	Total
Environmental improvements in production	Frequency %	26 36.1	35 48.6	11 15.3	72 100.0
Differentiation of products from competitors	Frequency %	39 54.2	22 30.6	11 15.3	72 100.0
Improved corporate image	Frequency %	45 61.6	22 30.1	6 8.2	73 100.0
Requirement for becoming a supplier for public institutions	Frequency %	36 50.0	19 26.4	17 23.6	72 100.0
Demand from customers	Frequency %	48 65.8	11 15.1	14 19.2	73 100.0
Demand from suppliers	Frequency %	4 5.8	11 15.9	54 78.3	69 100.0
Expectation of future demand	Frequency %	46 62.2	22 29.7	6 8.1	74 100.0
Prevention of public regulation	Frequency %	21 30.0	17 24.3	32 45.7	70 100.0
Labelling part of environmental strategy	Frequency %	34 47.9	25 36.2	12 16.9	71 100.0

Direct Costs and Organizational Barriers

The CSR literature often focuses on the merits of CSR and is less inclined to deal with the direct costs and the organizational barriers for implementing CSR. However, throughout the years, various researchers and practitioners have investigated some of the factors that might impede the planning and implementation of CSR. Some of these are listed in Table 5.3 below:

Table 5.3 Direct Costs and Organizational Barriers

Direct Costs	Organizational Barriers
• Initial review	• Organizational rigidity
• Documentation and administration	• Resistance to change
• Investments	• Lack of resources, particular in SMEs
• Reporting and communication	• Low management commitment
• Management, control and maintenance	• Conflicting interests among stakeholders
• Time spent	
• Training and education of employees	• Uncertainty regarding the benefits of implementing CSR initiatives
• Internal audit	• Competition mainly on price
• Fees to third-party verification	• Difficulties in monitoring and verifying CSR
• External audits	
• Certification	• Power structures in the supply chain

Source: Compiled from: Babakri et al. (2002), Bansal (2002), Biondi et al. (2000), Dale (1999), del Brio et al. (2001), Kirkland and Thompson (1999), Kolk (2000), Oakland (1993), Poksinska et al. (2002, 2003), Utting (2000) and Zutshi and Sohal (2004).

The costs of CSR differ significantly depending on whether the company wants to implement eco-labelling, cleaner technology, environmental management systems, social reporting, etc. For example, several studies have indicated that the costs associated with environmental management systems such as ISO14001 and EMAS are considerable (Bansal and Bogner 2002; Freiman and Walther 2001; Hamschmidt and Dyllick 2001; Morrow and Rondinelli 2002; Steger 2000; Zutshi and Sohal 2004). In comparison, environmental labelling schemes are far less demanding for companies (Pedersen and Neergaard 2006).

In our survey, the companies were asked to estimate the cost of their eco-labelling efforts. The majority of the companies reported costs below 7,000 Euro. Less than 5% of the companies had to make changes in their production or invest in new technology. Environmental management has been on the agenda in all the examined companies for a number of years. As a consequence, only minor adjustments were needed to produce products fulfilling the requirements of the two labels investigated. The primary costs to the companies include the time spent in the organization on fulfilling application requirements and gathering documentation from suppliers on their use of materials such as colours or chemicals. These activities are seen as considerable cost items in 70% and 55% of the companies, respectively.

The organizational barriers for instance include lack of information and know-how, difficulties with quantifying the benefits of environmental management or organizational inertia (Peattie 1997; Utting 2000). Moreover, if management fails to recognize the importance of CSR, the company is unlikely to allocate the required resources and ensure organizational support for the initiatives.[4]

In our analysis, the main barriers are external to companies. Even though the companies in our survey found it difficult to quantify the costs and benefits of their eco-labelling program, the most important barrier seems to be in the demand from the institutional market. A large number of the companies have adopted eco-labelling schemes in anticipation of an increasing demand from public institutions with green purchasing policies. But although a large number of public institutions have formulated such policies, they continue, nonetheless, to buy conventional products. Moreover, campaigns sponsored by the government or industry to promote eco-labels have been few. In consequence, consumers are not aware of the labels and the potential benefits of eco-labelled products (Pedersen and Neergaard 2006).

Benefits from Implementing CSR

According to the win-win literature on CSR, a number of benefits can be harvested from implementing social and environmental improvements. For instance, in an often-quoted article, Porter and van der Linde (1995: 120) point out that 'properly designed environmental standards can trigger innovations that lower the total cost of the product or improve its value'. A number of these benefits are listed in Table 5.4 below. Similar to motives, internal benefits are benefits achieved inside the company and related to the organization's products, processes, employees and employers. External benefits are basically about minimising the negative/maximising the positive impacts on the external environment and improving the relationships with outside stakeholders.

However, the boundaries between internal and external benefits are blurred. Internal benefits might generate positive impacts on the external environment (and *vice versa*), and external benefits might translate into financial benefits as time passes.

---

4 Lack of commitment does not necessarily imply that managers act socially irresponsible. Maybe they just do not recognize the need for CSR or believe that they can achieve the same results without adopting a standardised CSR framework (Kirkland and Thompson 1999; Bansal 2002).

However, we cannot conclude that benefits from CSR initiatives automatically improve financial performance.[5]

Table 5.4 Benefits of CSR

Internal Benefits	External Benefits
• Savings from reducing the costs of electricity, water, waste handling, chemicals, raw materials, packaging, etc. • Benefits from re-use and recycling of energy and materials • Development of new products or services • Savings from safer workplace conditions • Improved staff morale • Development of managerial and organizational skills • Higher quality of products • Systematization and documentation of competencies and processes • Improved staff recruitment and retention • Increased environmental awareness	• Maintaining and enhancing a good reputation • Improvement of image • Access to markets that demand CSR • Reduction of social and environmental risks • More responsible supply chain management • Improved community relations • Increased competitiveness • Legitimacy in society • Compliance with social and environmental regulation • Better contact and co-operation with public authorities • Goodwill from stakeholders • Increased brand value • Higher prices for products

Source: Compiled from: Acutt et al. (2001), Bansal and Bogner (2002), Biondi et al. (2000), Delmas (2002), Freiman and Walther (2001), Gallarotti (1995), Morrow and Rondinelli (2002), Porter and Van der Linde (1995), Rosen (2001), Smith (2003), Rondinelli and Vastag (2000) and Steger (2000).

---

5   Even though empirical research on the benefits of CSR is inconclusive, a majority of researchers have reported a positive relationship between social and financial performance (Griffin and Mahon 1997). However, even the much cited example of the better performance by the Dow Jones Sustainable Index (DJSI) compared to the general Dow Jones World Index has been questioned recently. A study by Cerin and Dobers (2001) suggests that the superior performance by the Sustainable Index may reflect asymmetric distributions in company sectors, world regions and market capitalization rather than greater efforts invested in sustainability.

Apparently, there is little consensus as to whether the benefits from e.g. EMS evolve mainly inside or outside the organization. Some findings indicate that EMS mainly generates internal benefits, such as improved management of internal processes, whereas others highlight the external benefits, including compliance to legislation and improved image (Freiman and Walther 2001; Poksinska et al. 2003; Zutshi and Sohal 2004).

The findings from our survey indicate that companies especially have achieved external benefits. The benefits from adopting the eco-labelling schemes are listed in Table 5.5. Almost 96 percent of the companies report that the labels to a large or some extent have made a positive contribution to the corporate image. This is undoubtedly the most visible benefit from the labelling schemes. Furthermore, almost one third of the companies state that is easier for them to participate in public tenders. In order to do so, companies must document that they have environmental policies and procedures in place. It is interesting that although only a small fraction of the companies adopted environmental labelling to achieve environmental improvements, 74 per cent believe that the labels have generated some environmental improvements, and 60 per cent have observed a certain decrease in resource consumption.

Table 5.5 Benefits Achieved from Environmentally Labelled Products (in percent points, N = 74)

	To a high degree	To some degree	Not at all
Increased profit	1.4	19.4	79.2
Increased sales to present customers	5.6	32.4	62.0
Increased sales to new customers	8.5	36.6	54.9
Decrease in resource consumption	14.3	45.7	40.0
Environmental improvements	27.5	46.4	26.1
Better relations to supplier	12.9	42.9	44.3
Improved image	29.6	66.2	4.2
Easier to participate in tenders	28.8	33.3	37.9
On average	21	65	14

It is also interesting that almost eighty percent of the companies in our study state that the environmentally labelled products have not increased profits. Fifty percent of the companies state that they are unable to ask a higher price for labelled products. The other half is able to demand a premium price only in certain cases. Environmentally labelled products are often sold for the same price as non-labelled products (Ackerstein and Lemon 1999; DOM 2002). Customers seem unwilling to pay a premium price for the labelled products, thus confirming Fineman and Clark's (1996) claim that environment is a qualifier rather than an order-winner. Evidence suggests that particularly large retail chains tend to offer eco-labelled products to the same price as conventional products (DOM 2002; Meyer 2001) refusing to give their suppliers a premium price for these products.

Costs and Benefits Compared

As mentioned earlier, it is basically impossible to conclude whether CSR pays off or not. It is very difficult for companies to estimate the cost and benefits of their CSR activities. Depict that we asked the companies in our survey whether they thought that the benefits from environmental labelling exceeded the costs. As the Figure 5.1 indicates, the majority of the companies believed that at least the monetary benefits did not exceed the costs. This is surprising considering that the costs of eco-labelling for the majority of companies were less than 7,000 Euro. Figure 5.1 shows that the benefits of eco-labelling did not exceed the costs in more than half of the companies; only one third of the companies observed a positive, financial outcome of the eco-labelling.

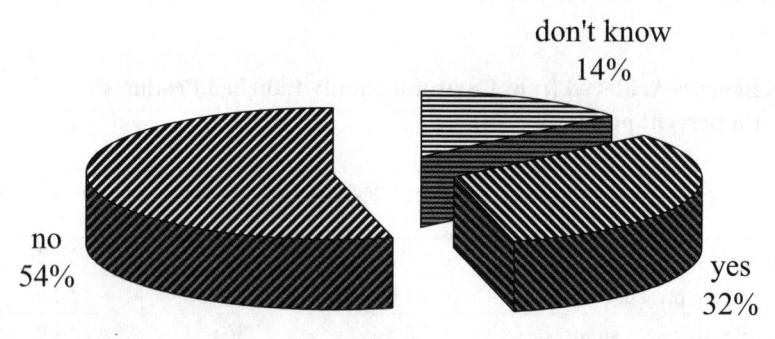

Figure 5.1 The Bottom Line of Environmental Labelling
Question: Is it your opinion that the earnings from environmental labelling exceed the costs? (N = 71)

There are, of course, limitations to these results. First of all, the companies found it difficult to quantify the costs and benefits from eco-labelling. One of the companies noted that it is difficult to estimate the sales lost from having no eco-labelled products in the product portfolio. Likewise, quantification of e.g. an improved corporate image and better relationships with stakeholders tends to become speculative. With regard to costs, it is a notorious bias that only few companies report the time spent on planning, implementing and maintaining CSR. And even if it is possible to measure the time spent, it is important to note that often it is the existing personnel that implements CSR. It is difficult to assess whether they could have used their time more profitably on other activities than the environmental labelling programme. Last but not least, there might be a delay between the defrayed costs and the realised benefits, making it difficult to make comparisons – at least in the short run (Freiman and Walther 2001).

It is also important to note that the narrow focus on economic costs and benefits might be misleading as it does not always reflect the companies' actual decision-making process and criteria for evaluating success and failure. The findings from our research indicate that economic benefits were not the only relevant issue.[6] Figure 5.2 indicates that the percentage of companies that have achieved their objectives to some extent is much higher than the percentage of companies reporting that the monetary benefits exceeded the costs. Eighty six per cent of the companies stated that their objectives regarding the labelling program have been achieved to a high or to some degree even though the earnings did not exceed the costs.

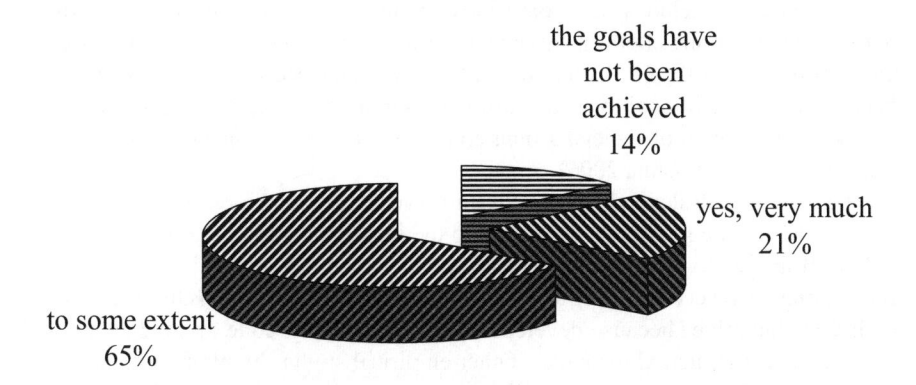

Figure 5.2 Environmental Labelling and Goal Achievement
Question: Has the company achieved the objectives regarding environmental labelling? (N = 73)

- the goals have not been achieved 14%
- yes, very much 21%
- to some extent 65%

The results indicate that the search for the bottom line of CSR might be less important than anticipated by scholars and practitioners that seem convinced that the future of CSR depends solely on whether it can be proved that CSR pays off. Instead of focusing on this issue, it seems more fruitful to regard CSR as just another element in the business strategy (Vogel 2005). CSR, and in this case eco-labelling, is only one of a range of options for a company to differentiate itself from others in the eyes of the stakeholders.

Conclusion

In this chapter we took as a point of departure the notorious measurement problems and the ambiguous nature of CSR, showing how difficult it is to uncover the 'business case' of CSR. Throughout the chapter, we have argued that it is important to acknowledge the heterogeneity of CSR and avoid oversimplified conclusions with regard to the relationship between CSR and financial performance. Instead

---

6   Biondi et al. (2000: 65) derive similar conclusions in their analysis of EMS in SMEs.

of continuing to debate whether social, environmental and financial goals are compatible or conflicting, it might be more fruitful to deal with the potentials and pitfalls encountered by companies trying to plan and implement different social and environmental improvements, which we might label CSR. In this chapter, we have focused on environmental labelling as such an initiative.

Based on a literature review, we have derived a set of common issues that companies should consider in the planning and implementing of CSR. These issues include the motives for adopting CSR, the costs and barriers involved as well as the benefits and the relationship between costs and benefits. The latter is not only measured in financial terms, but also as goal achievement.

The chapter concludes that companies are predominantly guided by external motives, which applies both in theory and to the companies surveyed. This is not really surprising as the CSR literature is heavily influenced by stakeholder theory that extends the traditional focus on customers, employees, managers and owners to include a vast number of societal groups and individuals (Freeman and McVea 2001, Freeman and Ramakrishna 2006).

The costs of CSR depend on the CSR initiative in question. For instance, the costs of eco-labelling are negligible compared to the implementation of an EMS such as ISO14001 and EMAS. However, the survey shows that the companies consider the time they spend on eco-labelling as a substantial cost. This situation is likely to apply to all CSR initiatives because development of CSR policy, code of conduct etc. is likely to draw on internal resources. Other empirical studies highlight a number of organizational barriers that might affect the implementation of CSR, for example lack of know-how and management commitment (Dale 1999; del Brio et al. 2001; Oakland 1993; Poksinska et al. 2003).

If we look at the benefits, companies that have introduced CSR initiatives often derive external benefits. This applies both to theory and the conducted survey According to the survey, there are also a number of internal benefits associated with CSR, even though the companies did not anticipate them from the start. An important part of CSR's future promotion should focus on the internal benefits that companies might realise through CSR initiatives.

By comparing costs and benefits, our findings have shown that several companies considered environmental labelling a success even though the monetary benefits did not exceed the costs. Monetary benefits are not the only issue that is relevant to a company. And even if it were, companies would still experience the same complexity that meets researchers, who are trying to assess the costs and benefits of CSR. In conclusion, it is close to dogmatic thinking to assume that companies solely are motivated by profit and evaluate all activities only by financial measures.

In summary, we argue that conclusions regarding the bottom line of CSR tend to be oversimplified due to measurement problems and the differences between the various CSR initiatives. The costs and benefits of implementing CSR differ significantly, depending on the CSR initiative and the specific context in which the company operates (Plesner and Neergaard 2005). Instead of focusing on the relationship between CSR and financial performance, future research should address the heterogeneity of CSR both in terms of activities and contexts. By doing so we may learn that some CSR activities for companies in certain contexts pay of financially and others do not. We may further learn more about the motives for companies for engaging in CSR and the extent of bottom line arguments for these activities.

Chapter 6

Lost in Translation: The Case of Skandia's 'Ideas for Life'

Pauline Göthberg

Introduction

Since the 1990s, corporate social responsibility (CSR) has gained increasing attention among societal actors (Margolis and Walsh 2003; Zadek 2001) and corporations are increasingly addressing the issue of corporate responsibility. Although it is not obligatory to follow the requirements (European Commission 2001), corporations are expected to comply beyond the letter of the law, and the idea seems to have spread to a large number of corporations. However, even though there seems to be a general understanding of CSR as an integration of social and environmental concerns in all business activities (European Commission 2001), in practice the activities undertaken by corporations differ considerably. As the editors of this book point out in the introduction, in order to understand the difference between a seemingly homogenous definition of the concept of CSR and the many different practices, it is also important to look at the actual practices being conducted under the umbrella label of CSR. But why do practices differ when looking at the corporate level of CSR? To answer this question we have to get a more detailed understanding of how corporations interpret new demands such as CSR.

Generally one tends to think that corporations comply with new demands by translating them into practice (Czarniawska and Sevón 1996). The demands on corporations to be socially responsible should therefore initiate new practice. Consequently, many studies have focused on the adoption of CSR: as a business strategy (Andersson and Bieniaszewska 2005); as a stimulus for generating new activities, such as community, health, and environment projects (Hills and Welford 2005); as header for reporting (Tschopp 2005); as a marketing tool (Maignan and Ferrell 2001); and as an instrument to increase financial performance (Orlitzky, Schmidt and Rynes 2003). However, even if corporations express a desire to comply with new demands, new demands do not necessarily generate new activities. In some cases old practices can be relabelled and presented as examples of the new and modern trend.

The empirical setting for this study is the historical development of one department within the multinational Swedish insurance company Skandia Insurance Company Ltd. The department, called 'Ideas for Life', works with preventative work for children and young people in partnership projects with NGOs and municipalities, and is presented by Skandia as part of the corporate ambition of being socially responsible (Skandia annual report 2004). CSR, however, arrived late at Skandia: Ideas for Life was established in 1987, whereas the concept of CSR was adopted by Skandia only in 2003. Therefore, the case of Skandia is much more an example of the translation of existing practice to fit new demands, than a matter of complying with them. But how did existing practice become transformed into a CSR activity?

Translation theory, as a distinctive area within the institutional literature (Czarniawska and Sevón 1996, 2005a; Sahlin–Andersson and Engwall 2002a), will be used in this chapter to explain how existing practice can play a role in establishing new trends. Management trends are adopted by corporations and are, in the process, reinterpreted or 'translated' by the recipient organization. In a translation perspective it is the recipients that are in focus since they have the ability to interpret and change the idea. The title of this chapter – *lost in translation* – is not only supposed to lead the reader to query what gets lost in the process. The title also refers to the role of 'old' practices in establishing new trends, which is one aspect that seems to have been lost or neglected in the translation literature.

This chapter focuses on how Ideas for Life managed to fit not only CSR but also other management trends. After market conditions changed within the insurance industry, Ideas for Life became dissociated from the business rationale and the department then seemed to have opened up for several different translation processes. During a period of five years Ideas for Life was justified and presented in relation to three popular management ideas of which CSR was one. Not only did Ideas for Life seem to fit quite disparate management ideas such as Knowledge Management, Sustainable Development and Corporate Social Responsibility, but Ideas for Life also started to be presented and seen as a successful CSR activity for others to imitate. In the case of Ideas for Life one could say that what got lost during the translation process were the problems that Ideas for Life was initially thought to have solved. Therefore, for old practices to play a role in implementing new trends, certain aspects of the practice seem to get lost although others apparently are gained.

The next section will present the theoretical framework, which is based on translation theory. This will be followed by a methodological discussion on how and why the case of Skandia and Ideas for Life was selected. Here I will stress the importance of looking beyond the discursive level of CSR and will also take a historical approach in order to understand why practices differ from the general notion of CSR. That section will be followed by the longitudinal study of the development of Ideas for Life within Skandia. Analysis and conclusions will be presented in the final section of this chapter, drawing some further reaching implications from this study.

Translation of Management Ideas

The processes by which new ideas travel and circulate between organizations has been a keen interest of organizational scholars, and it has been noted that organizations tend to implement the same changes about the same time (DiMaggio and Powell 1991a). Organizations imitate organizations that they perceive as successful. DiMaggio and Powell (1983) introduced the concept of field, which was defined as those organizations constituting a 'recognized area of institutional life', to explain that once a field had developed, isomorphic processes (coercive, mimetic and normative) made organizations within the field more alike.

According to institutional theory organizations are affected by, and develops with, norms and values in the environment and are judged on whether they comply with those demands (Meyer and Rowan 1977; DiMaggio and Powell 1983). The business environment for example expects managers to manage their organizations in an appropriate way. However, what is considered appropriate differs over time. Certain management techniques are promoted at certain times as the most efficient way to reach long–term goals and managers are seen as modern when using them. A management fashion could be described as a set of simplified techniques or models often associated with what is seen by the business community as a superior way of organizing, which are often connected to societal norms (Czarniawska and Sevón 2005a). Although the concept of 'fashion' might be associated with being 'chic' and 'vain', following a management fashion has more to do with organizations wanting to appear modern, legitimate and progressive (Abrahamson 1996; Meyer and Rowan 1977). The concept of CSR has many of the characteristics of a management trend and can be seen as a model for organizations to organize successfully (Windell 2006 this volume).

But how can we understand the process by which these fashions are adopted by organizations? Rather than viewing the process as diffusion where receivers are seen as rather passive (Erlingsdóttir and Lindberg 2005: 48; Powell, Gammal and Simard 2005: 233), Czarniawska and Sevón (1996) suggest a translation approach, which implies that actors have a more active role. Building on the work of Latour (1986), Czarniawska and Sevón (1996) argue that ideas and models could not spread in time and space without people, while people will modify, change, add and translate them into something new, appropriate for their local setting. Translation in this sense means 'displacement, drift, invention, mediation, creation of a new link that did not exist before and modifies in part the two agents' (Latour 1993, in Czarniawska and Sevón 1996: 24). It implies that ideas need actors to spread and during a translation process the idea does not remain unchanged (Czarniawska and Sevón 2005a). The way ideas then travel to other locations is a process of interaction where abstract management ideas are translated and edited by the recipient organization (Czarniawska and Sevón 1996; Sahlin–Andersson 1996). Ideas travel in time and space but for an idea to travel it first has to be disassociated (disembedded) from its local context and translated into a text or model. That means that the idea retains only its general characteristics and becomes more abstract. Thereafter the idea can travel to other organizations. When it lands or emerges in another organization the abstract idea has to be translated or reembedded into local activities and meaning. The new context will affect the idea and vice versa, and the new action will become stabilised and might also begin to travel again (Czarniawska and Sevón 1996).

The connection between a popular idea and organizational practice is a matter of translation and this process is considered to produce a number of different results (Czarniawska and Sevón 2005a: 10). One of the reasons why practices differ is that when an idea is taken in by an organization, it is translated or edited to fit that specific local context (Czarniawska and Sevón 1996; Sahlin–Andersson 1996). Although popular ideas such as CSR travel easily, practices do not necessarily remain the same when applied in different local contexts (Solli, Demediuk and Sims 2005). There are many ways in which an idea can transform into practice. Obviously organizations can choose to defy or to oppose institutional forces altogether (Oliver 1991). But if we concentrate on organizations that do choose to implement new ideas, there seems to be a number of different ways of doing so. One type of translation process is an adaptation process where a new idea is adopted, the idea then is turned into a detailed plan and the plan thereafter is turned into action (Czarniawska and Sevón 1996). As mentioned earlier, this kind of view seems to be common within the CSR literature. Although this is one important translation process, if we look at research on how other management fashions have spread they suggest different ways in which an idea is transformed into practice. Organizations can adopt a fashionable label but not the practice. Solli et al. (2005) show in their study of how the concept of 'Best Value reform' was imported from England by the federal state of Victoria in Australia. Victoria presented its work as 'Best Value' but in practice did something different from what was done in England. At the same time, the English 'Best Value' practice was implemented in Sweden but without ever using the name 'Best Value' (Solli et al. 2005).

Another type of translation process is a somewhat reversed process whereby existing practices can be translated to fit new ideas. In organizations certain activities become routine, and after some time nobody questions these activities any longer. However, these activities require legitimization and therefore a generally accepted motive can be ascribed to these activities. In many cases it is a process of re–labelling what organizations are already doing (Czarniawska and Sevón 1996: 40). Czarniawska and Sevón illustrate this by the institution of 'culture city'. The European City of Culture programme was initiated by the European Union in order to promote culture across Europe and was, according to Czarniawska and Sevón, about labelling and making sense of what European cities were already doing. Frenkel (2005) shows in his study of Israeli companies adopting the popular idea of 'Family Friendly Organization' that they presented already existing practice as part of the new idea and thereby distanced themselves from the 'old'. This study is in line with these findings. Although we know from previous research that solutions can precede problems (Cohen, March and Olsen 1972), the above studies seem to imply that the processes are not as random and entail actors who are more intentional (Czarniawska and Sevón 1996: 15). The purpose of this chapter therefore is to explore the role of 'old' practices in establishing 'new' management trend(s).

The Study

Empirically this chapter focuses on the development of a department within the multinational Swedish insurance company Skandia Insurance Company Ltd. Skandia has been an international insurance company since 1855, with operations in Europe, Latin America, North America, Asia and Australia. Operations concern long–term financial security and welfare. Skandia has developed from an insurance company working primarily with property and casualty insurance into a supplier of long–term savings products such as unit link, life assurance and mutual funds. Sales in 2004 were SEK 98 billion and the number of employees worldwide was 5,800 (Skandia annual report 2004). Although CSR is a fashionable trend, the question of corporate responsibility is not new, and therefore the insurance industry has been a relevant place to study corporate responsibility over time. Insurance companies have, as part of their business activities, a long tradition of working with activities directed at security issues in society such as health issues, road traffic research and preventative work in relation to violence and crime.

This chapter focuses on a department of Skandia, Ideas for Life, which works preventatively with children and youth issues and was initiated and justified in relation to Skandia's casualty insurance division in order to reduce crime and violence in society. The department consists of project coordinators who direct partnership projects and the department also offers financial support to civil society organizations. Each month Skandia employees spends working hours engaged in Ideas for Life projects. In 2004, fifteen percent of the workforce in Sweden devoted time to Ideas for Life activities (Skandia annual report 2004). Externally, Ideas for Life has established itself over the years as a legitimate department of Skandia working with children and young people and has had representatives on the boards of several non–profit organizations. The department has also co–operated with the government in reducing bullying in schools. Another example is a partnership project with Swedish municipalities where they have developed a model to improve the way municipalities work with children and young people. A foundation is connected to the department which was set up to provide funding to different projects and organizations which are invited to apply twice a year.

Case studies are normally used to study complex and contextual processes (Yin 2003) and in this study we follow the development of Ideas for Life from its start in 1987 to 2005. Most of the data collection was conducted in 2002–2003 where the history of Ideas for Life was analyzed including the pre–founding years and its subsequent eighteen years of conducting preventative work for children. The main type of data consists of interviews, documents and observations. Some forty semi–structured interviews have been conducted at different levels of Skandia from CEO and management level, middle management to employees within the Ideas for Life department. Interviews were also conducted with representatives from NGOs and municipalities. Documents such as internal reports, newspaper articles, annual reports, deeds of the related foundation, as well as material from Skandia's historical records at the Center for Business History in Stockholm were examined. In addition, to gain a better understanding of the standing and relationships of Ideas for Life within Skandia, as well as with other societal actors, several participant observations were made at internal meetings in Skandia, at Skandia's introductory course for newly employees, at conferences where Ideas for Life were participating and one of Ideas for Life's external meeting with municipalities.

The Story of Ideas for Life

Let us now follow the development of the department Ideas for Life during its eighteen years of existence in order to find out how it has been transformed and translated to fit contemporary problems at different times, that is, how it has been part of a translation process.

From Risk Management to Pro–Bono Work

The reasons for starting the Ideas for Life project in 1987 should be seen in relation to a few contributing factors. In the 1980s the general opinion of the Swedish casualty insurance business was negative, due to a perception that rules for making claims were too complicated and bureaucratic. Skandia, as the largest casualty insurance company in Sweden at the time, felt that the criticism was particularly directed at them. In addition, the largest evening newspaper was also running a series of articles about individuals who had been badly treated by Skandia. The management team was concerned since the criticism could affect customer trust. In fact, competitors were already increasing market share in traditionally strong areas for Skandia.

> Expressen had a reporter, Curt Rådström, who really affected the business. He found a Skandia case where a lady was in a respirator – a mother of two. We were accused of atrocious treatment of customers. The newspapers focused on the issue, the news broadcast filmed the gigantic insurance company with that poor woman. I was in a TV debate with Gary Engman, a real hard–hitting journalist. His mind was set on nailing us. (Björn Wolrath CEO Skandia 1981–1997, 25 September 2002)

The management team realised that customers might leave and therefore initiated several activities. Skandia employed an Ombudsman who could represent customers' interests, Skandia also initiated a crisis centre for customers offering psychological help to those who had been exposed to crime. There was also a revision made on Skandia's internal processes that brought about administrative changes. But public opinion was still rather condemning. In 1986, the head of Public Affairs and head of Communications made another suggestion to the CEO. They wanted to change public opinion by establishing a project called Pro–Bono which intended to 'do good' in society.

A subject that was frequently debated in the media at the time was perceived increased violence in society. An appeal went out to Skandia's customers: Help us with ideas that can create a safer and friendlier society and we will provide resources towards these goals. Out of the replies Skandia received, focus areas were established and a three–year project with a budget of SEK15 million was established and named Ideas for Life. The aim of the project was clearly defined – an activity that could change attitudes and thereby public opinion towards Skandia. The social needs identified were safer living, safer traffic and preventative work to combat violence. These areas were related to the casualty insurance business and could also be justified as preventative work for this part of the business. The partnership projects soon started to focus on activities for children and young people since it was considered a better strategy to work proactively against crime in society. Skandia also instigated a foundation to distribute funds in relation to these issues and the CEO of Skandia was appointed chairman of the foundation. Other members of the foundation were representatives from the government and NGOs. However, the reason for starting the project was not entirely altruistic from Skandia's point of view as it could rather be seen as risk management to counteract perceived negative public opinion of Skandia's casualty insurance business.

The Project Ends, Integration in Skandia Starts

After the first three years, in 1990, when the full project budget had been allocated and public opinion had indeed changed for the better, the project was intended to be terminated. After all, the project had achieved its aims and could therefore be considered to have no further role to play. However, the project was instead turned into a formal department within Skandia. The head of the Ideas for Life project wrote a report to the CEO and emphasised all the positive effects of the project. Customers had moved their business to Skandia and opinion polls were showing an increased awareness of Ideas for Life (Survey on general awareness of Ideas for Life, Temo FS9048 1990). The report also warned about discontinuing the project since it could be turned into something negative: The CEO decided that Ideas for Life should become a formal department within Skandia.

What started in 1987 as a solution to a specific problem expanded its scope and survived, despite the fact that the problems that justified its creation had dissolved. This project was allowed to live on even though its initial function was gone and new functions were discovered. Ideas for Life had, in a sense, exceeded management expectations since customers had moved their business to Skandia and the awareness of Skandia as being a company engaged in social activities had increased. The flip side of the proverbial coin was that Skandia was locked into this commitment since the management team anticipated that a termination of the Ideas for Life project could generate negative publicity.

Skandia Ideas for Life Ambassadors and Integration

In 1996 Skandia had been running Ideas for Life for nine years and Ideas for Life had established itself as a legitimate partner to organizations working with children and young people. Internally, however, Ideas for Life was still rather unknown and was considered to be a 'head office project'. The management team thought that if Ideas for Life was important in creating goodwill for Skandia, the employees should be aware of these activities. The management team therefore introduced the option for employees to become so called Ideas for Life ambassadors. This meant that employees could get involved in Ideas for Life's activities. Being an ambassador also involved informing colleagues about Ideas for Life and slowly the knowledge and acceptance of Ideas for Life increased.

> Something we developed, rather clever actually, was to create a system of ambassadors. (Björn Wolrath, CEO Skandia 1981–1997, 25 September 2002)

In the years following 1996 the interest for working as an Ideas for Life ambassador spread and the number of ambassadors increased.

Expansion Under the New CEO

In the autumn of 1997 the CEO stepped down and was replaced by vice president Lars–Eric Petersson. Since the former CEO was internally seen as the 'guardian angel' of Ideas for Life, there was concern about what would happen to the department. Was the new CEO going to be as interested in social issues as Björn Wolrath? Lars–Eric Petersson was already an Ideas for Life ambassador and engaged in 'Farsor på Stan', an organization consisting of parents who were out on the streets at night in order to reduce crime and damage. Lars–Eric Petersson also became chairman of the Ideas for Life Foundation. With the new CEO an increased interest for Ideas for Life followed. The reasons for running Ideas for Life were still in connection to its casualty insurance business and the goodwill it created.

> When I met the press and they asked why we are doing this (Ideas for Life) the answer was so easy. Damage is reduced when parents are out on the streets at night. We save money. We are part of the society. (Jan Molin, Head of Ideas for Life, 1996–1998, 24 October 2002)

The Raison d'être Disappears: What Happens to Ideas for Life?

During the 1990s, due to economic, social and political changes, the Swedish insurance industry was re–regulated. Insurance companies were allowed to own banks and vice versa, and competition on the financial market increased. There also were demographic changes within Western countries whereby the aging population increased and there was a strain on the social security systems. Fewer people had to support more elderly people and the market for private savings products increased. The long–term savings market was a profitable segment at the time and Skandia's operating result and share price increased. In fact, Skandia was Sweden's second most valuable company in 2000. The management team of Skandia decided in 1999 to divest its less profitable casualty insurance division and concentrate on life insurance and long–term savings products. The reasons, however, for running Ideas for Life were connected to the casualty insurance business, to reduce violence and crime. Using rational arguments based on Ideas for Life's connection to Skandia's business activities was the way Skandia presented Ideas for Life. Now that connection was gone and there was a discussion as to what Skandia should do with Ideas for Life. The discussions concerned whether Ideas for Life should follow the casualty insurance business or remain within Skandia. The CEO considered Ideas for Life as an important and integrated part of Skandia and it was therefore decided that it should remain within Skandia.

> We had discussions about this. Should Ideas for Life follow the casualty insurance business or Skandia? At the same time it was so connected to Skandia. The result was that it followed Lars–Eric and was detached from the insurance division. Lars–Eric didn't want to let it go. The connection to casualty insurance is gone, now it reflects a wider

societal responsibility. It feels natural to go on. (Jan Molin, Head of Ideas for Life 1996–1998, 24 October 2002)

Ideas for Life and its partners did not find it problematic since Ideas for Life had never emphasised the business connection too strongly since it could damage their legitimacy for conducting proactive work for children. The management team did, however, consider it important to link Ideas for Life to its core business activities. Other reasons for running Ideas for Life had to be considered in order to fit Ideas for Life to Skandia's new line of business. Ideas for Life was now being presented as part of a long–term savings mission.

> Skandia's business is long–term savings and we urge people to take responsibility for their future by saving. Ideas for Life focuses on long–term savings in our children and young people. In order to be able to take care of each other we have to concentrate on our children. That is the connection. (Alice Bah, Head of Ideas for Life, 19 September 2001)

So, when the raison d'être for running Ideas for Life dissolved due to changes within the financial sector, Skandia decided to keep Ideas for Life. However, Ideas for Life had to be connected to Skandia's core line of business since it was considered important to argue for Ideas for Life in relation to Skandia's business. Corporations hardly ever justify their social commitments 'just' because it is good for society but also in connection to why it is important for the corporation and its performance.

Ideas for Life as Part of Creating a Sustainable Development

In 1998 Skandia initiated a project addressing Skandia's environmental responsibility and that work was labelled Sustainable Development. The reason why Skandia adopted a sustainability perspective was due to the increasing demands on corporations to address environmental issues. Skandia claimed that in order to be profitable in the long term, Skandia had to combine economic growth, ecological balance and social progress. Mr Wolff, professor at the University of Gothenburg with a focus on sustainability issues, was appointed executive vice president of Skandia in 1998 and reported directly to the CEO. His task was to implement an environmental focus throughout the organization. Skandia did work with environmental issues prior to Mr Wolff's appointment, but the work was mainly related to the casualty insurance division and risk–management. Mr Wolff's task was to strengthen the environmental focus throughout the entire organization. During this time, Skandia also became a member of the World Business Council for Sustainable Development (WBCSD) whose definition of Sustainable Development Skandia adopted. Skandia established a Corporate Sustainability Unit and their work resulted in Skandia's first environmental report in 1999. Being in the service sector, Skandia's environmental impact was considered to be in relation to business travel and their water, paper and energy consumption.

Skandia's engagement in WBCSD was active: the CEO of Skandia and Robert Walker, the CEO of Severn Trent Ltd, became co–chairmen of the working group 'Corporate Social Responsibility'. The CEO Lars–Eric Petersson also represented

Skandia at an EU pre–summit on Sustainability in Gothenburg in 2001. During this period (1999–2001) Skandia was in fact considered a 'front runner' in the insurance industry for their sustainability work in the Dow Jones Group Sustainability Index.[1]

Increasingly, however, members of the Corporate Sustainability Unit felt that Skandia's focus was mainly on environmental performance and not on their social responsibilities. There were discussions within the group regarding issues on what should be included in Skandia's social responsibility. In the Environmental Report for 2001, several examples of Skandia's social responsibility were presented, such as a school prize founded by Skandia to reward good ideas at Swedish compulsory schools, or Skandia USA employees' participation in a house building project. Another example of work presented under the label of Sustainable Development was the work conducted by the department Ideas for Life. The Head of Environmental Affairs described the process of including Ideas for Life in the Environmental Report, and being connected to Sustainable Development, as follows:

> First it was a matter of how to measure. The second year we developed those measures. A third step was to get the whole company involved. During this time focus went from mainly environmental issues. This report (2001) became problematic and we had long discussions about focus being mainly on environmental issues and not on other parts. ... Unfortunately this was a bit of a compromise. Ideas for Life and other parts were included. (Karin Thomas, Head of Environmental Affairs, Skandia, 8 October 2002)

Ideas for Life did not, at this time, cooperate with the Corporate Sustainability Unit, nor did they have any joint discussions regarding the issues of Skandia's goal of creating a sustainable development. It was rather a matter of presentation and a translation of a general definition of Sustainable Development to fit several existing socially responsible practices of which Ideas for Life was one. However, environmental issues and Ideas for Life were soon to be related.

Ideas for Life and Creating a Common Value Ground

Skandia had already adopted the concept of Knowledge Management in the early 1990s and worked with the concept of intellectual capital (Intellectual Capital Prototype Report, Skandia 1998). The intellectual capital project addressed issues on how organizations could manage and visualise their intangible resources. Skandia's competitiveness was considered to be dependent on its human capital as in how to attract, retain and develop employees. An action program was initiated by the HR department in 2001 and the goal for Skandia was to become a first–choice employer worldwide (Annual Report, 2001). One way of attaining this objective was to focus on Skandia's cultural development and to further develop Ideas for Life. Ideas for Life and its ambassadors were seen as a way of implementing Skandia's core values; compassion, contribution, courage, commitment, creativity and passion, throughout the organization. An internal public relations campaign started and the goal was to

---

[1] The DJGSI analyses companies from economic, social and environmental perspectives. DJGSI was later renamed the Dow Jones Sustainability Index (DJSI).

engage more employees as Ideas for Life ambassadors. An internal survey showed that nearly ninety percent of the personnel had a positive attitude towards Ideas for Life (Åke Wissing & Co 2001). In June 2001, the CEO invited all employees to become Ideas for Life ambassadors and the goal was that all employees in Sweden would become ambassadors before the year 2005. An additional function of Ideas for Life was therefore to assist in Skandia's work of developing the Skandia culture and establishing a common value ground.

> When we are out informing about Skandia we try to emphasise elements that the others do not have. Ideas for Life is in this sense really important since not many, or rather, no other corporations have it. (Anja Rasmusson, Employer Branding, 30 October 2002)

From Sustainable Development to Corporate Social Responsibility

In 2002 Skandia started a process of phasing out the concept of Sustainable Development in favour of the concept of Corporate Social Responsibility. This process was strongly related to Skandia's bad financial performance and the large corporate scandals that were revealed during 2002–2004.

Skandia had established a department for Public Affairs in the beginning of 2002, headed by a former under–secretary of state. His job was to establish good relations with the government, unions and society in general. He also took over responsibility for the concept of Sustainable Development.[2] The department of Ideas for Life and the department of Environmental Affairs were now headed by the department of Public Affairs. During a period of nine months, a strategy for integrating social and environmental issues was developed.

During this period two things happened. Firstly, due to a declining stock market, Skandia's result was negatively affected and a cost cutting program was carried out. This affected Ideas for Life as its budget was reduced by forty percent and the number of staff in all the Nordic countries was downsized to twelve people. Secondly, the legitimacy of Ideas for Life was negatively affected due to scandals within Skandia. Even though Skandia had promoted itself as an ethical and responsible company (Skandia's Environmental Report 2001, Skandia's Annual Report 2001) members of the management team were criticised for non–ethical transactions and high executive remunerations. The media criticised Skandia for giving executives excessive bonus payments, executive misuse of Skandia's apartments, and it's use of the mutual savings company for Skandia's purposes rather than the mutual policy holders. The CEO Lars–Eric Petersson was dismissed after the annual general meeting in the spring of 2003. An independent investigation concluded that former executives had 'conducted acts that are unsuitable, unethical and in some cases probably illegal'. Former executives were also subject to a criminal investigation. These scandals affected the board of Skandia and at the Annual General Meeting on 15 April 2004, the former CEO and directors were denied discharge from liability.

The critique against the management team also affected Ideas for Life which was also being questioned in the media and described as the management's 'bad–

---

2   Mr Wolff had left Skandia in 2001 to continue his work at the University of Gothenburg and there was only one person left working on environmental issues.

conscience project', even though the department of Ideas for Life was around long before the criticised management team was employed. The positive effect that Ideas for Life was said to generate was questioned along with the high costs for running the department. The diminishing trustworthiness of the Skandia management team thereby affected the trust and legitimacy of Ideas for Life.

However, when the Public Affairs department had been in operation for nine months the management team decided, in line with its cost–cutting programme, to discontinue the department of Public Affairs towards the end of 2002. Critical voices were also being raised against the whole concept of Sustainable Development. It was said that the business case for environmental issues was difficult to see for Skandia. Skandia started to lose interest in environmental issues. The Head of Strategy and Communication at the time describes it as follows:

> Some of the Sustainability issues are not relevant for a service company such as Skandia. Our effect on the environment is our consumption of paper and coffee. Counting kWh and kilometres driven by employees in Skandia is not a reasonable or a sensible use of resources. (Odd Eiken, Vice President Strategy and Communication, 15 May 2003)

The first sign of environmental issues no longer being prioritised was when the management team decided to stop collecting environmental information from its subsidiaries. Then a decision was made to discontinue producing an environmental report. In fact, it was decided that the whole concept of Sustainable Development should be phased out in favour of the concept of Corporate Social Responsibility. That concept was not considered to emphasise an environmental focus to the same extent. Since Skandia's core business since 1999 was long–term savings products to 'provide financial security for people' Skandia wanted to contribute to creating sustained social stability in society. Skandia presented this ambition as trying to be a 'good corporate citizen' by acting as an initiative–taker, adviser or sponsor of community projects on behalf of children, senior citizens, medical research, education, and accident and disease prevention (Skandia's Annual Report 2004:38). In practice, this included Skandia's work on equality and diversity in the workplace, a publication series on health issues and preventative work for children and young people. In that work Ideas for Life was presented as a CSR activity since supporting initiatives in a child's youngest years was important since both individuals and society would benefit. Now Skandia's reasons for conducting proactive work for children and young people changed and was seen in connection with the concept of CSR, and Ideas for Life was being presented as Skandia's department for CSR activities.

This last section of the empirical part will end with an anecdote from Skandia which can illustrate not only that old practices can be important for establishing new trends, but also how old practices can be part of spreading new trends to other organizations. During the period when Skandia adopted the CSR trend and translated Ideas for Life to fit the new idea, Ideas for Life also began to be presented by Skandia as a CSR activity. Several Swedish corporations, according to Skandia, contacted them to learn how they worked with the concept of CSR and Ideas for Life. One corporation that was particularly interested was Ericsson, the Swedish telecommunications provider. Ericsson contacted Skandia and a representative from Ericsson was invited to Skandia's head office to, so to speak, learn the ropes on site. What Skandia provided was know–how (legal aid) on how Skandia had set up the Ideas for Life foundation that directs funds towards specific goals, and how Skandia allowed employees time to get involved in the different Ideas for Life projects. Ericsson then used the Ideas for Life set–up or structure when they formalised one of their own CSR activities – Ericsson Response. This is an initiative by Ericsson to provide telecommunication techniques in disaster areas such as in the aftermath of the tsunami in Thailand, the flooding in New Orleans and earthquake relief operations in Pakistan. The aim is to restore the infrastructure and enable relief workers to communicate at the site. In the case of Skandia's CSR activities, what was translated by Ericsson was the set–up or the organizational aspect of Ideas for Life. Ericsson has, according to Skandia, established a similar foundation that directs funds towards relief work, and Ericsson also recruits employees to help install and operate communications equipment at disaster sites.

The empirical story of the development of Ideas for Life concludes with this example in order to illustrate just one way in which ideas can spread. It shows how an 'old' practice, translated into the new management trend of CSR, travelled to another location as a CSR example. Corporations do not only comply with demands in the environment but are also active in defining what these demands should entail. By presenting existing practices as CSR, that very practice can become a CSR model for others to follow. Therefore, new demands do not necessarily generate new practices, and by presenting old practices under a new label these practices become part of shaping what is to be regarded as socially responsible corporate behaviour. One can easily get lost in these translation processes, but to understand what is today conceptualised as CSR practices we have to look beyond what are currently presented as CSR activities and discover how old practices can play a role in establishing new trends.

Analysis

The aim of this chapter is to understand the role of old practices in establishing new trends and ideas. As emphasised in the introduction, one tends to think that new demands directed at corporations generate new activities. However, in the case of Skandia and Ideas for Life it is more a matter of translating existing activities to fit the new demands. The chronological exposé showed that the practice of Ideas for Life has been translated a number of times in order to fit passing management fashions. Figure 6.1 recapitulates important phases of this development. After Skandia had disposed of its casualty insurance division Ideas for Life was connected to three management trends. Below, I will discuss how this 'inverted translation' came about, both how the old practice was disconnected from the old idea and how this practice was reconnected to new ideas.

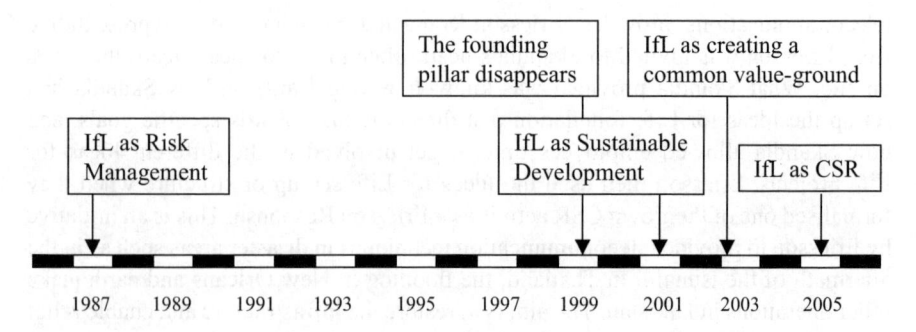

```
                          The founding           IfL as creating a
                        pillar disappears       common value-ground

    IfL as Risk                              IfL as Sustainable
    Management                                  Development          IfL as CSR

   ▼            ▼                            ▼           ▼             ▼
━━━━━━━━━━━━━━━━━━━━━━━━━━━━━━━━━━━━━━━━━━━━━━━━━━━━━━━━━━━━━━━━━━
  1987    1989    1991    1993    1995    1997    1999    2001    2003    2005
```

Figure 6.1 The Development of Ideas for Life (IfL) Chronologically

Disconnecting Old Practice

If we look at the development of Ideas for Life from a translation perspective, the case takes on interest some twelve years into the story. Until 1999, Ideas for Life was presented as preventative work in relation to its casualty insurance division and was seen as generating goodwill for Skandia. It was easy to argue for the existence of the department. Furthermore, two consecutive CEOs considered the activity to be important. What's more, many employees were involved as Ideas for Life ambassadors. A termination of the department would probably have met with internal resistance. During this period, the activities of Ideas for Life were not connected to any specific management trend. They were, one could say, Skandia's own invention. Thus, the first twelve years were important for establishing the initiative, although less interesting from a translation point of view. However, the decision in 1999 by Skandia to dispose of its casualty insurance drastically changed the situation.

Due to demographic changes in Western societies and the re–regulation of the banking and insurance industry, Skandia decided to change its business strategy. They decided to dispose of the casualty insurance division in able to expand their business in the long–term savings market. However, the *raison d'être* for running Ideas for Life had been justified in relation to the casualty insurance business. Now that connection was gone. Since the CEO decided that Ideas for Life should be kept within Skandia, Skandia seems to have had a solution but no problem. However, it was seen as important to be able to connect Ideas for Life to Skandia's new core business activities. Ideas for Life was re–contextualised in order to fit the 'new' business strategy of Skandia. This translation process required that the old problem, working preventatively in order to reduce crime and violence, had to be disassociated or lost. Ideas for Life was thereby disembedded from its local context when Skandia decided to dispose of its casualty insurance division.

Reconnection to New Ideas

After the sale of the casualty insurance business Ideas for Life was re–contextualised within corporate branding as part of sustainable development and later as part of

CSR. But how can one activity fit so many different ideas? One answer might be found in the vagueness of the definition of popular ideas (Windell this volume, Sahlin–Andersson 1996). Generally held ideas or management fashions are vague and fuzzy, and there are no clear definitions of what it is or how it should be translated into practice (Windell this volume). CSR, for example, is a broad term and could include almost any responsibility that a corporation could have towards its environment.

Another factor that seems to facilitate new trends becoming established is the ambiguity that surrounds the corporate goal. The goal of corporations is stated to be profit maximizing. However, that goal is quite vague and not very operational, in other words, it does not say anything about how to get there (Cyert and March 1963). The goal to maximize profits is as enlightening as to advise individuals to behave so that they will maximize their happiness in the long run (Rhenman and Stymne 1972: 58). The goal is both elusive and placed in the future, which enables many different kinds of solutions. In the case of Skandia the three management trends were all said to contribute to long–term profitability. Needless to say, any trend contributing to the opposite would presumably not travel very far. So a vague idea regarding how a corporation should act, in combination with a vague corporate goal expressed by the CEO as: 'Naturally, long–term profitability is our overriding principle' (Annual Report, 2001), leaves a lot of room for interpretation and translation. That makes it easier for companies to adapt to new ideas. That also made it easier for Skandia to fit the activities of Ideas for Life to a changing environment and new management trends.

Let us now take a closer look at the different translation processes whereby old practice became reconnected to new trends. What Czarniawska and Sevón (1996) suggest is that when an idea is disembedded from its local context, the idea only retains its general characteristics and becomes more abstract. When it emerges in another context, the abstract idea has to materialize and be translated into local activities and meaning. So far we have seen how Ideas for Life became disconnected from the old corporate problems and strategy. Now it is time to take a closer look at how the practice was re–embedded with different management trends. What Skandia, or rather different departments of Skandia, did in their translation processes was to link existing activities to ideas that were only adopted long after. The reason for engaging in Ideas for Life was presented very much in relation to contemporary problems. What these three translation processes had in common was a somewhat reversed translation process where Skandia choose to present activities already undertaken within the organization as part of a new trend.

First, Ideas for Life was not only seen as contributing to Skandia's new line of business as a savings company, but was also presented as part of the concept of sustainable development. Skandia said that in order to be profitable in the long run they had to combine economic growth, ecological balance and social progress, and Ideas for Life was being presented as part of Skandia's social responsibility. During my interview with the head of Environmental Affairs, she recalled that the general opinion of those working with the Environmental Report had been that focus were mainly on environmental issues and not on social issues to the same extent. The result of those discussions was that although some new initiatives were presented as Skandia's social responsibility (Environmental Report 2001), the old practice of Ideas for Life was also included.

A second translation process was when Ideas for Life, or rather its ambassadors, were seen as a way of creating a common value ground and establishing Skandia as an attractive employer. Knowledge Management was a popular management concept within Skandia at the time. It became important for organizations to manage and measure their most important resource, knowledge, to insure future profits and competitiveness (Roy 2003). Skandia anticipated that if they did not actively work with their human capital and their corporate culture, the company would not be an attractive employer and would not be able to motivate its personnel. Ideas for Life was translated by the HR department as a way of establishing Skandia as an attractive employer by using the Ideas for Life ambassadorship as a way of creating a common value ground.

A third translation process was when Skandia decided to phase out the concept of sustainable development in favour of the concept of CSR. Due to the financial crisis within Skandia a cost–cutting program was enforced which affected the work with the concept of sustainable development, leading to its termination. The Head of Strategy and Communication expressed a somewhat modified rhetoric and argumentation regarding environmental issues and argued that the sustainable development model was inappropriate for Skandia since the company's effect on the environment was negligible. Instead of a combination of ecological balance and social progress to ensure economic growth, the ecological work was lost in the translation process and only social responsibility was retained. At this point, Skandia started to use the management concept of CSR which said to be more suitable for Skandia's purposes since it was not, according to the company, emphasizing environmental issues to the same extent. Primarily, Skandia stressed that as a supplier of 'financial security solutions' they played an important role in society by their business activities. But as examples of CSR activities, Skandia translated Ideas for Life to fit under the concept of CSR and these were at the same time meant to contribute to the performance of the corporation.

What this study shows is a kind of reversed translation process whereby existing practice is translated to fit new trends. However, in order for the old practice to fit the new trends, the practice needed to be disembedded and disconnected from its local context and reembedded as a solution to contemporary problems. In fact, the reason for running Ideas for Life in connection with the old corporate problem of reducing violence and crime has fallen into oblivion and been lost in translation.

In the literature CSR is often handled as a new concept and highlights corporations that are increasingly addressing these issues (Zadek 2001, Andriof and McIntosh 2001a). What this study shows is that new demands, such as CSR, do not necessarily generate new practices. Instead, old practices can play a role in establishing new trends. One implications of this study is in order to understand the spread of new management fashions it is important to look beyond the contemporary aspects of fashions and put them in a longer time frame. The aim of this chapter was to explore the role of old practices in establishing new fashionable ideas and extending our understanding of translation processes. Although Czarniawska and Sevón (1996) acknowledge that existing practices can play a role in establishing new ideas, and we know from previous research that solutions can precede problems (Cohen et al. 1972), few studies of the spread of management fashions have focused on the role of already existing practice in establishing new trends. Thereby the implication of this 'reversed translation process' is an increased understanding of the spread of management fashions and this translation process gives a more nuanced picture than the one offered by the theory of diffusion or institutional isomorphism.

Lost in Translation

My intention in this chapter has been to explore the role of old practices in establishing new management fashions. The title of this chapter – lost in translation – referred both to the role of 'old' practices in establishing new trends, which is one aspect that seems to have been lost or neglected in the translation literature, but also to what got lost in the translation process. However, in order for an old practice to be able to fit new trends, the problem that the old practice was thought to solve got lost in the translation process while others were gained. Regarding Ideas for Life, what once started as a response to negative opinion related to the casualty insurance division of Skandia, was transformed over the years and was in 2003 presented by Skandia as a CSR activity. Ideas for Life could therefore be seen as a flexible solution to contemporary problems – an organizational chameleon taking on whatever colour deemed necessary at certain times – and CSR is only the latest fashion.

Chapter 7

'What about me?' The Importance of Understanding the Perspective of Non–Managerial Employees in Research on Corporate Citizenship

Elliot Wood

Introduction

In this chapter I discuss the need to conduct research on the corporate citizenship perspective of non–managerial employees. This group of stakeholders is rarely represented in the literature on corporate citizenship and corporate social responsibility (CSR), yet comprises many of those who undertake the day–to–day *implementation* of corporate citizenship activities. I posit some possible reasons for a sole managerial focus in the CSR literature and then discuss why such a focus limits our understanding of corporate citizenship activities. Next, I detail an empirical study into the non–managerial experience of corporate volunteering and show how the findings enhance our understanding of a published CSR framework originally developed with reference to managers. In the final part of this chapter I discuss how further research from a non–managerial perspective could enrich our understanding of other areas of corporate citizenship and CSR.

The Manager as Mouthpiece of the Corporate Experience

It is a curious irony that much of the CSR literature focuses on a privileged subsection of corporate citizens, despite concerns for the underprivileged and powerless amongst authors in the area (such as Hsieh 2004; Ite 2004; Kolk and van Tulder 2006; Seelos and Mair 2005; Sethi 2003; Wettstein and Waddock 2005). Research on social responsibility often focuses solely on the perspective of the CEO or other top executives, and fails to engage lower–level employees and their experience. As pointed out by Wood (1991: 707), 'if researchers want to know how companies respond to social demands, they ask top executives, preferably CEOs'. Despite a body of research and theory affirming the different perspectives taken by the manager and the non–managerial employee regarding organizational activity

(Berger and Luckmann 1967; Cook and Emler 1999; Liao–Troth and Dunn 1999; Ostroff, Shin and Kinicki 2005; Tsui and Milkovich 1987; Whiteley 1995), in much of the management literature, the views of the CEO and other executives are often portrayed as representative of the opinions and experiences of all individuals within the corporation.

A number of authors (Hemingway and MacLagan 2004; Smith, Wokutch, Harrington and Dennis 2001; Wood 1991) have called for researchers to consider the motives and responsibilities of individuals in the organization, in order to understand how corporate citizenship is perceived and implemented. However the rare research that discusses an individual–level perspective on CSR[1] still typically portrays the perspective of the management group. For example, Wood (1991: 700) suggests 'the individual's right and responsibility to decide and to act are affirmed within the bounds of economic, legal, and ethical constraints. The principle is based on human choice and will, focusing on the options and opportunities available to individual actors within their organizational and institutional contexts.' Yet Wood defines such individual opportunities for action only as *managerial* discretion. The focus on management runs at least from discussion of the social responsibilities of management in the 1950s (Bowen 1953; Drucker 1954), through research into managerial attitudes and values (Bowen 1978; Sturdivant and Ginter 1977; Sturdivant, Ginter, and Sawyer 1985) and the managerial reaction to social responsibility pressures (Frederick and Weber 1987; Gray and Hay 1974; Ostlund 1977; Wood 1991; Votaw and Sethi 1969) to questions of social responsibility in the body of the wider management literature itself (Carroll 1991, 1994; Coffey and Wang 1998; Kotler and Lee 2004; Wokutch 1998).

What are the Implications of this Managerial Focus?

There certainly are a number of valid reasons for basing CSR research on the views of managers. There is societal pressure on managers to espouse more than simply economic imperatives. As Windsor (2001: 226) for example notes, the language of corporate social responsibility has become, at least partly, an 'unavoidable managerial rhetoric', suggesting that 'no manager can openly advocate greed or non–responsibility'. As a result awareness of social responsibility and social impact forms a part of the managerial role. Furthermore as Desai and Rittenburg (1997) point out, it is individual managers who often shape the moral environments in which they work, and managers most often have a greater influence over work processes than non–managers (Gordon and DiTomaso 1992). In addition, discretion to undertake corporate citizenship activities depends in part on the amount of autonomy associated with one's role in the organization and the opportunity to

---

1 From a multi–level analytic perspective (Rousseau 1985), much CSR literature provides a contextual background rather than aiming at direct exposure to the experience of individuals within the corporation, discussing the role and responsibility of 'business' or 'the corporation' but failing to acknowledge or explore the experience of the individual employee as a key stakeholder in the changing corporate role. Wood (2004b) provides a discussion and critique of the individual, company and institutional level focus in the CSR literature.

influence events through political processes. Further afield, a focus on management has itself been suggested to be a cultural phenomenon, reflecting a US emphasis on the importance of management in directing firm performance (Jackson 2002; Trompenaars and Hampden–Turner 1997). A weaker emphasis on management in other countries is evidenced by industrial relations structures with less emphasis on management power (such as Germany's Betriebsrat) and compensation differentials across countries (Bass, Simerly and Li 1997; Zajac 1990).

In emphasizing the perspective of management it could be argued that much of the CSR literature implicitly supports an orthodox view of the organization as one of hierarchical power and rigid structures. Buchholz and Rosenthal (1997: 181) note that the field of business and society itself rests on an assumption of atomic positivism in which the two are 'separable, isolatable entities...that are roughly co–equal in their relationship to each other'. There is certainly a sense of irony in such orthodoxy given that topics of CSR and corporate citizenship have for a long time been considered 'radical' within the mainstream management literature (Dubbink 2004; Dunn 1991; Sethi 1972).

It could also be argued that a focus on management legitimizes a top–down approach to corporate citizenship activity and in line with principles dating back to scientific management (Taylor 1929), privileges the views and decisions of managers over those of non–managerial employees. From a sociological perspective, the debate here is largely one of individual agency versus structural functionalism. While Frederick (1960: 59) points out that individuals who are active within a system of social roles and institutions are still subject to its prevailing characteristics (for example, businesspeople must be concerned with profit, 'as a prime value within the presently existing system of business enterprise'), organizational structure and symbolism is more easily adapted to suit one's needs at higher levels of the organization, such that managers are better able to modify the structures within which they function (Bolman and Deal 1991).

From a structural functionalist position, the perspective and actions of non–managerial employees are largely relegated to inconsequence, at the whim of societal and institutionally–embedded rules and modes of conduct to which the employee has not contributed (Burrell and Morgan 1979). One may further question the emancipatory effects of such a managerial focus – in line with feminist critiques of management literature (such as Morgen 1994) the power of the non–managerial employee in the debate is lessened when his or her voice remains unheard.

Why is a Focus on Non–Managerial Employees Important?

Organizational research in a number of areas suggests a distinction between the managerial and non–managerial perspectives on organizational life and thus a different understanding of organizational activity. For example studies comparing managers with non–managerial employees have found that organizational climate tends to be perceived more positively by managers than non–managers[2] (Patterson, Warr and West 2004), that those with formal management education are likely to be more risk propensive when making decisions than those without such training (Johnson and Powell 1994), and that managers are likely to be more critical than non–managers of unethical situations when making decisions (Henthorne, Robin and Reidenbach 1992).

From the very start, managers have worked under a different set of expectations and experiences to 'workers'. Frederic Taylor in his quest for efficiency deliberately distinguished between manager and worker roles in order to ensure the most efficient and (in theory) effective approach to production. The result as noted by Burrell (1997) and described by Hoxie (1915, cited in Hollway 1991: 22–23) was the 'gather[ing] up and transfer to the management [of] all the traditional knowledge, the judgment and the skill of the workers...in connection with the work'. As Hollway (1991) notes, 'this both reflected and reproduced a situation in which *the perspective and values of workers and management were increasingly differentiated and these differences were structured into the organisation.*' (Hollway 1991: 22, italics added).

It is a standard of organizational theory that the perceptions of employees influence their subsequent behaviour (Dearborn and Simon 1958; Kelley 1972), and that employee actions (whether individually or as a whole) thus impact organizational performance (Kozlowski and Klein 2000). Much of the difference between managerial and non–managerial perceptions depends on knowledge and power (Clegg and Palmer 1996). Even language differences are common between managers and non–managers – 'Corporate–speak' and the inherent power of the managerial role itself excludes certain knowledge, practice and views of the organization from being aired (Morgan 1997; Oakes, Townley and Cooper 1998). The socio–semiotic aspect of communication in organizational settings further suggests that managerial narratives of organizational events are privileged over non–managerial narratives (Cooren 1999). Workers as such have commonly been seen to 'live' in the received world of structures, systems, and processes. They collect information about organizational values and ideals from the strategy and policy information of managers from whom they take instruction (Frost, Moore, Reis, and Lundberg 1991; Frost and Mitchell 1995).

However, challenges to the power of management come from a variety of sources. Post–modern authors such as Chia (1995; 1997), Charmaz (2000) and Tierney (2003) argue for the importance of *all* individuals at work, and in particular for the capacity for individuals to think and act independently of the structural constraints of management. Recent research on adaptive agency in which self–reflexive agents are capable of influencing broader systems through their own conscious actions (Holland 1995; McGuire 2003) provides a further espousal and explanation of the power inherent in *any* organizational role. With particular reference to corporate

---

2   To be fair, the CSR literature is not alone in ignoring possible differences between managers and non–managers, or in assuming that managerial perceptions are representative of other employee levels or of companies as a whole. For examples, Patterson, Warr and West (2004) note that even in the measurement of a construct such as organizational climate, changes over time have led the field toward almost a sole focus on the perceptions of managers.

citizenship, Andriof and McIntosh (2001b) suggest that 'we now live in a world where corporations are oriented very much towards the consumer and employee *because these people hold the ultimate power in the system*' (Andriof and McIntosh 2001b: 17, italics added). These authors suggest that the way in which (lower–level) employees experience corporate citizenship and the associated policies and activities of the firm should have a profound impact on corporate performance and as such are worthy of closer study. Indeed recent research supports this assertion. Turban and Greening (1997) for example found that perceptions of corporate social performance impacted not only a firm's reputation but also potential employee ratings of employer attractiveness, and other authors have found employee perceptions of a firm's image to be related to employee job satisfaction and one's intention to resign (Dutton and Dukerich 1991; Riordan, Gatewood and Barnes 1997).

A number of further studies in the CSR literature also support the call for research on non–managerial employees. Berthoin Antal (1990) and Collins (1990, as both cited in Wood 1991) suggest for example the need to direct research attention to 'bottom–up' forms of social responsiveness. Other authors suggest the relative importance of a corporation's social activities is dependent upon the relationship an employee has with the organization (Ibrahim and Angelidis 1995; Smith et al. 2001) – one's corporate social orientation. Smith et al. (2001) note that conflict between one's corporate social orientation and the firm's corporate social performance may predict behaviours such as customer and employee retention and suggest that 'it is imperative that firms investigate how their diverse employees perceive their actions' (Smith et al. 2001: 288).

Some corporate citizenship activities possibly do occur without the need for consideration of the lower–level employee, particularly where activities involve decisions regarding allocation of large resources, or for activities (such as public relations) typically oriented outside the company. Corporate philanthropy, corporate sponsorship and cause–related marketing, for example, often involve large budgets, and associated policy decisions are commonly taken at higher levels of the organization; they are traditionally seen as the prerogative of management. In such cases, perhaps a managerial focus *can* be reconciled with the importance of management in actually implementing corporate citizenship activities.

However decisions at managerial levels inevitably impact on non–managerial employees. Furthermore, lower–level employees undertake the implementation of many managerial decisions. As well, not all (perhaps even not many) activities associated with corporate citizenship involve *only* high–level decision–making. Whereas corporate philanthropy may involve high–level budget decisions, other forms of corporate citizenship (such as community involvement) involve considerable activity at lower levels of the organization. Given that the perspective of the non–managerial employee is missing from much of the literature, investigating the perceptions of non–managerial employees engaged in such activities is a worthy endeavour.

In the next section of this chapter I describe one area of corporate citizenship in which the non–managerial perspective may provide an enhanced understanding of the activity – corporate volunteering. I note several reasons for focusing on the perceptions of non–managerial employees in this area. Following this, I then describe a research study that explored both the managerial and the non–managerial employee experience of corporate volunteering activity in 3 organizations. I use Hemingway and MacLagan (2004)'s published framework for analyzing CSR as a tool with which to detail part of the findings of the study and show how the non–managerial perspective adds to our understanding of this framework, and consequently, to a greater understanding of CSR implementation as a whole.

The Case of Corporate Volunteering

Corporate volunteering is one of a number of activities associated with corporate community involvement and an indicator of corporate social responsibility and good corporate citizenship (Cronin and Zappala 2001; de Gilder, Schuyt and Breedijk 2005; Lukka 2000). Defined broadly as 'employees undertaking voluntary community activity supported in some way by their organisation' (Wood 2004a), corporate volunteering exhibits a number of characteristics that make it a particularly useful activity for investigating non–managerial perspectives, for contributing to the literature, and as a result, enhancing our understanding of corporate citizenship.

First, corporate volunteering activity, despite its varied nature is a form of corporate social responsiveness typically *undertaken and engaged in by the non–managerial employee.* That is, in comparison to other citizenship activities such as broader company sponsorship of community events or other forms of corporate philanthropy, corporate volunteering programs tend to involve personal involvement by a large number of individuals, most often at lower levels of the organization. Corporate volunteering in many companies in fact stems from a desire to include employees in the corporate citizenship process (Lee and Higgins 2001) and as such, employees are directly involved in activities. This is recognized in a number of corporate volunteering programs that emphasize both their 'grass–roots' nature and the importance of employee decisions. For example 3M's Volunteer Program points out that it is largely employee–inspired (3M 2003), whereas Citigroup notes that its employees themselves 'regularly seek out opportunities where business and social responsibility go hand–in–hand' (Citigroup 2003).

According to role theory, which posits that patterns of behaviour are influenced by (and influence) expectations regarding a person's work position and work activities (Biddle 1979), direct involvement in volunteering activity is likely to impact an individual's own experience of work and work role. For example, as volunteer activity takes up either work or non–work time, some form of extra time– or work–burden is likely in association with volunteering commitments. This is particularly the case where corporate volunteering happens outside of work hours (Lee and Higgins 2001). Given limited time and work resources, involvement in corporate volunteering may thus impact on one's work activity (and on the expectations of others regarding one's work performance). Such an impact is of particular interest for those who seek to understand the link between corporate citizenship activity and corporate performance as a whole, given that role–related constructs in particular (such as role conflict and role ambiguity) have empirically been shown to influence a range of attitudinal and performance measures, such as commitment, satisfaction, turnover and absenteeism (Hecht 2001; Randall 1988; Van Sell, Brief and Schuler 1981).

The impact of corporate citizenship activity on work performance is further distinguished by the *nature* of the corporate volunteering role itself. That is, to some degree expectations about volunteering can be juxtaposed with expectations about other work activity. Within organizations, the psychological contract (Rousseau 1995) establishes that (primarily) some form of economic reward is exchanged for a level of control over the type and quantity of work activity completed for the organization (Cooper 1999). Corporate volunteering on the other hand is undertaken freely without concern for financial gain (National Centre on Volunteering 1996) and by its very nature represents a discretionary opportunity out of step with traditional corporate expectations about work. This is most clearly seen in the reluctance to link corporate volunteering to performance appraisal (so as to avoid diluting the voluntary component of the activity), particularly where such appraisal is linked to remuneration or career progression (Tuffrey 1995: 29).

Given the relevance of corporate volunteering for understanding the employee experience of corporate social responsibility, what follows is a description of a research study conducted to examine the impact of participation in corporate volunteering on employee perceptions of their work and work role. The study provides a 'first glimpse' at the way in which non–managers think about and experience corporate citizenship activity and an example of ways in which such a perspective can aid our understanding of corporate citizenship as experienced by all in the organization.

A Research Study

In 2003 and 2004 I interviewed 32 non–managerial corporate volunteers in Australia about their individual experiences of corporate volunteering. I was primarily interested in the way in which their perceived experience of corporate volunteering (as a corporate citizenship activity) linked to their perceptions of work and their work role. As noted above, very few authors had previously explored how the perceptions of non–managerial employees undertaking corporate citizenship activity might impact on their own work performance. Many studies had used managers as surrogates of the views of the whole organization, or had actively considered managers as the important group to target. Furthermore, few studies had researched the involvement of non–managerial employees in the *implementation* of corporate citizenship.[3] Researching non–managerial employees' own involvement in corporate volunteering focused on corporate citizenship activity as it was directly experienced by the *individual* employee. Furthermore, researching *why* a non–managerial employee undertook corporate volunteering enabled an examination of the *motives* of those involved in implementation itself.

---

3 Implementation for non–managerial employees refers to their own *involvement* in the activities necessitated by managerial decisions about corporate citizenship, and thus for corporate volunteering this can be operationalized as *active involvement in corporate volunteering activity*. An operationalization of implementation for managers would focus more closely on decision–making activities such as resources allocated and policies approved.

The study involved in-depth qualitative interviews of 32 corporate volunteers undertaken at their place of work in three different organizations – a government agency, a university and a multinational accounting firm. Interviews lasted between 1 and 2.5 hours each and were conducted by the author. Interviews were recorded where possible for later transcription resulting in over 500 pages of interview transcription for analysis. Using software for qualitative data analysis, by the end of the content analysis, over 1100 individual codes had been established from the interviews, and from a series of 40 themes across the 3 organizations, 15 code families were developed. Some examples of the code families included Support (support for involvement, core business as a priority, encouragement and recognition of volunteering), Reputation (personal reputation, public relations, marketing of corporate volunteering), and Hierarchy (the role of management, bottom up, us and them, professional identity and barriers).

A grounded research design (Whiteley 2004) was utilized in the research, involving the identification and development of initial focal questions (Rubin and Rubin 1995), purposive sampling, and an iterative approach to data collection as data was collected, triangulated where possible, and content analyzed. Earlier interviews at the first organization were content analyzed and the results of analysis provided the impetus to search for interviewees and organizational contexts in which to confirm, refute, and expand upon emerging themes (Glaser 1992). A semi-structured qualitative interview format was utilized for data collection because of the underlying constructivist assumptions of the research paradigm (Guba and Lincoln 1998), and also because the paucity of data on non-managerial employees in the literature lent itself to an exploratory approach to data collection.

Two of the research questions which the study sought to address were 'what is the experience of participation in corporate volunteering like for employees?' and 'how do employees incorporate the experience of participation in corporate volunteering into their experience of work in general?' The next section discusses some of the emergent themes relevant to these two questions, and using these themes, demonstrates how a non-managerial focus can offer a new perspective that contributes to the existing managerial focus of much corporate social responsibility literature.

Discussion of the Study Findings

A number of themes emerged from the research study described above which appear rarely, if at all, in the literature on corporate social responsibility and citizenship and show the value of understanding a non-managerial perspective of corporate volunteering. These themes covered the considerations of *time and flexibility* in undertaking corporate volunteering, the role of *hierarchy and management* in the experience of corporate volunteering, and the importance of *passion, altruism and an action orientation* in relation to corporate citizenship.

From analysis of interview responses, one of the most important considerations for non-managerial employees turned out to be *when* corporate volunteering occurred. That is, corporate volunteering activity undertaken 'during work hours' was symbolically important – not only was it easier for non–managerial employees to undertake activity during work–sanctioned time, but providing time off to undertake corporate volunteering was seen by non–managerial employees to be evidence of the commitment of management to good corporate citizenship itself. The importance of time however was linked to *work flexibility* – non–professional staff (such as secretaries, or other administrative staff) on fixed work schedules had a view of 'work' itself that was focused on set times and a set place. One came to work at a certain time, worked in a certain location, and left work at a certain time. For professional staff work was seen as a vocation – not a specific time or place – *what* one was doing as a volunteering activity mattered more than *when* one volunteered. As such, the flexibility to engage in corporate citizenship activity when one wanted, and in whatever form one wanted was important for many non–managerial employees, as evidenced by the following quotes from interview participants:[4]

> is it important when you do it? It…I'd say it is because that shows the firm's support I think moreso if they said to do it on a Sunday probably less people would help out because its in your own time // the firm supports it as well because dealing with something that's outside generally like they give you a couple of hours off every 3 weeks // the only way I can say it might have an influence is if I was tightly controlled and wasn't allowed to do anything during work hours would make it harder for me // unfortunately the stuff that the charities came up with for people to do it wasn't a rewarding experience.

Further analysis of results indicated that *the more corporate volunteering was seen as an individual responsibility, and under the control of non–managerial employees, the better*. That is, there was a distinct bias towards considering corporate volunteering activity as one's individual responsibility – where the company or management was seen as a driver behind corporate volunteering, this was considered to be a negative influence. Such a notion was evident in an important aspect of the non–managerial experience – the *action orientation* of corporate volunteers. Many volunteers saw management activity as a hindrance and noted proudly that they 'got on and did things', *contrasting* this with the perceived management response of 'pushing a lot of paper around':

> to be involved and assist with the homework centre you actually have to get up off your bum and do something // you're the master of your own destiny whether it be from an organizational perspective or whether it's an individual and their ability to progress within the organization, see an opportunity and take it // we had you know the action plans that we have I've found that they have just been the best because it says here's what we're doing and this is when we're doing it by rather than minutes that just read through and you have no action.

Non–managerial employees often felt their individual responsibility to engage in corporate volunteering was curtailed by the 'corporate' concerns of management:

---

4 I have used the device '//' to indicate the end of a comment by one interviewee and the beginning of a separate comment by another interviewee.

> [Is it important that [the managing director] supports you?] Well he would have to because otherwise it just wouldn't work, it would be too hard, by his supporting it it runs down through the whole firm that maybe one partner doesn't agree with it, but knowing that the guy at the top supports it then they obviously have to turn a blind eye // I think if [the organization] tried to corporately, to do corporate volunteerism with the people who are already volunteering it would have a negative impact.

However paradoxically, non–managerial employees also discussed how the informal nature of most corporate volunteering activities meant that the *managerial hierarchy* of the organization was largely irrelevant whilst undertaking the activities themselves. Non–managerial employees could be working side–by–side planting trees with the CEO and have discussions on a first–name basis:

> so I might chat to a partner about these things whereas normally I wouldn't normally speak to that person I mean I was chatting to a partner last Friday night we had a work function a drinks function on [and?] I was talking to a partner I probably wouldn't have spoken to in the next 5–6 years.

Furthermore, corporate volunteering was seen by many as a bottom–up activity, the antithesis of a formalized 'corporate' approach. Thus for non–managerial employees, with an emphasis on 'doing' corporate volunteering, individual activity often worked *against* the formality of a corporate response.

> it's about us. It's got nothing to do with management. // provided the boss watches his place then everyone would have been happy but because the boss tried to manage the whole thing everyone went troppo // Most of the volunteer work, I don't think the management would initiate it. It comes from someone down below going 'there's this charity race coming up, Hey let's get involved, let's go and ask management if they'll sponsor it. So it's coming from down here and asking up.

A further theme to emerge from the non–managerial experience was a sense of the passion and affective commitment to corporate volunteering activity. For some, corporate volunteering provided an opportunity to emotionally engage in a way they could not do in their normal work role:

> Its just nice to know that you're actually doing something and doing something of value, cos in my role its like ok I organize Mrs X's life which is all very well and you know the papers and meetings and that sort of thing but its not valuable to the community to actually furthering where everything fits kind of thing, it sounds stupid, where the, I guess its, and that's probably the negative in my job that I find is that what value am I actually really adding?

The sense of 'doing something of value' focused in particular on helping others in the community. Many used the term passion to describe their volunteering work, and while emotions ranged from apprehension at undertaking volunteering in novel situations (such as homeless shelters) through to a long list of positive emotions such as joy, happiness, enthusiasm, many discussed the way positive emotions developed from the altruistic focus of their volunteering activity.

others are very genuinely concerned with their community and there is no there is nothing there for themselves as such // So everybody is happy to give their time to raise money. We get nothing out of it personally just the satisfaction. // But I'm not doing it for me. That's the key.

The focus on altruism suggested that non–managerial employees saw this as a particularly appropriate motive for volunteering. In discussing altruism further, they saw a management focus (where activities were undertaken for corporate purposes) as contrasting with an altruistic focus and having a *negative* impact on their motivation to volunteer. Marketing of corporate volunteering for example was seen as the antithesis of why non–managerial employees undertook corporate volunteering:

The worst aspect of it. Umm, (pauses) maybe when they don't support you enough in it. And if they milk it. // I think that is poor they are willing to take all the glory for all of these [front line staff] working their guts out volunteering but when it comes to the crunch they don't really support them // if we get exposure the boss gets the exposure you know the [front line staff] doing a good job for the community basks in the glory // when it comes to corporation there is much more of a question of what's in it for us?

What was *not* discussed by non–managerial employees was also of interest – that is, *unprompted, virtually none of the non–managerial employees discussed how corporate volunteering benefited either themselves or their organization.* Non–managerial employees did not consider *corporate* benefits of corporate volunteering as either important or particularly motivating. However virtually all those interviewed discussed at length the benefits to the community. In fact, in many instances, non–managerial employees were loath to admit to *any* personal benefits, despite corporate volunteering literature suggesting a range of individual benefits ranging from new skill development through to increases in life satisfaction (Tuffrey 1998). Non–managerial employees noted over and over again the importance of undertaking corporate volunteering work that had community impact – their motive was making a difference in the community rather than for corporate benefit – in essence, they saw their activity as *community* citizenship, not *corporate* citizenship.

Using a Non–Managerial Perspective to Shed Light on Management Models of CSR

What sense can we make of these findings and how do they contribute to our understanding of corporate social responsibility and corporate citizenship? In particular, does a non–managerial perspective of corporate volunteering add clarity to the management–oriented approach associated with much of the CSR literature?

To answer this question, let us take a management–focused model from the literature and see how the findings above might both support an existing understanding of the model and contribute new perspectives to CSR practice. A useful model in this regard is the work of Hemingway and MacLagan (2004), who have developed a framework for analysing corporate social responsibility (see Figure 7.1). The framework focuses attention on the importance of understanding both managerial motives (strategic versus altruistic) and the locus of responsibility for CSR implementation (individual or corporate) as key drivers of corporate social responsibility.

These authors note that corporate citizenship is not only associated with commercial imperatives, but rather, with the individual values of managers and suggest that those considering corporate citizenship need to take into account the personal values of managers, since corporate responsibility may be influenced far more by the *individual* concerns of those in a corporate role than by the *corporate* concerns of these managers per se.

MOTIVE

Idealistic/Altruistic

Corporate ——————————— Individual   LOCUS OF RESPONSIBILITY

Strategic

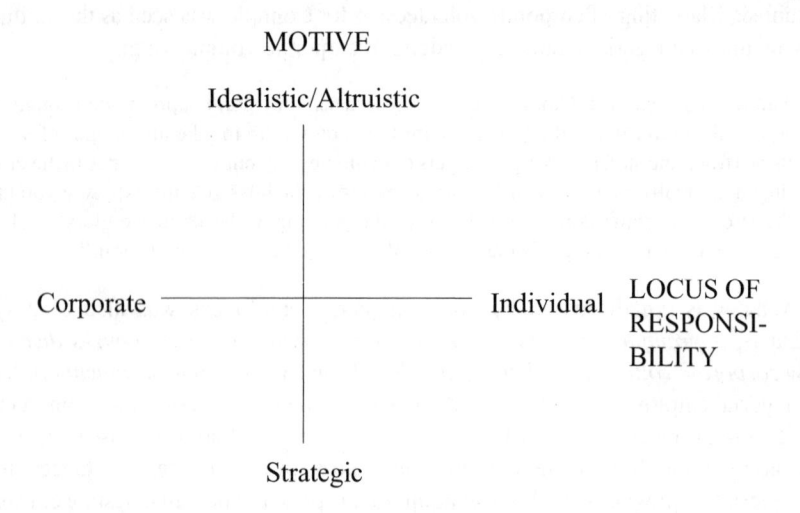

Figure 7.1 A Framework for Analyzing CSR
Source: Hemingway, C.A. and MacLagan, P.W. (2004), 'Managers' personal values as drivers of corporate social responsibility', *Journal of Business Ethics*, vol. 50, no. 1: 33–44. Reprinted with kind permission from Springer Science and Business Media.

Hemingway and MacLagan propose two key dimensions for the analysis of corporate social responsibility (CSR) practice in this way. They point to the locus of responsibility as an important consideration in determining whether a business itself is socially responsible. Thus socially responsible activity could be conceptualized as either a corporate response, or as an individual managerial response. To the degree that CSR practice is discretionary rather than driven by economic or legal imperatives (Carroll 1979, 1991), one can accurately determine the nature of a company's activities in corporate social responsibility terms. Furthermore, these authors note that that the *motives* of actions, introduced either by managers or by 'the corporation' could be considered along a second continuum, ranging from strategic at one end, to idealistic or altruistic at the other.

At first glance, the findings from the research detailed above would appear to suggest that from a non–managerial perspective, an individual locus of responsibility and the altruistic motive are certainly salient features of engagement in a CSR practice such as corporate volunteering. For example, non–managerial employees note that their individual practices are often interfered with by management, and that taking individual responsibility for action allows them to contribute effective outcomes to the community. They discuss how important it is to them that their CSR practice benefits others and they eschew the personal and corporate benefits of their actions. Furthermore, they describe the emotions involved in seeing how their practice has helped others in the community. As such, the experience of the non–managerial employee could be situated in the upper–right quadrant of Hemingway and MacLagan's framework.

This interpretation however contrasts with what Hemingway and MacLagan (2004) suggest is likely to be a managerial perspective on CSR practice. That is, while these authors acknowledge that individual managers may work from an altruistic values base, they cite Harrison (1975: 130) in arguing for a precedence of organizational values over personal values in the event of a conflict between the manager and the organization – 'it is more likely that the manager would accommodate his personal values to the purposes of the organisation in such a way as to further his [or her] own aspirations.' They suggest that such a balance makes it difficult to separate managerially–espoused strategic reasons for undertaking CSR practices from the underlying altruistic or idealistic concerns driving some managers. In essence, the manager as an agent of the firm's owners is required to act in the best interests of the firm and to be seen to be doing so, and thus espoused CSR practice from a managerial perspective is likely to be centred more strongly in the bottom (strategic) half of the framework.

However while managers may emphasise the 'strategic' drivers for CSR practice, the findings noted above suggest that non–managerial employees are far less inclined to espouse a strategic perspective. Whether this is a rhetorical position (i.e. it is outside of the 'norm' for non–managerial employees to discuss corporate benefits) is open to debate. However given the strong contrast between the action orientation of non–managerial employees, the emphasis on hierarchy and the negation of corporate benefits from volunteering, it would appear that the motives of non–managerial employees differ markedly from those suggested in the literature as relevant to management. Furthermore according to these findings, the 'management' norm of espousing strategic motives for CSR practice is likely to impact *in a negative way* on the experience of corporate citizenship for non–managerial employees. In fact, managers need to carefully consider the degree to which any strategic motive is communicated to non–managerial employees. Keeping a focus on the altruism associated with corporate volunteering seems particularly important for motivating non–managerial employees to contribute to corporate volunteering.

Conclusion

The above discussion demonstrates that evidence from non–managerial employee research is useful in providing a new perspective of existing CSR literature, in this case the framework provided by Hemingway and MacLagan (2004). In fact, consideration of the responses of non–managerial employees suggests that the motives for CSR practice for managers may be somewhat juxtaposed with those of non–managerial employees and thus without considering the non–managerial experience, the use of the Hemingway et al. framework (and perhaps other models in the CSR literature) may be somewhat limited in scope.

It should be noted that the findings discussed above and their particular relationship to the Hemingway and MacLagan (2004) model are only one example of the way in which non–managerial perceptions may contribute to our understanding of corporate citizenship and corporate social responsibility. Non–managerial perceptions may influence our understanding of CSR in different ways according to the research topic, the research sample, and the comparison framework or literature discussed. In the research study described above for example, it is debatable whether or not altruism, time, hierarchy or passion would surface as themes amongst non–managerial employees engaged in a different form of corporate citizenship activity (such as philanthropic giving), from a different type of company (such as small family–owned businesses) or within a different cultural setting. In Australia for example, a strong history of organized labour, and cultural myths of a classless society, equality and mateship have long resulted in attention to non–managerial perspectives in the implementation of organizational change (Avery and Ryan 2001).

The discussed research with non–managerial employees shows how literature that focuses solely on the perspective of managers may not adequately capture the full experience of corporate citizenship for all those who undertake such activity. Furthermore, in adding nuance to the dimensions of Hemingway and MacLagan's (2004) framework, it is evident that a non–managerial employee perspective can contribute to a wider understanding of corporate citizenship and CSR implementation. Locus of responsibility and the motives for undertaking corporate social responsibility implementation may be relevant to both managers *and* non–managers. However the importance of the altruistic motive, the action orientation and a community– as opposed to corporate– or individual– focus show that the views of lower–level employees regarding corporate citizenship in this case can differ markedly from those of management reported in the literature.

If we take corporate volunteering activity as one part of a corporate citizenship approach, it remains to be seen how the views surfaced in this paper fit with an understanding of what corporate citizenship might mean at a corporate level. With recourse to the literature however, accompanying the rhetoric of corporate citizenship is an undertone of the worth of the individual and the importance of a range of stakeholders to the organization (Dunham, Freeman, and Liedtka 2006; Freeman 1984; Freeman 1998) A corporate redefinition toward social responsibility and corporate citizenship is likely to impact widely on an individual employee's life experience. As noted earlier, individuals who are active within a system of social roles and institutions are nevertheless still subject to its prevailing characteristics.

The research findings noted above also have relevance for other fields of study. For example, in other work (Wood 2004a) it has been suggested that the possibility of a strategic focus for management and an altruistic focus for non–managerial employees provide the possibility for role conflict, the need for dialectic, and the opportunity to begin to reconceptualize corporate–community involvement as partnership rather than patronage. The degree to which CSR practice fits within a non–managerial employee's work role also has consequences for the meaning and significance generated by work, suggesting the importance of considering the impact of CSR practices on perceived job characteristics. Furthermore the centrality of time and emotion in the experience of corporate volunteering raises questions regarding the appropriateness of a rational, clock–centred conceptualization of work in the 21st century. Whilst these implications are outside the scope of the current chapter, what this chapter has nevertheless sought to make clear is the beneficial and nuanced contribution a non–managerial perspective can make to our understanding of corporate citizenship, built largely as it is on frameworks centred on managerial perceptions.

Viewing the non–managerial employee as worthy of consideration in a broader stakeholder approach suggests that the voices of these employees need to be sought and heard. Perhaps, with reference to Windsor (2001), the implementation of corporate citizenship carries with it a due assumption of the *lower–level employee*, not just the manager, as a citizen. Opportunities do exist for researchers to investigate how the employee impact of corporate citizenship activities might match the community rhetoric of corporate citizenship at a corporate level. Francis Grey, of the Dow Jones Sustainability Index has commented – 'When I say sustainability, many hear "socialism"' (Grey 2002). Although socialism may not be an ideal of the corporate citizen, certainly such an outcome should not be confused with an all–important humanism, as discussed by one of the managerial interviewees in the study outlined above:

> I think it's the humanising of the experience – like a fellow that I worked with is a senior manager as indeed I am but he works in [X] division and I'm now an [X] and we spent a great time together…so I can see absolutely the potential for that humanising thing to happen you have a partner and a senior manager and a graduate working side–by–side hoeing a garden or whatever it might be its just humanising.

By including a non–managerial perspective as a focus for research, there is every chance that such humanism can be nurtured and promoted in order to lead to more inclusive corporate citizenship for all. To establish a view of corporate citizenship that includes all corporate citizens is surely a worthy contribution of academic research to the practice of corporate citizenship.

Chapter 8

Exporting Knowledge and Values: A Discussion of Managerial Challenges when Attempting to Diffuse CSR across Company and National Borders

Eirik J. Irgens and Harald Ness

Introduction

When managers believe in what their company does, that is, in the organization's collective practices and the shared values these practices represent, they will most likely act as advocates for these values and practices when the company expands its business network through mergers and acquisitions. This should hold for Corporate Social Responsibility (CSR) in particular, since CSR, as Jackson and Carter (2000) point out, is closely associated with ideology, and as such, with values, virtues and what is held to be 'proper' social practice. When a corporation that flags CSR expands internationally, we expect that there would also be attempts to export CSR in one way or another.

In a global economy with networks of companies within and across national borders, we expect the diffusion of CSR to international subsidiaries to be particularly challenging. Ethical values, management principles, and respect for people and the environment are all examples of CSR–related issues that are mediated differently through different cultural lenses. Research on differences between national flavours of CSR (Chapple and Moon 2005) supports this idea. Behind the processes of isomorphism that apparently make organizations and corporations become more and more similar when it comes to formal and structural elements, the underlying national, local and company values may still vary to a large extent (Hofstede 1980; Powell and DiMaggio 1991b; Trompenaars and Hampden–Turner 1997). Attempts to export CSR to newly acquired and merged companies that are not based on thoughtful action will thus at least turn out to be problematic, or maybe even fail.

In this chapter, we highlight the process of exporting knowledge and values on CSR, based on a preliminary case study of a Norwegian corporation that has faced several managerial challenges in this process. Studying these processes in a Norwegian multinational is interesting given some particular properties of these multinationals. In the last thirty years, the Norwegian economy has flourished, thanks mainly to oil revenues. Norway ranks as one of the world's richest nations, and just a few years after the dot–com bomb hit the economy hard, business profits are reported to be higher than ever. Apparently Norwegian companies are performing quite well. In a recent study by Schramm–Nielsen, Lawrence and Sivesind (2004), the Scandinavian way of conducting business is characterized by values like equality and consensus. The authors argue that these values enhance organizational solidarity, reduce divisions within the workforce, underpin mechanisms of coordination, and facilitate communication and dialogue across different skill–job–qualification levels. They describe a democratic practice characterized by discussion before decision–making, loyalty to the decision process, and participation by trade unions and by personnel at different levels (Schramm–Nielsen et al. 2004). However, they also point at some weaknesses: decision–making may be slow, reluctance to use power may cause conflict avoidance, and a 'killer instinct' may be lacking. When studying processes of exporting knowledge and values across different subsidiaries, these traits make Norwegian multinationals an interesting empirical context.

This chapter provides an exploration of the export and editing of CSR–related issues between subsidiaries within multinational companies (MNCs). It is based on preliminary findings from a study of a Norwegian multinational in the paper industry. In this chapter, first the empirical findings will be presented in order to describe the context. Then, in our analysis, we build on neo–institutional theory (DiMaggio and Powell 1983; Scott 1995) as this stream of literature provides extensive research on the diffusion of organizational recipes and management ideas, as well as on how these ideas have been imported and edited in different settings (Røvik 1998; Sahlin–Anderson 1996). This school of thought also provides a vocabulary related to diffusion and import. Important limitations can be found in the bias towards a macroperspective that seems to have been dominating the neo–institutional school, and in its tendency to treat ideas as physical objects that are implemented in rather mechanical ways where organizations become abstract typologies on a macro level, rationalized and impersonal (Christensen, Karnøe and Strandgaard Pedersen 1997; Borum 1999; Powell and DiMaggio 1991b). We therefore will transform the diffusion and import metaphor into an *export and editing* metaphor. Doing so allows us to include the perspective of the exporter, as well as to illuminate the learning and knowledge challenges embedded in the local editing processes.

The globalization of Norwegian firms raises questions related to both *what* and *how* ideas are exported to newly acquired companies abroad. The expansion of Norwegian MNCs has primarily taken place through mergers and acquisitions. Our research therefore will aim at describing to what extent a particular parent corporation actively tries to export locally constructed ('home–grown') values and practices when they settle in unfamiliar cultures. In order to do so, we will study the case of Norske Skog, a Norwegian paper manufacturer that has rapidly expanded worldwide and that tries to foster its CSR policies among its subsidiaries. To study how this process of exporting local values and practices takes place, it is useful to first briefly discuss the Norwegian business context and then outline how this corporation has grown. Our objective in this chapter is to broaden our knowledge of how actors in Norwegian multinational corporations (MNCs) construct CSR–related identities and organizational recipes when the corporation transcends its national borders and local institutional context. How does the corporation deal with different logics of legitimacy and appropriateness along with logics of technological and economical efficiency, within the frames of multiple institutional and geographical environments? Addressing this type of questions ultimately should allow us to develop actionable knowledge that can be used when managers plan diffusion of CSR across company and national borders. In the final section of this chapter we will address this objective.

When Norwegian Corporations go International

The Scandinavian countries have a common history, which has contributed to the logics that regulate work and work conditions in general – especially the practices that together are called *The Collective Agreement*. The Collective Agreement stems from the so called 'Septemberforliget,' which was first approved in September 1899 in Copenhagen, as Danish employers accepted the existence and activities of labour unions, while the labour unions in return accepted employers' prerogative. Sweden copied this model in 1906, and Norway did the same in 1907 (Nielsen 1992, 1996).

After the construction of The Collective Agreement, the violent class struggle position of labour unions in Scandinavia gradually changed into a social democratic movement, arguing for a non–violent change of society and for the improvement of living conditions for the working class. This position of mutual respect enabled cooperation, since the employers (for example, the owners) were granted the right to own and control the production forces, while the workforce was granted the right to join unions and engage in the struggle for better work conditions, fair wages and a fair dispersion of working time, spare time and sleeping time. As Nielsen (1996) points out, The Collective Agreement has since the beginning of the 20th century been a basic element of the Scandinavian legal systems, and as such it represents a strong democratic tradition regulating the organization of work, which is not found in the same form in other legal systems, neither in Europe, Africa, Asia or America.

This way of organizing work has become institutionalized in Norway, embodied in stockpiles of historical and political arrangements, regulations by law, political documents, agreements and local settlements aiming to regulate the relationship between employers and workers' unions and each individual worker. Such taken for granted ideas and regulations – even if they are disputed from time to time – act as guidelines for the perceptions of reality and the interpretations and construction of meaning related to work in Norway.

In this chapter, we focus on challenges facing corporations trying to diffuse a CSR ideology based on a democratic tradition, to acquired and merged companies in other cultures. Many indications predict that these good intentions may at least partially fall short. For example, Leer–Salvesen (2000) summarizes five years of research on the activities of Norwegian companies in Asia, Africa, and Latin America with obvious disappointment. In other words, there is a need for research that can shed light on the processes where Norwegian corporations try to export their specific way of conducting business: If the business ethics of Norwegian corporations and managers, due to historical circumstances, are different from the ethics of for example American or other European multinational corporations and managers, then how does this influence attempts to export CSR from Norwegian headquarters to different subsidiaries?

A Brief History of the Globalization of Norske Skog

Norske Skog, which means Norwegian Forest Industry in English, was established as a pulp and paper company in 1962 at the rural town of Skogn in the middle of Norway.[1] The first two newsprint machines were installed at the firm in 1966–1967. The company was quite successful and over the years, mergers and acquisitions in Norway made Norske Skog the undisputed leader of the country's paper and pulp industry during the 1970s and 1980s. From then on, the company also went international in its mergers and acquisitions. In the 1990s, Norske Skog engaged in international acquisitions and new plant constructions in France, Austria, and the Czech Republic. In 1998 two mills in Thailand and South Korea were bought and in 1999, the Pan Asia Company (50 per cent Norske Skog–owned) was founded, based on four mills in South Korea, China, and Thailand. This initiative made Norske Skog the number four producer of newsprint in the world. In 2000, Norske Skog bought Fletcher Challenge Paper (with mills in New Zealand, Australia, Malaysia, Brazil, Chile, and Canada) and merged with Klabin in Brazil. In 2001, the corporation bought Walsum in Germany and Parenco in the Netherlands and merged with Pacifica in Canada. By the spring of 2004, Norske Skog ranked as the world's second largest newsprint producer and became a major producer of pulp and of coated and uncoated magazine papers. Finally, in 2005 Norske Skog bought the Pan Asia Company and now is the world's largest producer of newsprint. Between 1992 and 2002, Norske Skog's operating revenue grew from 1,1 to 3,33 billion USD, and its market capitalization from 0,25 billion to 1,84 USD billion. The production capacity of the 50 Norske Skog paper machines at the 24 mills varied from 90,000 to 335,000 tonnes. After several good years, newsprint markets experienced a marked setback in 2001–2002. In 2003, therefore, Norske Skog introduced an improvement programme. However, according to top management, this was not enough to improve profits. Accordingly, in the spring of 2006 the Union Paper Mill in Skien, Norway, which Norske Skog had acquired six years earlier, was closed down. 359 workers lost their jobs.

In forty years time, the corporation had developed from a fairly small local firm into a world leader. The national and international expansion also involved a transfer of values and management practices across different subsidiaries. Before we look at this transfer process in more detail, it is useful to outline the background of these values and practices.

---

1   In this chapter we distinguish between Norske Skog, meaning the global corporation, and Norske Skog Skogn, which is the mill from where Norske Skog originated in the 1960s, located in Skogn, Norway.

The Construction of Management Principles and Organizational Identity

Along with many other Norwegian companies in the 1970s and 1980s, the management of Norske Skog Skogn developed written management principles and value statements. These developments followed several international influences, which are briefly outlined here.

The first influence involved principles and translations of recipes developed mainly by the car industry in the USA before 1940 and during World War II. These ideas were brought to Norway by American consultants through the Marshall program after the end of World War II (Ness 2003). In 1971, two years after oil was found in the Norwegian part of the North Sea, one of the consultants from the Marshall program, George W. Kenning, was invited back by top management of the leading offshore company in Norway. Very soon, Kenning gained the position of a guru in management training in Norway, introducing what he called *Praxes* to a network of Norwegian leaders and managers.[2] These management principles were introduced at training sessions, known as the President Meeting courses (Ness 2003).[3] Kenning's ideas acquired a lasting impact on Norwegian management programs. Leaders from Norske Skog Skogn also took part in the training sessions, and the acquired management principles were translated and adjusted to fit in a paper mill and later on aligned to local and national ideas on how to manage and organize.

In 1982, management recipes from the McKinsey group were introduced to the President Meeting courses (such as Peters and Waterman 1982). These ideas represented a new input in Norwegian management programs, focusing on mergers, downsizing, core activities, and management principles (Ness 2003). Several well-known management concepts such as operational analysis, competitive analysis or transaction cost economics, originating from American business schools, found their way into Norwegian firms. Often these concepts were introduced by university graduates with a Bachelor's or Master's degree in business economics (Engwall 1999).

Norske Skog Skogn was one of the first Norwegian companies to introduce Japanese TQM logics in their activities. Following a management visit to a Toyota plant early in the 1980s, Quality Circles were translated and implemented in the production line in 1984–1985. Shortly after the middle of the 1990s, the concept of Best Practice was introduced to the Skogn mill. Originating from a Japanese Total Quality Control principle, best practice describes how to benchmark and standardize the best critical business procedures from any company or business branch worldwide to obtain 'world class quality' and business hegemony (JUSE 1991).[4]

Even if the impact of these American and Japanese management ideas on the Norwegian business community cannot be underestimated, any foreign idea had

---

2 Praxes is an abbreviation of 150 management principles developed by General Motors since the early beginnings of mass production up to the time shortly after World War II.

3 The Presidents Meeting was the name used by a network of Norwegian industry leaders from different branches, who met regularly with Kenning during the years 1972–1988. George W. Kenning died in 1988, but his ideas (Praxes) continued to have an impact on Norwegian leaders during the 1990s.

4 JUSE – Japanese Union of Scientists and Engineers.

to align with the Norwegian model in order to be successful. At Norske Skog Skogn, the local edition of the Norwegian model was significant in establishing their organizational practices from the very beginning. When the first paper mill came on line in 1966–1967, the competition in the Norwegian market was tough. The struggle to survive during the first critical years made a great impact on both leaders and workers in developing a spirit of unity and common goals – sink or swim together. Disputes about how to run the mill usually were solved through dialogue in a friendly way. This feeling of being on the same side; employers and employees fighting together against the competitors, still prevails at Norske Skog Skogn – a spirit referred to as the *Fiborg Feeling* (Fiborg is the name of the place where the mill is located). Some informants from Norske Skog Skogn claimed that these formative years were characterized by collaboration and mutual trust, and that parts of this feeling still prevail. They refer to this local way of editing and institutionalizing practices as an ethos of openness, respect and trust, shared by both employers and unions.

In 1997, the corporate headquarters were moved to Oslo, but the Skogn mill continued to be a vital force in the corporation. For example, most Norwegian managers who were sent abroad to take positions in acquired mills have been managers at Norske Skog Skogn. The Skogn mill is one of the most visited by other subsidiaries in the corporation, since many of the ideas, management principles, and ideologies that are disseminated within the corporation have been developed at Skogn, or by actors that had a strong relationship with the Skogn mill. One way of implementing these ideas and practices to newly acquired mills can be described as walking and talking through the business procedures at Norske Skog Skogn. By inviting managers, employee representatives and workers from other mills for audits and close inspections of human and industrial processes, the Skogn way of organizing and running a paper mill was promoted as a best practice throughout the corporation. Audits at Norske Skog Skogn still are a natural benchmark on particular processes, and it seems reasonable to conclude that Norske Skog Skogn has been, and still is, a vital force in the construction and transformation of company knowledge and values. This brief description of Norske Skog Skogn's position in the corporation and the way it is organized is helpful to understand how the corporation handles organizational issues related to CSR.

CSR in Norske Skog

The Norwegian government has recommended all international Norwegian companies to join the Global Compact. The Global Compact is an initiative of the United Nations aimed at establishing a contract between the UN and business enterprises world wide; to uphold and promulgate a set of core values in the areas of human rights, women's position, labour standards, anti corruption and environmental practices (United Nations 2000). The initiative was proposed by UN Secretary–General Kofi Annan in a speech to the Davos World Economic Forum in January 1999. Norske Skog signed the Global Compact in 2003, in addition to binding agreements with the Confederation of Norwegian Business and Industry

(NHO) on participating in the Female Future project to enhance equal opportunities in the company. The NHO has also formulated statements on CSR, influenced both by Kofi Annan's appeal, and by the European Commission's Green Paper on CSR (European Commission 2001). Norske Skog defines corporate social responsibility as a competitive edge, and the Norske Skog CSR policies include essential parts of the organization's collective memory and practices on human resource management, as well as their environmental policy.

Hall and Soskice (2001) portray the great variation within contemporary capitalism. The Norwegian model can be located within a cluster called the Scandinavian Model. But even within nations we can find local varieties on how details in a model or a recipe are translated and edited. The *Fiborg feeling* mentioned earlier is one example of such a local edition. The construction and institutionalizing of practices and principles at the Skogn Mill acquired the status of best practice in in–house collaboration already before the globalization process started. In the process of diffusing corporation values the unions have played a vital role. During the entire period of globalization of Norske Skog, the local union leader at the Skogn mill has been the person who has travelled the most – visiting every acquired or merged mill anywhere in the world, selling the Skogn way of doing business to his fellow union leaders abroad. Following these developments, in December 2004 a unique union–management agreement was announced on Norske Skog's webpage:

> Norske Skog has taken an important step forward in formalising a world–wide collaboration agreement between management and employees in the company by establishing a Global Employee Forum (GEF). Due to be signed today by chief executive Jan Oksum and chief shop steward Kåre Leira[5], this agreement represents the first worldwide agreement of its kind in pulp and paper industry. I'm proud that a Norwegian company is bringing Norway's model for collaboration between management and employees out into the world, says Mr Leira. We've reached a milestone in Norske Skog's in–house collaboration. This will give us a common platform for pursuing our important work on behalf of all employees world–wide (www.norskeskog.no, accessed 21 January 2005).

Opportunities and Challenges when Diffusing CSR globally

Some scholars advocate CSR through promises of a positive impact on economic performance in the long run. CSR is said to improve financial performance and increase employees' motivation and commitment to work as well as customer loyalty and corporate reputation (Schiebel and Pöchtrager 2003; Waddock and Graves 1997). Others choose to focus on how to implement or manufacture CSR (Roberts 2003; Were 2003), or how to audit CSR systems (Waddock and Smith 2000a). In this chapter, we will not take a normative stance on whether CSR is good for a company or not. Rather, we will focus on CSR as an espoused theory of action that, due to the concept's close association with values and virtues (Jackson and Carter 2000), may be particularly challenging to transfer to an applied theory

---

5 The chief shop steward referred to happens to be one of the most central union leaders in Norske Skog Skogn, as well as in Norske Skog Corporation.

when it is exported from one cultural context to another. We will especially focus on the challenges Norwegian corporation managers face when they are attempting to export CSR values and practices to merged and acquired companies abroad, and what consequences these challenges should have for further research. Allred, Boal and Holstein (2005) recently claimed that economic explanations are not sufficient in order to understand the fate of merged and acquired companies: They proposed a new metaphor to understand corporations as stepfamilies (Allred et al. 2005). Corporations are often referred to not as individuals, but as families of companies. In stepfamilies, as in corporations that have grown through mergers and acquisitions, individuals experience high stress levels, culture shock; role ambiguity, limited shared history, and complex structures. These problems are created by differences that call for new traditions, new coalitions, and new relationships, Allred et al. (2005) argue. In this process both stepfamilies and corporations must deal with issues such as loyalty conflicts, failure rates, problems with boundaries, and information asymmetries. The emotional component of parenting takes time to fully develop, and motivation is not always present. The level of stress is great, and when some of the children may be regarded as problem children, or the parents are not properly prepared, the possibilities for a happy family life are seriously reduced (Allred et al. 2005).

We will maintain that becoming a stepfamily is indeed a challenging endeavour, but that it is even more challenging when parents and their stepchildren represent different national cultures, as is evidenced in the vast literature on intercultural management and international business (see Adler 2002; Calori 1994; Hampden–Turner 2000; Hofstede 1980; Trompenaars and Hampden–Turner 1997). MNCs will then experience that values on individual, company, corporate and national level all are brought into play. The metaphor of multicultural stepfamilies may be a fruitful way of framing the challenges MNCs are confronted with. As in stepfamilies, the processes of establishing a harmonic unity can't fully be understood through applying rational economic theory. Parallel to stepfamilies, some actors in MNCs perform value–based leadership roles, while organizations, and leadership systems within organizations, are governed as much by beliefs as by rationality and outcomes (Klenke 2005). The possibilities of creating unwanted outcomes when trying to perform well then becomes apparent, even in monocultural stepfamilies. As Weaver (2001) points out; even if there is widespread cross–cultural agreement on the normative issues of business ethics, corporate ethics management initiatives (for example, codes of conduct, ethics telephone lines, or ethics offices) that are appropriate in one cultural setting nevertheless could fail to mesh with management practices and cultural characteristics of a different setting.

Pursuing shared ethical goals by means of culturally inappropriate management practices (for example Western management principles applied in a different culture) can undermine the effectiveness of ethics management efforts (Weaver 2001). Attempts to transfer Western management knowledge to Russian managers from programs conducted over a ten–year period were for instance studied by May, Puffer and McCarthy (2005). They found that the culture, values, attitudes, and behaviours of the stepchildren such as the Russian managers, affected the capabilities to engage in effective knowledge transfer of both transferors and receivers of knowledge.

However, how the different family members perceive themselves in comparison to the other members may differ significantly. Also, Al–Khatib, Rawwas and Vitell (2004) examined employees' self–reported work–related ethics and compared them to their perceptions of co–workers and top management along various morally challenging situations in the Gulf countries Saudi Arabia, Kuwait, and Oman. They found that respondents perceived all ethically challenging situations as unethical and had significant differences among themselves regarding their own ethical perceptions, as compared to perceptions of peers, and top management (Al–Khatib et al. 2004). When the family members represent different national cultures, these dissimilarities in perceptions and moral judgements will be even more evident. For instance, Christie, Kwon, Stoeberl and Baumhart (2003) applied Hofstede's cultural typology and examined the relationship between his five cultural dimensions (individualism, power distance, uncertainty avoidance, masculinity, and long–term orientation) and business managers' ethical attitudes in India, Korea and the United States. They found that national culture has a strong influence on business managers' ethical attitudes (Christie et al. 2003).

But within one and the same national culture there will always be companies that succeed more than others. These companies will, as with stepfamilies that succeed in establishing a functional and warm family, serve as exemplary and as representing a best practice within their field. Bowen (2004) studied what factors in the organizational culture of an ethically exemplary corporation are responsible for encouraging ethical decision–making. Through an exploratory case study of a pharmaceutical company held to be a worldwide leader in ethics, she found that organizational ethics are enhanced by an organizational culture that emphasizes the importance of ethics, rewards ethical behaviour, offers ethics training and facilitates ethical analysis.

What might happen when such an environment is infused with unethical values is shown by Sims and Brinkmann (2003). After analyzing the Enron Corporation collapse, they suggested that a company's culture has profound effects on the ethics of its employees – culture matters more than codes. That is, the values and norms embedded in an organization's culture make a stronger impact on actual behaviour than the espoused values expressed through for example documents and statements.

Developing a sound company culture hence seems to be an enduring challenge. However, in a stepfamily, the diffusion of best practices and the development of a corporate culture that supports ethical conduct are complicated by lack of tradition, unclear structures, and roles that are still in the making. This may fuse uncertainty and angst. The development of a stepfamily has the underlying goal of reducing uncertainty and forming a collective and functional unit through the development of strong family ties. In these processes stepparents become role models. In corporations, expatriate managers become the representatives and diffusers of the family values. The stepparents own values become imperative in the process of establishing a common ground for the new family. This is also shown in a study of Ecuadorian managers in which attitudes and external attributions were found to significantly predict managers' intentions to discipline employees who accepted a bribe (Wated and Sanchez 2005). The organizational climate regarding ethics, that is, the shared perception of what is ethically correct behaviour and how ethical issues should be handled within an organization, is in fact a result of the personal values and motives of organizational founders and other early organizational leaders (Dickson, Smith, Grojean and Ehrhart 2001).

The values of stepparents and stepchildren are important, but values are not a static entity, and ethical behaviour can be learned. For example, managers may be trained to meet situations that challenge their own and their corporation's ethical standards. Brand and Slater (2003) investigated the business ethics experiences of Australian managers who had spent a long time in China. These managers were challenged with situations related to corruption, requests for visa assistance, employee theft, nepotism and non–adherence to contractual obligations. Brand and Slater (2003) identified four key coping strategies: Managers spoke of not compromising their own morals, of attempting to understand the motivation of Chinese colleagues, of talking to others and of sticking to company policy. Based on these findings, these authors argue for the development of mentoring relationships between experienced and less experienced practitioners. In addition, they propose cultural training for managers and the establishment of a clear company policy on contentious issues such as bribery (Brand and Slater 2003). These issues apply to a wide variety of industries and hence also to the paper and pulp industry.

Mikkilä, Kolehmainen and Pukkala (2005) indeed studied four pulp and paper mills and their surroundings in four countries; China, Finland, Germany and Portugal. They focused on the acceptability of operations as an indicator of corporate social performance and responsibility and divided the notion of acceptability of operations into technical, financial, environmental, social, cultural and political dimensions. They found that the concept of acceptability of operations varies from place to place. National and company cultures influenced the elements that were emphasised at a particular time. These authors concluded that the variability in the concept of acceptability makes the definition of corporate social performance difficult, even within one branch of industry (Mikkilä et al. 2005). This again illustrates that the diffusion of CSR and related concepts is a value–laden and value–driven process that brings values at both individual, company, corporate and national levels into play. Consequently, CSR cannot be exported the way material goods are exported. As in stepfamilies, stepparents and stepchildren have to learn to live together. It is through learning processes that a new and functional common ground may be established and new norms may be formed. Turning to neo–institutional theory and organizational knowledge and learning literature can help in interpreting these initial observations.

A Neo–institutional and Knowledge–creating Point of Departure

Transfer – or the import and export – of knowledge and values generates both theoretical and empirical questions. Powell and DiMaggio (1991b) describe different forms of institutional isomorphism, which denote how organizations and corporations become more and more similar with respect to organizational forms. How does this isomorphism come about? According to Powell and DiMaggio (1991b), the different forms of isomorphism relate to coercion, mimicry, or norm following, depending on which environmental forces are influencing the organization. Scott (1995) argues that various types of repositories, or carriers, are bringing ideas from one place to another. Regulatory, normative, and cognitive carriers provide different kinds of meaning to social behaviour as well as various kinds of compliance to act according to rules, norms, or cognitive arguments.

Knowledge, practices and values – in short, organizational recipes (Ness 2003) – may also be seen as symbols of modernity, legitimizing the organization's activities versus local/national authorities and multinational/global treaties and trends (Røvik 1996, 1998). This perspective implies that some actors – usually those in a managerial position – are on the lookout for the latest and most trendy organizational recipe, not necessarily because the actual recipe will solve the problems in their organizations, but because they want to ensure that the organization's (and the manager's) image is up to date and legitimate. Applying modern management recipes hence shows off.

Recent studies show that organizations may make use of institutionalized standards that are in line with their already established practices or they may be decoupled from institutionalized demands and become superstandards (Meyer and Rowan 1977; Røvik 1998; Irgens 2003; Ness 2003). A superstandard may be conceived of as an organizational recipe that can be used as a norm for organizing or legitimating business practices at any time and anywhere in the world. In our view, the export or import of organizational recipes always involves individual actors. When corporations change their policies, products, or business ethics, this change will be difficult to understand if actors are not seen as both carriers and monitors of the multiple institutional logics that are ingrained in such processes. Processes describing the editing, sharing, and institutionalizing of standards, values, ideologies, competencies, and technologies in organizations inevitably then must rely on some assumptions about how learning processes unfold in individuals, in groups, and ultimately in and among organizations (Argyris and Schön 1978).

In line with Friedland and Alford (1991), we argue that actors can use and manipulate any recipe at their disposal. Even scientific theories can often be used in several ways. Prescriptive economic theories, such as transaction cost economics and agency theory, may be used to legitimize the maximization of huge management salaries, stock options, and bonuses as reward for successful management – the ingrained logic being that this will ensure that managers will focus on the maximization of profits for shareholders. The fact that (some) managers are apt to use this logic when downsizing or selling out companies – in order to maximize their own economic position – is underreported (Kaufman, Zacharias and Karson 1995). The social embedding of practices and virtues always reflects the multiplicity of values and logics in any given society at a particular historical period. In the USA, the acceptance of immense management salaries has been closely associated with ideas related to economic success stories. Before the scandal, Enron was celebrated as a laudatory economic success, and as such, the company was promoted as an example of the genius of American capitalism. The rewriting of the story is not so straightforward, however, since the illegal acts of the managers in Enron rely on explicit values celebrated by the same capitalistic society in which the misconduct took place (Ghoshal 2005).

In a global economy – especially in third world countries – the history of Enron may be a warning, leading corporations to proactively integrate CSR ethics in company practices. However, when actors from different societies or cultures meet, there will inevitably be some kind of melting and editing of values and logics (Christensen 2002). To master the dilemmas between legitimacy and efficiency, actors may construct stories that reinterpret efficiency practices in a legitimizing way.[6] There are several dimensions at play here:

1. the multiplicity of values and logics, which are embedded in the institutionalized national practices,
2. the fact that actors may be more or less receptive and sensitive to the explicit values, ideologies, logics, and competencies brought into play by the other,
3. the degree to which the actors are able to construct shared meanings and values depend on each actor's personal beliefs and preferences acquired through his or her social–historical–cultural responsive processes, resulting in a more or less integrated and appreciated self,
4. the relational exchange (especially power relations) between the actors, and
5. the pressure from the institutional contexts by which the actors are surrounded.

One example of potential dysfunctional organizational effects accompanying policy processes is described by Brown and Duguid (1991) in their analysis of Orr's (1996) ethnographic studies of service technicians. Brown and Duguid distinguish between espoused, canonical practices and actual, non–canonical practices. They state that it is the actual practices that determine the success or failure of organizations. As they contend, there are practices that are officially celebrated, and there are practices that are performed 'underground'. These non–canonical practices and the accompanying communities may be driven even further underground by formal organizational policies and decisions. There are many ways in which this discrepancy can be resolved. Brown and Duguid (1991) argue that an organization must strive to master this gap instead of trying to get rid of these underground practices.

Brown and Duguid's analysis was conducted within a single national context. We argue that the environments of a MNC will present an even greater diversity with respect to the legitimating of organizational practices. What is perceived as natural within one national culture may be seen as hostile or disrespectful elsewhere. Neo–institutional theory offers ways of conceiving and dealing with such diversities, especially when we talk about soft institutional elements such as CSR, that is; elements that may be thought of as primarily non–technical and non–economical.

---

6 Perhaps, this was the case with the chief executive in the Norwegian national oil company Statoil. At first, he was officially celebrated as a flourishing manager because Statoil got some prestigious contracts in Iran, but shortly afterwards, he was sacked when it was known that he had allowed the son of the Iranian oil minister to be bribed in order to win these contracts. The arguments used to defend what had happened were, among others, that this is an acceptable way of doing things, that is, in Iran.

Neo–institutional theory describes business environments as constituted by a technical and an institutional component (Scott and Meyer 1992). The technical environment exercises output control on the market, rewarding organizations for efficiency and effectiveness. The institutional environment rewards organizations for establishing correct structures and processes and not for the quantity and quality of their outputs (Scott and Meyer 1992). The essential argument of institutional theory is that it is not sufficient to do things well; you must also do things the right way, that is; according to what is legitimate within the institutional context. It is often argued that institutional environments vary across regions, while the technical environment – the market – is uniform and universal. This does not imply that markets are identical across regions or industries. Competition may indeed differ along important dimensions such as price, labour, and capital. However, the argument of institutional theory is that the performance of a company on the market is enhanced if the company is judged as being legitimate, whether that means a reputation for quality of products or being modern, trustworthy, fair, etc.

It is also argued that the introduction of particular structures and processes may legitimate the company and enhance its profitability. Structures and processes that will provide legitimacy vary with time, much like fashions (Abrahamson and Fairchild 1999; Røvik 1996). Lists of management fashions are long: Management by Objectives (MBO), Diversity Management (DM), Business Process Reengineering (BPR) and Corporate Social Responsibility (CSR) are all examples of such fashions. The concept of MBO was for instance quite popular in the 1970s and 1980s but during the 1990s it was supplanted by more 'modern' three letters recipes, such as TQM, BPR or CSR. In general this argument holds that managers (or others) are on the look–out for recipes that can solve problems that they perceive or construct in an organization in order to obtain an image of modernity. Turning this argument around some authors claim that superstandards may be perceived as solutions on the look–out for problems (Christensen and Westenholz 1999).

In the case of CSR, best practice incorporates both the internal and the external dimensions. CSR – even if there are several conceptions of what it really is (de Bakker, Groenewegen and den Hond 2005) – indicates that some practices are more valuable than others and thus are more likely to be exported, imported, and edited for local application. Although the ethical aspects of CSR may seem obvious, its implementation may challenge local management and governmental hegemonic values and practices, as well as the instrumental logics of business efficiency. The logics displayed in the Global Compact and in the European Commission's Green Paper declare that there should be some kind of empathetic dependency in the way multinationals do business, in particular, in third World countries (European Commission 2001). Since both the UN principles and the EC Green Paper advocate that empathetic logics ought to be a part of business activities in the new world economy, some of the profit–maximizing logics inscribed in prescriptive economic theory will inevitably be challenged. This might have consequences for a theory of action.

CSR Recipes as Standards for Organizing and Theories of Action

When one way of conducting business is regarded as better than others and its theory of action is depicted, it can set a standard for organization. The etymological roots of the noun 'standard' date back to the 12th century and once meant *a conspicuous object (as a banner) formerly carried at the top of a pole and used to mark a rallying point especially in battle or to serve as an emblem* (Merriam–Webster Dictionary). CSR may be understood as such a banner that some 'warriors' – often top and middle managers – carry into battle as a rallying point. It then serves as an object of identification and a clear and visible signal of where to move. As long as CSR is carried at the top of the pole, it is easy to see and difficult to neglect. It is brought forward in company documents, voiced by top management, and included in planning documents and performance measurement systems. Its visibility makes it an object to discuss and scrutinize, that is, it can easily be identified and discussed in terms of good, bad, and usable, and depending on the degree of pressure and control, the actors may consciously choose to follow the banner or not. If the pressure is strong, it might happen that an actor – or a company – decides to neglect the pressure to conform to the celebrated standard. This may lead to organizational justification and hypocrisy. As Brunsson (1993) points out, organizational ideas and actions are not always consistent, and ideas do not always take control over actions. Consistency is particularly difficult to accomplish when what can be done cannot be said and vice versa, while control is not easy to combine with consistency when ideas change more swiftly than actions (Brunsson 1993). After mergers and acquisitions, new ideas meet old, and the pace of change is often perceived as considerable by the actors involved. This indicates that there is a significant risk of hypocrisy when a specific CSR–practice is strongly advocated in newly acquired and merged companies.

When CSR is carried at the top of the pole in the battle for attention, another pitfall is the risk of driving local knowledge underground, as shown by Brown and Duguid (1991). The company may lose important knowledge if the insights needed to solve local problems are out of sight for the organization in general, and for top management in particular. All these organizational issues and related pitfalls also pose clear challenges to students of knowledge and value transfer processes in multinational firms.

When a manager from headquarters attempts to export corporation values such as CSR to a subsidiary, it can be understood as a meeting and a potential clash between different theories of action that rest upon dissimilar values and governing variables (Argyris, Putnam and Smith 1985; Argyris and Schön 1978). Dysfunctions and unintended consequences may be the result if the parties do not have the skills that are needed to inquire into the different logics that these action theories represent.

We thus argue in line with Friedman and Antal (2005) when we claim that attempts to diffuse CSR to subsidiaries should be understood from a micro–perspective as a way of negotiating reality, and as such as a way of learning and engaging the complexity of culture without being overwhelmed by it. Understood as a learning process, it involves developing strategies for effectively engaging intercultural interactions and for generating a richer repertoire of action strategies. This learning among the parties may include surfacing tacit knowledge and assumptions and inquiry into what lies underneath the surface of the visible tip of the cultural icebergs of the corporation and its subsidiary (Friedman and Antal 2005). When we apply an export and import metaphor in this chapter, we consequently direct attention towards a negotiation of reality that consists of learning processes from the very first endeavours, where corporation managers try to formulate a CSR ideology, and also to the attempts of persuasion that take place when expatriate managers actually carry CSR into new subsidiaries at the top of the pole in a battle for attention. If CSR can be understood as a corporation's knowledge about itself and the relation to the society it is a part of, learning related to export and import of CSR can be seen as knowledge creating processes that are both mediated, situated, provisional, pragmatic and contested (Blackler 1995). That is, CSR has to be negotiated and edited in changing cultural contexts where its significance is challenged by local actors and new meaning attributed in order to find a practical balance between the headquarters' expectations and what seems to be realistic according to local practices. In essence, this implies that the success of attempts to export CSR from the exporter's point of view ultimately has to be measured according to the degree the result complies with the ethical standards of the headquarters. To expect that CSR as a value–infused prescription for conducting business can be exported as a more or less concrete given thing will in all probability fail, whether the result is hypocrisy, decoupling, local practice driven underground or open conflict. How these dysfunctions may be avoided through thoughtful management is a serious challenge, and, we argue, calls for closer empirical studies.

Methodological Considerations

Brown and Duguid's (1991) analysis challenges the endeavour to integrate CSR in a large, international corporation like the one we described in this chapter and raises a significant query for top management: How can we export CSR in ways that do not lead to hypocrisy or drive local knowledge and practices underground? This question becomes even more important due to the very characteristics of CSR. As Jackson and Carter (2000) point out, ethical issues and social responsibility are closely related to an organization's ideology. According to Littlejohn (1992), an ideology exists when individuals and groups share a set of ideas that structures their notions of reality, as a system of representations or a code of meanings that presides over how they see the world. In other words, ideologies are also prescriptions for a way of life, and as such, they are also prescriptions for ways of organizing (Wilden 1987).

An ideology rests upon certain values. In an organization, there may be several rivalling ideologies. Some of these ideologies may have become established as taken–for–granted accepted standards for organizing. A dominant organizational ideology is a set of ideas–in–residence that has achieved local hegemony (Czarniawska 1997). When the values upon which the ideology is based can be identified by analyzing the actors' actual behaviours, we may speak about values–in–use and, accordingly, ideologies–in–use (Argyris and Schön 1978). However, ideologies may also be espoused but at the same time untraceable in actual behaviour. This is the case when top management flags the standard of CSR on a high pole but does not follow up the espoused theories with theories–in–use. Any study of the export of CSR must thus take into consideration these deep structural elements represented by ideology, values, and paradigmatic assumptions that may both jeopardize and facilitate the successful implementation of CSR policies and practices across cultures (Pondy 1984).

Table 8.1 The Export and Editing of CSR: Mapping from the Headquarter's Point of View

CSR products	• *Which* "values and best practices" (way of doing things, principles, etc) do they (HQ) want "the customer" (the subsidiaries) to "buy"?
Exporters	• *Who* are trying to export CSR?
Customers	• *Who* are the customers? What characterizes the customer?
Strategies for sale	• How do the "exporters" *plan* and *manoeuvre* in order to sell the "products"? • Relations, networks, alliances • Lobbying • Pressure/power • Incentives? Such as? • Other?
Choice of products	• How are *decisions* made on what to export? • What do they want to export? • By chance? • By design – by whom?
Feedback and knowledge	• How do the "exporters" edit and construct knowledge? • Accumulation of knowledge from senior managers? • Individual attempts? • Other?
Learning	• What is *learned* from experience? • What are the successes? • What are the failures? • What are the reasons for success and failure? • What do the researchers want to learn? • How can they make new knowledge actionable and useful for the company?

By using an export and editing metaphor derived from neo–institutional and organizational knowledge/learning theory we derive some empirical questions that are tentatively presented in Table 8.1. In an attempt to avoid some of the pitfalls of an export and editing metaphor, we choose to combine a neo–institutional perspective with knowledge and learning theory. The neo–institutional perspective offers conceptual tools to analyze the transport of ideas between companies, whereas the knowledge and learning approach helps us understand CSR as the company's knowledge about itself, that is, its espoused and enacted theories about how to organize and manage in a socially responsible way, as well as methodologies to analyze the problems management may run into in such endeavours (Argyris and Schön 1978). This table serves as an illustration of the different issues involved in studying this complex process of export and editing CSR in order to make it fit in different national contexts.

CSR activities in a corporation like Norske Skog differ between sites and societies. The differences in CSR practices can be interpreted in multiple ways: The lack of shared perceptions of institutional values, norms and standards may be understood as one reason for different practices among sites. Even more, the continuous influence from social, cultural, and political institutions in a given country during a certain period could make the actors predisposed to 'new' espoused theories of work. The case of Norske Skog's subsidiary Steti in the Czech Republic is illustrative in this respect. In Steti, effects from more than 40 years of communist rule are still embedded in the actors' institutionalized values and beliefs. As one of our informants put it: 'The effect of the communist system seems to be that the workers had lost every trust in management and leaders, and it is not easy to get rid of such attitudes overnight. When we first met with them, they seemed to lack confidence in us, simply because we were managers.'[7] The resistance that the 'exporters' met in Steti might be rudiments of non–canonical local practices. Originally constructed to avoid the celebrated practices flagged by the communist regime, these non–canonical practices are still institutionalized and taken–for–granted as the right way of doing things. This means that the 'underground' theories–in–use from the communist period still may be operative in the workers' minds, obstructing also the introduction of CSR practices and standards.

According to our informants, the introduction of CSR 'standards' has been met with enthusiasm in Thailand and South Korea. Why? Maybe the influence from the Buddhist and Shinto religions, and their culture at large, make an impact on the workers' minds in their attitudes towards work, as will the general conditions of living. Or maybe is it the influence from Japanese Total Quality Management and other 'bench mark practices', which for some time have been circulating in industries located in South Korea and Thailand that make an impact? Even though the answers are speculative, these examples illustrate how institutional contexts vary and present different challenges for expatriate managers attempting to export CSR.

Concluding Comments

In this chapter, we have focused on challenges facing corporations when trying to export a Scandinavian CSR ideology to acquired and merged companies in other cultures. We have illustrated the challenges by using the example of Norske Skog, a Norwegian based corporation that has grown from a small pulp and paper mill in rural Skogn to a global world–leader over the last decade. We have shown how the corporation's values are a result of a meeting between ideas from local plants, with

---

7 From interviews with managers at Norske Skog Skogn.

Norske Skog Skogn as the most influential, and a Scandinavian democratic legal system regarding the organization of work that represents a strong tradition. We have argued that the way the democratic tradition is institutionalized in Scandinavia, is not found in the same form in any other legal systems, neither in Europe, Africa, Asia or America.

By deploying the metaphor of the stepfamily, we wanted to show that the challenges Norwegian corporations face when they attempt to export CSR are complex human processes where expectations, fears, values and hopes are brought into play. With support from intercultural management theory we argued that these challenges become even bigger when the actors involved represent different national cultures.

We have chosen to see CSR as a standard for organizing and a perceived best practice that is spread as an organizational recipe or management idea through deliberate attempts to export espoused corporate values. As such, we have argued that the *macro–processes* of CSR export can be analyzed through the lens of neo–institutional theory, with its focus on diffusion, editing, and legitimacy. We have also stressed that the very characteristics of CSR make it a particularly difficult object to export, since CSR is closely associated with values, virtues and what is perceived as 'proper' social practice.

When the ideas of CSR are transformed into actual practice by managers and the same managers are committed to and believe in the way they are conducting business, we anticipate that they will act as advocates for these practices when they are assigned by the corporation as managers in new subsidiaries. CSR as an espoused theory is then challenging a newly acquired or merged company's theories–in–use and its local ideology. Seeing CSR as a value–laden concept closely related to personal beliefs, company ideology and national culture, we further anticipate that its successful diffusion will depend on avoiding dysfunctional consequences like decoupling, hypocrisy, and non–canonical knowledge being driven underground. We thus propose that the *micro–processes* of diffusing CSR can be fruitfully analyzed with the help of lenses offered by organizational knowledge and learning theory. We consequently argue that a perspective combining macro– and micro–processes is required to fully grasp the export and editing processes at hand.

We have used the Norwegian–owned paper mill Norske Skog as an illustration. It is illustrative in the sense that it is based on a long Scandinavian tradition of management, which the corporation tries to export when it is expanding globally. Scandinavians are the people in the world that rank highest when it comes to trusting other people (La Porta, Lopez-de-Silanes, Shleifer and Vishny 1997). However, this does not imply that Scandinavian expatriate managers are knowledgeable when it comes to exporting democratic values. On the contrary, this may also indicate some sort of naivety based on a lack of knowledge that may produce counterproductive consequences, above all when different values meet. As Kelley and Stahelski (1970) found, a naïve way of approaching other people that, on their hand, meet you with a strategic win-loose approach, will make you loose. It will also establish a competitive climate. Good intentions are obviously not enough. We thus hold forth that the attempts to export democratic values embedded in a Scandinavian notion of

CSR call for closer empirical investigations. Looking at multinational corporations then is all the more fruitful.

PART 3
Measuring: CSR in Scales

Chapter 9

The Development of a CSR Industry: Legitimacy and Feasibility as the Two Pillars of the Institutionalization Process

Aurélien Acquier and Franck Aggeri

Introduction

[One of the main forces or catalysts likely to shape future developments in social responsibility is] the creation of a *social responsibility industry* of consultants and enterprises offering services to companies, including those involved in certifying compliance with management systems and other standards, and providing advice on how to comply with such standards. This industry in combination with two other established industries (accounting and investing) have become a major catalyst for CSR activity, funding and sponsoring conferences, publications, initiatives and organizations whose purpose is to create markets for reports and their verification, for socially responsible funds, and for company information on CSR activities (ISO 2004: 24).

Over the last ten years, CSR has experienced a new wave of development, driven by the idea of a 'business case' for social responsibility. As Vogel (2005) proposes it, CSR has entered the era of the 'market for virtue', relying on the hypothesis that it pays to be good and that CSR can be integrated in market dynamics. This new era for CSR has been marked by a process of quantification of CSR and the subsequent development of various CSR markets dealing with consulting, audits, certification, ratings of corporate social performance (CSP) and socially responsible investment (SRI).

This process of 'marketization' has gained increasing attention in CSR research (Aggeri, Pezet, Acquier and Abrassart forthcoming; Déjean 2005; Déjean, Gond and Leca 2004; Louche 2004; Louche and Tagger 2005; Vogel 2005; Windell this volume; Zarlowski this volume). So far, those works have focused on one single market. Among the various markets, the SRI and the extra financial rating markets have concentrated most of the attention. Building on neo-institutional perspectives in organizational analysis, those works have brought great insights around three questions: what strategies do actors develop to gain legitimacy in times of market creation (Aldrich and Fiol 1994; Suchman 1995)? What are the different perspectives and competing alternatives about CSR management and CSP evaluation? How do national economic and institutional contexts influence the design of local CSR evaluation tools?

However, because of their tendency to concentrate on one single market, taken independently from the others, those works fail to develop a more comprehensive and systematic perspective on the interrelationships between those markets, the division of labour and the need for coordination between them. In this paper, we propose to follow another path for investigating those dynamics. We propose to focus on the development of the CSR *industry*, which regroups a *set of markets* devoted to the communication, measurement and evaluation of Corporate Social Responsibility (CSR) and Corporate Social Performance (CSP). What is at stake behind the emergence of the CSR industry is an attempt to set up a global market infrastructure for a dynamic monitoring, quantification and integration of externalities into the market game (Callon 1998a, 1998b; Acquier and Gond 2005).

We believe that the ability to grasp industry level dynamics is essential for understanding the patterns and the ultimate reach of CSR institutionalization within the management field. The choice to analyze the whole sector dealing with consulting, reporting, certification and rating is useful for analyzing the dynamics in this sector, because it points to the division of labour, the interrelationships and interdependencies between those markets. Instead of focusing on actors' legitimation strategies on one emerging market, we raise the question of the ability to develop, coordinate and legitimize a set of inter-related markets. By doing so, we show that although the question has been overlooked, issues related to the functional feasibility of the CSR industry play a central role in the institutionalization process of the CSR industry.

Our aim, in this work, is to bridge different strands of research (neo-institutional literature and knowledge based approaches of collective action) to investigate the development of the CSR industry. We wish to show that by focusing on industry rather than market dynamics, and by mobilizing new theoretical approaches, it is possible to unveil new dynamics and to raise fresh research questions about the institutionalization of CSR. We will develop this chapter as follows: we will start by underlying the gap between discourses and practices in the CSR industry, and try to interpret that gap through early neo-institutional lenses. Building on an analogy between the CSR industry and technical systems, we will provide a different interpretation of that gap. In particular, we will show that the functional feasibility of the CSR industry is a central problem of its development. In a third part, we will develop a model of the CSR institutionalization process based on legitimacy and feasibility variables and apply this framework to the development of standards in this area.

CSR industry: The Gap Between Discourse and Practices

The development of the CSR reporting industry is relying on a project to develop several interconnected markets devoted to the measurement, certification, communication and evaluation of CSR and CSP. In this part, we try to account for an important feature of this process: the gap between official discourses and real practices. Investigating this gap is a way to grasp the issues and the difficulties encountered in a process of industry building. We will interpret it using early neo-institutional theories (which emphasize the advantages of decoupling 'talking' from 'doing') and will introduce the possibility to bring other theoretical frameworks in the analysis, like those that account for knowledge and learning dynamics in the design of technical systems.

Official Discourses: The CSR Industry as an Extension of the Financial Industry

> Since corporate sustainability performance can now be financially quantified, [investors] now have an investable corporate sustainability concept. Second, sustainability leaders are increasingly expected to show superior performance and favorable risk/return profiles. A growing number of investors is convinced that sustainability is a catalyst for enlightened and disciplined management, and, thus, a crucial success factor (Dow Jones Sustainability Index DJSI).[1]

This statement is representative of many official discourses, which suggest that the industry for measurement and evaluation of CSR performance is a simple transposition of the traditional financial logic, already providing satisfying results. This rhetoric of financial transposition can also to be found explicitly in the Global Reporting Initiative, which is a 'global initiative to develop, promote, and disseminate a generally accepted framework for sustainable reporting – voluntary reporting of the economic, environmental, and social performance of an organization. The GRI was established to make sustainability reporting as routine as financial reporting' (GRI 2002). This project of financial evaluation and corporate conformation to externally well-defined standards may let the reader think that CSR is already measurable and calculable in terms of performance.

Such discourses provide a good understanding of the discursive strategies that actors tend to adopt in order to get legitimacy in an emerging market situation (Aldrich and Fiol 1994), and the managerial philosophy guiding them. As Déjean et al. (2004) have shown it in their study of a French rating agency, the focus on measurability, calculation and performance is a key element to be recognized as a legitimate actor (Suchman 1995) by financial investors or within the financial community at large. But this discursive analysis should be completed by a careful analysis of real practices, standards and tools that are being developed in the CSR industry.

Real Practices: Bricolage and Imperfect Markets

The confrontation between discourses and real practices reveals the distance between talking and doing in the CSR industry. Three elements cast some doubts on the reality of the transposition of the financial logic and tools to the field of CSR.

---

[1] <http://www.sustainability-indexes.com/> (home page). The Dow Jones Sustainability Index (DJSI) was created in 1999, as a cooperation between SAM (social and environmental rating), STOXX and Dow Jones Indexes. Built on SAM's analyses of corporate social performance, the index aims at monitoring the financial performance of sustainable companies, and group of companies that outperform other traditional indexes.

First, actors are confronted with numerous problems of definition and measurement regarding CSR and CSP. Actors still lack basic knowledge to define CSP and its connection to financial performance. Establishing this link, or defining the 'business-case for CSR' is a core activity for many CSR consultants (for example, SustainAbility in Great Britain) and managers within firms. The impressive number of statistical research about the link between Corporate Social Performance and Financial Performance has produced controversial and contradictory results (Margolis and Walsh 2003), because of the wide range of concrete definitions used (Carroll 1979, 1999; Griffin and Mahon 1997; McWilliams and Siegel 2000; Ullman 1985; Wood 1991), some of which may be in contradiction with the others. Thus, CSP is far from being as stabilized as his financial counterpart.

Second, information is far from being standardized and freely available to all actors. Important information asymmetries remain between corporations, stakeholders and regulators. Instead of being well defined and freely available (as classic economic and financial theories would suggest), the pieces of CSR information necessary to evaluate Corporate Social Performance are neither easily accessible for external actors, nor precisely defined. As Geneviève Férone, former head of a rating agency put it, institutional communication can largely manipulate external actors who are trying to evaluate corporate social performance: 'Companies have made great improvements in sustainable reporting. But in the meantime, there has been a shift from silence to noise over these subjects. We have become an instrument of corporate institutional communication. Today companies communicate a lot but it becomes really difficult for us to know what they actually do. It is necessary, in this context, to develop in-house evaluations requested by the companies themselves' (Férone 2004).[2] Several European countries have made it compulsory to report on social and environmental dimensions (Capron and Quairel-Lanoizelée 2004), but there is still no set of agreed-upon prescriptive guidelines for social and environmental accounting.[3]

The low quality of social and environmental reporting raises a third series of questions about the relevance of third party insurance, as well as rating methodologies. If several accountants are considering CSR as a promising new area for certification, they are cautious about the kind of certification they can deliver. As a result, the level of insurance about CSR data is significantly lower than that of financial reporting. Accountants do not certify the CSR figures reported but only the quality of internal reporting systems. Given those elements, many questions are also raised about the relevance and feasibility of external ratings of corporate social performance, and the quality of the evaluation provided by social and environmental rating agencies. In response to this problem, several rating agencies (such as Vigeo or BMJ in France)

---

2 Geneviève Férone is the founder of the first French rating agency and is now chief manager of Core Ratings, a European rating agency based in London, whose French activities have been bought back by BMJ, a consulting firm, on 17 May 2006. The new company will drop external evaluation and concentrate on in-house evaluations requested by companies (see also Zarlowski this volume).

3 The Global Reporting Initiative (GRI), which produces the most widely accepted guidelines for social and environmental reporting, does not have a compulsory status. Instead, any organization will be considered as a GRI reporter if it chooses to report on some of the GRI guidelines (see below).

have developed, next to their external rating activities, a more qualitative and in-house approach of CSP evaluation.

Interpreting the Gap

From those observations, it appears that the industry for CSR measurement and evaluation faces many limitations and encounters difficulties to keep its promises. Two kind of interpretation frameworks can be put forward to explain the gap between official discourses and real practices: new institutional theories in organizational analysis, and other perspectives investigating the spread of existing managerial techniques to new fields and the role of learning dynamics in this process. While new institutional theories describe the advantages of decoupling 'talking' from 'doing', the second perspective insists on both the necessity and difficulty to couple them.

The first interpretation framework derives from the early version of the new-institutional theories in organizational analysis. From those perspective, the issue behind CSR management systems or ratings is legitimacy (Suchman 1995). Corporate commitment for CSR, as well as other formal structures, can be understood as a new form of 'ceremonial myth' (Meyer and Rowan 1977), little more than a symbolic action meant to testify the company's good faith and its adhesion to shared beliefs, in order to get legitimacy. Within this framework, the processes at stake boil down to a 'window dressing' strategy, largely disconnected from real practices: management systems and voluntary approaches are very loosely coupled with real activity constraints, they reflect corporate aversion for real evaluation. Evaluation is based on non-technical, very general and non-verifiable criteria (Meyer and Rowan 1977). In this context, corporate discourses and policies regarding their Social Responsibilities can be considered as a manifestation of 'organizational hypocrisy' (Brunsson 2003). 'Continuous performance' standards, reporting and rating systems are designed to codify trust; they tend to become a substitute for ethical and political discourse while having limited effects on real practices (Brunsson and Jacobsson 2002). Consultants generate isomorphic pressures (DiMaggio and Powell 1983) by developing common language (for example about the link between CSR and financial performance) and standards about CSR, whatever their effectiveness of their tools.

Those analytical perspectives point to an important dimension of the diffusion of the CSR industry. If this dimension proves to be the dominant one, the CSR industry will have a limited ability to transform real practices and may experience a limited development. Whatever the merits, legitimacy and social demand for CSR and CSP evaluation, the contemporary diffusion of CSR will appear as a new managerial fad (Abrahamson 1991), with no productive impact on corporate practices.

While acknowledging the relevance of these insights, we think it is necessary to complement this perspective with a more dynamic framework of analysis. Instead of considering the decoupled character between discourses and practices as taken for granted, it is necessary to discuss the conditions necessary for the CSR industry to deliver its promises and understand where the current difficulties come from. For this, we think it is useful to develop an analogy between the CSR industry and a technical system, and to mobilize various pieces of the literature focusing on the role of managerial tools and techniques (Miller 2001; Power 1996) learning and knowledge dynamics (Blackler 1995; Hatchuel and Weil 1995; Hatchuel 2005), complex technical systems, modular innovation and standardization (Henderson and Clark 1990; Baldwin and Clark 1997), as well as later works in the new institutional literature. We will show that this perspective enables to raise new research questions that we will develop in the following section.

The CSR Industry as a Technical System

As mentioned earlier, the CSR industry can be analyzed as a set of markets meant to quantify CSR and evaluate CSP. In this view, it is possible to consider the CSR industry as a technical system, with interdependent sub-units (markets), where each sub-unit is delivering a specific function, necessary for the appropriate functioning of the whole system.

Market Functions and Interdependencies

The different functions of the system and the interdependencies between the various actors and markets composing the CSR industry are developed in Figure 9.1. As shown in the figure, a technical system meant for measuring and calculating CSR performance has to combine an important number of functionalities. First, it has to tackle the question of defining what is the nature, scope of CSR and defining and measuring performance (rating agencies methodologies). Second, the system must be based on relevant, accurate and valuable information (markets for reporting, accounting and verification). Third, the system needs to be able to integrate new issues as they develop (internal reporting and management systems). This third question is particularly critical for the social dimension of CSP, which is more dynamic and subject to cultural interpretations than environmental dimensions.[4]

The overall feasibility of the system (in our case the ability to transpose a financial logic in the field of CSR) relies on the ability to achieve a good level of feasibility for each function. To illustrate this idea, let us take the example of a new stakeholder calling for the integration of a new dimension in CSP, like, for example, the development of a supply-chain perspective about child labour practices in third-world countries. Integrating this question into CSP evaluation models is meaningless if there is no way to monitor and audit those practices at a reasonably low price, and to calculate the potential costs associated with a non compliance to such standards. The inability of any actor, within the CSR industry value-chain, to deliver a valuable and reliable answer may put into question the functioning of the whole system. Thus, there is a need for coordination between actors who are trying to adapt existing financial methodologies to the field of CSR.

---

4 For instance, a cultural variable like positive discrimination which is encouraged in countries like the US or the UK, is forbidden in the French law where it is seen as a communitarian drift, incompatible with a republican view of the general interest. On the contrary, the French law requires an extended social reporting ('bilan social') for large corporations on social variables such as training, wages and competencies, whereas such a legal provision does not exist in Anglo-Saxon countries.

This perspective brings us to a complementary interpretation than that of our first grid of analysis. The question becomes to understand under which conditions the functioning of the overall system becomes feasible.

Several questions can be explored in this context: where are the functional difficulties encountered in the project of industry development? Which difficulties may jeopardize the functioning of the whole system, and may lead to a revision of the initial project of transposition of the financial logic? How do actors adapt themselves when they encounter difficulties in this process of transposition?

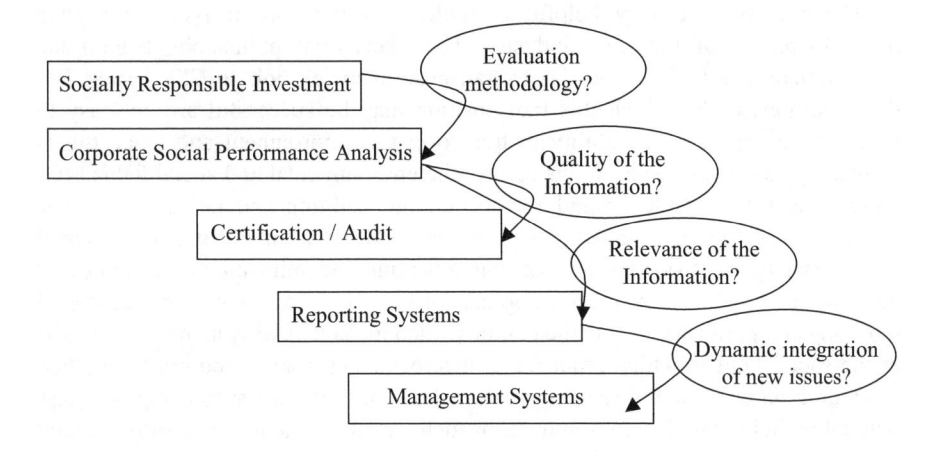

Figure 9.1 Market Interdependencies in the CSR Field

Investigating the Conditions of Transposition of Financial Evaluation Technologies

Such a technical system has already been set up in the financial field. Although its efficiency is the object of harsh discussions since the Enron collapse, the system is quite structured and institutionalized in the financial field. As we have shown, the question raised with the CSR industry is the ability to replicate this financial model for the social and environmental sectors, that is the ability to transpose existing managerial technologies – the specific techniques, methods and tools used for measurement and monitoring, particularly reporting, auditing and rating techniques – from the financial field to the CSR field. Several studies (Power 1997; Miller 2001; Miller and O'Leary 1987) indicate that the transposition these managerial technologies from the financial field to other domains is nothing but a natural process. On the contrary, it has to be analyzed as a process of adaptation, where time and learning are required to learn how to manage and control activities, build typologies, and 'plug' calculative technologies (such as accounting) on existing activities.

Let us develop our argument in the case of reporting and accounting. Those activities have been investigated by Power who has shown that their practice requires 'auditable' environments (Power 1996). Such environments have to be constructed, they must be transformed in order to become auditable. In this process, Power emphasizes the central role of monitoring systems or quality management systems that enable actors to measure, calculate, and make corporate practices visible to a wider audience. In the environmental field, quality management systems have spread through the 1990s and have led to ISO 14001 and EMAS norms. Built in a context where standards of performance where impossible to define, such systems did not prescribe accurate performance standards but they played a key role in facilitating calculation (and ultimately, the identification and valuation of externalities). Thus, management systems constituted first steps in the identification of meaningful environmental reporting indicators and standards of performance.

Those works are very helpful to understand the current issues and state of development of the CSR industry. The managerial philosophy behind the development of a CSR industry is to transpose financial tools to CSR issues. But the conditions under which this transposition may be successful are not easy to meet: in this process, the ability to transform the environment and make things auditable is a crucial issue. In this regard, the environmental and social fields offer more or less favourable ground for accounting, auditing and rating techniques. In the field of the environment, the existence and early spread of environmental quality management systems has facilitated the quick identification of accurate and meaningful guidelines, and the development of a financial approach to environmental reporting and performance. On the contrary, such management systems did not exist in the social field in which reporting is heterogeneous from a country to another, depending on cultural and regulatory variables. Thus, social issues compose a less 'auditable' field than the environment. In such a context, the move towards general quality management systems is to be understood as a first and necessary step towards auditability. Even in the absence of agreed-upon indicators for social performance, such systems testify that global social policies can be implemented, impacts can be measured and that actions are auditable and visible to all.

We have developed the example of auditing techniques to underline the issue of transposing existing managerial technologies to CSR environments. Of course, this example should be completed, systematized and extended to other activities, such as rating methodologies. By using this example, our aim was to show that, in the global process of adapting existing financial approaches to the field of CSR, two questions have not been widely discussed by the existing literature and could be worth investigating for each activity (rating, audit, reporting, management systems):

- How do actors reformat environments to make them suitable for traditional financial techniques?
- How are financial techniques translated and adapted to their new environments?

Standardization as Way to Conciliate Local Adaptation and Innovation with the Global Interoperability of the Industry System

Building on the analogy between the CSR industry and a technical system, we have considered each market (consulting, rating, certification, etcetera) as a specific function, and showed how the various functions of the system are interdependent.

Then we have shown that the transposition of existing financial technologies to these new areas is not a natural process. Either managerial technologies or environments have to be transformed in this process. In this process, it is critical, however to maintain the interoperability of the general system.

Thus, we see that an important issue is the articulation between the micro (at the level of the function) and macro (at the level of the system) levels. Whereas the micro level requires learning, innovation and adaptation, the macro level requires an articulation and an *inter-operability* between standards, so that the industry, as a whole, can keep its promises. The issue is thus to device organizational arrangements that would enable to decentralize innovation while keeping the different pieces of the system work together. This is precisely the issue of modular design and product architecture, which has been investigated in the field of management of innovation, in the computer and automobile industry in particular (Henderson and Clark 1990; Baldwin and Clark 1997). Modularity enables to build a complex product or process from smaller subsystems that can be designed independently and yet function together as a whole. The issue is to specify accurately a minimal set of constraints and articulation rules of the various sub-systems. Various actors in high-tech industries have developed strategies for platform leadership (Gawer and Cusumano 2002). Such elements suggest that designing such an architecture is a key element for the development of an industry.

To our knowledge, this field of research has, so far, focused on high-tech fields, but, once again, we contend that it would be relevant to apply this strand of research to the CSR industry. In particular, such approaches shed new light on the standardization processes at work. Instead of considering standardization as a power-struggle between central actors, they help to enlarge the perspective and to understand that standards both constrain and enable action: they are central tools for coordination, and need to integrate the minimal requirements of each markets for securing the interoperability of the whole system. These elements suggest that more attention should be devoted to the study of standardization in the field of CSR, with several research questions in mind:

- Are there transversal standards which enable modular innovation in the field of CSR? What kind of constraints and requirements are discussed in their development?
- What to do in the absence of transversal and modular standards? How are the interdependencies between the markets / standards managed within the CSR industry?
- What are the economic and political issues of platform leadership in the CSR industry?

Analyzing the Institutionalization of the CSR Industry: Combining Legitimacy and Feasibility Variables

Building on the preceding elements, we are now going to develop an analytical model of the institutionalization process of the CSR industry. First, we argue that solely focusing on legitimacy is problematic, because it bypasses a key issue in the institutionalization process of the CSR industry: feasibility, that is the ability to produce the desired outcomes of an institutional project. Consequently, we propose to investigate how couples of legitimacy and feasibility evolve around a standardization/market building project. Then, we apply those insights for the analysis of the CSR standardization process. We develop a typology of standardization initiatives and propose hypotheses about the issues in terms of legitimacy and feasibility in each case.

Coupling Legitimacy and Feasibility to Investigate the Institutionalization Process

Organizational literature has shown that legitimacy is a basic resource for action, in particular in times of industry creation. Legitimacy refers to the 'generalized perception or assumption that the actions of an entity are desirable, proper, or appropriate within some socially constructed system of norms, values, beliefs, and definitions' (Suchman 1995: 574). Various works have underlined the central role of legitimacy, in particular in the development of new activities (Aldrich and Fiol 1994). Without legitimacy, actors cannot get access to financial or political support, or develop the trust necessary to gather human resources to develop a new project (Pfeffer and Salancik 1978). Thus, gaining legitimacy is a critical issue for those actors that strive to create new activities and gather support around their project. Consequently, several works have investigated the various legitimation strategies that actors develop to gain support and resources in a given institutional context (Suchman 1995; Oliver 1991, 1997). In this strategic perspective, legitimacy is seen as 'an operational resource that organizations extract from their environments and that they employ in pursuit of their goals' (Suchman 1995: 576).

Suchman's distinction between pragmatic, normative and cognitive forms of legitimacy is useful to understand the discursive and organizational strategies at work in the CSR industry. In their effort to develop legitimacy around their project, actors can proceed to *pragmatic tradeoffs with key stakeholders* of their field (by responding to their substantive needs or giving them a place in the decision-making process) in exchange of their support. They can also strive to develop *normative legitimacy*, either by putting forward meritorious objectives (sustainable development) or by using socially accepted techniques, procedures (such as auditing and accounting), or forms of organization (such as multi-stakeholder governance). Such forms of normative legitimacy 'may serve to demonstrate that the organization is making a good-faith effort to achieve valued, albeit invisible, ends' (Suchman 1995: 580). These processes may involve dynamics of impression management (Gardner and Martinko 1988; Elsbach and Sutton 1992) and symbolic manipulation in an effort to legitimize an institutional project.

In spite of its key role, legitimacy is not sufficient to explain the institutionalization process of the CSR industry. An organization, a market or a standard becomes institutionalized once its existence is not permanently questioned and, to a certain extent, becomes 'taken for granted' (Zucker 1987). To become institutionalized, it has to be seen as legitimate and be co-opted by their surrounding environment (Selznick 1949). The institutionalization of a new industry creation is a fragile and contested process (Stinchcombe 1965). Legitimacy is indeed a dynamic and unstable resource that may be quickly withdrawn. In her work about the sources of de-institutionalization, Christine Oliver has shown that an institution will be weakened and subject to political contests if it becomes subject to functional pressures: 'technical or functional considerations that tends to compromize or raise doubts about the instrumental value of an institutionalized practice' (Oliver 1992: 571). This element is important for our argument because it helps us to advance on the question of decoupling 'talking' from 'doing', and enables us to introduce the issue of feasibility of an institutionalization project. We define feasibility as the ability to perform and achieve the outcomes of an institutional project (or the ability to couple the promises of 'talking' with the real practices of 'doing'). For us, an institutionalization process should be grasped by analyzing the dynamics of the couple legitimacy – feasibility. A project like the creation of a CSR industry will not be truly institutionalized if it cannot reach simultaneously legitimacy and feasibility.

Two important elements should be mentioned regarding the couple of legitimacy – feasibility. The first one is that legitimacy and feasibility are not independent factors. Feasibility contributes to legitimize an institutional project. However, its contribution varies over time, and might grow in importance as resources have been devoted to build a standard or establish a new market.

The second element is that the couple legitimacy – feasibility is to be analyzed in a dynamic perspective. Feasibility and legitimacy may be met by different paths. It is possible to distinguish a range of institutionalization strategies, some firstly focused on legitimating the initiatives undertaken and other focused on developing feasibility before legitimizing a technical solution and then strive for wider institutionalization.

An Application: The Case of CSR Standardization

We are now going to see how the couple legitimacy – feasibility is tackled in various standardization initiatives in the CSR industry. Given the large number of standardization initiatives in the field of CSR, we shall not try to be exhaustive. Rather, we will only consider a limited number of significant initiatives (the GRI, the AA1000, ISO 26000 standard, the Sigma project) to develop a more general typology. Those initiatives are presented in details in Appendix 9.1. We propose to distinguish these various initiatives by using two variables, that are related to the types of relationships and the nature of knowledge involved in the standardization process. Our typology implicitly derives from Hatchuel (2005) and Hatchuel and Weil (1995), who propose that, taken together, knowledge and relationships constitute the two fundamental units of analysis of collective action.

The first variable relates to the number and diversity of stakeholders involved. Most standardization initiatives put forward a democratic, participatory, multi-stakeholder process. For example, the Global Reporting Initiative or the ISO 26000 standard are developing their standards through a multi-stakeholder process and strive to reach consensus between a wide variety of stakeholders (companies, NGOs, governments, labour unions, consumers, etc.). The design of those global and far reaching standards involve a non closed list of participants. We propose to compare them to an 'agora', a public place or a forum where citizens can have a voice in the debate. On the opposite, the Sigma project or the AA1000 assurance standard have been developed through a more restrained process, involving close cooperation between a limited number of actors. Standards are then developed in a 'club' logic where the number of participants is limited and stable from the beginning. As we will see, the number and diversity of stakeholders involved in the process of standard creation has important consequences on the legitimacy – feasibility couple.

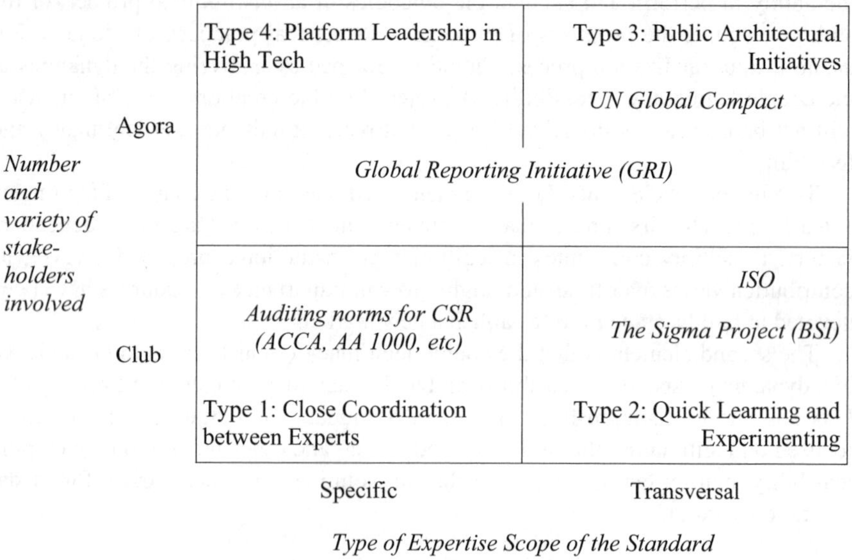

Number and variety of stakeholders involved

		Type 4: Platform Leadership in High Tech	Type 3: Public Architectural Initiatives
	Agora		UN Global Compact
		Global Reporting Initiative (GRI)	
	Club	Auditing norms for CSR (ACCA, AA 1000, etc)	ISO The Sigma Project (BSI)
		Type 1: Close Coordination between Experts	Type 2: Quick Learning and Experimenting
		Specific	Transversal

Type of Expertise Scope of the Standard

Figure 9.2 A Typology of Standardization Initiatives

The second variable we use to distinct the various standardization initiatives refers to the nature of the expertise required in the development process and the scope of the standard. At the first extreme of the spectrum, several standards develop broad and encompassing management frameworks for defining and managing CSR in a dynamic way (the Sigma project, the ISO 26000 standard). The technical knowledge underpinning the development of such standards is general, and has to do with an adaptation of the plan-do-check-act approach to CSR. At the other extreme of the spectrum, auditing and assurance standards (such as the AA 1000 assurance standard) have to tackle more technical issues, such as the conditions under which accounting and auditing techniques may be transposed with a good level of confidence to the field of CSR. Between the two extremes, the GRI tries to combines the two logics, and strives to tackle a variety of issues such as reporting content, reporting frameworks and the audit of sustainability reporting.[5] Once again, the type of knowledge involved and the scope of the standards play an important influence on the couple feasibility – legitimacy. A representation of the main standardization initiatives is provided on Figure 9.2.

Our typology of standardization initiatives lead us to distinguish four distinct types of standardization, that raise different issues in terms of legitimacy – feasibility. We will describe factual elements concerning those initiatives and draw more general hypotheses on the issues related to the legitimacy – feasibility couple for each type.

Type 1 is that of close coordination in a small group of experts, on a technical issue. Specific technical standards can be included in this model. In the case of the CSR industry, accounting protocols on social or environmental auditing range in this category. In this case, the resources necessary for their development are often provided by professional bodies. Legitimacy is provided by competence and may be an important question inside professional organizations (for example, will the accountants decide to devote resources for social and environment accounting?), but wider social acceptance and support for such projects is a secondary question. This issue may become more important in a second stage, when the actors will try to institutionalize the standards by anchoring them to over-arching standardization initiatives (type 3) or by progressively opening the process to new actors (type 4). In type 1, we can hypothesise that the key question relates to the conditions of feasibility of a standard, that legitimacy is important within professional bodies. Socio cultural legitimacy is a less strategic issue, at least in the short run.

Type 2 is devoted to quick learning and experimentation. The Sigma Project is a good example of this model. As explained in Appendix 9.1, the Sigma (Sustainability Integrated Guidelines for Management) Project is a British Initiative that was designed to develop a management standard to provide support for sustainable strategies implementation within corporations. It provides companies with a set of 'Guiding Principles' as well as a 'Management Framework', that consists of phases and sub-phases, going from the development of a sustainable policy to performance monitoring and auditing of CSR related programs. Those approaches were conducted with a limited number of actors (The Brithish Standards Institute, AccountAbility and Forum for the Future, accountants, and a few leading companies) to foster quick experimentation and learning. Launched in 1999 in reaction to the GRI, this initiative has proved very efficient for producing tools and designing a standard at a fast rate. Connecting its tools with other initiatives (such as the GRI, environmental accounting methodologies, AA1000 standards, etc.), it has also shown its ability to integrate the question of standard architecture and interoperability of markets within the industry. An important risk of such initiatives is to appear as a coalition of interests where consultants (Forum for the Future, AccountAbility and the BSI consulting branch) try to develop their own markets and brand their own methodologies with a new name, with a low transparency of the overall process. Thus, a current issue for the Sigma initiative is to get recognition and acceptance for its standard. An important

---

5 Because of this variety, the GRI can be an interesting object for researchers who would like to understand how an architecture of standards and a system of modular innovation is progressively being set-up in the field of CSR.

stake, in this regard, is to influence the forthcoming ISO 26000 standard (which should be issued on 2008) on CSR. The ISO standardization is meant to follow a more democratic design process and should thus be granted more legitimacy than a private initiative like Sigma. Based on those elements, we can hypothesise that type 2 standards rely on a relational logic, that, in combination with the general and encompassing scope of the standard, will favour quick development and feasibility. However, their legitimacy may be questioned as actors try to institutionalize their projects in more general and representative arenas.

Type 3 refer to transversal standards based on multi-stakeholder dialogue and governance. ISO 26000 and the GRI are good examples of such large scope initiatives. Let us give a few elements about the GRI standardization process, based on our own work and others researchers' investigations (Acquier and Aggeri 2006; Aggeri et al. forthcoming; Waddell 2002). The Global Reporting is an open source standard that organizations can use to organize sustainability reporting. It is far reaching because it covers both the content and the process of reporting, and wish to gather various stakeholders (financial investors, rating agencies, companies, auditing and accounting firms, NGOs, trade unions, etc.) around the project of sustainability reporting. Given the breadth of the project, its ambition to become the overarching reference in the field, and the will to serve the interest of various stakeholders, it was very important to develop the GRI visibility, to enrol legitimate 'gatekeepers' (Allen 1977) while preventing any actor from capturing the project. Since no actor would directly benefit from the development, the GRI was seen as a common good, benefiting to everyone but that no-one would be ready to finance. In this context, access to resources has been a key issue since the birth of the project. Gaining wide socio cultural support was key to the project. This issue led actors to take various actions meant to gain moral legitimacy (Suchman 1995): they linked the project with socially valued moral outcomes (sustainability) while integrating it with a free-market and financial rhetoric. They also increased procedural and structural legitimacy by putting forward broad stakeholder engagement and governance, open communication, and trustworthy procedures. Finally, they also opted for a voluntary (instead of a compulsory) approach of reporting, which can be analyzed as a pragmatic bargain with companies, necessary to secure their participation and collaboration in the process. Those decisions proved successful since many stakeholders joined the initiative and the UN offered its (temporary) financial support to the project.

The GRI is now preparing to issue the third version of the guidelines (which should be issued in late 2006). Today, an important point today is the difficulty to reconcile different points of views about reporting. The issue is to move beyond divisions and integrate rather than aggregate the points of views of the various stakeholders. For example, whereas companies call for a step by step and non-binding approach, NGOs are favouring a much more stringent, mandatory and accurate approach of reporting. Therefore, the initial founders of the GRI have a limited influence over its development process, which has become subject to power struggles between the various stakeholders involved. The initial legitimacy granted to the GRI may become contested if actors fail to produce quick learning and operational results through a democratic process (Baker 2003, 2005).

Thus, we can hypothesise that type 3 standards may gain early legitimacy because of their multi-stakeholder character. But orchestrating learning and reaching feasibility is a critical issue in such processes. Indeed, such forms of organizations may be subject to political quarrels, consensus, learning and integration being difficult to develop. Since type 3 standards are far reaching and multi-actor, they need to be co-opted by a large environment to institutionalize. This process is risky because they bear important risks of goal displacement (Selznick 1949), which may challenge the functional feasibility of the standardization project.

Type 4 refers to situations where a large variety of stakeholders are involved for the design of a specific standard. To our knowledge, if such situation may be found in high-tech platforms, there is no such situation in the CSR standardization process.

We think this framework is useful for the issues of standardization and industry building analysis. For example, Garud, Jain and Kumaraswamy (2002) show that technical standardization is difficult to manage because it involves paradoxical tensions involved in the creation of standards (for example managing cooperation and competition between actors). They insist that maintaining 'coopetition', that is the balancing of common and private interests is a very important issue to manage: 'private interests, if they appear too early, may dampen a collective's ability to generate sufficient momentum around a standard' (Garud et al. 2002: 209). They also call for a better understanding of the various institutionalization strategies that actors may used in the field of standardization.

Our model may offer a good framework to investigate more in-depth those institutionalization strategies. A first line of research can consist in a better analysis of each type, investigate the various ways to handle issues related to feasibility and legitimacy and to manage a balance between common and private interests. A second line of research could consist in studying the articulation between those types in a process of industry building: how are the various standards articulated with each other? How to transpose design concepts such as modularity (Baldwin and Clark 1997) or architectural innovation (Henderson and Clark 1990) to the field of CSR standardization? A third line of research could consist of a longitudinal analysis of standards in the making, to understand how they may shift from one model to the other, and what kind of path may prove most efficient in terms of institutionalization. In this process, time pacing and articulation with other standards are important questions to investigate.

Conclusion

To conclude this article, we would like to sum-up our approach and propositions about the study of the CSR industry. Starting from the gap between 'talking' and 'doing' in this emerging industry, we have: 1) proposed to switch the focus of analysis from the level of a single market, taken independently, to that of the industry, 2) developed an analogy between the functioning of an industry and that of a technical system in which each market would play the role of a specific function, 3) introduced the issue of feasibility and shown what theoretical questions and issues are raised, 4) proposed to investigate legitimacy and feasibility as the two pillars of the institutionalization of the CSR industry 5) applied this model in the case of CSR standardization.

This work remains, in many regards, a first exploratory attempt. Our objective was to show that considering the CSR industry as a system of interrelated markets may open very rich perspectives for practice and research. Thus, we have tried to raise research questions, and to suggest what theoretical frameworks may be most relevant to follow that path of research.

We think our approach to the development of the CSR industry enables to develop fresh questions for practitioners, researchers and public policy: by focusing on industry level dynamics, we have pointed to the interdependencies between these markets. At the level of practices, our analysis reveals that beyond their direct involvement in their own market and the need to legitimate and market specific services to clients, actors' involvement in standardization initiative is a highly strategic activity. At the level of public action, a systemic analysis of the state of development of the CSR analysis may help to develop a clearer representation of the issues and difficulties encountered by actors (which market is performing worse and slowing down progress of the overall industry?) and allocate resources where it appears most appropriate. Last, integrating a vision of tightly coupled system is also an important element for researchers who are concerned with the institutionalization and potential impact of CSR markets or industry. In this regard, we have tried to show that the theoretical force of institutional theories could be increased with a more systematic investigation of learning processes and knowledge dynamics.

Appendix 9.1 An Overview of the Main Standardization Initiatives in the CSR Industry

Standardization initiative	Presentation
The GRI	Launched in 1997, this multi-stakeholder project produces guidelines for sustainable reporting that have quickly become the main reference in that field. In its sustainability guidelines, the GRI provides guidance on both the 'what' and the 'how' of sustainability reporting. 'The Global Reporting Initiative (GRI) is a multi-stakeholder process and independent institution whose mission is to develop and disseminate globally applicable Sustainability Reporting Guidelines. These Guidelines are for voluntary use by organisations for reporting on the economic, environmental, and social dimensions of their activities, products, and services. The GRI incorporates the active participation of representatives from business, accountancy, investment, environmental, human rights, research and labour organisations from around the world. Started in 1997, GRI became independent in 2002, and is an official collaborating centre of the United Nations Environment Programme (UNEP) and works in cooperation with UN Secretary-General Kofi Annan's Global Compact.' *Source*: <http://www.globalreporting.org/about/brief.asp>.

The AA1000 framework/ assurance standard	The AA 1000 framework is a management system developed by the British consulting firm AccountAbility, to integrate sustainable development in corporate processes through stakeholder engagement. AccountAbility has progressively developed 'adds-on' standards (the AA 1000 series), including a module on the assurance of sustainability reports (the AA 1000 assurance standard, launched in March 2003). 'Launched in 1999, the AA 1000 framework is designed to improve accountability and performance by learning through stakeholder engagement. It was developed to address the need for organisations to integrate their stakeholder engagement processes into daily activities. The Framework helps users to establish a systematic stakeholder engagement process that generates the indicators, targets, and reporting systems needed to ensure its effectiveness in overall organisational performance.' 'The AA 1000 Assurance Standard is based on assessment of reports against three Assurance Principles: materiality, completeness, and responsiveness. It is providing a basis for independent third parties to assure, or verify, sustainability reporting.' *Source*: <http://www.accountability.org.uk> (home page).
The Sigma Project	Launched in 1999, the Sigma (Sustainability Integrated Guidelines for Management) Project is a British Initiative that was designed to develop a management standard to provide a support for sustainable strategies implementation within corporations. It provides companies with a set of 'Guiding Principles' as well as a 'Management Framework', that consists of phases and sub-phases, going from the development of a sustainable policy to performance monitoring and auditing of CSR related programs. The Sigma guidelines and toolkits were launched on September 2003. *Source*: <http://www.projectsigma.com/>.
The ISO 26000 Standard	'In September 2004 a Working Group was established within ISO, to develop an International Standard providing guidelines for social responsibility (SR). The objective is to produce a guidance document, written in plain language that is understandable and usable by non-specialists, and not a specification document intended for third party certification. The standard should be usable for organizations of all sizes, in countries at every stage of development. ISO is taking action to ensure [...] a balanced representation in the working group, of six designated stakeholder categories: industry, government, labour, consumers, nongovernmental organizations and others, in addition to geographical and gender-based balance. The designation of the standard is ISO 26000 and the target date for publication is October 2008.' *Source*: <http://www.iso.org/sr>.

Chapter 10

Marketing Corporate Social Responsibility in a National Context: The Case of Social Rating Agencies in France

Philippe Zarlowski[1]

Introduction

In socio–economics, management and law, considerable attention has been devoted to the questions of national business systems and the convergence in local corporate governance institutions under the pressures of globalization in financial and real markets (Berger and Dore 1991; DiMaggio 2001; Djelic and Quack 2003; Gordon and Roe 2004; Hall and Soskice 2001; Plihon and Ponssard 2002; Whitley 1999). Three competing interpretations of on–going change processes can be identified. It was proposed that national business systems will retain their distinctiveness, because of path dependencies (Bebchuk and Roe 2004) or of comparative economic advantages of national institutional arrangements (Hall and Soskice 2001), and that this will lead to persistence in national corporate governance structures. Others argue that because of efficiency considerations, competition and globalization, national business systems will align on an Anglo–Saxon type of institutional arrangement (Easterbrook and Fischel 1991; Useem 1998). A third view, investigating the characteristics of change processes at the national, regional and global levels, stresses that while new ideas, methods and practices follow a translation process when they are imported in a national context, the repeated diffusion of imported features into a national business system will lead to the gradual transformation and hybridization of the institutional arrangement of the latter (Djelic and Quack 2003).

---

1 Earlier versions of this paper have been presented at the Egos Colloquium, Ljublajana, July 2004, and research seminars organized at ESSEC Business School and Ecole Polytechnique, France, and Pompeu Fabra University, Barcelona. Thanks to Frank den Hond, Karolina Windell, Bruno Oxibar, Jean–Pierre Ponssard, Marie–Laure Djelic, Annick Bourguignon, Daniel Beunza, Marc Le Menestrel and participants for their comments. Thanks to three anonymous reviewers and the editors of this volume who offered invaluable comments and insights. Julien Margaine provided useful research assistance. This research has been supported by ESSEC Research Center and the chair on sustainable development at Ecole Polytechnique, France. Remaining errors and shortcomings are mine.

Studies have analyzed the impact on local business contexts of global management consulting firms and business service organizations (Kipping and Engwall 2002; Sahlin–Anderson and Engwall 2002a), the rise of global shareholders in local companies (Tainio, Huolman, Pulkinen, Ali–Yrkkö and Ylä–Anttila 2003) and the introduction of an Anglo–Saxon logic in the organizing of financial professions (Kleiner 2003). In this paper, we argue that ideas, products and activities associated with Corporate Social Responsibility (CSR) are also likely to question and interact with local institutional arrangements. Therefore, we propose that the national business system framework provides a useful theoretical and analytical framework for the study of CSR approaches which emerge and develop in a national context. Basically, CSR assumes that investors, employees, not–for–profit organizations, local authorities, communities or consumers, among others, would try and evaluate both present and future performance of companies in terms of their economic, environmental, social or societal impacts, which puts a requirement on companies to disclose information regarding their CSR and, following, to control their corporate social performance. As such, CSR might question prevailing corporate governance institutions, which we will understand here as the set of rules and relations that influence and constrain the behaviours of large corporations in a local business context. We assume that, given the fuzziness of CSR concepts (de Bakker, Groenewegen and den Hond 2005; Vogel 2005), competing definitions of what CSR should be might well co-exist at a given point in time in a national setting, all the more when CSR, as a label, can be regarded as an imported innovation from the North–American or global environments.[2] However, competing CSR definitions might differ in their degree of coherence with the existing corporate governance system of the country. The national business system framework suggests that existing corporate governance institutions influence the outcome of the developmental process of local CSR constructions and operationalizations. Three levels of analysis can be identified:

- the resources that CSR actors are able to secure within the existing business context so as to favour the development of a market for CSR and secure their access to this market;
- the idealistic conceptions of what CSR should be and their adequacy with core norms, values and representations that structure interactions between companies, shareholders and further stakeholders within the business context;
- the products and activities intended to operationalize idealistic CSR conceptions.

Our study is focused on the field of social rating agencies in France. In this country, social rating agencies can be regarded as prominent actors that are engaged in the construction and operationalization of CSR ideas (Déjean, Gond and Leca 2004). Since 1997 indeed, social rating agencies have emerged in France

---

2 Following such steps as the creation of Global Reporting Initiative of the United Nations in 1997 or the OECD statement of 10 January 2000, on the responsibility of firms regarding sustainable development. See also Vogel (2005).

as intermediaries between companies that are expected to supply information on their social responsibility and, on the demand side, investors and stakeholders. The services provided by rating agencies consist in the collection, analysis, interpretation, evaluation, and diffusion of information that would help investors and stakeholders in assessing how well a given company performs in terms of CSR. The judgments made are synthesized in company reports and ratings.

Given their overriding impact and the personalities of their CEOs, our analysis is focused on CoreRatings and Vigeo, which are the two agencies that dominated the field of social rating in France during the mid–2002 to mid–2004 period. We also analyzed data about other social rating organizations in order to trace the impact of these leading agencies on the field of social rating. Our data collection focused on facts regarding social rating organizations and their markets on the one hand, and the discourses of social rating agencies and their leaders on the other hand. The analysis of discourses is important to reveal self–presentation strategies of social rating agencies, as well as possible discrepancies between idealistic CSR concepts underlying social rating agencies discourses and the practical conditions of their rating activities. Three sources of data have been used. The websites of social rating agencies, as well as published transcripts of interviews and conferences of social rating actors in France have been a primary source of information about their mission statements, products and activities. Both CEOs have indeed developed many public relations activities in order to promote CSR ideas and the role of their organizations in the evaluation of corporate social performance. Two independent organizations, Novethic and ORSE, provide much information on CSR in France.[3] Since these organizations can themselves be regarded as CSR actors, we have conducted an exhaustive analysis of business press articles about social rating agencies in France, accessed through the Factiva database, which has been important in terms of data saturation and triangulation. The analysis of this corpus has been supplemented with interviews that we conducted in September and October 2003 with the CEOs of both leading social rating agencies.

The remainder of our paper is structured as follows. In the first section, we analyze the institutional context for social rating in France. In the second section, we analyze corporate social rating products and markets and the driving forces fuelling the demand for corporate social rating. In the third section, we compare the idealistic CSR conceptions promoted by social rating agencies. In the last section we analyze and discuss the developments of social rating agencies in the French context before concluding our paper.

Social Rating in the French Context

The French Corporate Governance Context

The French corporate governance system, like other systems prevailing in continental Europe, has been typified as belonging to a stakeholder model of

---

3   <http://www.novethic.fr> (home page) and <http://www.orse.org> (home page).

corporate governance, as opposed to the shareholder model that would represent an Anglo–Saxon archetypical setting (see, for instance, Barca and Becht 2001, Hall and Soskice 2001, Plihon and Ponssard 2002). Table 10.1 summarizes the main features of both models. The French business context has traditionally been characterized by interlocking directorates, 'noyaux durs' (hard cores) and cross–shareholdings between firms, leading to a protection of national champions from hostile take–over bids, especially if such bids were to be triggered by foreign investors. Contrary to the shareholder model, the regulation of companies would not occur through the disciplinary role of financial markets, but mostly through internal governance processes and the direct or indirect control exerted by block–holders, employees' representatives, and the community of peers belonging to the same business, political, and educational elite (Alcouffe and Alcouffe 2000; Barca and Becht 2001; Bauer and Bertin–Mourot 1987). In this corporate governance arrangement, minority shareholders, who are solely interested in the financial performance of their investments, are not regarded as the leading constituency. The notion of social interest of the company as a going concern has been defined and recognized since 1966 in French company law; it indicates that the company has to be governed in the interests of a wider set of stakeholders as opposed to the sole financial interest of its minority shareholders.

Table 10.1 Corporate Governance Models

	Shareholder Model	**Stakeholder Model**
Representative constituency	• Minority shareholder	• Several: State, banks, industrial firms, insurance companies, employees
Firm objectives	• Shareholder value creation	• More diversified objectives
Corporate regulation	• External (financial markets)	• Internal and/ or more diffuse
Financial markets	• Very developed • Key role of financial analysts	• Much less developed
Shareholding	• Scattered	• More concentrated • Control blocks
Protection of minority shareholders	• Important	• Limited
Conditions of efficiency	• High standards of financial disclosure • No take-over barriers	• Clear definition of stakeholders' roles • Ability to act

Source: Adapted from Plihon, Ponssard and Zarlowski (2001)

Since the 1980s, though, the French business context has been permeated by ideas and changes that originated in the Anglo–Saxon or supra–national (European or global) environments. Notably, following the liberalization and globalization of financial markets, the rise from the second half of the 1990s of institutional investors in the ownership structure of large French listed companies has been analyzed as a factor of transformation and hybridization of the French corporate governance system (Plihon and Ponssard 2002; Morin 2000; Djelic and Zarlowski 2005). In turn, foreign institutional investors have fuelled the demand for Socially Responsible Investment (SRI) funds, that is funds that adopt investment criteria based on an evaluation of the performance of companies in terms of CSR. Institutional investors may directly hold shares in large listed companies or, as analyzed in the next section, invest in mutual or dedicated funds. CSR and SRI have diffused in the French institutional context: since 15 May 2001 the *Loi sur les nouvelles régulations économiques* made it compulsory for French listed companies to publish an annual report on sustainable development. The setting up of the French *Fonds de Réserve des Retraites* (FRR) – a large investment fund aimed at helping the adaptation of the French retirement system to demographic trends by cumulating a total of 150 billions of euros by 2020, and that is governed by representatives of the French State, the State–owned financial institution Caisse des Dépôts et Consignations, and trade unions – would also foster the development of SRI and, as a consequence, of the demand for corporate social rating. According to a member of its executive board , FRR's goal 'is to tackle certain issues, such as sustainable development, with determination.'[4] Before turning to the demand for social rating products in the next section, we describe in the remainder of this section the field of social rating agencies in France and the resources of social rating organizations.

The Field of Social Rating Agencies in France

Déjean et al. (2004) studied the first phase of development of the social rating industry, which ended in 2002. They analyzed the strategy of legitimization developed by Geneviève Férone, who in 1997 founded Arese, the first social rating agency in France, inasmuch as 'measuring the unmeasured' can be regarded as having conferred legitimacy to this agency (Déjean et al. 2004). Geneviève Férone can indeed be considered as having been a key actor in the diffusion in France of ideas regarding SRI and sustainable development. She granted many press interviews, held conferences and co–authored books, some of them with academics, on these subjects (Férone, d'Arcimoles, Bello and Sassemou 2001; Férone, Debas and Génin 2004).

However, according to Geneviève Férone, by 2002 Arese was at a cross–road. The demand for corporate social rating did catch up, yet remained too small to cover the costs incurred by collecting and processing the required data. Because of what she called diverging views with her shareholders regarding the strategic reorientation of Arese, she left the agency when, by mid–2002, Arese has been transformed into Vigeo, with a new management team and an enlarged set of shareholders. Several

---

4   Press release by Novethic, 3 March 2003, <http://www.novethic.fr> (home page).

of Arese's managers, including its historical founder, left the structure which led to a bourgeoning of competing organizations (see Figure 10.1). Notably, Geneviève Férone founded and served as the CEO of the competing social rating agency CoreRatings. Until May 2004, CoreRatings was established in Paris and in London. Vigeo, although claiming to be a European agency, was established in Paris only. Thus, from 2002 onwards, in the wake of the disappearing of the pioneering Arese, the field of social rating in France underwent a deep restructuring.

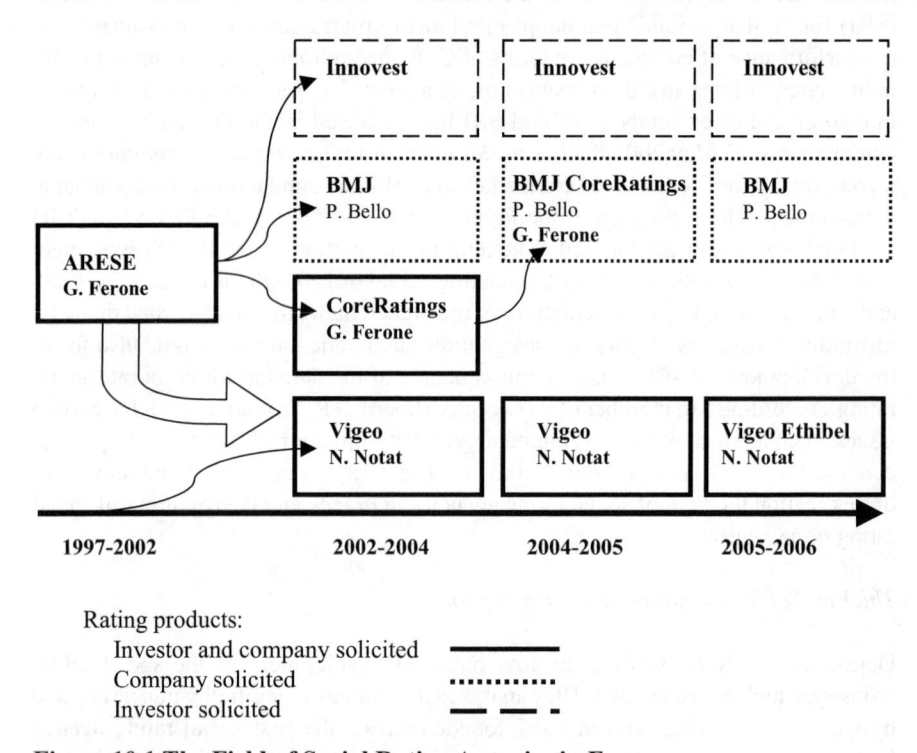

Figure 10.1 The Field of Social Rating Agencies in France

During the mid–2002 to mid–2004 period, the field of social rating in France has been dominated by these two French agencies, Vigeo and CoreRatings. Although much smaller in terms of size and clout, notably regarding business and general media coverage, two other structures are worth mentioning. The first one is Innovest, an American rating agency owned in part by State Street Global Advisor. By the end of 2002, Innovest had created an office in Paris its other establishments being London, New York, and Toronto. The former director of research of Arese left Arese–Vigeo at the end of 2002 to join the Paris office of Innovest. The second one is BMJ, a smaller rating agency founded by Pascal Bello, who subsequently served as the managing director of Arese between 2001 and 2002. He left Arese in July 2002 in the same time as Genevieve Férone and got back to BMJ.

With the noteworthy exception of Nicole Notat and the new management team she brought in at the time of the creation of Vigeo, virtually all the executives of French leading rating agencies have thus shared in their professional lives the experience of Arese which constituted the crucible of this professional network. While she had been instrumental in the creation of Vigeo out of Arese, Nicole Notat could be regarded at that time as a newcomer in the field of social rating.

On the whole, in terms of sales, number of employees, or profitably, social rating remains itself an emerging economic market. For 2003, Vigeo, the larger French agency, reported 38 employees and a turnover of 1.3 million euros, whereas CoreRatings reported 30 employees and a turnover of 1.2 million euros. However, the leading agencies, Vigeo and CoreRatings, and their leaders, Nicole Notat and Geneviève Férone, have benefited from extensive coverage of their activities in the business press as well as in academic, business and political institutions and networks, incommensurate thus to the very reduced size of their economic activities.

Social Capital, Financial Capital and Independence

A parallel can be drawn between the educational and, most importantly, professional backgrounds of the leading corporate social rating entrepreneurs in France, the business and financial resources that they have been able to secure and their approach of the question of independence which, together with transparency and the relevance of the rating process, would be determining for the credibility of the social rating activity. Geneviève Férone, chairwoman and CEO of Core Ratings, graduated from a French business school, completed a PhD in international business law, worked for several international organizations and eventually for a firm of business lawyers in the United States of America. She indicated that she discovered there how USA pension funds were dealing with SRI, and she herself put forward that her approach of analyzing corporations along several dimensions liable to impact their long–term financial performance was germane to the investment policies of pension funds. According to her, the credibility of a rating agency would rely on its financial independence coupled with the disciplinary role of competition between 'serious' social rating agencies. The shareholders of Arese, the first social rating agency that she founded, had been Caisse d'Epargne, a network of regional mutual banks, and Caisse des Dépôts et Consignations, a large state–held financial institution. Coherent with their own status and governance structures, both institutions have been engaged and interested in the diffusion in France of sustainable development and CSR ideas, and they could be regarded as having guaranteed the independence of Arese from French companies and its credibility as a rating agency. CoreRatings, the second social rating agency founded by Geneviève Férone when she left Arese–Vigeo in 2002, was owned by the financial rating agency Fitch. Behind Moody's and Standard and Poor's, Fitch is the third worldwide financial rating agency and was part of the French family–owned financial group Fimalac. Such shareholders were again very likely to guarantee the formal independence of CoreRatings in its social rating activities.

The stance taken by Nicole Notat, founder and CEO of the new Vigeo, has been quite the opposite in terms of shareholding: the ownership structure of Vigeo has comprised from its origin in 2002 three sets of associates: financial institutions (including Eulia, a joint subsidiary of Caisses d'Epargne and Caisse des Dépôts, who owns a 39 percent stake), trade unions, and large companies, most of them French. This ownership structure makes sense given the personal and professional background of Nicole Notat. Between 1992 and 2000, she had been the head of CFDT, the leading French trade union in terms of numbers of affiliates. She began her carrier as a school teacher before becoming a full–time trade unionist and eventually serving as the head of CFDT. As such, she had been closely involved in the governance of social security institutions, as well as in labour negotiations which associate in France trade unions, the syndicate of employers, and the government. As head of CFDT, she was willing to promote direct negotiations between trade unions and employers, de–emphasizing the role of the government in labour negotiations. She happened to be criticized by other trade unions as well as by affiliates of her own organization for the reformist stances that she made on several touchy social security and pension issues. This contrasted with more radical orientations that used to be adopted by leading trade union representatives and which often lead to modes of relations with either the government or employers based on conflicts and the threat of social unrest rather than on partnership and negotiations. Nicole Notat's view on relations between employees and employers is reflected in the ownership structure of Vigeo and could explain why the French business elite has been so supportive of her project. Jean Gandois, a former French *grand patron* ('top CEO') and former head of the French syndicate of employers is often presented as having been one of Nicole Notat's key sponsors in her project and has served as a non–executive director on the board of Vigeo. While the very diversity of this ownership structure should, according to Nicole Notat, guarantee the independence of Vigeo as a rating agency, Geneviève Férone deemed that it would be perceived as a crippling default in the Anglo–Saxon market which she was intending to serve: 'An Anglo–Saxon would immediately disqualify a rating agency that would have its own shareholders as first clients, even if such a scheme might not be chocking in the French tradition' (research interview, September 2003).

Nicole Notat's close relationships with the French business elite enabled her to secure important financial resources for Vigeo which could provide it with a competitive advantage over the rival CoreRatings. While the latter was created with an initial capital of 1 million euro, the former could rely on a much larger financial capital of 13 million euro. Vigeo reported a net loss of 2.8 million euro for its first year of operation (2003) and its business plan anticipated that the break–even point could be reached by 2007, indicating that at that time the market for social rating products was considered to be at an early stage of its development. Having companies, financial institutions and trade unions as its shareholders could also allow Vigeo to capture a larger share of this emerging French market. In the following section we analyze the characteristics of this market and the demand for social rating products.

Products, Markets and the Demand for Social Rating

Social Rating Products

The various products proposed by rating agencies are based on the whole on the same methodological framework. A rating process will typically begin with the analysis of information disclosed by companies: financial, environmental, social and sustainability reports, website information, press releases. Information is supplemented and cross–checked with governmental databases, information published by non–governmental organizations and other information providers such as industry analysts and competitors. Preferably, an exchange of information takes place between the rating agency and the analyzed company. Each rating agency then processes the information collected through its own grid of analysis based on detailed criteria and indicators. For instance, for one of its rating products, Vigeo claimed to analyze six domains (customers and suppliers, human rights, societal commitment, environment, corporate governance and human resources). These domains were operationalized by decomposing them into 38 CSR criteria for which 298 indicators were defined. The result of the analysis consists in measuring and scoring how well a company is doing on each indicator. In the last step of the methodology, these scores are pondered in a rating which synthesizes the performance of the company in terms of CSR.

Both Vigeo and CoreRatings have sold two types of ratings: investor–solicited rating and company–solicited rating, whereas Innovest and BMJ are focused on one type of rating only, respectively on investor–solicited and company–solicited rating (see Figure 10.1).

While these ratings are on the whole based for each rating agency on the same CSR dimensions, they do differ in terms of clients. Clients for investor–solicited rating are fund managers and financial companies that are interested in accessing information about the performance of a company in terms of CSR. In this respect, social rating would thus amount to widen or supplement with non–financial data about environmental, social and societal issues the information set about companies that financial analysts provide to fund managers. Alternatively, a company might also want to assess its own performance in terms of CSR in a more pro–active behaviour and buy a rating of its activities from a social rating agency. This company–solicited rating is on the whole based on the same methodological framework as for investor–solicited rating, yet the company will normally provide the social rating analysts with more information, for example data room information, allowing a deeper analysis of its CSR practices which would end up with a more detailed and reliable evaluation of its performance.

Because of higher selling prices and higher margins, company–solicited rating is a much more financially profitable product than investor–solicited rating; the development of the contribution of solicited rating would even be critical to cover the high fixed costs associated with the rating activity. To develop their market for investor–solicited rating, social rating agencies have had to gradually widen the universe of companies that they cover. For instance, at its beginning in 1997/1998, Arese had only rated the 40 companies that were part of the CAC 40 stock exchange index of the main French blue–chip publicly traded companies. In May 2004, Vigeo was stating on its website that it was providing ratings on 450 companies out of the DJ Stoxx 600, whereas in the interview that we conducted with her in September 2003, Geneviève Férone claimed that CoreRatings was following between 500 and 600 companies worldwide. To widen the universe of rated companies, rating agencies have had to gather and develop teams of analysts with high technical skills and strong professional reputations, since analysts' skills and reputations are also critical to enhance the confidence of clients and third parties in the quality of the rating process. From an economic standpoint, therefore, social rating is associated with high fixed costs and would demand considerable funding in the initial stage of its development.

In the two subsections that follow, we analyze in more detail the demand for each type of rating product and the characteristics of their markets.

SRI Market and the Demand for Investor–Solicited Rating

The SRI market basically comprises two segments, SRI mutual funds and SRI dedicated funds. Whereas individual investors are the main economic agent behind the mutual fund segment, SRI dedicated funds are set up for institutional investors only.

In France the SRI mutual fund industry mainly covers the set of funds that practice positive screening, that is an investment policy based on the screening and selection of companies in terms of their compliance with at least some of the SRI dimensions (Déjean 2005). Targeting individual investors, SRI mutual funds are predominantly distributed through retail banking networks. According to Novethic, at the end of March 2004, there were 118 open–ended SRI funds on the French market (including foreign and domestic funds) managing on the whole 4.5 billion euro of assets, a tenfold increase from 1999. As opposed to countries such as the USA and the Netherlands, in France there are hardly any funds working on the basis of negative screening, for example excluding tobacco firms or producers of weapons. In March 2004, retail customers accounted for about 60 percent of the SRI mutual fund market, institutional investors accounting for 30 percent, the remaining 10 percent being attributable to SRI funds managed under employee savings plan (data provided by Novethic). Individual investors can thus be regarded on the demand side as the main market segment for the SRI mutual fund industry. The demand for SRI funds could be based on the rationale that socially responsible companies would in the long run exhibit higher economic performance as they take into account the long–term impact of their operations on their natural and social environments. However, until now this rationale remains speculative, as empirical studies have as yet failed to establish a clear correlation between CSR and economic performance (Margolis and Walsh 2003; Vogel 2005). Novethic, a major French provider of information regarding SRI and CSR which also presents itself as a source of expertise for French actors as well as for its shareholder, Caisse des Dépôts et Consignations, acknowledges that 'the impact of the SRI factor on portfolio performance is still difficult to isolate' (Novethic press release, 26 January 2004). As a consequence the driving force behind the retail demand for mutual funds would lie in the social desirability of this type of investment, which did develop since the creation of Arese. According to Déjean et al. (2004: 748), 'Arese helped to develop the activity of social rating in France and the SRI industry itself'. They draw a parallel between the institutionalization of Arese as a social rating agency and the development of SRI mutual funds in France, since most positive screening SRI mutual funds relied on information provided by social rating agencies to select socially responsible companies and make their investment decisions accordingly. They note that the number of SRI funds grew from seven in 1997 to 42 in 2001, whereas the market share of Arese, which was grounded in 1997 also, steadily rose over the period to reach an impressive 85 percent in 2001.

However, despite the dramatic rise in both the number of SRI funds and the amount of assets that they manage, the total market share of SRI investment funds remains narrow, below one percent of the mutual funds market at the end of 2003 (estimate by Novethic), implying that by then, SRI mutual funds were still to be considered an emerging industry. It was unclear whether the demand for SRI mutual funds alone could guarantee the sustainability of the social rating industry.

Whereas institutional investors account for 30 percent of the market of SRI mutual funds, funds dedicated to institutional investors can also be managed under SRI principles. According to Novethic, SRI dedicated funds amounted by the first term of 2004 to about 3.7 billion euro, thus an amount slightly smaller than the SRI mutual fund market. Out of these dedicated funds, 84 percent were owned by foreign institutional investors and 70 percent of SRI funds managed by French asset managers have been entrusted to them by foreign institutional investors. Foreign institutional investors can thus been regarded as having contributed to fuelling the demand for investor–solicited ratings in the emerging stage of this industry.

The Demand for Company–Solicited Rating

Given the characteristics of this activity in terms of costs and margins, Geneviève Férone considered that investor–solicited should pave the way for the development of company–solicited rating. In this respect, CoreRatings should replicate what she called the concepts and business model of financial rating agencies. In this business model, a rating is solicited and paid for by a company, even if the main end–user of the rating is not the company itself, but financial analysts and institutional investors. The economic function of a rating agency can indeed be conceptualized as that of reducing information asymmetries between publicly traded companies and financial markets. The rating process is based on the principle that the company should be transparent in the information that it provides. Analysts of the rating agency would thus typically have access to confidential information. The disclosure of this information could be detrimental to the company if its competitors or other constituencies could benefit from it. Thanks to the rating process, precise, potentially sensitive information can remain private, while in the same time being disclosed in a synthesized form to financial markets and other external constituencies through the rating provided by the agency. This economic function of rating agencies as information providers and intermediaries between markets and corporations is based on the assumption that the rating process itself is deemed reliable, which would be ascertained provided that the rating agency remains independent from its customers as well as from other external parties that could be interested in influencing the result of the rating process. The agency is also expected to provide a high level of transparency regarding both its rating methodology and its governance structure. Competition between a small numbers of rating agencies also constitutes a key regulation principle in the conceptualization of rating agencies as useful economic institutions in the governance of firms in a business system.

In Geneviève Férone's view, the credibility of company–solicited rating was based on two fundamental characteristics of the rating activity. First, the rating should concern the company as a whole, including all its subsidiaries and activities. This condition was aimed at limiting the risks of the rating agency being instrumented by a company: a company could require a rating for a subset of well–performing activities or well–managed CSR dimensions only. Second, while the rating belongs to the company, it nonetheless has to be published after the first year if the company has chosen to engage in a repeated annual rating process. The idea was that the first year was a trial year, the opportunity for the company to learn about CSR management and in the wake of the rating process the opportunity to improve its CSR policies and practices. Yet after the first year, the company had to contractually commit itself to disclose its rating. This implies that transparency regarding the result of the rating process was in this approach both a condition of credibility of what the rating agency did and a direct consequence of how it defined the company–solicited rating product. Given the tight conditions framing CoreRatings company–solicited rating, it was highly unlikely that the demand for this product could be driven by companies themselves. In September 2003, CoreRatings had had only seven customers for this product, and Geneviève Férone acknowledged that the demand from companies was still limited, given a self–selection of clients in this emerging stage of the corporate rating market: 'the companies that come to us are already the best ones, those that have done the most in terms of CSR'. The constituencies that would be likely to drive the demand for social rating were investors and financial analysts: 'My great fight is that fund managers understand social rating is useful to them. We will be taken seriously once they will ask questions about CSR during CEOs road shows' (research interview, September 2003).

This conception of investor oriented company–solicited rating seemed to be largely specific to CoreRatings and its founder and CEO. Vigeo and BMJ promoted company–solicited rating products which in their scopes and usages did differ from the approach of CoreRatings. On a conference on social rating, Ecole des Mines de Paris, 19 November 2003, Nicole Notat mentioned about her company–solicited rating that: 'It is established internally and remains confidential and the property of the company. It can be implemented on a branch or department if the company wants it'. Thus a company soliciting a rating from Vigeo was entitled to limit the scope of the rating mission and to control the disclosure process.

For instance, in its annual report on environmental and social responsibility, the French company Danone referred to the rating that it solicited from Vigeo.[5] The rating was favourable for the company, since on five dimensions out of the six identified

---

5 <http://www.danonegroup.com/dev_durable/doc/External_audits.pdf>, accessed May 2004.

by Vigeo in its rating methodology Danone got the second–best evaluation on a four points scale and the best evaluation on the remaining ('societal commitment') dimension. However, it was mentioned that the rating mission concerned the corporate level only; Danone's subsidiaries had not been audited by Vigeo. Such a limited scope for a company-solicited rating mission would not have been acceptable for CoreRatings, given the gap that can exist between what is defined and promoted at the corporate level and what is actually implemented at the operating level in a multinational company employing more than 90,000 people in 120 countries.[6]

In terms of rating confidentiality, BMJ promoted the same position as Vigeo, as it states on its website that 'The rating report remains confidential and the company's property under all circumstances'.[7] The position of Vigeo and BMJ regarding either rating disclosure or the scope of the rating activity might be interpreted as an alleviated one as compared to CoreRatings which would claim a more radically independent position. However, the informational function of social rating defined by CoreRatings and the corresponding structural arrangement between companies, investors, and rating agencies that it tried to promote can also be regarded as coherent with, yet highly contingent to, a specific conception of the underlying mission of rating agencies.

Two Competing Idealistic CSR Conceptions

Mission Statements and the Question of Ethics

While every rating agency takes into account the three basic dimensions of CSR in the evaluation process of companies – that is the environmental, social and societal impacts of their activities – rating agencies do separate on two fundamental questions: ethics and the identification of the constituencies that count.

In its mission statement (see Appendix 10.1) Vigeo claims that it was willing to serve a universal set of constituencies. It stated that 'une notation sociale des entreprises (…) est dans l'intérêt de tous les acteurs de l'économie et de la société, à l'échelle mondiale', in its English translation 'corporate social rating […] is in the interests of every economic and social party.' The original French mission statement is worth mentioning, to point out the different formulations: the French version adds: 'à l'échelle mondiale' that is to say 'worldwide'. The constituencies mentioned comprise investors and shareholders, board directors as well as employee representatives. Here again, it is interesting to note that the original French mission statement is much more explicit in its orientation than the English translation. Instead of employee representatives, of which the French equivalent would be 'représentants des salariés', the original French mission statement mentions 'organisations syndicales de travailleurs', that is 'trade unions of workers', which makes sense given Nicole Notat's background as trade union leader and illustrates how her commitment in

---

  6   <http://www.danonegroup.com/group/index_group.html> (home page), accessed May 2004.
  7   <http://www.bmj-sa.com> (home page), accessed May 2004.

social rating relates to her previous activities. While being less explicit than Vigeo, BMJ also aims at serving 'the stakeholders' of the corporation.

On the contrary, CoreRatings only aims at serving its 'corporate and financial clients', 'companies and their providers of long–term debt and equity finance', other stakeholders being totally eluded in this mission statement. In this respect, CoreRatings is very close to the American agency Innovest. While the mission statement of the latter does not explicitly mention the constituency that it intends to serve, it nonetheless makes clear that Innovest's analysis of CSR issues is conducted with 'a particular focus on their impact on competitiveness, profitability, and share price performance'. The methodologies developed are focused on shareholders and shareholder value creation, CSR dimensions being conceptualized as factors of shareholder value creation ('the unseen part of the value iceberg').

Vigeo and BMJ do not focus primarily on the financial community, at least regarding their company–solicited rating. For instance, BMJ claims that it 'entertains no relationships with investors and analysts'. It does not propose investor–solicited rating products but company–solicited ratings and audits that can also aim at educating company employees and directors on CSR issues. This idea of communication and learning is underlying the discourse of Vigeo founder, Nicole Notat, regarding how companies can benefit from social rating. As she expressed it on a conference on social rating, Ecole des Mines de Paris, 19 November 2003, a social rating brief would allow the company 'to better communicate with the stakeholders for which it is accountable' and 'to identify where it can improve' in terms of CSR.

Logically, Vigeo and CoreRatings also separate on the question of ethics. CoreRatings founder Geneviève Férone claimed that her agency was positioned on risk analysis to avoid any normative stance. 'We position ourselves on risk analysis and we set aside any moral commitment that would precede the rating' (research interview, September 2003). To illustrate this point, she mentioned as an example the ethically sensitive question of child labour. According to her, in terms of corporate social rating, child labour would not be considered as a problem as such. However, it could become a risk of exposure in terms of image and could eventually negatively impact sales and the shareholder value of the company if the latter has a business to consumer activity and depends from a supply chain in which some links do resort to child labour. The company would thus be badly rated on this human development criterion if it has not taken steps to cope with this risk. For instance, even though child labour is not unlawful in the country where the suppliers operate, the consumer goods company could require from its suppliers that they provide better labour conditions and education for the children that they employ. On the contrary, Vigeo would tackle the problem of human rights as such. A noticeable change that has been introduced in Arese methodology when Arese was transformed into Vigeo was the introduction of 'human rights' as a sixth dimension of CSR performance evaluated in the rating process, the five previous dimensions being environment, corporate governance, human resources, clients and suppliers and community involvement. This is coherent with the new rating methodology developed by Nicole Notat and Vigeo new management team. Nicole Notat claimed that 'Vigeo is not entitled to create its own norms' (*Le Monde*, 13 March 2003: 20) and would thus refer to international standards, principles and codes of conduct set up by such supranational organizations such as the International Labor Organization, the United Nations or the Organization for Economic Cooperation and Development.

Instrumental and Normative CSR

While Vigeo and CoreRatings bear many similarities in terms of products and markets, the methodologies on which their rating processes are based do exhibit differences and they promote their activities in different perspectives that draw two distinct idealistic conceptions of what CSR should be. These idealistic conceptions echo the conceptual models evidenced by Berman, Wicks, Kotha and Jones (1999) and Margolis and Walsh (2003) following their reviews of the academic literature on stakeholder and CSR management. Both works draw on Freeman's definition of a stakeholder as 'any group or individual who can affect or is affected by the achievement of the organization's objectives' (Freeman 1984: 46). According to Berman et al. (1999: 491), this definition has led either to an instrumental approach of stakeholder management in the empirical literature, stakeholder management being conceptualized as 'a means to an end' or to a normative approach of 'intrinsic stakeholder commitment'.

Nicole Notat and Vigeo would promote a normative approach of CSR, based on the idea that any company has to be held 'accountable', as Nicole Notat mentioned, for its impact on its ecological, social and societal environments. In this respect, the social rating agency would serve as an intermediary between the firm and its stakeholders. It would provide stakeholders with information about how the company takes into account their own interests, help the company 'communicate more reliably to the stakeholders to whom it is accountable', and help the company to improve in terms of CSR performance. The diffusion of CSR would thus, according to Nicole Notat, rely on the media, public opinion, supranational institutions and pension funds managers – she referred in this respect to the creation of the French FRR pension fund.

In Geneviève Férone's approach, stakeholders should also be taken into account by companies yet inasmuch as not doing so could negatively hamper their long–term financial performance, which is clearly coherent with an instrumental conception of CSR. While she justified the social rating methodology based on risks that she promoted by a willingness to avoid any normative stance, the underlying postulate remains nonetheless normative, since it amounts to considering that companies should act in the – long–term – interests of their shareholders.

CoreRatings and Vigeo thus promote differing views on CSR and the economic and social roles of social rating agencies (see Table 10.2). During the mid–2002 to mid–2004 period however, both models competed in France. It led to a polarization in the field of social rating, with agencies, like Vigeo and BMJ, promoting a CSR normative approach, while others, like CoreRatings and Innovest, were referring in their discourses, products and activities to an instrumental CSR conception. In the last section, we present the developments in the field of social rating in France and discuss how the national business context framework can provide interpretations of these developments.

Table 10.2 CSR in Discourses and Activities: Two Competing Views

	CoreRatings	Vigeo
Leading constituency	• Long-term institutional investors (Anglo-Saxon pension funds)	• Stakeholders (notably, employees and citizens)
Mission	• Reducing information asymmetries	• Improving communication and learning
Prescribing party for company-solicited rating	• Investors	• Public opinion, the media, international organizations, French fund for pensions (FRR)
View on company-solicited rating	• Global and public (disclosure)	• Partial and private (confidentiality)
Ethics	• Focus on risk analysis	• Human rights as a CSR dimension
CSR conception	• Instrumental	• Normative ('Accountability')

The Developments of the Field of Social Rating and a Discussion

Model Selection

In May 2004, the emerging field of social rating has encountered another major development with the announcement of the merger of CoreRatings France with BMJ. Following the merger, CoreRatings France would stop doing investor–solicited rating and refocus on company–solicited rating. Fitch, which formerly owned 100 percent of CoreRatings France, kept a minority stake (34 percent) in this company.

The merger between CoreRatings France and BMJ was a further change of positions in a professional network which originated from the Arese community, and can be interpreted as a failure of the social rating model promoted by CoreRatings. Geneviève Férone became in May 2004 managing director of the new BMJ–CoreRatings, Pascal Bello, who worked with Geneviève Férone at the time of Arese, remaining CEO of the new structure. In many respects, BMJ conception of social rating pertains to a normative approach, coherent with its positioning on company–solicited rating only. The temporary website that was on line in late June 2004 following the merger between BMJ and CoreRatings was only referring to the new BMJ–CoreRatings entity core values: 'independence, expertise, confidentiality', implying that positioning of the previous BMJ agency has been largely left unchanged.[8]

The restructuring in the field of social rating did go on after this operation. In October 2004, the London based branch of CoreRatings was sold to the Norwegian

---

8 <http://www.bmjCoreRatings.com> (home page).

DNV (Det Norske Veritas), a global certification company. In turn in October 2005 DNV sold the investor–solicited activity of CoreRatings to Innovest. In January 2006, BMJ has been sold to Fininfo/ Dun and Bradstreet, a group specialized in the provision of information on companies and Geneviève Férone left this organization to become the director for sustainable development of Eiffage, a large French construction company which had been one of CoreRatings first customers, thus leaving the social–rating activity she introduced in France about ten years before.

In contrast, Nicole Notat's Vigeo seemed to have been more successful: it announced in October 2005 the acquisition of and subsequent merger with the Belgian agency Ethibel. It is interesting to note that Ethibel had been created by NGOs that were active in the provision of financing and support to social projects. This militant origin bears similarities with the background of Vigeo founder, and both agencies indicated that they shared 'converging views and methodological approaches' (*Les Echos*, 17 June 2005: 34). Ethibel was focused on investor–solicited rating and the new group, rating 1,500 companies worldwide, has become the European leader on this activity. At the beginning of 2006, Vigeo was thus building up an alternative to the British/ North–American providers of information on CSR such as Innovest.

The Influence of the National Context: Persistence and Change

The success of the approach developed by Nicole Notat for Vigeo and the comparative failure of the model of social rating promoted by Geneviève Férone can be analyzed within the national business framework at the three levels of resources, idealistic CSR conceptions promoted, and rating products and activities.

The stance of Vigeo concerning the constituencies that count, its approach regarding the accountability of companies towards their stakeholders promote an normative, idealistic view on CSR coherent with the values and norms that have dominated the French business system and the stakeholder corporate governance model. The governance structure of the agency echoes the balancing of interests which is assumed in this model, with a regulation of corporate behaviours through networks and instances that operate privately and the role of social capital in the provision of financial resources and business relationships (Bauer and Bertin–Mouraud 1987; Plihon and Ponssard 2002). These features explain would–be inconsistencies in the definition of products and processes. While discourses indicate that companies should be accountable to their stakeholders and the agency claims that it aims at serving these stakeholders, the ratings provided remain confidential and the decision regarding their publication is left to the management of the company. In addition to this, the scope of a company–solicited rating mission can be limited and the rating methodology, while referring to general, internationally recognized principles, is based on the idea that a rating should be relative to the behaviour of same–sector companies. A company that is doing better than its competitors would thus obtain a higher rating, irrespective of the responsibility of its behaviour regarding the intrinsic interests of its stakeholders. In this pragmatic approach, higher records of corporate social performance would be achieved though education and learning rather than competition and transparency.

Conversely, Geneviève Férone and CoreRating's approach of CSR and social rating was very coherent with the values, corporate governance model, and idealistic CSR conception favoured by the Anglo–Saxon institutional investors that the agency intended to serve, with the ideas that regulation can be achieved through markets and transparency based on fair information disclosure and the role of independent parties certifying and assessing financial as well as CSR information. The products and processes developed by CoreRatings did conform to these principles, as well as the governance and ownership structure of the agency. However, preserving the formal independence of the social rating agency from companies limited the resources – in terms of access to financing means and business relationships – that Geneviève Férone has been able to secure for CoreRatings, in comparison to Vigeo. Theoretically, the instrumental conception of CSR underlying CoreRatings' approach nonetheless pertains to an instrumental stakeholder view of the firm (Freeman 1984; Donaldson and Preston 1995) as opposed to a shareholder/agency theory view (Jensen 2002; Tirole 2001). The underlying corporate governance model would not be the archetypical shareholder model based on scattered shareholdings but the hybrid model of investor capitalism in which institutional investors, concerned with the (long–term) financial performance of their investments, are dominant, active and influential.

As previously indicated in this paper, part of the demand for SRI funds in France has indeed been fuelled by foreign institutional investors. CoreRatings' approach of social rating can be viewed as coherent with on–going transformations in the French business context, yet it might have anticipated the pace and scope of these transformations while in the same time neglecting influencing national features of the French business context. Vigeo's approach was better suited to this context, in terms of access to resources, the CSR conception promoted, and less transparency and more pragmatism in its rating activities as compared to CoreRatings'. While in the press interviews she has granted as well as in our meeting Nicole Notat put forward the idea of sustainable development and the accountability of companies towards their stakeholders, Vigeo has nonetheless been selling its rating products to investors. In 2004, for instance, Vigeo reported that its investor–solicited products accounted for 60 percent of its sales.

In CoreRating's approach, the emphasis was rather placed on the conformity of facts and processes to formal rules of transparency and independence. Vigeo's less clear–cut approach of the rating process coupled with potentially unresolved conflicts of interests given its own governance structure can be interpreted in terms of inconsistencies, decoupling between discourses and practices and hypocrisy (Brunsson 2003). An alternate interpretation would point out at the differences in socially admitted norms and values underlying the local construction and uses of performance measures (Bourguignon, Malleret and Nørreklit 2004). External control and the contractual logic would be more legitimate in Anglo–Saxon countries than in France where external controls could be perceived as a threat to the individual's honour (d'Iribarne 1989; Bourguignon 2005). Hence the rationale behind Vigeo's approach of CSR and the rating process could be that the responsibility for a fair rating relies on the analyst just as the responsibility for ethical behaviour eventually relies on the manager.

Conclusion

The developments of the field of social rating tend to confirm the interest of the business system framework in accounting for the comparative success and failure of the marketing strategies of social rating agencies in France. Following a first period of development characterized by the foundation and domination of the first French rating agency, Arese, the field of social rating underwent a process of polarization between a small set of agencies dominated by two leading organizations, CoreRatings and Vigeo that in 2002 both originated from Arese. While CoreRatings and Vigeo competed on the same CSR market, the analysis of the backgrounds and resources of their leaders, the idealistic CSR conception underlying their discourses, their products and activities, indicate that these agencies have promoted two distinct approaches of social rating, with the objective of shaping the economic and social demand regarding their social rating products and securing their access to this demand.

In the wake of the polarization process, a selection occurred, with the disappearing of the agency that intended to promote an approach that would be more congruent with Anglo–Saxon standards. Given its focus on institutional investors, external control and long–term shareholder value creation, this approach was wider from the traditional features of the French corporate governance system than the competing one.

The competition between the rival leading agencies and the ensuing selection process illustrate the influence of the national business system features in the developmental process of social rating in France. This case study would support the view that institutional change processes are path–dependent, the diffusion of new ideas and activities being much more likely to occur if they accommodate the core features of prevailing local institutional arrangements. In turn, these 'hybridized' ideas and activities might shape future changes (Djelic and Quack 2003). A developing demand for social rating products might force companies to act more pro–actively on CSR information market (Ponssard 2004).

However, interpreting the impact of CSR and social rating activity on the French business system is not straightforward. By the end of 2005, the market–share for SRI funds was still below the one percent level. The SRI market and, following, the demand for rating products were still emerging, which might not allow concluding that CSR and social rating agencies have institutionalized in the French context and lead to practical changes in the behaviours of companies. In addition to this, while a business case for CSR might exist, the markets for CSR might be structurally limited in their scope (Vogel 2005). However, by the beginning of 2006, the emergence at the European level of a leading Continental social rating agency beside the Anglo–Saxon rating organizations would be a further illustration of the hybridization process. Coherent with the idea of gradual and cumulative change (Djelic and Quack 2003), other empirical studies encompassing further dimensions of both the local and regional contexts are needed to follow the possible transformation of corporate governance institutions and interpret their evolution. Following Margolis and Walsh (2003), this militates for descriptive studies of CSR which, in our view, could unearth the meanings attached to CSR by different constituencies and their motivations to take actions that they understand or declare as being related to CSR ideas.

Appendix 10.1 Values and Mission Statements of Social Rating Agencies

Vigeo <http://www.arese-sa.com> (home page), accessed May 2004.

'Values

"A corporate social rating, provided that its method and reference model are serious and solid, is in the interests of every economic and social party. It allows shareholders to optimize their control, investors to fine-tune their investment choices, and it allows company directors to better assess risks, to improve the quality of information and to the performance of the management systems. Other actors such as employee representatives will also benefit from this new analysis: Vigeo's reference model takes into account, for example, the respect of human rights on the workplace and in the community, as well as a series of human resources development criteria, which naturally includes social dialogue. Our criteria specifically focus on the chain of social, environmental and community interests that the company, wherever it may be operating, should consider." Nicole Notat'

CoreRatings <http://www.CoreRatings.com> (home page), accessed May 2004.

'Our vision

To help companies and their providers of long-term debt and equity finance fully understand the investment risks and associated value parameters arising from key non-financial impact areas, to help our corporate and financial clients develop products and strategies that will grow their businesses profitably.'

BMJ <http://www.bmj-sa.com> (home page), accessed May 2004.

'Vision and values

Our vision of sustainable development is to initiate the corporate social and environmental value system enabling effective actions and efficient communication serving the needs of all stakeholders. We work with businesses across all industry sectors and we are convinced that companies in sensitive sectors in particular need assistance to initiate management of change and continuous learning processes to promote genuine sustainable strategies.'

Innovest <http://www.innovestgroup.com> (home page), accessed May 2004.
'Innovest Strategic Value Advisors is an internationally recognized investment research and advisory firm specializing in analyzing companies' performance on environmental, social and strategic governance issues, with a particular focus on their impact on competitveness, profitability, and share price performance.'

Chapter 11

Superimposition or Continuity? Corporate Social Responsibility in Non–Profit Organizations

Paolo Rossi

Corporate Social Responsibility and Non–Profit Organizations: A Confused Overlap

The debate on the concept of corporate social responsibility (CSR) first arose from reflection in the managerial disciplines on the relationships between multinational companies and society (Bowen 1953; Friedman 1962; Backman 1975; Sethi 1975; Carroll 1979). For–profit enterprises, especially those of large size, have for many years been the principal subject of studies on the topic.

Non–profit organizations have for long been relatively neglected by the debate on CSR. This may initially have been due to a confused superimposing of the concept of social responsibility with that of non–profit organization, the consequence being that numerous scholars (as well as members of non–profit organizations) dismissed any juxtaposition of the two concepts as tautological and redundant. Yet the majority of non–profit organizations define themselves – or can be implicitly defined – as socially responsible, given the social value of their activities.

Although this claim is plausible from numerous points of view, it is contradictory and in certain respects misleading, because the concept of social responsibility does not coincide with the organizational and legal nature of an enterprise. Merging together the concepts of non–profit organization and (self–styled) socially responsible organization is an error which persists and which has generated a certain amount of conceptual as well as analytical confusion.

It is therefore advisable to provide definitions that will clarify the differences between the two concepts. Definition of 'non–profit organization' (henceforth NPO) has been a matter of much discussion in Italy and Europe. Here I shall use the definition furnished by Fiorentini (2002), which enumerates five criteria with which to distinguish and define an NPO:

- formal constitution;
- private legal status;
- self–governance;
- non–profit distribution constraint;
- presence of a certain amount of voluntary labour.

To be defined such, an NPO must fulfil these five criteria, although it is clear that they are not the only ones with which an NPO can be defined, nor can the definition be considered exhaustive. However, Fiorentini's definition furnishes a sufficiently comprehensive framework within which to distinguish the concept of NPO.

The concept of CSR has also been much discussed, and numerous attempts have been made to define it (Sen 1987; Zadek 2001; Rusconi 1997; Sacconi 1997; Joyner and Payne 2002). The definition currently most widely accepted is the one furnished by the European Commission: 'a concept whereby companies integrate social and environmental concerns in their business operations and in their interaction with their stakeholders on a voluntary basis' (EC 2001: 6).

Presentation of these two definitions evidences that the concepts of NPO and CSR are different and distinct both ontologically and substantially. Moreover, the distinction between them is being made even more apparent by the spread of instruments like social accounts, ethical codes, and codes of behaviour, which have enabled considerable formalization of the notion of social responsibility by translating it into operational and empirical terms. Consequently, when speaking today of corporate social responsibility, one must refer to a set of highly formalized practices and instruments which quite clearly define the concept and its range of application. Misunderstandings and overlaps may still exist, but one discerns an increasing tendency to address CSR as a matter distinct from the legal nature and business mission of an organization. In other words, the theme of CSR now traverses both for–profit enterprises and NPOs (and also, of course, state–owned enterprises and public institutions).

Theoretical Background: NPOs and CSR from an Organizational Perspective

Awareness of the difference between the concepts of NPO and socially responsible enterprise raises two questions. Firstly, why are many NPOs adopting the instruments typical of social responsibility? Secondly, how can the relation between NPO and CSR be interpreted by going beyond the idea of their overlap?

There are numerous possible answers to these questions. At the substantial level, there are various factors that may induce a non–profit organization to adopt a social account, ethical certification, or a code of behaviour: a wish to put itself forward as socially responsible; the need to obtain certification in order to tender for contracts; desire for an enhanced reputation in the community; the intention to increase cohesion among members.

In theoretical and analytical terms, the motives can be explained by using various interpretative frames. Firstly, it can be argued that the spread of the concept of corporate social responsibility and the instruments correlated with it among NPOs results from the process of mimesis described by the neo–institutionalist approach in organization studies (Powell and DiMaggio 1991a). As Meyer and Rowan (1977) show, the outcomes of this process may be contradictory: these instruments may be adopted regardless of their actual usefulness for the organization. In this sense, Abrahamson (1991, 1996) has illustrated how the adoption of certain 'innovative' processes and instruments may follow a logic largely determined by fashion.

Secondly, as Michael Power points out (1997), the diffusion of CSR–related practices may be viewed as an effect of the broader phenomenon of closer social control now pervading the Western societies. This is especially the case of so–called 'social accountability', which is one of the best–known and most widely–used practices in the field of CSR. From this point of view, the instruments of social accountability (the social account, for example) are clear examples of the greater emphasis now placed on the 'accounting' of social interactions. Indeed, these instruments are used to monitor and to control not only the economic and financial implications of a business activity but also a wider range of social, ethical and environmental questions. This phenomenon can also be read in evocative and metaphorical terms by conceiving accounting as the key language of contemporary inter–organizational relations (Morgan 1988).

Finally, one may refer to the 'new public management' theories (Osborne and Gaebler 1992) which, in certain respects, synthesize some of the notions set out above in regard to the behaviour of public institutions. The theoreticians of new public management stress that the evaluation criteria used by public institutions are shifting to a greater emphasis on efficiency, in like manner to what is happening at the corporate level. The objective of improved service quality is flanked by the requirement to fulfil criteria of managerial efficiency. This change has had a knock–on effect on the choices and strategies of all organizations that interact more or less directly with the public institutions. Several NPOs – which often depend for their livelihoods on the supply of products and services to the public institutions – must consequently adopt a similar logic in the devising of management strategies, and particularly in communication of their development policies.

This theoretical background helps explain why CSR practices and instruments are spreading among NPOs, but it obviously does not cover all the possible factors that may induce an NPO to concern itself with CSR. Moreover, it furnishes a preliminary overview which should be verified by empirical analysis. The experience of the MOSES project may be of interest in this regard.

The MOSES Project

The aim of the MOSES (*Modelli Organizzativi a Sostegno dell'Economia Sociale*) Project was to introduce a number of non–profit organizations operating in the province of Trento, Italy, to the theme of social responsibility and the related practices and instruments (in particular, social accounting and the social account). Financed by the European Union under the Equal initiative, the project divided into three main phases:

- an initial phase during which applications of social responsibility in the non–profit sector were studied and documented;
- a second phase during which a selected group of NPOS were instructed on the theme of social responsibility and trained in how to compile a social account;

- an experimental phase of implementation of around one year, during which the organizations that had attended the training course compiled their own social accounts.

In substance, the programme involved a training course, and then application of the contents acquired: that is, compilation of a social account by each of the participant organizations. A total of fourteen organizations took part in the project, and each of them could enrol one or more persons on the training course. These persons formed the 'project team' working on the social account in each organization.

To be stressed is that participation in the programme was free. Moreover, during the implementation phase, each organization was flanked by a consultant who assisted the project team in compiling the social account. His/her task was to act as a sort of process consultant by following compilation of the social account through its various stages.

From a methodological point of view, the entire process of research, training and experimentation can be conceived as an action research project (Greenwood and Levin 1998; Elden and Levin 1991; Bryman 1989). In fact, the MOSES project pursued objectives to do both with the production of academic scientific knowledge and with the implementation of concrete organizational development schemes at the local level. Moreover, the participants were constantly involved in the research and experimentation activities and therefore performed the role of 'co–researchers'.

The present writer acted as the consultant for four organizations, which therefore constitute four cases on which to conduct empirical analysis. These four cases – denoted by the following acronyms TNM, CMU, PRI and JSR – will be reported and examined by means of a grid comprising the following elements:

- a brief description of the organization;
- a summary of the main reasons that induced the organization to participate in the project (and consequently to interest itself in social responsibility and social reporting);
- an analysis of the factors that aided or hindered compilation of the social account during the experimentation phase;
- the outcome of the experimentation phase.

The Case of TNM

TNM is an organization furnishing assistance to emigrants from the province of Trentino (and their descendants) resident abroad. Its activities are undertaken in two main areas:

- economic support for emigrants suffering hardship in territories afflicted by economic and political crisis (such as certain countries in South America); also provided is legal and logistical support for emigrants wishing to return to Italy;
- the promotion of cultural activities to maintain links between emigrants and Trentino.

The organizational structure of TNM is rather complex. The organization's central office, with a staff of five people, undertakes secretarial and administrative functions and provides tax consultancy. There is then a group of volunteers – the *Gruppo Giovani* – which actively participates in TNM's cultural initiatives in both Italy and abroad. The TNM board consists of representatives of local public institutions: the provincial government, the university, the library, etc. Finally, TNM's presence abroad is organized into '*circoli di famiglie*' (family circles) distributed around the globe and consisting of families of Trentino origin. In some cases, South and North America for example, the circles have created a 'federation'.

TNM's activities are funded to the amount of 95% by the public administration. Its main expenses arise from the organization of rallies and meetings (both in Italy and abroad) and the promotion of local development projects among communities with Trentino emigrants suffering economic and social hardship.

Reasons for Participation in the Project TNM is experiencing a major crisis of social legitimacy at local level. In fact, the Trentino population does not have direct evidence of how TNM spends the public funds (of a conspicuous amount, for that matter) which it receives annually. The TNM managers complain of a widespread belief that they merely organize trips, conferences and rallies. In metaphorical terms, the fear is that the public image of TNM is that of a travel agency for a select group of cronies.

On the other hand, it is difficult for TNM to communicate the social value of its many initiatives undertaken abroad: support for the construction of hospitals, schools and wells; consultancy on agricultural conversion projects; the promotion of cooperatives and social enterprises. But only the more 'festive' and 'convivial' aspects of TNM's activities are perceived in Italy. The consequence is a certain scepticism, fuelled by polemics in the mass media, regarding the effectiveness and efficacy of TNM.

TNM saw the MOSES project as an opportunity to equip itself with a useful instrument with which to communicate the social and cultural value of its activities. Two people from TNM attended the training course: a worker at the central office and a member of the group of voluntary workers. These two people then formed the project team during the experimentation phase. The director of TNM supported its participation in the project but was never directly involved.

Strengths of the Experimentation Phase Attendance on the course by two people belonging to different branches of the organization (the office and the group of voluntary workers) increased the 'voices' involved in the experimentation phase. This enabled common problems to be interpreted from different viewpoints, and it brought out tensions between the office and the voluntary workers. At the same time, the office and the voluntary workers realized that they had a shared interpretation of certain issues which was sometimes at odds with the views of the TNM board. Finally, the presence of 'operational' rather representative figures in the project team enabled the focus to be trained on concrete issues (e.g. the scant participation of young Trentini in the organization's initiatives, or the lack of a database on the circles abroad) rather than expressly political and strategic matters.

Weaknesses of the Experimentation Phase The complexity of TNM's organizational structure impeded the smooth progress of the work, after deadlock had been reached in certain decisions regarding the collection and processing of the data to be published in the social account. The project team had decided to conduct wide–ranging consultation in order to define the contents of the social account. This decision, however, had provoked a clash among the various branches of the organization, and different views of TNM's political role vis–à–vis its stakeholders emerged. This had repercussions on the selection and classification of the stakeholders. For some members of TNM, Trentino emigrants and their descendants should continue to be TNM's main interlocutors, while for others the organization should pay closer attention to local actors like schools and libraries in order to spread a culture of emigration which enhanced concern for immigrants into Trentino as well.

Outcome of the Experimentation Phase The outcome of the experimentation process was negative in that TNM was unable to draw up a social account. Two main factors were responsible for this failure:

- the complexity of the organization, as illustrated above, which impeded definition of the contents of the social account;
- the only partial contribution made by the director of TNM, who, although he supported the initiative, was never involved in first person with compiling the social account. This not only deprived the project team of valuable input but diminished the authoritativeness of the entire project within the organization (and made the cooperation of other members less forthcoming).

The Case of CMU

CMU is an organization furnishing assistance to children with mental or social difficulties. It runs programmes for social recovery and reintegration at various facilities distributed around the province, and which accommodate the children for periods of time or organize recreational activities. Besides these activities, CMU has stipulated a number of agreements with families to host children experiencing problems with their families of origin, so that they can live in a more tranquil environment until the age of eighteen.

CMU is a non–religious organization, although its roots are in the Catholic tradition. The organization was founded by a Catholic priest, in fact, and still today its legal representative is a clergyman. The director is instead a layman, and CMU's activities are conducted by specialized personnel who are not required to be members of the Catholic Church. The only stipulation is that they must abide by the educational principles on which CMU's action is based.

CMU is financed by public funds provided either by the provincial government or by the municipal administrations of the towns in which its facilities are located. The funding body also establishes the criteria used to assess the organization's activities. Each local facility therefore interfaces with a different public actor expressing both specific needs (connected with local problems) and different criteria for assessment of CMU's welfare policies. As a consequence, CMU must respond to diverse evaluation criteria, although its activities are inspired by a common set of principles.

Reasons for Participation in the Project CMU saw participation in the MOSES project as an opportunity to develop a uniform system of social accounting for all its local facilities. CMU's interest therefore sprang from concerns other than CSR, although its activities were profoundly inspired by ethical and social values. At the time, however, CMU was confronted by a strictly organizational problem: the absence of a uniform system for collecting and processing the information necessary for overall assessment of the organization's activities.

CMU viewed the possibility of compiling and publishing a social account as an opportunity for the organization to grow more generally. It should be stressed that CMU's intention was to publish a document for internal use, without data and information being disseminated externally. This intention also reflected one of the organization's basic strategies as encapsulated by its founder's motto: 'Do and be silent'. This strategy stemmed from a certain scepticism about externally–directed communication practices, which in most cases were regarded as distractions from the organization's mission.

However, this conviction had induced CMU to neglect the importance of communication with the local community, given that each local facility was focused on its own activities and mainly interested in interacting with a few selected stakeholders. The director was aware of this shortcoming and believed that a social account, even though intended for internal use, would foster the organization's openness to the outside – albeit only in terms of knowledge of CNU's various activities and initiatives.

Strengths of the Experimentation Phase Participation in first person by the director and his belief in the validity of the project indubitably favoured the entire process. The director participated in both the training course and the experimentation phase, during which he coordinated the internal project team. The latter produced a set of forms with which to collect uniform data from all CMU facilities, and it devised the questions and indicators. Another strength of the experimentation process was the considerable commitment shown by the organization's other members to the project, which they deemed consistent with CMU's organizational culture. In many respects, one may say that the project satisfied a need latent in the organization.

Weaknesses of the Experimentation Phase The main obstacle against fulfilment of the project was precisely the problem that it was intended to address: the fragmented organizational structure of CMU. The organization can be depicted as a network with connections that were formally well–defined and stable but in substance rather slack. The difficulty of assembling the heads of the various local facilities and the difficulty of identifying common indicators for assessing initiatives slowed down compilation of the social account.

A second drawback was that CMU had decided to hire a person who, amongst other things, would have assisted the director in managing the activities connected with compilation of the social account. However, owing to a lack of economic resources, this person was not hired, and as a consequence the director had to coordinate the activity on his own.

Outcome of the Experimentation Process By the end of the year CMU was able to publish its social account, which was presented as an internal document. However, it was published in draft form in order to assess its efficacy and its effective use by the organization. The members of the CMU board reacted positively to publication of the social account and evaluated it with interest.

To be noted is that the social account was published in rather meagre form and some sections of it were incomplete. The overall outcome of the process was therefore good in part. The positive judgement on it is based, not on the document issued at the end of the year but mainly on the intent expressed by the CMU board to continue with the initiative beyond the experimentation tied to participation in the MOSES project.

The Case of PRI

PRI is a voluntary association, which assists the social integration of the disabled, especially if young. The organization works in two main areas: (i) recreational and care activities for the disabled, together with support for their families; (ii) events (meetings, discussions, theme evenings) intended to direct attention to the difficulties of families with disabled members, and to increase public awareness and solidarity.

The organizational structure of PRI is very simple. The association's activities are run by a steering committee whose members are elected by the general assembly. Each member of the committee is responsible for a particular organizational area (administration, communication, events, etc.). Decisions by the committee are taken collegially. PRI has three categories of members: voluntary workers, disabled persons, relatives of the disabled. These categories often combine because a person may participate in PRI's activities as a voluntary worker and simultaneously as the relative of a disabled person. It is consequently difficult to distinguish between the organization's internal and external aspects.

Reasons for Participating in the Project The principal reason for PRI's participation in the project was the decision taken by the steering committee to adopt an accounting system for the organization's activities. Because PRI's initiatives are mainly undertaken by its voluntary workers, they do not involve large economic resources but may arouse considerable interest in the localities where PRI operates. However, the association has never had an instrument for verifying attendance at its initiatives, nor a system for planning and managing its activities. These shortcomings have always been off-set by the enthusiasm of the association's members. In recent years, however, PRI has stepped up its activities, and they have met with increasing success. It has therefore grown apparent that planning and management should be rationalized.

Participation in the MOSES project was therefore viewed as an opportunity for the association to develop further. The possibility to adopt a planning and accounting instrument was consequently the main reason for participation, besides the social value that the document might have.

In order to reflect PRI's internal structure, the training course was attended by a disabled member of the association and by a voluntary worker, who was also the parent of a disabled boy. The same two people formed the team which led implementation of the project.

Strengths of the Experimentation Phase PRI proved to be a highly cohesive organization with a distinct organizational identity and a clear vision of its goals and programmes. This facilitated compilation of the social account, because there were few differences of opinion about the information to be published – and consequently about the information to be collected and processed. The experimentation process was also markedly participative and reflected the collegial nature of decision making by the PRI steering committee. This broad participation, however, did not disperse ideas and energies; rather, it transmuted into a willingness to draw up forms, collect data, process information and synthesize it in a final document.

Weaknesses of the Experimentation Phase The difficulties encountered by PRI in compiling the social account were due to a lack of technological resources for data collection and processing. The association had only one and rather old computer. To deal with this problem, numerous members had to 'take work home with them'. This situation hampered constant coordination of the compilation process, and in some cases it necessitated the updating and standardizing of the date collected, as well as of the methods used to collate them.

Outcome of the Experimentation Process PRI published its social account at the end of the experimentation year. The outcome of the operation was quite satisfactory, both because the document produced was of good quality, and because the need to update and standardize the data collected finally endowed PRI with a system for collecting and evaluating information on its activities.

The association decided to issue a social account for the following year as well, even though it could no longer count on the assistance of the organizations running the MOSES project.

The Case of JSR

JSR is a sports club which organizes courses in judo and martial arts mainly for children and adolescents. However, its activities are not restricted to sports coaching, because it also seeks to enhance the educational function of sport in fostering personal growth and socialization. To this end, JSR also organizes cultural initiatives on the significance of martial arts and distributes information materials among its members.

The club is very small. The director is the core of the organization and attends to all the main aspects of its management and administration. He is also the best qualified of the club's instructors. He is helped by other instructors, who also assist him with the organization of specific events (like the end–of–year display or training sessions).

JSR's activities depend on the voluntary work of the instructors, who although they have some preparation are not professionals and have other jobs. One of the club's main problems is negotiating with the municipality over space in which to run its courses, given that there are other associations claiming space for their activities.

Reasons for Participating in the Project Besides organizing courses in judo and the martial arts, JSR pursues two objectives: (i) gaining greater support from the municipality, which in practice means obtaining more hours for its gym sessions; (ii) gaining greater appreciation of its activities among the parents of the children attending the club's courses: the director complained that parents treated the club as a 'kid parking area' and were uninterested in what their children actually learned during lessons.

JSR intends to achieve these goals by enhancing the educational and cultural content of its activities. The message that the club wants to convey is that it does not only teach wrestling techniques but also seeks to teach social values (mutual respect, tolerance, fraternity) to young people through sport.

The social account was therefore viewed as a useful means with which to collect and transmit information pertinent to these two objectives. Participation in the MOSES project was consequently prompted by a desire to emphasize the cultural and social value of sport as an educational process.

Strengths of the Experimentation Phase The main strength of the experimentation phase was the director's strong commitment to the objectives that prompted JSR's participation in the project. A further strength was indubitably the small size of the organization, which favoured easy agreement on the form and content of the social account. A third strength was the considerable amount of data and information that the association had produced to illustrate its activities, and which formed the basis for the social account.

Weaknesses of the Experimentation Phase Although the small size of the organization facilitated discussion of the social account, it meant that the entire weight of experimentation rested on a few people. Because these people also worked voluntarily within the club, they did not have the time or resources to follow the entire project through. As a consequence, the project imploded because the people who were supposed to conduct it were unable to find the time and resources to carry out the experimentation phase.

Outcome of the Experimentation Phase The social account was not published. As said, the members of the club were unable to complete the experimentation phase because they lacked sufficient time. The attempt foundered after an initial phase which instead presaged good results thanks to the club's foresight in already producing information material about its activities.

The Schemes Compared

Now that these four experiences in compiling a social account have been briefly described, they can be compared for the purpose of overall reflection on the outcomes of the MOSES project, and on the theoretical significance of these experiences. The basis for the reflection is comparison among the motives, strengths and weaknesses of these four cases. Table 11.1 summarizes the findings.

Table 11.1 Summary of the Main Motives, Strengths and Weaknesses Encountered by the Organizations in the MOSES Project

Organization	Motive	Strengths	Weaknesses
TNM	• Increase social legitimacy	• Multiple participant voices • Pragmatic attitude	• Internal conflicts on the definition of strategies • Non-participation by the director in the project team
CMU	• To coordinate and standardize accounting practices	• Belief in the project • Coherence with the organizational culture	• Territorial dispersion of the organization
PRI	• To create an internal management system	• Internal organizational cohesion	• Lack of technological resources
JSR	• To increase visibility among institutions and the general public	• Belief in the project • Disposition to communication	• Shortage of human resources to devote to the project

Besides analysis of the individual schemes, Table 11.1 also permits an overall interpretation from which interesting insights can be gained. The first concerns the reasons for participating in the MOSES project, and therefore the decision to publish (or at least try to publish) a social account. It is obvious that these motivations evidenced latent needs in the organizations. But the most striking feature is that these motivations did not correspond to 'ethical' issues, nor did they reflect concerns about the social and environmental effects of the organization's activities, as one might expect from a shift to CSR principles. This only partly happened in the case of TNM, which needed to regain legitimacy among certain local stakeholders. The other organizations were prompted to participate in the MOSES project by internal and strictly organizational issues.

This last point introduces the second consideration: the view that adoption of CSR (more specifically, social accounting) was an opportunity for organizational growth. This process involves two specific areas of organizational life: management and communication. As regards the former, to be noted is that more than one organization saw compilation of a social account as an opportunity to endow itself with a more thorough and effective planning, control and accounting system. This signifies that simple financial accounting (i.e. the traditional financial statement) did not meet the needs for control of organizations which, however small and limited in their business goals, had somewhat complex relations with their stakeholders. As a consequence, the social account was an instrument which, besides its ethical value, furnished important managerial support for these organizations. This point applies to communication as well: the social account was regarded as a document with which to intervene efficaciously in relations with stakeholders, especially those crucial for the organization. This is because the social account enabled an organization to provide a broader and more detailed description of its activities, besides those forming the more traditional components of organizational communication (public relations and communication with institutions).

A third consideration concerns the outcome of the experimental schemes conducted as part of the MOSES project. One notes that the organizations able to publish a social account were those with greater internal cohesion, both at the level of organizational culture and identity, and at the level of interaction and cooperation among members. These features were therefore the necessary preconditions for the success of a social accounting process, and more generally of reflection on CSR. It is evident, however, that the results of the MOSES project cannot be generalized. Nevertheless, one gains the impression from the four cases examined that coherence between the organizational culture and organizational practices is a prerequisite for obtaining a sharply focused 'snapshot' of the organization in its social account. The case of TNM is emblematic in this regard: a plurality of voices (which in itself may signify greater participation and collaboration) instead generated conflict over the purposes of the project and interpretations of it. This situation reflected marked fragmentation internally to the organization, which was going through a critical period in both its relationships with stakeholders and definition of the organization's internal equilibriums and mission.

NPOs and CSR: Between Continuity and Superimposition

In light of the foregoing analysis of the experience acquired from the MOSES project, it is now possible to discuss the significance of interest in CSR for an NPO and the meaning which CSR initiatives may acquire for an NPO. The reflections that follow rotate around two opposing propositions: (i) CSR represents an extension of an NPO's potential, so that the relation between the concepts of NPO and CSR is one of continuity; (ii) there persist situations in which the relation between the two concepts still takes the form of their superimposition, with all the consequent uncertainties and misunderstandings.

CSR as an Extension of an NPO's Activities The cases of CMU and PRI represent situations in which the organization's relation with CSR takes the form of continuity. This consideration derives from the fact that the motives cited by CMU and PRI did not comprise particular concern with the ethical and social value of a social account or the information contained in it. It is evident that these NPOs did not intend to construct their identities and organizational cultures around CSR. Their interest in the theme and their implementation of a formal CSR instrument did not entail an ethical and cultural change. If anything, the intent of these organizations was to reiterate and to articulate more clearly the values on which these organizations based their action. The change that they wanted to achieve was instead change of a technical and organizational nature.

There was therefore a continuity between being an NPO and reflecting on the ethical and social implications of its activity. This relation was especially coherent when the organization's identity and culture were well established and clearly defined. In other cases, TNM for example, internal fragmentation obstructed the definition of development policies and action in critical areas.

However, these considerations should not be taken to imply that any NPO can, as such, define itself as socially responsible. One cannot presume that an organization successfully engaged in social action is equally able to establish correct relations with its internal or external stakeholders. This would require positing an equivalence between the concepts of NPO and CSR giving rise to considerable conceptual and analytical confusion.

The continuity is apparent if one considers the implementation of CSR practices and instruments as an extension of an NPO's potential. These practices and instruments become initiatives that rationalize a set of concerns and interests (of an ethical and social nature) already expressed in organizational activities. CSR may be accordingly read as providing NPOs with an opportunity for growth because it marks out a development path, which is neither self–referential nor tautological.

However, consideration is necessary of the strategic implications of such situations. From this perspective, in fact, continuity between NPO and CSR runs the risk of unconsciously basing itself on the auditing dynamics described by Michael Power. On the other hand, however much situations of continuity may appear coherent with an NPO's organizational culture, the technical changes to which they give rise (implementation of a control and accounting system) prefigures a shift discontinuous with respect to simpler and more informal management of the organization. Such change may indubitably have a beneficial impact on the organization and the efficiency of its operations. Nevertheless, it introduces a control dynamic that will prove difficult to elude and which will probably become the synonym and guarantee of the organization's efficiency regardless of the social efficacy of its activities. The risk is therefore that the formal efficiency introduced by these control systems may prevail over an NPO's social efficacy.

CSR as Overlapping with the Concept of NPO Situations of superimposition between the concepts of NPO and CSR may nevertheless persist. They are to be found in cases where the concept of CSR is used in merely instrumental terms. It is difficult to identify criteria and indicators that unequivocally attest to such situations. However, in light of the research reported here, one may say that the superimposition is most evident when an organization shifts towards CSR because of external pressure rather than an internal exigency.

The absence of a specific internal need (or lack of awareness of one) also hampers reflection on CSR and consequently the implementation of CSR practices and instruments. The case of TNM is emblematic: lack of agreement on classification of their stakeholders reflected a cleavage within the organization that impeded the adoption of such CSR programmes as social accounting.

The superimposition arises because CSR instruments and practices are adopted to 'stanch' critical organizational occurrences (like crises of reputation or legitimacy) substantially exogenous to the organization's non–profit nature. Moreover, poor management does not depend on the decision to configure the organization as an NPO rather than a for–profit enterprise.

The superimposition is the more misleading, that more CSR is put forward as a natural and innate dimension of an NPO's activities, almost as if there were an equivalence between being an NPO and acting in a socially responsible manner. In such cases, the superimposition is radically misleading. Above all, these situations are evident examples of the mimesis of currently fashionable practices and processes described by the neo–institutionalist scholars (DiMaggio and Powell 1983; Meyer and Rowan 1977) mentioned at the outset. Moreover, CSR instruments and practices are often adopted without clear awareness of their usefulness for the organization or of the work that their introduction will require. This becomes a further obstacle against their effective implementation.

Conclusions

This chapter has examined the controversial relationship between the concepts of NPO and CSR. The analysis began by acknowledging that the two concepts are often confusedly superimposed so that it is believed that all NPOs by definition act in socially responsible manner towards their stakeholders. Without entering into discussion of the ethical and social value of the activities of many NPOs, the chapter has discussed how the relationship between the two concepts can be interpreted in a more articulated manner.

The empirical research conducted on this topic has shown that, although more or less deliberately created situations of overlap still persist, CSR may also represent an extension of an NPO's potential. In the case of deliberate superimposition of the two concepts, there is an evident endeavour to make instrumental CSR for purposes largely coherent with the goals of an NPO. In the case of continuity, apparent instead is a strategy more coherent with organizational growth whereby reflection on CSR furnishes a framework within which to channel already ongoing paths and processes.

It should be borne in mind, however, that continuity between NPO and CSR may imply a discontinuous transition due to the introduction of new instruments for the planning and communication the organization's activities. These instruments may distort the sense of CSR initiatives, in that their implementation may require the adoption of control systems and procedures which extend beyond the initiatives themselves and end up conditioning the life of the organization. It is therefore advisable to ensure that a strategic vision of CSR does not amplify the sphere of 'controllability' described by Michael Power. This, moreover, may deplete the sense and distinctiveness of an NPO's organizational action. In short, for an NPO, reflection on CSR centres on an endeavour to strike a balance among fundamental values and strategies for organizational development. The latter should ensue from the former: the process in reverse may not only be incoherent but also have scant efficacy and credibility.

Conclusion

Chapter 12

Managing Corporate Social Responsibility in Action: Reconciling Rhetorical Harmony and Practical Dissonance

Frank den Hond, Frank G.A. de Bakker, Peter Neergaard and Jean–Pascal Gond

Introduction

In the introduction to this volume, we noted a discrepancy between a general and global CSR discourse that seems to be homogeneous in content, and an apparent heterogeneity of operationalizations of CSR at the firm level. Further, we suggested that the measurement of CSR plays a mediating role between the two. Therefore, the chapters in the three parts of this book explored homogeneity and heterogeneity in CSR, as well as the role of measurement of CSR, at different levels of analysis. The time has come to take stock of our findings and to interpret the discrepancy. In this concluding chapter, we first show that indeed there is a rather homogeneous CSR discourse at the broadest level of analysis, and we offer an explanation for this observation. Then, we show how at the operational level there actually is much more heterogeneity than generally assumed: not only across countries, and across and within industries, but also within firms and over time. Again, we offer an explanation. Finally, we discuss how emerging CSR reporting systems serve as mediators between the contradicting trends at both levels. In the discussion, we present some implications of these findings. The chapter is concluded with some general suggestions for future research on managing CSR in action.

Part 1: A History of Conceptual Homogeneity

The first section in this volume (*Talking: CSR in Discourse*) sought to demonstrate that there is conceptual homogeneity in the CSR discourse. Buhr and Grafström (Chapter 2) analyzed how the concept of CSR was given meaning in and by the *Financial Times*; Windell (Chapter 3) how and why consultants contributed to the translation of CSR into the Swedish business context; and de Bakker, Ohlsson, den Hond, Tengblad and Turcotte (Chapter 4) how Swedish, Canadian and Dutch firms represented themselves in their annual reports on issues related to CSR. Despite the different settings and the different roles of the actors involved – business press, management consultants, firms – there are striking similarities in the findings presented in these three chapters. This section continues by highlighting these similarities, and closes with an explanation for the observed conceptual homogeneity.

Buhr and Grafström report how the *Financial Times*, a well-distributed and much read business newspaper based in London, ascribed meaning to the concept of CSR. A word count on the prevalence of 'corporate social responsibility' and 'CSR' in its pages showed that the *Financial Times* has only given significant attention to the theme since 1999, although occasional references were made in the 1988–1999 period. This leads to two themes for discussion. One is the meaning of the concept in the different periods of time; the other is the timing of the appearance of CSR in this newspaper.

Although Great Britain is heralded as having become one of the epicentres of the contemporary resurgence of CSR, in fact CSR–related business activities have a long history in this country. Before the late 1990s, the 'socially responsible agenda' of British businesses was largely implicit and national in its orientation, comprising issues such as community involvement, socially responsible products and processes, and socially responsible employee relations (Moon 2005). Several articles in the *Financial Times* in the 1988–1998 period testify this implicit and national orientation of the CSR concept. It is likely that more articles appeared on such issues, but without a reference to 'corporate social responsibility' or 'CSR'. Only after the very first mentioning of 'CSR' in May 1988, did such issues become associated with the 'CSR' concept and could they be traced in Buhr and Grafström's study. The occasion of the first mentioning of 'CSR' is interesting: a British–American conference on Private Sector Initiatives, which was attended by the British Prime Minister Margaret Thatcher and the Prince of Wales, and which was addressed by the President of the United States of America, Ronald Reagan, through a videotape. It suggests how the contemporary CSR concept may well have been imported from the United States.

About a decade later, after the late 1990s, the British CSR agenda had become much more explicit (Moon 2005; Matten and Moon 2005). According to Buhr and Grafström, during the 1999–2003 period, the meaning of the concept in the *Financial Times* had broadened. Before 1999, CSR was discussed in connection to local or national social issues, but after that year, the term increasingly referred to firms' behaviours at a global scale. In the same period of time, a connection was established between CSR and the globalization debate. Finally, Buhr and Grafström find that only after 1999 a debate appeared in the newspaper's columns about the appropriateness of firms investing in social issues. In this debate, the same arguments were used that already had been advanced in similar debates in the 1950s and 1960s in the United States about the firm's social responsibilities (compare Chapter 1). In this debate, the *Financial Times* took a supportive stance, reinforcing the relevance of the CSR concept as a prescription for managerial decision making by providing accounts of how CSR could reduce business risks, or expand market opportunities. By doing so the *Financial Times* increased the attractiveness of the concept to managers, as managers could more legitimately claim that their firms were both modern and rational in increasing shareholder value. However, the advent of CSR was not only stimulated by the business press. Also management consultants and firms themselves contributed to an increasing appearance of CSR as a homogeneous and explicit concept.

Windell highlights the role of management consultants in advancing and commercializing CSR in Sweden. Management consultants help firms to gain and strengthen their legitimacy by, first, suggesting concepts whose adoption by firms may help them to be perceived as modern and rational, and second, by helping firms to adopt and implement such concepts. Windell's analysis shows that rather unspecific, 'fluffy' ideas about social responsibilities of business started to circulate in Sweden in the early 1990s. Initially, management consultants transformed such ideas into diverse labels such as 'corporate citizenship', 'corporate social responsibility' and 'corporate ethics'. Windell explains how the commercialization of these 'fluffy' ideas proceeded in three sequential stages: (1) labelling ideas about social responsibilities of business as CSR, (2) packaging this new label into marketable consulting services, and (3) mobilizing it through rhetorical strategies.

Interestingly, Windell's results demonstrate that the consultants did not share identical motives for commercializing CSR. Some consultants – 'money–makers' – were driven by an interest in expanding their services and creating and meeting a market demand. For others the commercialization of CSR was not an end in itself. This latter group of consultants – 'world–saviours' – purposively sought to promote other interests than commercial ones; they had the ambition and motivation to improve the conditions of the world by spreading ideas of corporate social responsibility. However, despite their different motives, the dominant rhetoric used to sell the services was one of commercial benefits rather than social benefits. Rhetorical strategies emphasizing economic rationales for convincing corporations of the benefits of CSR were used by all consultants, both for winning firms over to the CSR label and for convincing them to buy the particular service offered by the consultant. What is thus observed is conceptual homogeneity at the level of CSR that is differentiated when it comes to making the concept operational, while a similar rhetoric is used for advancing both the broad concept and the different services derived thereof. Both world–saviours and money–makers predominantly suggest that firms increase profits by implementing CSR. The role of consultants in translating the CSR label into an attractive concept for firms to engage in goes beyond the concept's intrinsic qualities but should also be seen as 'a consequence of processes of social construction and reconstruction' (Røvik 2002: 143).

Firms themselves however also influence the diffusion of the explicit CSR concept. De Bakker et al. compare the self–representation on CSR–related issues in annual reports issued by a sample of Swedish, Canadian and Dutch stock–listed firms for the years 1981, 1991 and 2001. From this three–country comparison over time, they conclude that by 2001, several marked changes have taken place in how firms report on their social responsibilities. First, in all three countries, a discourse on CSR clearly has established, but one that is amazingly devoid of content. Many firms seem to feel obliged to address CSR, but rhetoric is dominating actual content in many of the reports studied. Although firms increasingly claim that they observe ethical standards and acknowledge their social responsibilities, they provide little or no specifications of what such standards are and how they acknowledge their responsibilities. Second, references to the national business context (such as the domestic political and economic situation) have decreased in importance in annual reports from all three countries. Third, and related, in 2001 references to globalization as a dominant business context have become more prevalent. Altogether, authors conclude that the data suggest a steady rise of the CSR discourse, taking place simultaneously with a decrease of other discourses on social, economic and political development in a company's home country, and with a rise of references to internationalization and globalization. Of course, these results may well have been biased by the sampling method as the analyses predominantly cover firms that are among the larger players in their national contexts. Nevertheless the data suggest a development towards more explicit forms of CSR, even if the analyses cannot be confirmed statistically. Further, the observations from the previous chapters also confirm this development.

The timing of these changes between 1991 and 2001 strikingly parallels the emergence of the explicit concept of CSR in the *Financial Times* (Buhr and Grafström this volume), as well as the start of the CSR–related activities by Swedish management consultants (Windell this volume). Therefore, these three chapters suggest that, by the end of the 1990s, in various countries, different actors expressed highly similar conceptions of CSR. Conceptual homogeneity was established around the principle that corporations have certain responsibilities towards society, and that these responsibilities are to be taken up voluntarily and should serve the firms' self interests.

In the remainder of this section we argue that this conceptualization is highly similar to the American–borne, explicit model of CSR (Matten and Moon 2005), and offer an explanation as to why these countries, as well as quite a few others, inundated with implicit CSR, would be so eager to adopt, or adapt to, the American notion of explicit CSR. Although recent research has sought to identify national flavours of CSR, we suggest that the similarities across the many national incarnations of CSR – each of which is largely explicit – can be explained by referring to the supra–national advent of economic globalization. In order to substantiate this position, we need to look at the history and evolution of the concept. Of course, globalization has often been mentioned in the context of CSR, yet mainly to point out the fact that the CSR concept was embraced at large scale in many settings, rather than to outline how globalization affected the emergence of explicit notions of CSR in different geographical and cultural settings.

Most authors trace the origins of the debate on the relationship between corporate economic activity and society to the United States at the turn of the 19th and 20th century (for example Blumberg 1972; Bowen 1953; Heald 1957). It has been suggested that the cultural imprint of that pedigree can still be observed in representations of the CSR concept today (Pasquero 2005) and even that the influence of American culture on the concept of CSR might be explained by the religious climate of those days (Acquier, Gond and Igalens 2005). Acquier et al. (2005) suggest, building on the Weberian argument of the influence of the protestant ethic on the spirit of capitalism, that it was considered a moral obligation to the (successful) businessman to share his wealth with the people in his community. But why did this attention rise at that place and that moment in time?

Several authors suggest that this development was related to the rise of the corporation as a separate legal entity in the United States (Bakan 2004; Crowther 2004). Especially the limited liability to stockholders of the consequences of directors' deeds, and the legal obligation for directors to act in the financial interests of their stockholders, have been important elements in constituting the modern corporation. The further expansion of the corporation into diversified conglomerates under 'general management', often spatially separated from the actual operations of the firms' subsidiaries, increased the salience of issues of social responsibility of businesses and their managers. Indeed, the debates in the United States between Bowen (1953) and Davis (1960) on the one hand, and Levitt (1958) and Friedman (1962, 1970) on the other hand, focused on this very issue. Friedman argued that the business of business is business; firms should increase shareholder value, only restricted by law and custom. Davis (1960), on the other hand, argued that businessmen, that is the firm's general managers, should be concerned with the social implications of their decision making within firms, precisely because of the position of power that their firms have within communities, the state and the economy at large. Because managers act as leaders of sizeable institutions, they have considerable social power through the wide–ranging impacts of the policies and decisions implemented through the firms they manage. According to Drucker (1954), *noblesse oblige*: managers have been granted the right to continue their business projects as corporations of virtually unrestricted lifetimes, as well as the right to make decisions in their corporations' best interests. However, these rights also require managers to assume responsibility for increasing social welfare, in the sense that doing so should make business sense (Drucker 1984). To these authors, power and responsibility need to go hand in hand.

The consequence of this careful balancing act of responsibility and power is that if managers *were not* to accept social responsibility commensurate to their social power – and the position of neo–classical economists such as Friedman (1962, 1970) is that they *should not* if this negatively affects shareholder value – they are likely to *lose* business power. According to Drucker (1984) and Davis (1960), if they do not, notably the state and trade unions are likely to step in and enforce what managers fail to take responsibility for. In 1960, Davis predicted that 'businessmen during the next fifty years probably will have substantial freedom of choice regarding what social responsibilities they will take and how far they will go. As current holders of social power, they can act responsibly to hold this power if they wish to do so ... The choice *is* theirs' (Davis 1960: 74, original emphasis).

Nearly fifty years later, Davis' predictions can be examined with the benefit of hindsight. From the 1950s onwards, Western industrialized countries started to build their welfare states, arguably more so in Western Europe than in the USA. This development was financed by a long period of economic growth. Business revenues were needed in this respect, and a considerable social consensus existed around the idea that a thriving economy was good for all. In terms of the 'responsibility' debate, managers could postpone Davis' choice of taking any responsibilities that were to parallel their firms' social power, because the state had a decisive influence on social and economic development (Peters 1996). Government hence was seen as the 'prime mover', capable of eliminating market failures, stimulating innovation, and creating demand through public expenditures, thus incorporating firms in their master project of building the welfare state. However, during the late 1960s and early 1970s, externalities of unlimited growth became visible and widespread societal concern about population growth and environmental pollution arose. This development fired back at the firms, as states increased the levels of regulation and taxation in order to counter these externalities and to pay for the provisions of the welfare state such as pensions, health care, mass education, or unemployment compensations. It has been argued that not only the cost to firms increased – with the consequence of hampering growth and innovation – but also that such regulation was ineffective in addressing the problems. In fact, government was increasingly seen as the problem rather than the solution (Adelman 2000) and political and academic debates increasingly turned to questioning the conditions under which regulation might stimulate innovation (Ashford, Ayers and Stone 1985; Jaffe and Palmer 1997). An important condition was the nature of the regulation: direct through law, or indirect, through financial and informational incentives. A strong belief in the benefits of industry self–regulation emerged. Subsequent economic downturns and two oil crises (1973 and 1979), in combination with the state–induced higher cost, created fertile ground for the 'neo–liberal revolution' of the 1980s that has become associated with the political leadership of Ronald Reagan and Margaret Thatcher. In this period, neo–classical theory came to dominate economic development and governmental policies. Market competition was put central, while governmental involvement was to be kept to a minimum. Extensive programs of deregulation, tax rate reductions, as well as reforms of welfare programs were initiated. The end of the Cold War undoubtedly contributed to these developments (Jenkins 2001; Peters 1996), while the increasing globalization also challenged the efficiency of national regulations (Haufler 2001). The public sector thus was forced into a more defensive role.

Following Davis' (1960) logic, this neo–liberal turn would imply the eventual reinstatement of social responsibilities to the corporation. The decline in public sector responsibility created a need for a rise in voluntary actions governed by industries and individual companies. Even more so, a new position in the debate around the social and environmental obligations of firms thus emerged as governments, firms, and business organizations were all stressing both the need for private engagement in these domains, and the necessity of the voluntary character of such engagement. Civil society organizations, non–governmental organizations, public interest groups, and similar organizations, increasingly challenged business firms directly on the nature of the social and environmental consequences of their policies and practices. This is partly because governments argue that such problems should be dealt with in the market, and partly because firms claim that they will indeed act voluntarily in these domains. Firms make such claims either to prevent governmental mandatory regulation, or, arguably, to retake social responsibilities that need to parallel their increased levels of social power. All in all, CSR is a prime example of self–regulation concerned with social and environmental issues but how CSR is managed in different situations seems to vary across firms.

With the advent of deregulation and economic globalization, first, the power of firms has further increased, and second, non–American firms have increasingly emulated the American system of corporate governance, for instance because they are stock–listed in New York.[1] Consequently, they are likely to subscribe to the American CSR discourse as well, at least in general terms. On the one hand, this requires firms to obey American regulations, such as those issued by the Securities and Exchange Commission (SEC), and to deal with the expectations of various American stakeholders, including those of shareholders, government agencies, and non–governmental organizations. In short, they needed to find legitimacy in an American institutional context. On the other hand, the combination of the further growth of these firms and the relative lack of regulation in the international markets and supply chains, recreated a situation very similar to that of the 1950s and 1960s in the United States out of which the earlier CSR debates emerged. After all, in that period, as in the 1980s, the CSR debate was focused at the societal consequences of corporate growth. In both periods the advent of economic globalization was paralleled by increased pressures on firms to become more socially responsible. Both factors – the need to secure legitimacy in the American institutional context, and pressures on firms to demonstrate responsibility commensurate to their social power – have contributed to the broad adoption of a general notion of CSR, and may have added to the willingness of firms to partake – at least rhetorically – in efforts by their home country governments to take some responsibility for solving some of the pressing national problems. However, once it comes to such (national) specification, implementation and reporting of CSR, contingent stakeholder and institutional pressures seem to prevail, leading to increased levels of differentiation and heterogeneity. Thus, despite the strong cultural and historical background of the CSR concept in the early 20th century American business climate, it can be explained why almost a century later in culturally and structurally quite different geographical areas, such as continental Europe or Japan, the American CSR discourse has firmly rooted, substituting for longer established implicit notions of CSR.

In this overall development, homogeneity of the CSR concept seems to have been developed around a synthesis of the positions of Davis and Friedman. The *noblesse oblige* argument that social responsibilities of firms should be commensurate to their social power (Davis 1960) is seamlessly interwoven with the firm's prime responsibility of making money, where short–term losses are only accepted if instrumental in maximizing the firm's value for its shareholders in the long run (Friedman 1962). In this way, rhetorical harmony regarding the meaning of the concept may have developed, but it is less likely that conceptual homogeneity is reflected in an equally homogeneous praxis.

Part 2: Evidence and Explanation of Heterogeneity in Praxis

Firms that engage with such a broad conceptualization of CSR can be viewed as attempting to convince 'relevant outsiders' (Pfeffer and Salancik 1978; Rayman–Bacchus 2004) of their legitimacy, by playing to the tune that behaving 'socially responsible' is a laudable thing to do. To claim that a firm or its activities are

---

1 The transfer of American business models to other countries has been frequently studied, for instance by Djelic (1998) and Kipping (1999). See also Chapter 8 for a detailed example.

'socially responsible' is to claim that the firm or its activities are 'desirable, proper, or appropriate' within the specific institutional setting in which it operates (Suchman 1995: 574). To some degree, however, there might be a lack of correspondence between a firm's claim of social responsibility and its actual behaviour. From a firm's perspective, there may be good reasons why its 'espoused theory' differs from its 'theory–in–use' (Argyris and Schön 1978). Firms may be exposed to societal expectations that not only differ in place and time, but also change over time. In situations that social norms and stakeholder pressures are contradictory or inconsistent, or if they are conflicting with demands for efficiency, firms may develop separate organizational structures or processes that help them deal with each demand separately, while assuring that the internal dependencies between the resulting structures or processes remain 'loosely coupled' (Weick 1976). For instance, Utting (2000) found that codes of conduct are often lofty principles, which are neither effectively implemented nor thoroughly verified by parties independent from the firm ('third–party verification'). When no efficient compliance mechanisms exists, consumers and the general public could be mislead by companies that are trying to 'greenwash' their products and business activities (Greer and Bruno 1996).

Against such a background, it may even be argued that the insistence on the 'voluntary' character of CSR, as it is stressed in most of the broad conceptual definitions, is a deliberate move to allow firms some room to manoeuvre strategically in dealing with outside pressures (Oliver 1991), as is also contended by opponents of the concept (Corporate Watch 2006). Of course, a number of companies did not live up to their earlier commitments to act 'socially responsible' – and some of them even blatantly and fraudulently so. But therefore radically to dismiss the concept altogether would not do justice to the complexities, particularities and intricacies that managers face in their organizations and the environments in which their firms have to operate and that therefore also influence their abilities for acting socially responsible ('emergent strategy', Mintzberg and Waters 1985).

A literature has emerged around the question of particularities of CSR in different institutional contexts. A number of case studies has sought to establish the particular national flavour of CSR, for example in Finland (Panapanaan, Linnanen, Karvonen and Phan 2003), Hong Kong (Gill and Leinbach 1983), India (Mohan 2001), Japan (Wokutch 1990), New Zealand (Hackston and Milne 1996), Romania (Korka 2005) or Singapore (Tsang 1998). Perrini (2005) seeks commonalities in CSR reporting in a sample of companies from various European countries. Beyond this, attempts have been made to compare national styles of CSR (for example Habisch, Jonker, Wegner and Schmidpeter 2005). And of course, differences have been found. European styles of CSR have been found to differ from those in the USA (Maignan and Ralston 2002; Tschopp 2005), but differences can also be observed between European countries. One example is found in the expectations that stakeholder groups hold of how firms should act responsibly (Maignan 2001). Matten and Moon (2005) introduced the notion of 'implicit CSR' to suggest that such differences can for the greater part be explained by differences in how traditionally the state has, or has not, provided for social welfare. Similarly, Chapple and Moon (2005) conclude from their study of CSR representations on corporate websites in a number of Asian countries, that there is considerable variation and that this variation is explained by factors in the respective national business systems, rather that by the stage of development of the national economies. They also conclude that multinational companies are more likely to adopt CSR than those companies operating solely in their home country, but that the profiles of multinationals' CSR tend to reflect the profiles of the country of operation rather than the country of origin. All this suggests that the institutional context does matter in how the CSR concept is made operational, but also that operationalizations in any particular context are connected to other operationalizations at the more abstract, conceptual level.

Other dimensions have also been proposed in the literature to explore and explain differences in operationalizations of CSR, industry differences being a prominent one. The type of industry is likely to impact the adoption of CSR, as not all industries face similar stakeholder pressures to address issues of social responsibility. Such observations have been reported both across and within industries. For instance, Brammer and Millington (2003) report on inter–industry differences in corporate community involvement among British firms, and Heugens, Lamertz and Calmet (2003) observe systematic intra–industry differences in corporate citizenship behaviour among Canadian breweries. This industry dimension also illustrates some of the institutional differences among firms.

However, research reporting on institutional differences in CSR needs to be treated with some caution because of two potential biases. First, such research may be biased towards a willingness to find differences across boundaries such as nationality, culture, industry, or strategic group, and thereby runs the risk of overlooking any similarities of CSR concepts across that boundary. Second, the emphasis on differences across boundaries – at least implicitly – suggests homogeneity *within* the realm delineated by those boundaries. Such studies therefore potentially overlook differences within this realm. In addition to these potential biases, there is an implicit expectation in such studies that the observed differences will persist, because their origins are to be sought in the institutional fabrics in which firms operate. The result could be an overly static description of ever–emphasized differences across boundaries, to the neglect of differences and change within these boundaries.

The second set of chapters (*Doing: CSR in Praxis*) contributes to the debate of what CSR actually gets to mean once it is put into practice. CSR in praxis does not represent a uniform set of activities: labelling schemes, code of conducts, reporting systems (Pedersen and Neergaard, Chapter 5), corporate volunteering (Wood, Chapter 7), social programs (Göthberg, Chapter 6) and membership of the UN Global Compact (Irgens and Ness, Chapter 8), are all examples of corporate engagements that have been presented and discussed under the label of CSR. The overall conclusion of this section, namely that CSR means very different things for different companies, a practical dissonance, can be refined to highlight two important issues: the re–labelling of existing practices within firms, and divergence in firms' reception of CSR practices.

Regarding re–labelling, Göthberg provides a historical analysis of the shaping and reshaping of 'Ideas for Life', a project in which one of Sweden's major insurance companies, Skandia, currently concentrates its CSR activities. But it hadn't been always this way, neither was this project started because of Skandia's engagement in CSR *per se*. Such observations can be interpreted using institutional theory.

According to this theory, organizations seek legitimacy by accommodating to norms, values and expectations in their environment, for example, in order to appear modern and progressive, or to live up to the expectations of relevant stakeholders. The concept of CSR can be seen as a management fashion, as a collective answer to such institutional pressure that comprises a set of techniques for firms, which helps them to become or remain legitimate, as Windell (this volume) suggested. However, as argued by Göthberg, managers can modify, change and translate the concept into something appropriate for their local setting (Czarniawska and Sevón 2005a). She illustrates how in 1987 the 'Ideas for Life' department was originally formed as an important element in the company's risk management policies. Its aim was to counteract bad publicity; by then, the press accused Skandia for its bureaucracy and its very poor customer service. Göthberg shows how, in a period of fifteen years, the same project was presented and justified as fitting new management trends as knowledge management, sustainable development and finally CSR. This chapter therefore illustrates that new demands like CSR do not necessarily generate new practices. Instead, old practices are translated and to a certain degree modified to fit new demands. By presenting an old practice under a new CSR label, Skandia promoted itself as a socially responsible company, as the relevant stakeholders appeared to have an interest in this issue.

The chapters by Irgens and Ness and by Wood consider the reception of CSR within companies, but whereas Irgens and Ness focus on a corporate head office and its subsidiaries, and thus analyze organizations, Wood delves into the psychology of individual employees.

Irgens and Ness highlight that management principles and concerns for people and environment are mediated differently through different cultural lenses. They rely on a long tradition of research addressing the relationship between management practices and culture (Hofstede 1998; Hampden–Turner and Trompenaars 2000) and differences in institutional environments. Numerous authors have discussed how national culture shapes the perception of various management concepts including business ethics and CSR. Irgens and Ness embark on this research tradition as they focus their research on the challenges that face a large Norwegian corporation, Norske Skog, in attempting to diffuse its CSR policies to its newly acquired subsidiaries. These challenges stem from a situation in which the company's CSR policies are rooted in a Scandinavian CSR ideology, that in turn has developed in a particular welfare system, whereas the newly acquired companies are embedded in different institutional settings, thus suggesting that their respective cultural and cognitive dispositions vary considerably. Similar observations have been made in comparative research. Mohan (2006), for example, finds that there is considerable variety in the CSR activities of the Indian subsidiaries of two UK–based multinationals. Part of the variety is related to the different industries in which the subsidiaries operate, another part to managerial discretion at corporate headquarters in what is being managed regarding their subsidiaries' CSR engagements. Similarly, regarding the implementation of environmental practices beyond regulatory compliance, Delmas and Toffel (2004) find variety among plants that must also be explained by plant–level characteristics.

However, Irgens and Ness go beyond such observations by proposing to use the metaphor of stepfamilies (Allred, Boal and Holstein 2005) to understand the relationship between multinational corporations and their acquired subsidiaries. In stepfamilies, individuals experience high levels of stress, cultural shock, role ambiguity and lack of shared history. They argue that the metaphor of multi–cultural stepfamilies may be a fruitful way of framing the challenges facing multinationals when they try to diffuse CSR to newly acquired subsidiaries. Hence, they study how organizational recipes and management ideas are diffused within an organization, and how these ideas are imported and edited in different settings.

Contrarily, Wood studies CSR from the perspective of non–managerial employees, viewing corporate volunteering as a manifestation of CSR. He claims that most of the research on CSR so far has been from the perspective of management. He argues that the way non–managerial employees experience CSR and the associated policies and activities are likely to have a profound impact on corporate performance and as such are worth a closer investigation. Wood reports a survey on corporate volunteering among non–managerial employees in Australia. The surveyed employees did not consider corporate benefits of volunteering as either important or particularly motivating for themselves. The opportunity to do volunteering during working hours was highly motivating and seen as a testimony of management commitment to CSR, as were other factors such as the ability to control their volunteering, the lack of formal hierarchical structure in the work and a possibility to make a difference in the community. In discussing whether and how his findings could be generalized, Wood points at several peculiarities in Australian culture that might account for the observations.

These chapters add to the debate on what exactly comprises CSR once the concept is implemented in praxis. This question is different from the question which factors increase the likelihood that a given firm will engage in CSR – Jones (1999) proposed thirteen hypotheses, formulated at the level of nationality, industry, firm and individual manager, as to how companies might differ in their propensity to engage in CSR – and also from the question of what the (financial) consequences of engaging in CSR entail. Such questions are all the more difficult to address, if CSR in praxis does not only mean different things to different companies, but also to different sub–units within companies, and over time. With such a multitude of dimensions it becomes tempting to see CSR in praxis as idiosyncratic because it is likely that, at the very least, firms' private interests do play a significant role in the way they develop their specific version of CSR.

Pedersen and Neergaard point at the importance of such differences. They argue that the very different initiatives are likely to generate different costs and benefits for companies, making it very problematic to render any general statements on the impact of CSR on the bottom line. Their conclusion resonates with McWilliams and Siegel's (2001) theory of the firm perspective. Both studies suggest that rational firms will engage in particular CSR activities, and only so up to the point where the costs are no longer offset by the benefits derived from doing so. Thus, only some CSR activities may be beneficial for some firms under some circumstances (Vogel 2005). If this is correct, then only a loose coupling between the overarching CSR discourse and CSR in practice can be found. This puts the measurement of CSR in a twisted position. It can no longer just be considered the more or less straightforward operationalization of one overarching concept, with only one problem left to solve: how to deal with the abstractness of the concept. Measurement also must acknowledge, and maybe protect or justify, a certain degree of corporate discretion in which CSR activities are being implemented – or which activities can be presented – as CSR, otherwise it loses contact with the empirical domain it is supposed to measure.

Part 3: The Mediating Role of Measuring

The third set of chapters (*Measuring: CSR in Scales*) discusses how emerging social reporting systems can indeed be mediators between the contradictory trends at these two levels. On the one hand, CSR rating systems need to appeal to the broad, general CSR discourse for social legitimacy. On the other hand, these systems also need to be tailored to the demands of specific stakeholders in the particular context in which the firm operates, in order to be practically meaningful.

These two tendencies characterize a key trade–off associated with the exercise of measurement (Porter 1994, 1996): that between *standardization* and *accuracy*. Measurement, in this case of CSR, needs to be standardized in order to allow for comparison, either over time, across a set of heterogeneous practices, or in relation to some abstract norm. In the measurement, particular aspects of what needs to be measured are abstractly expressed, quite often quantitatively, whereas other aspects are deemed of less importance, and are therefore not measured (Porter 1994). The 'standard' thus defines what is being measured, and therefore, the activity of measuring can be related to a bureaucratic work of collecting facts and data. In the case of CSR, data are collected about relevant projects or programs, or about (changes in) the impact of the corporation on its external environment. Such work could be performed internally by corporations, for the purpose of deploying or improving the CSR policy, or by external organizations in order to provide various stakeholders with information about CSR, as in the case of socially responsible investment schemes or social audits. This kind of work implies to elaborate a simplified picture of the CSR activities and consequently leaves room for representing the nature of CSR to the advantage of the business unit or of the corporation, as Cochoy and Vabre (2004) illustrated. New issues can be incorporated within the standard at the firm's convenience.

The essential need for standardization conflicts with the search for accuracy and precision, which are also at the core of any measurement project (Porter 1994, 1996). Investors relying on CSR data will expect the data used as input to construct their 'ethical' or 'socially responsible' portfolio to actually reflect CSR to some extent, as do CEOs or managers elaborating their firm's social strategy based on an internal reporting system. They also expect that the data they rely on will be of sufficient quality and precision to allow for the assessment of differences in CSR performance across organizations – be they different corporations or corporate sub–units – or over time. However, trying to know exactly what is behind a low CSR score of a corporate sub–unit or what differences exist between two corporations exhibiting a similar 'score' of CSR for a given stakeholder will directly point to the inherent limitation of any measurement exercise: a lack of precision.

Social rating organizations and other groups that aim at standardizing the system of CSR reporting, operate as institutional entrepreneurs in trying to bridge the tension between these two contradicting trends, by providing comparisons and evaluations of reporting practices (Déjean, Gond and Leca 2004). The role of these organizations is all the more relevant as they can influence the institutional shaping of CSR practices: what gets accepted as a good (local) implementation of a broad issue of CSR? Contributions to Part 3 of this volume explore how such measurement organizations do so. In some cases they set up CSR evaluation or reporting standards in competition with each other (Acquier and Aggeri, Chapter 9, and Zarlowski, Chapter 10). Quite a different, interesting example can be found in the institutional context of a non–profit sector, where it is shown how the mere introduction of the idea of measurement plays a role in enhancing the general understanding of the nature of social responsibility for those organizations (Rossi, Chapter 11). These contributions also illuminate the mediating role of measurement at three different scales by investigating measurement of CSR at the industrial (Acquier and Aggeri), the organizational (Zarlowski) and the micro–organizational levels (Rossi).

Aggeri and Acquier explore the role of the first tendency inherent to measurement – standardization – at the industry level. Their study reaffirms the existence of a gap between, on the one hand, discourses showing an easy translation of a financial mode of management to fit the CSR field, and, on the other hand, the actual practices of CSR assessment by actors, relying more often on *bricolage* between existing ad–hoc data and pre–existing methods designed for other purposes that on a 'linear' translation of financial models. In line with previous research (Gond and Leca 2004), they consequently reveal the rather symbolic attachment of the CSR industry to the financial world, and move beyond by investigating the role of standards construction in the development of the CSR industry. Borrowing Henderson and Clark's (1990) analysis of system inter–operability, they argue that technical feasibility should be taken into account together with legitimacy in order to accurately portray the institutionalization process of CSR standards and their potential success. Their main empirical contribution consists in investigating how these variables have been managed by different organizations aiming at developing standards for CSR management or audit (such as GRI or AA 1000). Doing so, they convincingly demonstrate that legitimacy is not a sufficient condition for the success of a CSR standard and suggest that any analysis of a CSR standard project should consider the relationship between both variables to evaluate its potential. Their stimulating analysis opens a new avenue of research by suggesting that the value of a standard on a given market (such as the market for CSR evaluation or CSR audit) should be analyzed in relationship to its compatibility with standards developed on other markets from the CSR industry. Such a perspective invites to explore the multi–markets CSR standards competition in future studies.

Zarlowski complements the previous one by analyzing two competing standards of CSR evaluation in detail. He does so by considering key actors in their national institutional context. His empirical comparison of two social rating agencies providing data to investors for the purpose of socially responsible investing but relying on two different models of evaluation, suggests that the long term success of a standard in a given market is strongly related to its adaptation to the local variety of capitalism in which the agency operates. Once again the tension between standardization and relevance is at play. Both agencies aim at offering standardized data to investors needing quantified data (Déjean et al. 2004), but whereas one agency has developed a methodology reflecting the stakeholder view inherent to continental capitalism (Albert 1991), the other one appears as a more direct 'import' from the Anglo–American context. Zarlowski argues that the success of these two attempts to standardize CSR in order to become the unique standard on the French Socially Responsible Investment market is strongly dependent on the adaptation of the models embedded in those agencies to their national business system. According to Zarlowski, one agency, Vigeo, has been more successful mainly because its model has been selected by the context as suitable for the more 'continental' French variety of capitalism (Schmidt 2003). Consequently, the local adaptation of CSR standards – in other words their cultural *relevance* – appears as a crucial variable to explain its success. This tendency reflects the variety of capitalism thesis of the maintenance of strong national differences in business practices regardless of the globalization (see Crouch and Streeck 1997; Whitley 1999).

Taken together, these two chapters suggest that competing standards could succeed if they achieve a right balance between *legitimacy*, *technical feasibility* and *local tailoring*. The conclusion that both chapters suggest is that the 'CSR standards of the future' have to be flexible enough to be compatible with other CSR standards from various markets of the CSR industry as well as being 'translatable' in a way that could fit the local institutions of the countries where they are diffused. Both perspectives call for the development of studies about the work underlying the management of these three components, looking at the processes through which actors are constructing locally acceptable CSR standards by translating methods or models from others markets or institutional contexts.

The third chapter completes these insights by providing an analysis of the role played by CSR measurement at a micro–organizational level. Whereas the two previous chapters were investigating relatively elaborated forms of CSR measure and quantification – corresponding to 'second order' CSR measurement, that is the calculations performed on previously organized and collected data about CSR (Callon and Muniesa 2005; Power 2004) – the case presented by Rossi reflects an attempt to elaborate a very basic form of 'first order' CSR measurement, that is the search for data that would enable the assessment of CSR. It is indeed a very basic form of CSR reporting that the non–profit organizations (NPOs) under study are trying to put in place. This work reveals some of the hidden faces associated with measurement, such as its role in structuring members' representations of what their organization and its basic purpose encompass. The four cases of NPOs, by taking into account organizations whose world is not yet made of figures, reveal the social construction of the meaning of CSR for actors through the process of measurement. What might well be taken for granted in larger organizations and often is understudied in the CSR field of research – such as the very need to quantify, the existence of stakeholders and the achievement of external visibility – appears to be completely negotiable in the context of very small organizations. Rossi's empirical study shows that the exercise of measuring CSR leads the members of the studied organizations to clarify their own representation of the organizational purposes and to clarify the relationship between the NPO and society. Doing so, measurement can potentially reveal conflicting views of what *are* and what *should be* the relevant stakeholders of the organizations (the target audience of the social report). The development of measurement also implies crucial choices in terms of stakeholder engagement that could generate tensions within the organization. The difficulties to construct a consensual, collective representation of the social responsibility of the micro–organization during the measurement process could even explain to some extent the failure of two of the studied organizations to establish a reporting system. Here, CSR measurement appears as a key mediator, not only between official discourses and actual practices or between an organization and its stakeholders, but also between individual members of an organization.

Rossi's focus on the intricacies of introducing measurement of CSR in organizations thus highlights one of the basic points that Power (1997) made about the potential existence of an expectation gap, in the sense that an outside observer may have an incomplete understanding of what is actually measured in a particular audit system, and the consequences thereof. These points give rise to some further contemplation.

To the extent that measuring firms' CSR efforts, or the results achieved by these efforts, produces reliable information on the basis of which decisions are made, any system designed to do so is an audit system. Audit systems, as Power (1997) argues, are to produce trust, and thereby facilitate social exchange, whether in the market or other domains that are subject to audit controls, such as health care or education. In some instances these systems fail to do so, which needs not necessarily be explained by failure of the system itself, but may also be related to the existence of an expectation gap.

Audits can be 'first order', produced on the basis of relatively simple manipulation of primary data, as described by Rossi. Here, the expectation gap can be recognized in the relative difficulty that the leaders of non–governmental organizations had in producing a social account in the first place: those that were less characterized by internally coherent organizational cultures and identities faced considerable more difficulty in doing so, arguably because there was little common ground in expectations as to what these organizations were supposed to do. A solution for the expectation gap might then be found in attempts to align the various expectations.

However, as audit systems increasingly seem to become 'second order' – that is, characterized by increasingly complicated calculus of data – the potential problems relating to the existence of an expectation gap become more subtle. Ignorance of what is really being presented in the audit then might add to distrust of the firm's claims regarding its engagement and achievements in CSR, as the distance between the audit and the primary data increases because of the calculus and manipulation. Distrust may increase further if the audit is based on a complicated calculus of primary data on management processes, rather than on output. How are different audiences to know what such audits really stand for?

One solution to solve the expectation gap might be in increasing transparency, not just on the outcomes of the audit, but also on the methodology of the audit. If not properly addressed, there remains room for claims that the audit is decoupled from corporate realities. Decoupling is the result of a ritualistic or ceremonial response to institutional pressures (Meyer and Rowan 1977). It could be part of an attempt to engage in some form of impression management (Elsbach 1994), or to manipulate the institutional demands and expectations by purposeful and opportunistic attempts to co–opt, influence, or control institutional pressures and evaluation (Oliver 1991). Decoupling could then be seen as the 'organization of hypocrisy', as a practice of incorporating different organizational structures, processes and ideologies for internal and external use (Brunsson 2002). The limited ability to monitor companies' CSR initiatives in detail adds to this hypocrisy, as it limits the opportunity for outsiders to arouse scandal in case of (assumed) discrepancies between norms and facts. Conversely, in case of scandal, it has been shown that firms respond more convincingly if they refer to shared norms than to facts (Elsbach 1994). Firms can reinforce their post–scandal credibility by pre–emptively creating a deeply entrenched association between the firm and the norms that they believe add to their legitimacy (Ashforth and Gibbs 1990). This is where talking, doing and measuring of CSR come together. Through rhetorical strategies, firms can try to strengthen the legitimacy of what they do (compare Suddaby and Greenwood 2005). However, such responses only sustain as long as their intended audience does not question them, that is, as long as the expectation gap remains hidden from view. In this respect, it is of primordial importance that the measurement is trusted. This vulnerability of the legitimizing effects of measuring CSR to external scrutiny is exacerbated by the empirical weakness of CSR at the conceptual level. It is difficult to unequivocally assess the nature and quality of a firm's CSR because of the multi–faced character of the construct itself.

Another solution to the expectation gap is to bring the firm's operations in line with the criteria, standards, and procedures that are included in the audit system. This also could disturb the balancing act as the measuring of CSR may then 'colonize' the firm. In order to be measurable, CSR needs to be *made* measurable. This may require the firm to change its operational processes and internal structures in such a way that it emulates the measurement model. In doing so, the internal balance of the firm's routines, developed over time as the arrangement of activities that makes its business model profitable (Prahalad and Bettis 1986), may be distorted by adaptation to the external requirements of how to articulate CSR. Similar observations have been reported in different contexts. Power (1997), for example, discusses medical audits and illustrates the tensions between managers and clinicians. In general, he notes that, due to colonization, 'the imposition of audit and related measures of auditable performance leads to the opposite of what was intended, i.e. creates forms of dysfunction for the audited service itself' (Power 1997: 98).

If the general conclusion that 'accounting systems in their broadest sense function more often to legitimate individual and organizational behaviour than to support efficient and rational decision making' (Power 2003: 379) also holds for measuring CSR, it is to be expected that the former problem will be more prevalent than the latter. But nevertheless, we suggest that both types of distortions due to measuring CSR may occur, hindering an effective reconciliation of talking and doing.

Conclusion: Implications and Directions for Further Research

Having revisited the three parts of this volume and having placed the observations in a broader context, we can now develop an overall conclusion, and suggest directions on how to continue with CSR in research and praxis. As often highlighted, many debates around CSR are still unresolved and many traditions can be discerned (Crowther and Rayman–Bacchus 2004c; Habisch et al. 2005). As Van Oosterhout and Heugens (2007) stated: 'the gist of the problem is that it is not clear what CSR is, that we do not understand its causes and consequences, and that the notion is not very helpful in understanding what exactly is desirable or required at the business–society interface.' Although this volume does not intend to settle all of these problems, revisiting the three parts emphasizes the need to see CSR as a matter of talking, doing *and* measuring.

So, we first showed that there clearly is conceptual homogeneity, since CSR can be seen as a concept that is intricately linked to the advent of economic globalization, if not a tool in its deliberate advancement. The inclusive and somewhat vague character of the concept makes it a useful tool in such processes: both for consultants to sell to companies and for companies to communicate to their different stakeholder audiences. Meanwhile, there is a distinct heterogeneity in praxis, which is also confirmed in other studies. For instance, according to Whitehouse (2006: 293), 'CSR reveals itself among large companies not as a uniform concept but as a variety of conceptions.' This variation is not only visible along the various boundaries that so far have been described in the literature, but also within companies and over time. Superficially, many activities brought under the heading of CSR use similar language. But once put into practice, actual differences play out. Finally, measurement can serve as a mediator between these two poles in at least two directions. Measurement can provide rhetorical legitimacy for disparate corporate practices, while it can also shape corporate CSR engagement by influencing praxis. In this sense, CSR is a balancing act that can fail in either way. Therefore, rather than discussing the measurement or implementation of CSR *tout court*, it would be better to start asking what particular form of CSR is (to be) measured or implemented (see also Rowley and Berman 2000; van Oosterhout and Heugens 2007).

Of course, in this volume we have adopted a liberal stance on what to consider CSR – the variety of topics addressed as CSR in Part 2 is testimony of this – but we did so to show that in praxis there is not only variety to be found under the label of CSR, but there also are commonalities under related labels, such as corporate citizenship. The hunt for an all–encompassing type of CSR might well be pointless and could, in our view, better be replaced by research scrutinizing the antecedents and evolution of particular forms of CSR. That is, seeing CSR as a dependent variable rather than as an independent variable, influencing firm performance. Doing so acknowledges the differences in CSR. Our reconciliation of conceptual homogeneity and heterogeneity in praxis is addressed from the understanding that CSR is to be given meaning, or socially constructed, in different places, times, and occasions. Measuring, then, plays an important role in such processes of social construction. Variety, and the possibility of changing meanings over time, should be a necessary quality of the concept. Perhaps it has always been, because 'social responsibility' is a subjective if not political concept.

Given this state of affairs, a comparison could be made with Joanne Martin's evaluation of research on organizational culture (Martin 1992; Meyerson and Martin 1987). She distinguishes different perspectives: integration, differentiation and fragmentation, each of which sheds a different light on the phenomenon of organization culture. From the integration perspective, the dominant cultural traits are highlighted, whereas differences and conflict, for example emerging from sub–cultures, are downplayed. Culture then is open to managerial influence, and – if characterized by specific traits – a contributor to organizational performance. However, from the differentiation perspective, organizational culture is like a patchwork: differences between sub–cultures are highlighted, whereas commonalities are downplayed. Organization culture is seen as being continuously contested, rather than as a homogenizing force within the organization. Finally, from the fragmentation perspective, it is emphasized that culture is elusive, changing, created and re–created by who–ever happens to be around and influenced by contingencies of the moment. Likewise, CSR could be studied from each of these three perspectives. An integration view would emphasize how CSR is good for profit, whereas a differentiation view would highlight how, for example, national styles of CSR are good for profit given different national contexts. From a fragmentation point of view, CSR would be considered as the dependent variable of social action, contested and ambiguous. It could be argued that Part 1 of this volume took an integration, Part 2 a differentiation, and Part 3 a fragmentation perspective. Thus, this volume has shown that multiple perspectives can be useful in explaining different aspects of CSR. Then where does that bring us, or the debate on CSR?

Of course, the sheer acknowledgement of the usefulness of different perspectives offers a vantage point from which existing literature can be critically examined and further developed. By joining these three different perspectives and discussing their relation, we offer a broader perspective of CSR than is found in several recent suggestions for research agendas. For example, McWilliams, Siegel and Wright (2006) – and many other authors that are interested in the consequences of CSR engagement – appear to make use of an integration perspective by advocating a strict definition of what CSR is, and what it is not. Their main concern is rigour in constructs in order to facilitate measurement, and thereby hypothesis testing. In Hirsch and Levin's terminology, such authors position themselves as members of the 'validity police', trying to narrow down the meaning of the concept and to box it into a typology. According to McWilliams et al., the problem surrounding CSR research is in construct development: 'The lack of consistency in the use of the term CSR makes it difficult to compare results across studies, hampering our ability to understand the implications of CSR activity' (McWilliams et al. 2006: 8). We agree, but add that the problem may even be located in the empirical realm: the independent variable – CSR – is not or perhaps cannot be defined unequivocally; it means too many different things outside companies, within companies and over time. Studies that make CSR operational in particular ways in order to conduct cross–sectoral analyses will therefore remain vulnerable to challenges of their validity. For example, the debate between Entine (2003) and Waddock (2003), about the validity of using the

KLD rating data as a measure of corporate social performance, focuses on this very issue. In this sense, in order to acknowledge the messy reality of CSR in praxis, it may be more productive to acknowledge that CSR is an 'umbrella construct' (Gond and Crane 2006; Hirsch and Levin 1999), and consequently to adopt a differentiation or even a fragmentation perspective.

Quite some studies have been published that take a differentiation perspective, notably those that seek to find systematic differences in CSR, for example in national flavours or across sectors.[2] However, as noted before, such studies may overlook differences in CSR praxis within boundaries of nation or sector, as even within companies and over time CSR may be differentiated. In this sense, we would argue for even more diversity in CSR research, and hence take the position of what Hirsch and Levin (1999) call 'umbrella advocates'. To consider CSR as an umbrella construct, exploring all of its different meanings and its social construction in particular settings, goes with the risk that eventually the construct collapses, as is argued to be the case by van Oosterhout and Heugens (2007). Yet, as Hirsch and Levin (1999: 199) suggest: 'some umbrella constructs may ultimately be made coherent or remain permanently controversial rather than collapse.' The upside of taking seriously the umbrella character of CSR is that a much more nuanced understanding of its nature and development emerges, whether or not a coherent construct or definition evolves during this process.

One might even wonder whether reaching a coherent definition of CSR is necessary at all to make it meaningful in practice. A state of permanent controversy does not necessarily lead to an inferior form of CSR. Some recent research for instance hints at how different strategic choices can be deployed to establish a suitable form of CSR within a specific context (Galbreath 2006). Dissimilar, even conflicting, definitions may still lead to acceptable results. Pivotal in such debates will be the role of measurement, as that is where theory and practice need to be brought in accordance. Measurement or auditing systems serve as mediators, ideally balancing the tendencies of propagating window–dressing or hypocrisy, versus colonizing firms with some invasive version of CSR. We suggest that treating CSR as a dependent variable could lead to an increased understanding of the way firms and their stakeholders are currently trying to come to terms with this complicated concept in different settings.

The implication is that much more attention in research is to be given to antecedents of CSR, and to how CSR is getting meaning in particular settings, rather than to expand on the sequence of studies that link CSR and some financial indicators in order to 'prove' that CSR is good for business. Of course, firms are in business to do business, but the ways they shape CSR, the struggles they face in establishing this concept (Irgens and Ness) and the emphases they place, for instance on employee involvement (Wood) will greatly vary. Measurement systems will need to grapple with such a variation; they will need to see through the conceptual homogeneity.

---

2 But of course, without a comparison of flavours, such studies adopt an integration perspective.

If one is to really understand how one concept – CSR – can be *both* quite uniform in the way it is talked about *and* very differentiated once it is applied in practice, it is on the way CSR is shaped that research should focus, rather than on its influence on financial performance. Investigating how companies become more responsible, for instance under pressure from investors, consumers, non–governmental organizations, or activist groups (Bartley 2003; den Hond and de Bakker 2007; Guay, Doh and Sinclair 2004) might be more productive than focusing on the financial performance related to alleged CSR/CSP practices (de Bakker, Groenewegen and den Hond 2005). Doing so provides more insight in what factors influence the way CSR is constructed or reconstructed in a certain context over time. Also research into the question how CSR principles and practices are experienced by, and affect, employees and other stakeholders, and thereby influence these stakeholders' continued support to the decision makers' firm (Klein, Smith and John 2004; Sobczak 2003), adds to the understanding of how CSR is being constructed. Finally, research into how instruments for measuring CSR (such as codes of conduct, standards and international norms) gain institutional weight (Déjean, Gond and Leca 2004), and how they may contribute to regulating the global firm (Gendron, Lapointe and Turcotte 2004) adds to such an understanding of CSR.

Normatively, the way forward then would be to investigate how CSR can be made productive – in both social and financial terms – in particular situations. Despite the suggestion that the CSR construct is inherently normative (Matten, Crane and Chapple 2003), there is not much research that takes an explicit normative stance (de Bakker et al. 2005), especially not in how the norms embedded in particular conceptions of CSR can be effectively implemented in particular situations. In the introductory chapter we quoted Votaw (1973), stating how brilliant the CSR concept was in meaning something different to everyone. To understand CSR in action, this multi–faceted character is central. After all, a reconciliation of talking, doing and measuring CSR is to be found in understanding the roles of each of these three activities and in accepting the inherent differences associated with them. If more normative and instrumental approaches are to be developed, appreciating these differences is required. Measurement, transparency and dialogue are then some crucial notions, as highlighted also in recent studies. Pedersen (2006) for instance recommends stakeholder dialogues in operationalizing CSR, while Ählström and Egels-Zandén (in press) show how definitional processes of CSR can turn into interpretation battles between different stakeholders. Not only do such studies provide some instrumental guidance to CSR in action but they also can contribute to a normative grounding of the concept. What is to be seen as proper, responsible corporate behaviour? Evidently, there is an important role here for concepts such as transparency and legitimacy. After all, dialogues and definitional struggles can only develop fully if they are fed with useful information, whereas the norms and values as to what behaviour is proper, legitimate and indeed responsible – that is, being able and willing to answer (Lucas 1993) – provide the margins in which these dialogues and struggles take place.

In recent studies it has been proposed to look more closely at the processes through which social theories – such as in economics or management – frame behaviours in business life until they ultimately self–validate their postulates

(Ferraro, Pfeffer and Sutton 2005; MacKenzie and Millo 2003). Such approaches are all the more relevant in a time when 'bad management theories' are suspected to destroy 'good management practices' (Ghoshal 2005). In this regard, the messy world of CSR practices and theories has at least the advantage to provide some alternatives to the dominant financial or shareholder value mindset (Acquier and Gond 2005), to allow for alternative interpretations of responsible behaviour beyond shareholder maximization alone. The investigation of the ways through which different normative approaches of CSR are institutionalised through business education and embedded in emerging practices, and their potential to ultimately influence managers' behaviours offers numerous and promising avenues of research to explore. Accepting the variation in CSR could lead us to a better understanding of CSR in action. More work on talking, doing and measuring then is required, not to find the holy grail of one all-encompassing concept, but to understand what is actually going on. Researchers and managers alike need to delve deeper into what CSR entails if they are to take their involvement in CSR seriously.

Bibliography

3M (2003), Volunteer programs, <http://www.3m.com/about3m/sustainability/perf_comm_volunteer.jhtml>, accessed 7 February 2003.

Abbott, W.F. and Monsen, R.J. (1979), 'On the measurement of corporate social responsibility', *Academy of Management Journal*, vol. 22, no. 3: 501–515.

Abrahamson, E. (1991), 'Managerial fads and fashions: The diffusion and rejection of innovations', *Academy of Management Review*, vol. 16, no. 3: 586–612.

Abrahamson, E. (1996), 'Management fashion', *Academy of Management Review*, vol. 21, no. 1: 254–285.

Abrahamson, E. and Fairchild, G. (1999), 'Management fashion: Lifecycles, triggers, and collective learning processes', *Administrative Science Quarterly*, vol. 44, no. 4: 708–740.

Ackerstein, D.S. and Lemon, K.A. (1999), 'Greening the brand. Environmental marketing strategies and the American consumer', in M. Charter and J. Polonsky (eds), *Greener marketing. A global perspective on greening marketing practice*, Sheffield: Greenleaf, 233–254.

Acquier, A. and Aggeri, F. (2006), 'A knowledge based perspective on institutional building. The case of the Global Reporting Initiative (GRI)', working paper, Paris: CGS, Ecole des Mines de Paris.

Acquier, A. and Gond, J.–P. (2005). 'Building a constructivist perspective in business and society: Insights from Michel Callon's works', in L.V. Ryan and J.M. Logsdon (eds), *Proceedings of the 16th annual meeting of the International Association for Business and Society*, 62-75.

Acquier, A., Gond, J.–P. and Igalens, J. (2005), 'Des fondements religieux de la responsabilité sociale de l'entreprise à la responsabilité sociale de l'entreprise comme religion', paper presented at the 16th Conference of the Association de Gestion des Ressources Humaines '(Ré)concilier l'économique et le social', Paris, 15–16 September.

Acutt, N., Carter, A., Kapelus, P. and Hamann, R. (2001), *Towards evidence of the costs and benefits of tri–sector partnerships*, London: Natural Resources Cluster.

Adams, C.A., Hill, W.–Y. and Roberts, C.B. (1998), 'Corporate social reporting practices in Western Europe', *British Accounting Review*, vol. 30, no. 1: 1–21.

Adelman, I. (2000), *The role of government in economic development*, London: Routledge.

Adler, N.J. (2002), *International dimensions of organizational behaviour*, Cincinnati: South–Western.

Aggeri, F., Pezet, E., Acquier, A. and Abrassart, C. (forthcoming) *Organizing sustainable development*, Cheltenham: Edward Elgar.

Agle, B.R., Mitchell, R.K. and Sonnenfeld, J.A. (1999), 'Who matters to CEOs? An investigation of stakeholder attributes and salience, corporate performance, and CEO values', *Academy of Management Journal*, vol. 42, no. 5: 507–525.

Ählström, J. and Egels–Zandén, N. (in press), 'The process of defining corporate responsibility: A study of Swedish garment retailers' responsibility', *Business Strategy and the Environment*.
Åke Wissing & Co (2001), Internal survey conducted in Skandia on attitudes towards Skandia Ideas for Life, June 2001.
Albert, M. (1991), *Capitalisme contre capitalisme*, Paris: Seuil.
Alcouffe, A. and Alcouffe, C. (2000), 'Executive compensation: Setting practices in France', *Long Range Planning*, vol. 33, no. 4: 527–543.
Aldrich, H.E. and Fiol, M.C. (1994), 'Fools rush in? The institutional context of industry creation', *Academy of Management Review*, vol. 19, no. 4: 645–670.
Al–Khatib, J.A, Rawwas, M. and Vitell, S.J. (2004), 'Organizational ethics in developing countries: A comparative analysis', *Journal of Business Ethics*, vol. 55, no. 4: 307–320.
Allen, T. (1977), *Managing the flow of technology. Technology transfer and the dissemination of technological information within the R&D organization*, Cambridge: MIT Press.
Allred, B.B., Boal, K.B. and Holstein, W.K. (2005), 'Corporations as stepfamilies: A new metaphor for explaining the fate of merged and acquired companies', *Academy of Management Executive*, vol. 19, no. 3: 23–37.
Alvarez, J.L., Mazza, C. and Strandgaard Pedersen, J. (2005), 'The role of mass media in the consumption of management knowledge', *Scandinavian Journal of Management*, vol. 21, no. 2: 1–6.
Alvesson, M. and Karreman, D. (2000), 'Varieties of discourse: On the study of organizations through discourse analysis', *Human Relations*, vol. 53, no. 9: 1125–1149.
Andersson, C.L. and Bieniaszewska R.L (2005), 'The role of corporate social responsibility in an oil company's expansion into new territories', *Corporate Social Responsibility and Environmental Management*, vol. 12, no. 1: 1–9.
Andriof, J. and McIntosh, M. (eds) (2001a), *Perspectives on corporate citizenship*, Sheffield: Greenleaf.
Andriof, J. and McIntosh, M. (2001b), 'Introduction', in J. Andriof and M. McIntosh (eds), *Perspectives on corporate citizenship*, Sheffield: Greenleaf, 13–24.
Argyris, C. and Schön, D. (1978), *Organizational learning: A theory of action perspective*, Reading: Addison–Wesley.
Argyris, C., Putnam, R. and Smith, D. (1985), *Action science: Concepts, methods, and skills for research and intervention*, San Francisco: Jossey–Bass.
Armbüster, T. and Kipping, M. (2003), 'Strategy consulting at the crossroads: Technical change and shifting market conditions for top–level advice', *International Studies of Management and Organization*, vol. 32, no. 4: 19–42.
Arndt, M. and Bigelow, B. (2000), 'Presenting structural innovation in an institutional environment: Hospitals' use of impression management', *Administrative Science Quarterly*, vol. 45, no. 3: 494–522.
Ashford, N.A., Ayers, C. and Stone, R.F. (1985), 'Using regulation to change the market for innovation', *Harvard Environmental Law Review*, vol. 9, no. 2: 419–466.

Ashforth, B.E. and Gibbs, B.W. (1990), 'The double–edge of organizational legitimation', *Organization Science*, vol. 1, no. 2: 177–194.
Austin, J.E. (2000), 'Business leadership coalitions', *Business and Society Review*, vol. 105, no. 3: 305–322.
Avery, G. and Ryan, J. (2001), 'Applying situational leadership in Australia', *Journal of Management Development*, vol. 21, no. 3–4: 242–262.
Babakri, K.A., Bennett, R.A. and Franchetti, M. (2002), 'Critical factors for implementing ISO 14001 standard in United States industrial companies', *Journal of Cleaner Production*, vol. 11, no. 7: 749–752.
Backman, J. (1975), *Social responsibility and accountability*, New York: New York University Press.
Bakan, J. (2004), *The corporation. The pathological pursuit of profit and power*, London: Constable & Robinson.
Baker, M. (2003), 'Corporate responsibility reporting. The great unread', *Ethical Corporation*, no. 19 December: 20–33.
Baker, M. (2005), 'CSR reporting faces its next challenge', *Ethical Corporation*, no. 5 July: 30–33.
Baldwin, C.Y. and Clark, K.B. (1997), 'Managing in an age of modularity', *Harvard Business Review*, vol. 75, no. 5: 84–93.
Bansal, P. (2002), 'The corporate challenges of sustainable development', *Academy of Management Executive*, vol. 16, no. 2: 122–131.
Bansal, P. and Bogner, W.C. (2002), 'Deciding on ISO 14001: Economics, institutions, and context', *Long Range Planning*, vol. 35, no. 3: 269–290.
Bansal, P. and Hunter, T. (2003), 'Strategic explanations for the early adoption of ISO 14001', *Journal of Business Ethics*, vol. 46, no. 3: 289–299.
Barca, F. and Becht, M. (eds) (2001), *The control of corporate Europe*, Oxford: Oxford University Press.
Bartley, T. (2003), 'Certifying forests and factories: States, social movements, and the rise of private regulation in the apparel and forest products fields', *Politics and Society*, vol. 31, no. 3: 433–464.
Bass, K.E., Simerly, R.L. and Li, M. (1997), 'The effects of CEO compensation on corporate economic performance and corporate social performance', *Academy of Management Proceedings*: 401–405.
Bauer, M. and Bertin–Mourot, B. (1987), *Les 200. Comment devient–on un grand patron?* Paris: Seuil.
Baum, J.A.C. and Powell, W.W. (1995), 'Cultivating an institutional ecology of organizations: Comment on Hannan, Carrol, Dundon, and Torres', *American Sociological Review*, vol. 60, no. 4: 529–529.
Bebchuk, L.A. and Roe, M.J. (2004), 'A theory of path dependence in corporate ownership and governance', in J.N. Gordon, M.J. Roe and J. Mark (eds), *Convergence and persistence in corporate governance*, Cambridge: Cambridge University Press, 69–113.
Bell, A. and Garrett, P. (1998), *Approaches to media discourse*, Oxford: Blackwell.
Berger, P. and Luckmann, T. (1967), *The social construction of reality*, Garden City: Anchor.

Berger, S. and Dore, R. (eds) (1991), *National diversity and global capitalism*, Ithaca: Cornell University Press.

Berman, S.L., Wicks, A.C., Kotha, S. and Jones, T.M. (1999), 'Does stakeholder orientation matter? The relationship between stakeholder management models and firm financial performance', *Academy of Management Journal*, vol. 42, no. 5: 488–506.

Biddle, B. (1979), *Role theory: Expectations, identities and behaviours*, New York: Academic Press.

Biondi, V., Frey, M. and Iraldo, F. (2000), 'Environmental management systems and SMEs: Motivations, opportunities and barriers related to EMAS and ISO 14001 implementation', *Greener Management International*, no. 29: 55–68.

Blackler, F. (1995), 'Knowledge, knowledge work and organizations: An overview and interpretation', *Organization Studies*, vol. 16, no. 6: 1021–1046.

Blumberg, P.I. (1972), *Corporate responsibility in a changing society*, Boston: Boston University Press.

Bolman, L.G. and Deal, T.E. (1991), *Reframing organizations*, San Francisco: Jossey-Bass.

Bonifant, B.G., Arnold, M.B. and Long, F.J. (1995), 'Gaining competitive advantage through environmental investments', *Business Horizons*, vol. 38, no. 4: 37–48.

Borum, F. (1999), 'Omkring to skandinaviske bøger og nyinstitutionel teori', *Nordiske Organisasjonsstudier*, vol. 1, no. 1: 85–103.

Bourguignon, A. (2005), 'Analyzing the ideological function of accounting practice and discourse in context: Framework and illustration', paper presented at the 2005 'Critical Perspectives on Accounting Conference', Baruch College, City University of New York, 28–30 April, <http://aux.zicklin.baruch.cuny.edu/cpa2005/papers.htm/8381bourguignon.htm>.

Bourguignon, A., Malleret, V. and Nørreklit, H. (2004), 'The American balanced scorecard versus the French tableau de bord: The ideological dimension', *Management Accounting Research*, vol. 15, no. 2: 107–134.

Bowen, H. (1953), *Social responsibilities of the businessman*, New York: Harper and Row.

Bowen, H. (1978), 'Social responsibilities of the businessman. Twenty years later', in E.M. Epstein and D. Votaw (eds), *Rationality, legitimacy, responsibility: Search for new directions in business and society*, Santa Monica: Goodyear, 116–130.

Bowen, S.A. (2004), 'Organizational factors encouraging ethical decision making: An exploration into the case of an exemplar', *Journal of Business Ethics*, vol. 52, no. 4: 311–324.

Bowman, E.H. (1978), 'Strategy, annual reports, and alchemy', *California Management Review*, vol. 20, no. 3: 64–71.

Bowman, E.H. and Haire, M. (1975), 'Strategic posture toward corporate social responsibility', *California Management Review*, vol. 18, no. 2: 49–58.

Brammer, S.M.A. and Millington, A. (2003), 'The effect of stakeholder preferences, organizational structure and industry type on corporate community involvement', *Journal of Business Ethics*, vol. 45, no. 3: 213–226.

Brand, V. and Slater, A. (2003), 'Using a qualitative approach to gain insights into the business ethics experiences of Australian managers in China', *Journal of Business Ethics*, vol. 45, no. 3: 167–182.

Brown J.S. and Duguid, P. (2000), *The social life of information*, Boston: Harvard Business School Press.

Brown, J.S. and Duguid, P. (1991), 'Organizational learning and communities-of-practice: Towards a unified view of working, learning and innovation', *Organization Science*, vol. 2, no. 1: 40–57.

Brunsson, N. (1993), 'Ideas and actions: Justification and hypocrisy as alternatives to control', *Accounting Organizations and Society*, vol. 18, no. 6: 489–506.

Brunsson, N. (2002), *The organization of hypocrisy. Talk, decisions and actions in organizations* (2nd ed.), Copenhagen: Copenhagen Business School Press.

Brunsson, N. (2003), 'Organized hypocrisy', in B. Czarniawska and G. Sevón (eds), *The northern lights. Organization theory in Scandinavia*, Copenhagen: Copenhagen Business School Press, 201–222.

Brunsson, N. and Jacobsson, B. (2002), *A world of standards*, Oxford: Oxford University Press.

Bryman, A. (1989), *Research methods and organization studies*, London: Unwin Hyman.

Buchholz, R. and Rosenthal, S. (1997), 'Business and society: What's in a name', *International Journal of Organizational Analysis*, vol. 5, no. 2: 180–201.

Burns, L.R. and Wholey, D.R. (1993), 'Adoption and abandonment of matrix management programs: Effects of organizational characteristics and inter-organizational networks', *Academy of Management Journal*, vol. 36, no. 1: 106–138.

Burrell, G. (1997), *Pandemonium: Towards a retro–organization theory*, London: Sage.

Burrell, G. and Morgan, G. (1979), *Sociological paradigms and organizational analysis*, London: Heinemann.

Callon, M. (1998a), 'Introduction: The embeddedness of economic markets in economics', in M. Callon (ed), *The laws of the markets*, Oxford: Blackwell, 1-57.

Callon, M. (1998b), 'An essay on framing and overflowing: economic externalities revisited by sociology', in M. Callon (ed), *The laws of the markets*, Oxford: Blackwell, 244-269.

Callon, M. and Muniesa, F. (2005), 'Economic markets as calculative collective devices', *Organization Studies*, vol. 26, no. 8: 1229–1250.

Calori, R. (1994), *A European management model: Beyond diversity*, New York: Prentice Hall.

Campbell, D. (2003), 'Intra– and intersectoral effects in environmental disclosures: Evidence for legitimacy theory?' *Business Strategy and the Environment*, vol. 12, no. 6: 357–371.

Cannon, T. (1994), *Corporate responsibility*, Harlow: Pearson Education.

Capron, M. and Quairel–Lanoizelée, F. (2004), *Mythes et réalités de l'entreprise responsible. Acteurs, enjeux, stratégies,* Paris: La Découverte.

Caron, M.-A. and Turcotte, M.-F. (in press), 'Forces de transformation et d'inertie dans la divulgation de la performance d'entreprise: Les rapports de développement durable', in C. Gendron (ed), *Les nouvelles formes de régulation*, Sainte-Foy: Presses de l'Université du Québec.

Carroll, A.B. (1979), 'A three–dimensional conceptual model of corporate performance', *Academy of Management Review*, vol. 4, no. 4: 497–405.

Carroll, A.B. (1991), 'The pyramid of corporate social responsibility: Toward the moral management of organizational stakeholders', *Business Horizons*, vol. 34, no. July–August: 39–48.

Carroll, A.B. (1994), 'Social issues in management research: Experts' views, analysis and commentary', *Business & Society*, vol. 33, no. 1: 5–29.

Carroll, A.B. (1999), 'Corporate social responsibility. Evolution of a definitional construct', *Business & Society*, vol. 38, no. 3: 268–295.

Carroll, A.B. and Buchholtz, A.K. (1999), *Business & society, ethics and stakeholder management* (fourth ed.), Cincinnati: South–Western.

Carroll, C.E. and McCombs, M. (2003), 'Agenda–setting effects of business news on the public's images and opinions about major corporations', *Corporate Reputation Review*, vol. 6, no. 1: 36–46.

Cerin, P. and Dobers, P. (2000), 'What does the 'Dow Jones Sustainability Group Index' tell us', paper presented at the Business Strategy and the Environment Conference, 18–19 September, Leeds: ERP Environment.

Cerne, A. (2003), *Integrating corporate social responsibility with marketing strategies in retailing,* unpublished licentiate thesis, Lund: Lund University.

Chapple, W. and Moon, J. (2005), 'Corporate social responsibility (CSR) in Asia: A seven country study of CSR web site reporting', *Business & Society*, vol. 44, no. 4: 415–441.

Charmaz, K. (2000), 'Grounded theory: Objectivist and constructivist methods', in N. Denzin and Y. Lincoln (eds), *Handbook of qualitative research* (2nd ed.), Thousand Oaks: Sage, 509–535.

Chia, R. (1995), 'From modern to postmodern organizational analysis', *Organization Studies*, vol. 16, no. 4: 580–604.

Chia, R. (1997), 'Thirty years on: From organisational structures to the organisation of thought', *Organization Studies*, vol. 18, no. 4: 685–707.

Christensen, C. (2002), 'Organizational embeddedness', unpublished manuscript.

Christensen, S. and Westenholz, A. (eds) (1995), *Medarbejdervalgte i danske virksomheter: Fra lønarbejder til borger i virksomhedssamfundet*, Copenhagen: Handelshøjskolens forlag.

Christensen, S., Karnøe, P. and Strandgaard Pedersen, J. (1997), 'Actors and institutions', *American Behavioral Scientist*, vol. 40, no. 4: 392–396.

Christensen, T. and Laegreid, P. (eds) (2002), *New public management: The transformation of ideas and practice*, Aldershot: Ashgate.

Christian Aid (2004), 'Behind the mask: The real face of corporate social responsibility', London: Christian Aid, <http://www.christian-aid.org.uk/indepth/0401csr/csr_behindthemask.pdf>, accessed 17 August 2006.

Christie, P.M.J., Kwon, I.W.G., Stoeberl, P.A. and Baumhart, R. (2003), 'A cross-cultural comparison of ethical attitudes of business managers: India, Korea and the United States', *Journal of Business Ethics*, vol. 46, no. 3: 263–287.

Citigroup (2003), 'Citigroup and the issues', <http://www.citigroup.com/citigroup/corporate/issues/com.htm>, accessed 7 February 2003.

Clegg, S. and Palmer, G. (1996), *The politics of management knowledge*, London: Sage.

Cochoy, F. and Vabre, M. (2004), 'From stakeholder to stakesliders: The resistible implementation of corporate social responsibility in a French mining company', paper presented at the 2nd ADERSE Conference, Toulouse, 21–22 October.

Coffey, B. and Wang, J. (1998), 'Board diversity and managerial control as predictors of corporate social performance', *Journal of Business Ethics*, vol. 17, no. 14; 1595–1593.

Cohen, M., March, J.G. and Olsen, J.P. (1972), 'A garbage can model of organizational choice', *Administrative Science Quarterly*, vol. 17, no. 1: 1–25.

Colyvas, J. and Powell, W.W. (2005), 'Roads to institutionalization', in B. Staw (ed), *Research in organizational behaviour*, vol. 27, Greenwich: JAI Press, 305–353.

Cook, T. and Emler, N. (1999), 'Bottom–up versus top–down evaluations of candidates' managerial potential: An experimental study', *Journal of Occupational and Organizational Psychology*, vol. 72, no. 4: 423–439.

Cooper, C. (1999), 'The changing psychological contract at work', *European Business Journal*, vol. 11, no. 3: 115–118.

Cooren, F. (1999), 'Applying socio–semiotics to organizational communication', *Management Communication Quarterly*, vol. 13, no. 2: 294–304.

Corporate Watch (2006), 'What's wrong with corporate social responsibility?', <http://www.corporatewatch.org/?lid=2670>, accessed 17 August 2006.

Courtis, J.K. (1995), 'Readability of annual reports: Western versus Asian evidence', *Accounting, Auditing & Accountability Journal*, vol. 8, no. 2: 4–17.

Cronin, C. and Zappala, G. (2001), 'The coming of age of corporate community involvement: An examination of trends in Australia's top companies', working paper no. 6, Camperdown: The Smith Family.

Crouch, C. and Streeck, W. (eds) (1997), *Political economy of modern capitalism: Mapping convergence and diversity*, London: Sage.

Crowther, D. (2004), 'Limited liability or limited responsibility?', in D. Crowther and L. Rayman–Bacchus (eds), *Perspectives on corporate social responsibility*, Aldershot: Ashgate, 42–58.

Crowther, D. and Rayman–Bacchus, L. (eds) (2004a), *Perspectives on corporate social responsibility*, Aldershot: Ashgate.

Crowther, D. and Rayman–Bacchus, L. (2004b), 'Introduction: Perspectives on corporate social responsibility' in D. Crowther and L. Rayman–Bacchus (eds), *Perspectives on corporate social responsibility*, Aldershot: Ashgate, 1–20.

Crowther, D. and Rayman–Bacchus, L. (2004c), 'The future of corporate social responsibility', in D. Crowther and L. Rayman–Bacchus (eds), *Perspectives on corporate social responsibility*, Aldershot: Ashgate: 229–249.

Cyert, R.M. and March, J.G. (2003/1963), *A behavioral theory of the firm*. Oxford: Blackwell.

Czarniawska, B. (1997), *Narrating the organization. Dramas of institutional identity*, Chicago: University of Chicago Press.
Czarniawska, B. and Sevón, G. (eds) (1996), *Translating organizational change*, Berlin: Walter de Gruyter.
Czarniawska, B. and Sevón, G. (eds) (2005a), *Global ideas: How ideas, objects and practices travel in the global economy*, Malmö: Liber AB.
Czarniawska, B. and Sevón, G. (2005b), 'Translation is a vehicle, imitation its motor, and fashion sits at the wheel', in B. Czarniawska and G. Sevón (eds), *Global ideas: How ideas, objects and practices travel in the global economy*, Malmö: Liber AB, 7–12.
Czarniawska–Joerges, B. (1988), *Att handla med ord*, Stockholm: Carlssons Förlag.
d'Iribarne, P. (1989), *La logique de l'honneur*, Paris: Seuil.
Dale, B.G. (1999), *Managing quality*, Blackwell: Oxford.
David, C. (2001), 'Mythmaking in annual reports', *Journal of Business and Technical Communication*, vol. 15, no. 2: 195–222.
Davis, K. (1960), 'Can business afford to ignore social responsibilities?', *California Management Review*, vol. 2, no. 3: 70–76.
Day, R. and Woodward, T. (2004), 'Disclosure of information about employees in the Directors' report of UK published financial statements', *Accounting Forum*, vol. 28, no. 1: 43–59.
de Bakker, F.G.A., Groenewegen, P. and den Hond, F. (2005), 'A bibliometric analysis of 30 years of research and theory on corporate social responsibility and corporate social performance', *Business & Society*, vol. 44, no. 3: 283–317.
de Gilder, D., Schuyt, T. and Breedijk, M. (2005), 'Effects of an employee volunteering program on the work force: The ABN–AMRO Case', *Journal of Business Ethics*, vol. 61, no. 2: 143–152.
de Nooy, W., Mrvar, A. and Batagelj, V. (2005), *Exploratory social network analysis with Pajek*, Cambridge: Cambridge University Press.
Dearborn, D. and Simon, H. (1958), 'Selective perception: A note on the departmental identification of executives', *Sociometry*, vol. 21, no. 2: 140–144.
Deephouse, D.L. (2000) 'Media reputation as a strategic resource: An integration of mass communication and resource–based theories', *Journal of Management*, vol. 26, no. 6: 1091–1112.
Déjean, F. (2005), *L'investissement socialement responsable. Etude du cas français*, Paris: Vuibert.
Déjean, F., Gond, J.–P. and Leca, B. (2004), 'Measuring the unmeasured: An institutional entrepreneur strategy in an emerging industry', *Human Relations*, vol. 57, no. 6: 741–764.
del Brio, J.A., Fernández, E., Junqquera, B. and Vázquez, C.J. (2001), 'Motivations for adopting the ISO 14001 standard: A study of Spanish industrial companies', *Environmental Quality Management*, vol. 10, no. 4: 13–28.
Delmas, M. (2002), 'Stakeholders and competitive advantage: The case of ISO 14001', *Production and Operations Management*, vol. 10, no. 3: 343–358.

Delmas, M.A. and Toffel, M.W. (2004), 'Stakeholders and environmental management practices: An institutional framework', *Business Strategy and the Environment*, vol. 13, no. 4: 209–222.

den Hond, F. and de Bakker, F.G.A. (2007), 'Ideologically motivated activism: How activist groups influence corporate social change activities', *Academy of Managament Review*, vol. 32, no. 3: in press.

Desai, A. and Rittenburg, T. (1997), 'Global ethics: An integrative framework for MNEs', *Journal of Business Ethics*, vol. 16, no. 8: 791–800.

Dickson, M.W., Smith, D.B., Grojean, M.W. and Ehrhart, M. (2001), 'An organizational climate regarding ethics: The outcome of leader values and the practices that reflect them', *Leadership Quarterly*, vol. 12, no. 2: 197–217.

DiMaggio, P. (2001), *The twenty-first century firm: Changing economic organization in international perspective*, Princeton: Princeton University Press.

DiMaggio, P.J. and Powell, W.W. (1983), 'The iron cage revisited: Institutional isomorphism and collective rationality in organizational fields', *American Sociological Review*, vol. 48, no. 2: 147–160.

Djelic, M.-L. (1998), *Exporting the American model: The postwar transformation of European Business*, Oxford: Oxford University Press.

Djelic, M.-L. and Quack, S. (eds) (2003), *Globalization and institutions: Redefining the rules of the economic game*, Cheltenham: Edward Elgar.

Djelic, M.-L. and Zarlowski, P. (2005), 'Entreprises et gouvernance en France: Perspectives historiques et évolutions récentes', *Sociologie du travail*, no. 47: 451–469.

DOM (2002), 'Erfaringer med Blomsten. En analyse af danske tekstil- og beklædningsvirksomheders erfaringer med opnåelse af EU–Blomsten', Copenhagen: Department of Operations Management (DOM), Copenhagen Business School.

Donaldson, T. and Preston, L.E. (1995), 'The stakeholder theory of the corporation: Concepts, evidence and implications', *Academy of Management Review*, vol. 20, no. 1: 65–91.

Drucker, P.F. (1954), 'The responsibilities of management', *Harper's Magazine*, vol. 209, no. 1254: 67–72.

Drucker, P.F. (1984), 'The new meaning of corporate social responsibility', *California Management Review*, vol. 26, no. 2: 53–63.

Dubbink, W. (2004), 'The fragile structure of free–market society: The radical implications of corporate social responsibility', *Business Ethics Quarterly*, vol. 14, no. 1: 23–46.

Dunham, L., Freeman, R. Liedtka, J. (2006), 'Enhancing stakeholder practice: A particularized exploration of community', *Business Ethics Quarterly*, vol. 16, no. 1: 23–42.

Dunn, C. (1991), 'Are corporations inherently wicked?', *Business Horizons*, vol. 34, no. 4: 3–8.

Dutton, J. and Dukerich, J. (1991), 'Keeping an eye on the mirror: Image and identity in organizational adaptation', *Academy of Management Journal*, vol. 34, no. 3: 517–554.

Easterbrook, F.H. and Fishel, D.R. (1991), *The economic structure of corporate law*, Cambridge, MA: Harvard University Press.

Elden, M. and Levin, M. (1991), 'Co–generative learning. Bringing participation into action research', in W.F. Whyte (ed.), *Participatory action research*, Newbury Park: Sage, 127–142.

Elkington, J. (1994), 'Towards the sustainable corporation. Win–win–win business strategies for sustainable development', *California Management Review*, vol. 36, no. 2: 90–100.

Elsbach, K.D. (1994), 'Managing organizational legitimacy in the California cattle industry: The construction and effectiveness of verbal accounts', *Administrative Science Quarterly*, vol. 39, no. 1: 57–88.

Elsbach, K.D. and Sutton, R.I. (1992), 'Acquiring organizational legitimacy through illegitimate actions: A marriage of institutional and impression management theories', *Academy of Management Journal*, vol. 35, no. 4: 699–738.

Engwall, L. (1999), 'The carriers of European management ideas', CEMP report no. 7, Uppsala: Uppsala University.

Entine, J. (2003), 'The myth of social investing: A critique of its practice and consequences for corporate social performance research', *Organization & Environment*, vol. 16, no. 3: 352–368.

EPA (1998), 'Environmental labelling issues, policies, and practices worldwide', project number EPA 742–R–98–009, Washington (DC): United States Environmental Protection Agency (EPA), Office of Prevention, Pesticides and Toxic Substances.

Epstein, M.J. and Roy, M.J. (2001), 'Sustainability in action: Identifying and measuring the key performance drivers', *Long Range Planning*, vol. 34, no. 5: 585–604.

Erlingsdóttir, G. and Lindberg, K. (2005), 'Isomorphism, isopraxism, and isonymism: Complementary or competing processes?', in B. Czarniawska and G. Sevón (eds), *Global ideas. How ideas, objects and practices travel in the global economy*, Malmö: Liber AB, 47–70.

Ernst, B. and Kieser, A. (2002), 'In search for explanations for the consultants explosion', in K. Sahlin–Andersson and L. Engwall (eds), *The expansion of management knowledge: Carriers, flows and sources*, Stanford: Stanford University Press, 47–73.

European Commission (EC) (2001), 'Promoting a European framework for corporate social responsibility', Brussels: European Commission, <http://europa.eu.int/comm/employment_social/soc-dial/csr/greenpaper_en.pdf>, accessed 29 September 2004.

European Commission (EC) (2002), 'Communication from the Commission concerning corporate social responsibility: A business contribution to sustainable development', COM(2002) 347 final, Brussels: Commission of the European Communities, <http://ec.europa.eu/employment_social/soc-dial/csr/csr2002_en.pdf>, accessed 19 September 2006.

Fairclough, N. (1995), *Critical discourse analysis*, London: Longman.

Fauset, C. (2006), 'Dear stakeholder', in Corporate Watch, 'What's wrong with Corporate Social Responsibility?', <http://www.corporatewatch.org/?lid=2670>, accessed 17 August 2006.

Férone, G. (2004), 'L'évaluation environnementale et sociale', presentation at the conference 'Comment évaluer la responsabilité sociale des entreprises? Rating social et bilan sociétal: 2 outils innovants', Paris: Maison des Essec, 29 April 2004.

Férone, G., d'Arcimoles, C.–H., Bello, P. and Sassemou, N. (2001), *Le développement durable: Des enjeux stratégiques pour les enterprises*, Paris: Editions d'Organisation.

Férone, G., Debas, D., and Génin, A.–S. (2004), *Ce que développement durable veut dire*, Paris: Editions d'Organisation.

Ferraro, F., Pfeffer, J. and Sutton, R.I. (2005), 'Economic language and assumptions: How theories can become self–fulfilling', *Academy of Management Review*, vol. 30, no. 1: 8–24.

Fineman, S. and Clarke, K. (1996), 'Green stakeholders. Industry interpretations and response', *Journal of Management Studies*, vol. 33, no. 6: 715–730.

Fiorentini, G. (2002), 'L'accountability nelle aziende nonprofit', in S. Zamagni (ed), *Il nonprofit italiano al bivio*, Milan: Egea, 101–152.

Fiss, P.C. and Hirsch, P.M. (2005), 'The discourse of globalization: Framing and sensemaking of an emerging concept', *American Sociological Review*, vol. 70, no. 1: 29–52.

Fombrun, C.J., Gardberg, N.A. and Barnett, M.L. (2000), 'Opportunity platforms and safety nets: Corporate citizenship and reputational risk', *Business and Society Review*, vol. 105, no. 1: 85–106.

Frederick, W. (1960), 'The growing concern over business responsibility', *California Management Review*, vol. 2, no. 4: 54–61.

Frederick, W. and Weber, J. (1987), 'The values of corporate managers and their critics', in W. Frederick (ed), *Research in corporate social performance and policy*, vol. 9, Greenwich: JAI Press, 131–152.

Freeman, R.E. (1984), *Strategic management: A stakeholder approach*, Boston, MA: Pitman.

Freeman, R.E. (1998), 'Poverty and the politics of capitalism', *Business Ethics Quarterly*, vol. 1, no. 1: 31–35.

Freeman, R.E. (1994), 'The politics of stakeholder theory: some future directions', *Business Ethics Quarterly*, vol. 4, no. 4: 409–421.

Freeman, R.E. and McVea, J. (2001), 'A stakeholder approach to strategic management', in M.A. Hitt, R.E. Freeman and J.S. Harrison (eds), *The Blackwell handbook of strategic management*, Oxford: Blackwell, 189–207.

Freeman, R.E. and Ramakrishna, S.V. (2006), 'A new approach to CSR: Company stakeholder responsibility', in A. Kakabadse and M. Morsing (eds), *Corporate social responsibility: Reconciling aspiration with application*, Basingstoke: Palgrave MacMillan, 9–23.

Freiman, J. and Walther, M. (2001), 'The impacts of corporate environmental management systems: A comparison of EMAS and ISO 14001', *Greener Management International*, no. 36: 91–103.

Frenkel, M. (2005), 'Something new, something old, something borrowed: The cross–national translation of the "Family Friendly Organisation" in Israel', in Czarniawska, B. and Sevón, G. (eds), *Global ideas. How ideas, objects and practices travel in the global economy*, Malmö: Liber AB, 147–166.

Friedland, R. and Alford, R.R. (1991), 'Bringing society back in: Symbols, practices and institutional contradictions', in W.W. Powell and P.J. DiMaggio (eds), *The new institutionalism in organizational analysis*, Chicago: University of Chicago Press, 232–263.

Friedman, M. (1962), *Capitalism and freedom*, Chicago: University of Chicago Press.

Friedman, M. (1970), 'The social responsibility of business is to increase its profits', *New York Times Magazine*, 13 September: 22–26.

Friedman, V.J. and Antal, A.B. (2005), 'Negotiating reality. A theory of action approach to intercultural competence', *Management Learning*, vol. 36, no. 1: 69–86.

Frost, P. and Mitchell, V. (1995), *Managerial reality: Balancing technique, practice and values*, New York: Harper Collins.

Frost, P., Moore, L., Reis L., Lundberg, C. and Martin, J. (1991), *Reframing organisational culture*, Newbury Park: Sage.

Fukukawa, K. and Moon, J. (2004), 'A Japanese model of corporate social responsibility? A study of website reporting', *Journal of Corporate Citizenship*, no. 16: 45–59.

Galbreath, J. (2006), 'Corporate social responsibility strategy: Strategic options, global considerations', *Corporate Governance*, vol. 6, no. 2: 175–187.

Gallagher, J.A. and Goodstein, J. (2002), 'Fulfilling institutional responsibilities in health care: Organizational ethics and the role of mission discernment', *Business Ethics Quarterly*, vol. 12, no. 4: 433–450.

Gallarotti, G.M. (1995), 'It pays to be green: The managerial incentive structure and environmentally sound strategies', *The Columbia Journal of World Business*, vol. 30, no. 4: 39–57.

Gardner, W.L. and Martinko, M.J. (1988), 'Impression management in organizations', *Journal of Management*, vol. 14, no. 2: 321–338.

Garriga, E. and Melé, D. (2004), 'Corporate social responsibility theories: Mapping the territory', *Journal of Business Ethics*, vol. 53, no. 1–2: 51–71.

Garud, R., Jain, S. and Kumaraswamy, A. (2002), 'Institutional entrepreneurship in the sponsorship of common technological standards: The case of Sun Microsystems and Java', *Academy of Management Journal*, vol. 45, no. 1: 196–214.

Gawer, A. and Cusumano, M.A. (2002), *Platform leadership: How Intel, Microsoft, and Cisco drive industry innovation*, Cambridge: Harvard University School Press.

Gendron, C., Lapointe, A. and Turcotte, M.–F. (2004), 'Social responsibility and the regulation of the global firm', *Relations Industrielles–Industrial Relations*, vol. 59, no. 1: 73–100.

Ghoshal, S. (2005), 'Bad management theories are destroying good management practices', *Academy of Management Learning & Education*, vol. 4, no. 1: 75–91.

Gill, R.W.T. and Leinbach, L.J. (1983), 'Corporate social responsibility in Hong-Kong', *California Management Review*, vol. 25, no. 2: 107–123.

Glaser, B. (1992), *Basics of grounded theory analysis: Emergence vs. forcing*, Mill Valley: The Sociology Press.

Gond, J.-P. and Crane, A. (2006), 'Explaining a recurrently failing concept: Corporate social performance disoriented', ICCSR research paper, Nottingham: ICCSR.

Gond, J.-P. and Leca, B. (2004), 'La construction d'une notation sociale des entreprises, ou l'histoire d'ARESE', *Sciences de la Société*, no. 62: 188–207.

Gordon, G. and DiTomaso, N. (1992), 'Predicting corporate performance from organizational culture', *Journal of Management Studies*, vol. 29, no. 6: 783–798.

Gordon, J.N. and Roe, M.J. (eds) (2004), *Convergence and persistence in corporate governance*, Cambridge: Cambridge University Press.

Grafström, M. (2005), 'Nyheter på ekonomiska', in B. Rombach (ed), *Den framgångsrika ekonomiskan*, Stockholm: Santérus, 110–129.

Grant, D., Hardy, C., Oswick, C. and Putnam, L. (eds) (2004), *The Sage handbook of organizational discourse*, London: Sage.

Gray, E. and Hay, R. (1974), 'Social responsibility of business managers', *Academy of Management Journal*, vol. 17. no. 1: 135–143.

Gray, R., Kouhy, R. and Lavers, S. (1995), 'Corporate social and environmental reporting: A review of the literature and a longitudinal study of UK disclosure', *Accounting, Auditing & Accountability Journal*, vol. 8, no. 2: 47–77.

Green, S. (2004), 'A rhetorical theory of diffusion', *Academy of Management Review*, vol. 29, no. 4: 653–669.

Greenwood, D.J. and Levin, M. (1998), *Introduction to action research. Social research for social change*, Thousand Oaks: Sage.

Greenwood, R., Suddaby, R. and Hinings, C.R. (2002), 'Theorizing change: The role of professional associations in the transformation of institutionalized fields', *Academy of Management Journal*, vol. 45, no. 1: 58–80.

Greer, J. and Bruno, K. (1996), *Greenwash: The reality behind corporate environmentalism*, Penang: Third World Network.

Grey, F. (2002), 'Can ethical investment be profitable?', presentation at the 'Ethics on toast: A Wilderness Society breakfast', Perth, March 11, 2002.

GRI (2002), *A historic collaborative achievement: Inauguration of the Global Reporting Initiative,* Boston: GRI.

Griffin, J.J. and Mahon, J.F. (1997), 'The corporate social performance and corporate financial performance debate: Twenty–five years of incomparable research', *Business & Society*, vol. 36, no. 1: 5–31.

Guay, T., Doh, J.P. and Sinclair, G. (2004), 'Non–governmental organizations, shareholder activism, and socially responsible investments: Ethical, strategic, and governance implications', *Journal of Business Ethics*, vol. 52, no. 1: 125–139.

Guba, E.G. and Lincoln, Y.S. (1998), 'Competing paradigms in qualitative research', in N. Denzin and Y. Lincoln (eds), *The landscape of qualitative research*, Thousand Oaks: Sage, 195–220.

Habisch, A., Jonker, J., Wegner, M. and Schmidpeter, R. (eds) (2005), *Corporate social responsibility across Europe*, Heidelberg: Springer.

Hackston, D. and Milne, M.J. (1996), 'Some determinants of social and environmental disclosures in New Zealand companies', *Accounting, Auditing and Accountability Journal*, vol. 9, no. 1: 77–108.

Hall, P.A. and Soskice, D. (eds) (2001), *Varieties of capitalism. The institutional foundations of comparative advantage*, Oxford: Oxford University Press.

Halliday, M.A.K. and Matthiessen, C. (2004), *An introduction to functional grammar*, London: Arnold.

Hampden–Turner, C.M. (2000), 'What we know about cross–cultural management after thirty years', in D. Lynch and A. Pilbeam (eds) *Heritage and progress. From the past to the future in intercultural understanding*, Bath: LTS Training, 17–27.

Hampden–Turner, C.M. and Trompenaars, F. (2000), *Building cross–cultural competence*, New Haven: Yale University Press.

Hamschmidt, J. and Dyllick, T. (2001), 'ISO 14001: profitable? Yes! But is it eco-effective?', *Greener Management International*, no. 34: 43–54.

Hatchuel, A. (2005), 'Towards an epistemology of collective action: Management research as a responsive and actionable discipline', *European Management Review*, vol. 2, no. 1: 36–47.

Hatchuel, A. and Weil, B. (1995). *Experts in organizations. A knowledge based perspective on organizational change*, Berlin: Walter de Gruyter.

Haufler, V. (2001), *A public role for the private sector: Industry self–regulation in a global economy*, Washington (DC): Carnegie Endowment for International Peace.

Heald, M. (1957), 'Management's responsibility to society: The growth of an idea', *Business History Review*, vol. 31, no. 4: 375–384.

Hecht, L. (2001), 'Role conflict and role overload: Different concepts, different consequences?', *Sociological Inquiry*, vol. 71, no. 1: 111–121.

Hemingway, C.A. and MacLagan, P.W. (2004), 'Managers' personal values as drivers of corporate social responsibility', *Journal of Business Ethics*, vol. 50, no. 1: 33–44.

Henderson, D. (2001), *Misguided virtue: False notions of corporate social responsibility*, London: Institute of Economic Affairs.

Henderson, R.M. and Clark, K.B. (1990), 'Architectural innovation: The reconfiguration of existing product technologies and the failure of established firms', *Administrative Science Quarterly*, vol. 35, no. 1: 9–30.

Henriques, A. (2001), 'Civil society and social auditing', *Business Ethics. A European Review*, vol. 10, no. 1: 40–44.

Henthorne, T., Robin, D. and Reidenbach, R. (1992), 'Identifying the gaps in ethical perceptions between managers and salespersons: A multidimensional approach', *Journal of Business Ethics*, vol.11, no. 11: 849–896.

Heugens, P.P.M.A.R., Lamertz, K. and Calmet, L. (2003), 'Strategic groups and corporate citizenship: Evidence from the Canadian brewing industry', *Journal of Corporate Citizenship*, no. 12: 75–92.

Hillary, R. (ed) (1997), *Environmental management systems and cleaner production*, Chichester: John Wiley.

Hills, J. and Welford, R. (2005), 'Coca–Cola and water in India', *Corporate Social Responsibility and Environmental Management*, vol. 12, no. 3: 168–177.

Hirsch, P.M. (1986), 'From ambushes to golden parachutes: Corporate takeovers as an instance of cultural framing and institutional integration', *American Journal of Sociology*, vol. 91, no. 4: 800–837.

Hirsch, P.M. and Levin, D.Z. (1999), 'Umbrella advocates versus validity police: A life–cycle model', *Organization Science*, vol. 10, no. 2: 199–212.

Hoedeman, O. (2002), 'Rio+ 10 and the greenwash of corporate globalization', *Development*, vol. 45, no. 3: 39–42.

Hofstede, G. (1980), *Culture's consequences: International differences in work-related values*, Beverly Hills: Sage.

Hofstede, G. (1998), 'Identifying organizational subcultures: An empirical approach', *Journal of Management Studies*, vol. 35, no. 1: 1–12.

Holland, J.H. (1995), *Hidden order: How adaptation builds complexity*, Reading: Addison-Wesley.

Hollway, W. (1991), *Work psychology and organizational behaviour*, London: Sage.

Hsieh, R. (2004), 'The obligations of transnational corporations: Rawlsian justice and the duty of assistance', *Business Ethics Quarterly*, vol. 14, no. 4: 643–662.

Hussain, S.S. (1999), 'The ethics of going green: The corporate social responsibility debate', *Business Strategy and the Environment*, vol. 8, no. 4: 203–210.

Hwang, H. and Powell, W.W. (2005), 'Institutions and entrepreneurship', in S.A. Alvarez, R. Agarwal and O. Sorenson (eds), *Handbook of entrepreneurial research*, Dordrecht: Kluwer, 179–210.

Hyland, K. (1998), 'Exploring corporate rhetoric: Meta–discourse in the CEO's letter', *Journal of Business Communication*, vol. 35, no. 2: 224–245.

Ibrahim, N. and Angelidis, J. (1995), 'The corporate social responsiveness orientation of board members: Are there differences between inside and outside directors?', *Journal of Business Ethics*, vol. 14, no. 5: 405–410.

Idowu, S.O. and Towler, B.A. (2004), 'A comparative study of the contents of corporate social responsibility reports of UK companies', *Management of Environmental Quality*, vol. 15, no. 4: 420–437.

Igalens, J. (2004), 'Comment évaluer les rapports de développement durable', *Revue Française de Gestion*, vol. 30, no. 152: 151–166.

Inglehart, R. (1997), *Modernization and post–modernization: Cultural, economic, and political change in 43 societies*, Princeton: Princeton University Press.

Irgens, E.J. (2003), 'Change projects as creators and carriers of knowledge', in F. McGrath and D. Remenyi (eds), *Proceedings of the fourth European conference on knowledge management*, Reading: MCIL, 507–514.

International Standards Organization (ISO) (2004), 'Working report on social responsibility', ISO Advisory Group on Social Responsibility, <http://inni.pacinst.org/inni/corporate_social_responsibility/WorkingReportonSR.pdf>.

Ite, U. (2004), 'Multinationals and corporate social responsibility in developing countries: A case study of Nigeria', *Corporate Social Responsibility and Environmental Management*, vol. 11, no. 1: 1–11.

Jackson, N. and Carter, P. (2000), *Rethinking organisational behaviour*, London: Financial Times.

Jackson, T. (2002), *International HRM: A cross–cultural approach*, London: Sage.

Jaffe, A.B. and Palmer, K. (1997), 'Environmental regulation and innovation: A panel data study', *Review of Economics and Statistics*, vol. 79, no. 4: 610–619.

Jenkins, H. and Yakovleva, N. (2006), 'Corporate social responsibility in the mining industry: Exploring trends in social and environmental disclosure', *Journal of Cleaner Production*, vol. 14, no. 3–4: 271–284.

Jenkins, R. (2001), *Corporate codes of conduct: Self-regulation in a global economy. Technology*, Geneva: United Nations Research Institute for Social Development, Business and Society Programme. No. 2.

Jenkins, R. (2005), 'Globalization, corporate social responsibility and poverty', *International Affairs*, vol. 81, no. 3: 525–540.

Jensen, M.C. (2002), 'Value maximization, stakeholder theory, and the corporate objective function', *Business Ethics Quarterly*, vol. 12, no. 2: 235–256.

Johnson, J. and Powell, P. (1994), 'Decision making, risk and gender: Are managers different?' *British Journal of Management*, vol. 5, no. 2: 123–138.

Jones, M.T. (1999), 'The institutional determinants of social responsibility', *Journal of Business Ethics*, vol. 20, no. 2: 163–179.

Joyner, B.E. and Payne, D. (2002), 'Evolution and implementation: A study of values, business ethics and corporate social responsibility', *Journal of Business Ethics*, vol. 41, no. 4: 297–311.

Judd, V.C. and Tims, B.J. (1991), 'How annual reports communicate a customer orientation', *Industrial Marketing Management*, vol. 20, no. 4: 353–360.

JUSE Problem Solving Group (ed) (1991), *TQC solutions: the 14–step process*, Cambridge: Productivity Press.

Kaptein, M. and van Tulder, R. (2003), 'Toward effective stakeholder dialogue', *Business and Society Review*, vol. 108, no. 2: 203–224.

Kaufman, A., Zacharias, L. and Karson, M. (1995), *Managers vs. owners. The struggle for corporate control in American democracy*, New York: Oxford University Press.

Kell, G. (2003), 'The Global Compact. Origins, operations, progress, challenges', *Journal of Corporate Citizenship*, no. 11: 35–49.

Kelley, H.H. (1972), 'Attribution in social interaction', in E.E. Jones, D.E. Kanouse, H.H. Kelley, R.E. Nisbett, S. Valins and B. Weiner (eds), *Attribution: Perceiving the causes of behaviour*, Morristown: General Learning Press, 1–26.

Kelley, H.H. and Stahelski, A.J. (1970), 'Social interaction basis of cooperators' and competitors' beliefs about others', *Journal of Personality and Social Psychology*, vol. 16, no. 1: 66–91.

Kieser, A. (2002), 'Managers as marionettes? Using fashion theories to explain the success of consultancies', in M. Kipping and L. Engwall (eds), *Management consulting: Emergence and dynamics of a knowledge industry*, Oxford: Oxford University Press, 167–183.

Kipping, M. (1999), 'American management consulting companies in Western Europe, 1920 to 1990: Products, reputation, and relationships', *Business History Review*, vol. 73, no. 2: 190–220.

Kipping, M. and Engwall, L. (eds) (2002), *Management consulting. The emergence and dynamics of a knowledge industry*, Oxford: Oxford University Press.

Kirkland, L.H. and Thompson, D. (1999), 'Challenges in designing, implementing and operating an environmental management system', *Business Strategy and the Environment*, vol. 8, no. 2: 128–143.

Kjaer, P. and Langer, R. (2005), 'Infused with news value: Management, managerial knowledge and the institutionalization of business news', *Scandinavian Journal of Management*, vol. 21, no. 2: 209–233.

Klein, J.G., Smith, N.C. and John, A. (2004), 'Why we boycott: Consumer motivations for boycott participation', *Journal of Marketing*, vol. 68, no. 3: 92–109.

Kleiner, T. (2003), 'Building up an asset management industry: Forays of an Anglo–Saxon logic into the French business system', in M.–L. Djelic and S. Quack (eds), *Globalization and Institutions: Redefining the Rules of the Economic Game*, Cheltenham: Edward Elgar, 57–82.

Klenke, K. (2005), 'Corporate values as multi–level, multi–domain antecedents of leader behaviors', *International Journal of Manpower*, vol. 26, no. 1: 50–66.

Kolk, A. (2000), *Economics of environmental management*, Harlow: Pearson Education.

Kolk, A. (2003), 'Trends in sustainability reporting by the Fortune Global 250', *Business Strategy and the Environment*, vol. 12, no. 5: 279–291.

Kolk, A. and van Tulder, R. (2006), 'Poverty alleviation as business strategy? Evaluating commitments of frontrunner multinational corporations', *World Development*, vol. 34, no. 5: 789–801.

Korka, M. (2005), 'Corporate social responsibility in Romania: From theory to practice', *Transition Studies Review*, vol. 12, no. 1: 47–57.

Kotler, P. and Lee, N. (2004), *Corporate social responsibility: Doing the most good for your company and your cause*, Hoboken: John Wiley.

Kozlowski, S.W.J. and Klein, K.J. (2000), 'A levels approach to theory and research in organizations', in K.J. Klein and S.W.J. Kozlowski (eds), *Multilevel theory, research and methods in organizations*, San Francisco: Jossey–Bass, 3–90.

Latour, B. (1986), 'The powers of associations', in Law. J. (ed), *Power, action and belief*, London: Routledge and Kegan Paul, 261–277.

La Porta, R., Lopez–de–Silanes, F., Shleifer, A. and Vishny, R.W. (1997), 'Trust in large organizations', *American Economic Review*, vol. 87, no. 2: 333–338.

Lawrence, T.B. and Phillips, N. (2004), 'From Moby Dick to Free Willy: Macro–cultural discourse and institutional entrepreneurship in emerging institutional fields', *Organization*, vol. 11, no. 5: 689–711.

Lee, L. and Higgins, C. (2001), 'Corporate volunteering: Ad hoc interaction or route to dialogue and partnership?', *Journal of Corporate Citizenship*, no. 4: 79–90.

Lee, T. (1994), 'The changing form of the corporate annual report', *The Accounting Historians Journal*, vol. 21, no. 1: 215–232.

Leer–Salvesen, T. (2000), 'An ombudsman to control companies? The Norwegian experience', *Corporate Europe Observer* [website], no. 7, <http://www.corporateeurope.org/observer7/norway.html>, accessed 29 June 2004.

Leipziger, D. (2003), *The corporate responsibility code book*, Sheffield: Greenleaf.

Levitt, T. (1958), 'The danger of social responsibility', *Harvard Business Review*, vol. 36, no. 5: 41–50.

Liao–Troth, M. and Dunn, C. (1999), 'Social constructs and human service: Managerial sensemaking of volunteer motivation', *Voluntas*, vol. 10, no. 4: 345–362.
Littlejohn, S.W. (1992), *Theories of human communication*, Belmont: Wadsworth.
Lockett, A., Moon, J. and Visser, W. (2006), 'Corporate social responsibility in management research: Focus, nature, salience and sources of influence', *Journal of Management Studies*, vol. 43, no. 1: 115–136.
Louche, C. (2004), *Ethical investment. Processes and mechanisms of institutionalisation in the Netherlands 1990–2002*, PhD thesis, Rotterdam: Erasmus Universiteit.
Louche, C. and Tagger, J. (2005), 'Socially responsible investment. Now and looking forward', *Public Service Review*, no. 9: 20–22.
Lucas, J.R. (1993), *Responsibility*, Oxford: Clarendon Press.
Lukka, P. (2000), 'Employee volunteering: A literature review', working paper, London: Institute for Volunteering Research.
Lyons, J. (1995), *Linguistic semantics: An introduction*, Cambridge: Cambridge University Press.
MacKenzie, D. and Millo, Y. (2003), 'Constructing a market, performing a theory: The historical sociology of a financial derivatives exchange', *American Review of Sociology*, vol. 109, no. 1: 107–145.
Maguire, S., Hardy, C. and Lawrence, T.B. (2004), 'Institutional entrepreneurship in emerging fields: HIV/AIDS treatment advocacy in Canada', *Academy of Management Journal*, vol. 47, no. 5: 657–679.
Maignan, I. (2001), 'Consumers' perceptions of corporate social responsibilities: A cross–cultural comparison', *Journal of Business Ethics*, vol. 30, no. 1: 57–72.
Maignan, I. and Ferrell, O.C. (2001), 'Corporate citizenship as a marketing instrument: Concepts, evidence and research directions', *European Journal of Marketing*, vol. 19, no. 3: 205–230.
Maignan, I. and Ferrell, O.C. (2004), 'Corporate social responsibility and marketing: An integrative framework', *Journal of the Academy of Marketing Science*, vol. 32, no. 1: 3–19.
Maignan, I. and Ralston, D.A. (2002), 'Corporate social responsibility in Europe and the US: Insights from businesses' self–presentations', *Journal of International Business Studies*, vol. 33, no. 3: 497–514.
Malavasi, D. (2005), 'Banks' annual reports: An analysis of the linguistic means used to express evaluation', paper presented at the 7th European Convention of the Association for Business Communication, Copenhagen, Denmark, 26–28 May.
Margolis, J.D. and Walsh, J.P (2001), *People and profits? The search for a link between a company's social and financial performance*, Mahwah: Lawrence Erlbaum.
Margolis, J.D. and Walsh, J.P. (2003), 'Misery loves companies: Rethinking social initiatives by business', *Administrative Science Quarterly*, vol. 48, no. 2: 268–305.
Martin, J. (1992), *Cultures in organizations: Three perspectives*, New York: Oxford University Press.

Matten, D. and Moon, J. (2004), 'Corporate social responsibility education in Europe', ICCSR working paper no. 33, Nottingham: ICCSR.
Matten, D. and Moon, J. (2005), 'A conceptual framework for understanding CSR' in A. Habisch, J. Jonker, M. Wegner and R. Schmidpeter (eds), *Corporate social responsibility across Europe*, Berlin: Springer: 335–356.
Matten, D., Crane, A. and Chapple, W. (2003), 'Behind the mask: Revealing the true face of corporate citizenship', *Journal of Business Ethics*, vol. 45, no. 1–2: 109–120.
May, R.C., Puffer, S.M. and McCarthy, D.J. (2005), 'Transferring management knowledge to Russia: A culturally based approach', *Academy of Management Executive*, vol. 19, no. 2: 24–35.
McCombs, M.E. and Shaw, D.L. (1972), 'The agenda–setting function of mass media', *Public Opinion Quarterly*, vol. 36, no. 2: 176–187.
McGuire, A. (2003). '"It was nothing." Extending evolutionary models of altruism by two social cognitive biases in judgments of the costs and benefits of helping', *Social Cognition*, vol. 21, no. 5: 363–384.
McIntosh, M., Thomas, R., Leipziger, D. and Coleman, G. (2003), *Living corporate citizenship: Strategic routes to socially responsible business*, Edinburgh: Prentice Hall.
McWilliams, A. and Siegel, D. (2000), 'Corporate social responsibility and financial performance: Correlation or misspecification?' *Strategic Management Journal*, vol. 21, no. 5: 603–609.
McWilliams, A. and Siegel, D. (2001), 'Corporate social responsibility: A theory of the firm perspective', *Academy of Management Review*, vol. 26, no. 1: 117–127.
McWilliams, A., Siegel, D.S. and Wright, P.M. (2006), 'Corporate social responsibility: Strategic implications', *Journal of Management Studies*, vol. 43, no. 1: 1–18.
Media Live (2006), 'European Business Readership Survey (E.B.R.S.) 2002', <http://www.medialive.ie/Comment/ebrs2002.html>, accessed 9 January 2006.
Meyer, A. (2001), 'What's in it for the customers? Successfully marketing of green clothes', *Business Strategy and Environment*, vol. 10, no. 5: 317–330.
Meyer, J.W. (1996), 'Otherhood: The promulgation and transmission of ideas in the modern organizational environment', in B. Czarniawska and G. Sevón (eds), *Translating organizational change*, Berlin: Walter de Gruyter, 241–252.
Meyer, J.W. and Rowan, B. (1977), 'Institutionalized organizations: Formal structure as myth and ceremony', *American Journal of Sociology*, vol. 83, no. 2: 340–363.
Meyerson, D. and Martin, J. (1987), 'Cultural change. An integration of three different views', *Journal of Management Studies*, vol. 24, no. 6: 623–647.
Micheletti, M. (2003), *Political virtue and shopping: Individuals, consumerism and collective action*, London: Palgrave Macmillan.
Micheletti, M. and Stolle, D. (2004), 'Swedish political consumers: Who they are and why they use the market as an arena for politics', in M. Boström, A. Føllesdal, M. Klintman, M. Michelletti and M.P. Sørensen (eds), *Political consumerism: Its motivations, power, and conditions in the Nordic countries and elsewhere*, Copenhagen: Nordic Council of Ministers, 145–164.

Michell, N.J. (1989), *The generous corporation: A political analysis of economic power*, Newhaven: Yale University Press.

Mikkilä, M., Kolehmainen, O. and Pukkala, T. (2005), 'Multi–attribute assessment of acceptability of operations in the pulp and paper industries', *Forest Policy and Economics*, vol. 7, no. 2: 227–243.

Miller, P. (2001), 'Governing by numbers: Why calculative practices matter', *Social Research*, vol. 68, no. 2: 379–396.

Miller, P. and O'Leary, T. (1987), 'Accounting and the construction of the governable person', *Accounting, Organizations and Society*, vol. 12, no. 3: 235–265.

Mintzberg, H. and Waters, J.A. (1985), 'Of strategies, deliberate and emergent', *Strategic Management Journal*, vol. 6, no. 3: 257–272.

Mohan, A. (2001), 'Corporate citizenship: Perspectives from India', *Journal of Corporate Citizenship*, no. 2: 107–117.

Mohan, A. (2006), 'Global corporate social responsibilities management in MNCs', *Journal of Business Strategies*, vol. 23, no. 1: 9–32.

Mohr, J.W. (1998), 'Measuring meaning structures', *Annual Review of Sociology*, vol. 24, no. 1: 345–370.

Mohr, J.W. (forthcoming), 'Implicit terrains: Meaning, measurement, and spatial metaphors in organizational theory', in J. Porac and M.J. Ventresca (eds), *Constructing industries and markets*, London: Elsevier Science.

Moon, J. (2005), 'United Kingdom: An explicit model business–society relations', in A. Habisch, J. Jonker, M. Wegner and R. Schmidpeter (eds), *Corporate social responsibility across Europe*, Heidelberg: Springer: 51–65.

Morgan, G. (1988), 'Accounting as reality construction: Towards a new epistemology for accounting practice', *Accounting, Organizations and Society*, vol. 13, no. 5: 477–485.

Morgan, G. (1997), *Images of organization: The executive edition* (2nd ed), San Francisco: Berrett–Koehler.

Morgen, S. (1994), 'Personalizing personnel decisions in feminist organizational theory and practice', *Human Relations*, vol. 47, no. 6: 665–684.

Morin, F. (2000), 'A transformation of the French model of shareholding and management', *Economy and Society*, vol. 29, no.1: 36–53.

Morrow, D. and Rondinelli, D. (2002), 'Adopting corporate environmental management systems: Motivations and results of ISO and EMAS certification', *European Management Journal*, vol. 20, no. 2: 159–171.

Mueller, F., Sillince, J., Harvey, C. and Howorth, C. (2003), '"A rounded picture is what we need": Rhetorical strategies, arguments, and the negotiation of change in a UK hospital trust', *Organization Studies*, vol. 25, no. 1: 75–93.

Muraskin, W. (1988), 'The silent epidemic: The social, ethical, and medical problems surrounding the fight against hepatitis–B', *Journal of Social History*, vol. 22, no. 2: 277–298.

National Centre on Volunteering (1996), 'Information leaflet', London: National Centre on Volunteering.

Neergaard, P. and Pedersen, E.R. (2003), 'Corporate social behaviour: Between the rules of the game and the law of the jungle', *Journal of Corporate Citizenship*, no. 12: 43-57.

Ness, H. (2003), 'The 'import' and 'export' of organizational recipes. How the car industry's management logics came to be used in Norwegian offshore plants', paper presented at the 19th EGOS Colloquium, Copenhagen, Denmark.

Neu, D., Warsame, H. and Pendwell, K. (1998), 'Managing public impressions: environmental disclosures in annual reports', *Accounting, Organizations and Society*, vol. 23, no. 3: 265–282.

Nielsen, R. (1992), *Arbejdsgiverens ledelsesret i EF–retlig belysnin. Studier i EF–rettens integration i dansk arbejdsret*, Copenhagen: Juristforbundets Forlag.

Nielsen, R. (1996), *Employers' prerogative in a European and Nordic perspective*, Copenhagen: Copenhagen Business School.

Oakes, L., Townley, B. and Cooper, D. (1998), 'Business planning as pedagogy: Language and control in a changing institutional field', *Administrative Science Quarterly*, vol. 43, no. 2: 257–292.

Oakland, J.S. (1993), *Total quality management: The route to improving performance*, Oxford: Butterworth–Heinemann.

Ohlsson, C. and Tengblad, S. (2004), 'Corporate social responsibility: The problem of securing external legitimacy in a globalized world', paper presented at the 20th EGOS Colloquium, Ljubljana, Slovenia, 1–3 July.

Oliver, C. (1991), 'Strategic responses to institutional processes', *Academy of Management Review*, vol. 16, no. 1: 145–179.

Oliver, C. (1992), 'The antecedents of deinstitutionalization', *Organization Studies*, vol. 13, no. 4: 563–588.

Oliver, C. (1997), 'Sustainable competitive advantage: Combining institutional and resource–based views', *Strategic Management Journal*, vol. 18, no. 9: 697–713.

Orlitzky, M., Schmidt, F.L. and Rynes, S.L. (2003), 'Corporate social and financial performance: A meta–analysis', *Organization Studies*, vol. 24, no. 3: 403–441.

Orr, J.E. (1996), *Talking about machines: An ethnography of a modern job*, Ithaca: ILR Press.

Osborne, D. and Gaebler, T. (1992), *Reinventing government*, Reading: Addison–Wesley.

Ostlund, L. (1977), 'Attitudes of managers toward corporate social policy', *California Management Review*, vol. 19, no.4: 35–49.

Ostroff, C., Shin, Y. and Kinicki, A. (2005), 'Multiple perspectives of congruence: relationships between value congruence and employee attitudes', *Journal of Organizational Behavior*, vol. 26, no. 6: 591–623.

Panapanaan, V.M., Linnanen, L., Karvonen, M.–M. and Phan, V.T. (2003), 'Roadmapping corporate social responsibility in Finnish companies', *Journal of Business Ethics*, vol. 44, no. 2–3: 133–148.

Pasquero, J. (1988), 'Comparative research: The case for middle–range methodologies', in J.E. Post, W.C. Frederick, M. Starik and D. Collins (eds), *Research in corporate social performance and policy. International and comparative studies*, vol. 10, Hoboken: John Wiley, 181–209.

Pasquero, J. (1997), 'Business ethics and national identity in Québec: Distinctiveness and directions', *Journal of Business Ethics*, vol. 16, no. 6: 621–633.

Pasquero, J. (2005), 'La responsabilité sociale de l'entreprise comme objet des sciences de gestion: Un regard historique', in M.–F. Turcotte and A. Salmon (eds),

Responsabilité sociale et environnementale de l'entreprise, Sainte–Foy (Québec): Presses de l'Université du Québec, 80–111.

Patterson, M., Warr, P. and West, M. (2004), 'Organizational climate and company productivity: The role of employee affect and employee level', *Journal of Occupational and Organizational Psychology*, vol. 77, no. 2: 193–216.

Peattie, K. and Charter, M. (1997), 'Green Marketing', in P. McDonagh and A. Prothero (eds), *Green management. A reader*, London: The Dryden Press, 388–412.

Pedersen, E.R. (2006), 'Making corporate social responsibility (CSR) operable: How companies translate stakeholder dialogue into practice', *Business and Society Review*, vol. 111, no. 2: 137–163.

Pedersen, E.R. and Neergaard, P. (2006), 'Caveat Emptor. Let the buyer beware! Environmental labelling and the limitations of 'green' consumerism', *Business Strategy and the Environment*, vol. 15, no. 1: 15–29.

Pedersen, E.R., Neergaard, P., Andersen, M., Bech, L. and Olsson, M.L. (2004), *Miljømærkningens pris. En analyse af gevinster og omkostninger ved miljømærkning*, Copenhagen: Danish Environmental Protection Agency.

Perrini, F. (2005), 'Building a European portrait of corporate social responsibility reporting', *European Management Journal*, vol. 23, no. 6: 611–627.

Peters, B.G. (1996), *The future of governing: Four emerging models*, Lawrence, University Press of Kansas.

Peters, J. (2004), 'Social responsibility is free. How good capitalism can co–exist with corporate social responsibility' in D. Crowther and L. Rayman–Bacchus (eds), *Perspectives on corporate social responsibility*, Aldershot: Ashgate, 205–216.

Peters, T.J. and Waterman, R.H. (1982), *In search of excellence*, New York: Harper & Row.

Pfeffer, J. and Salancik, G.R. (1978), *The external control of organizations: A resource dependence perspective*, New York: Harper & Row.

Phillips, N. (2002), 'Discourse or institution? Institutional theory and the challenge of critical discourse analysis' in R. Westwood and S. Clegg (eds), *Debating organization. Point–counterpoint in organization studies*, Oxford: Blackwell, 220–231.

Phillips, N., Lawrence, T.B. and Hardy, C. (2004), 'Discourse and institutions', *Academy of Management Review*, vol. 29, no. 4: 635–652.

Piper, A. (2000), 'Some have credit cards and others have giro cheques: "Individuals" and "people" as lifelong learners in late modernity', *Discourse & Society*, vol. 11, no. 4: 515–542.

Plesner, A.M. and Neergaard, P. (2005), 'Corporate financial and social performance. A contextual explanation of variations in corporate social performance', paper presented at the 3rd Conference on Performance Measurement and Management Control, Nice, 23–24 September.

Plihon, D. and Ponssard, J.–P. (eds), (2002), *La montée en puissance des fonds d'investissement. Quels enjeux pour les entreprises?* Paris: La Documentation Française.

Plihon, D., Ponssard, J.–P. and Zarlowski, P. (2001), 'Quel scénario pour le gouvernement d'entreprise? Une hypothèse de double convergence', *Revue d'économie financière*, no. 63: 35–51.

Poksinska, B., Dahlgaard, J.J. and Antoni, M. (2002), 'The state of ISO 9000 certification: A study of Swedish organizations', *The TQM Magazine*, vol. 14, no. 5: 297–306.

Poksinska, B., Dahlgaard, J.J., and Eklund, J. (2003), 'Implementing ISO 14000 in Sweden: Motives, benefits and comparisons with ISO 9000', *International Journal of Quality and Reliability Management*, vol. 20, no. 5: 585–606.

Pollock, T.G. and Rindova, V.P. (2003), 'Media legitimation effects in the market for initial public offerings', *Academy of Management Journal*, vol. 46, no. 5: 631–642.

Pondy, L.R. (1984), 'Union of rationality and intuition in management action', in S. Srivastva & Associates (eds), *The executive mind*, San Francisco: Jossey Bass: 161–191.

Ponssard, J.–P. (2004), 'Indicateurs de développement durable: Une analyse stratégique', *Les Echos*, 25 November: 5–6.

Porter, M.E. and Kramer, M.R. (2002), 'The competitive advantage of corporate philanthropy', *Harvard Business Review*, vol. 80, no. 12: 56–69.

Porter, M.E. and Van der Linde, C. (1995), 'Green and competitive: Ending the stalemate', *Harvard Business Review*, vol. 73, no. 5: 120–134.

Porter, T.M. (1994), 'Making things quantitative', in: M. Power (ed), *Accounting and science, natural inquiry and commercial reason*, New York: Cambridge University Press, 36–56.

Porter, T.M. (1996), *Trust in numbers: The pursuit of objectivity in science and public life*, Princeton: Princeton University.

Powell, W.W. and DiMaggio, P.J. (eds) (1991a), *The new institutionalism in organizational analysis*, Chicago: University of Chicago Press.

Powell, W.W. and DiMaggio, P.J. (1991b), 'Introduction', in W.W. Powell and P.J. DiMaggio (eds), *The new institutionalism in organizational analysis*, Chicago: University of Chicago Press, 1–38.

Powell, W.W., Gammal, D.L. and Simard, C. (2005), 'Close encounters: The circulation and reception of managerial practices in the San Francisco Bay Area non–profit community', in B. Czarniawska and G. Sevón (eds), *Global ideas. How ideas, objects and practices travel in the global economy*. Malmö: Liber AB, 233–258.

Power, M. (1996), 'Making things auditable', *Accounting, Organizations and Society*, vol. 21, no. 2–3: 289–315.

Power, M. (1997), *The audit society: Rituals of verification*, Oxford: Oxford University Press.

Power, M. (2003), 'Auditing and the production of legitimacy', *Accounting, Organizations and Society*, vol. 28, no. 4: 379–394.

Power, M. (2004). 'Counting, control and measurement: Reflections on measuring and management', *Human Relations*, vol. 57, no. 6: 765–783.

Prahalad, C.K. and Bettis, R.A. (1986), 'The dominant logic. A new linkage between diversity and performance', *Strategic Management Journal*, vol. 7, no. 6: 485–501.

Preston, L.E. and Post, J.E. (1975), *Private management and public policy: The principle of public responsibility*, Englewood Cliffs: Prentice–Hall.

Quazi, A.M. and O'Brien, D. (2000), 'An empirical test of a cross–national model of corporate social responsibility', *Journal of Business Ethics*, vol. 25, no. 1: 33–51.

Randall, D.M. (1988), 'Multiple roles and organizational commitment', *Journal of Organizational Behavior*, vol. 9, no. 4: 309–317.

Rayman–Bacchus, L. (2004), 'Assessing trust in, and legitimacy of, the corporate', in D. Crowther and L. Rayman–Bacchus (eds), *Perspectives on corporate social responsibility,* Aldershot: Ashgate, 21–41.

Rhenman, E. and Stymne, B. (1972), *Företagsledning i en föränderlig värld*. Stockholm: Aldus/Bonnier.

Richards, L. (1999), *Using NVivo in qualitative research*, Thousand Oaks: Sage.

Riordan, C., Gatewood, R. and Barnes Bill, J. (1997), 'Corporate image: Employee reactions and implications for managing corporate social performance', *Journal of Business Ethics*, vol. 16, no. 4: 401–412.

Risberg, A., Tienari, J. and Vaara, E. (2003). 'Making sense of a transnational merger: Media texts and the (re)construction of power relations', *Culture and Organization*, vol. 9, no. 2: 121–137.

Roberts, J. (2003), 'The manufacture of corporate social responsibility: Constructing corporate sensibility', *Organization*, vol. 10, no. 2: 249–265.

Rogers, P.S. (2000), 'CEO presentations in conjunction with earnings announcements. Extending the construct of organizational genre through competing values profiling and users–needs analysis', *Management Communication Quarterly*, vol. 13, no. 3: 426–485.

Rondinelli, D. and Vastag, G. (2000), 'Panacea, common sense, or just a label? The value of environmental management systems', *European Management Journal*, vol. 18, no. 5: 499–510.

Rosen, C.M. (2001), 'Environmental strategy and competitive advantage', *California Management Review*, vol. 43, no. 3: 8–15.

Rousseau, D. (1985), 'Issues of level in organizational research', in L.L. Cummings and B. Staw (eds), *Research in organizational behavior*, vol. 7, Greenwich: JAI Press, 1–37.

Rousseau, D. (1995), *Psychological contracts in organizations: Understanding written and unwritten agreements*, Thousand Oaks: Sage.

Røvik, K.A. (1996), 'Deinstitutionalization and the logic of fashion', in B. Czarniawska. and G. Sevón (eds), *Translating organizational change*, Berlin: Walter de Gruyter, 139–172.

Røvik, K.A. (1998), *Moderne organisasjoner*, Bergen: Fagbokforlaget.

Røvik, K.A. (2002), 'The secret of the winners: Management ideas that flow', in K. Sahlin–Andersson and L. Engwall (eds), *The expansion of management knowledge: Carriers, flows and sources*, Stanford: Stanford University Press, 113–144.

Rowley, T.J. and Berman, S. (2000), 'A brand new brand of corporate social performance', *Business & Society*, vol. 39, no. 4: 397–418.
Roy, S. (2003), 'Navigation in the knowledge era. Metaphors and stories in the construction of Skandia's Navigator', research report, Stockholm: Stockholm University School of Business.
Rubin, H.J. and Rubin, I.S. (1995), *Qualitative interviewing: The art of hearing data*, London: Sage.
Ruggie, J.G. (2004), 'Reconstituting the global public domain: Issues, actors, and practices', *European Journal of International Relations*, vol. 10, no. 4: 499–531.
Ruiz–Carrado, M.F., Palmer–Silveira, J.C. and Fortanet–Gómez, I. (2005), 'Discursive strategies in annual reports: The role of visuals', paper presented at the 7th European Convention of the Association for Business Communication, Copenhagen, Denmark, 26–28 May.
Rusconi, G. (1997), *Etica e impresa. Un'analisi economico–aziendale*, Padova: Clueb.
Sacconi, L. (1997), *Economia etica organizzazione*, Rome: Laterza.
Sahlin–Andersson, K. (1996), 'Imitating by editing success. The construction of organizational fields', in B. Czarniawska and G. Sevón (eds), *Translating organizational change*, Berlin: Walter de Gruyter, 62–92.
Sahlin–Andersson, K. and Engwall, L. (eds) (2002a), *The expansion of management knowledge: Carriers, flows and sources*, Stanford: Stanford University Press.
Sahlin–Andersson, K. and Engwall, L. (2002b), 'Carriers, flows, and sources of management knowledge', in K. Sahlin–Andersson and L. Engwall (eds), *The expansion of management knowledge: Carriers, flows and sources*, Stanford: Stanford University Press, 3–32.
Sahlin–Andersson, K. and Engwall, L. (2002c), 'The dynamics of management knowledge expansion', in K. Sahlin–Andersson and L. Engwall (eds), *The expansion of management knowledge: Carriers, flows and sources*, Stanford: Stanford University Press, 277–298.
Scarbrough, H. (2003), 'The role of intermediary groups in shaping management fashion. The case of knowledge management', *International Studies of Management & Organization*, vol. 32, no. 4: 87–103.
Schiebel, W. and Pöchtrager, S. (2003), 'Corporate ethics as a factor for success. The measurement instrument of the University of Agricultural Sciences (BOKU), Vienna', *Supply Chain Management–An International Journal*, vol. 8, no. 2: 116–121.
Schmidt, V.A. (2003), 'French capitalism transformed, yet still a third variety of capitalism', *Economy and Society*, vol. 32, no. 4: 526–554.
Schnietz, K.E. and Epstein, M.J. (2005), 'Exploring the financial value of a reputation for corporate social responsibility during a crisis', *Corporate Reputation Review*, vol. 7, no. 4: 327–345.
Schramm–Nielsen, J., Lawrence, P. and Sivesind, K.H. (2004), *Management in Scandinavia. Culture, context and change*, Cheltenham: Edward Elgar.
Schueth, S. (2003), 'Socially responsible investing in the United States', *Journal of Business Ethics*, vol. 43, no. 3: 189–194.
Scott, W.R. (1995), *Institutions and organizations*, Thousand Oaks: Sage.

Scott, W.R. and Meyer, J.W. (1992), *Organizational environments: Ritual and rationality*, Newbury Park: Sage.

Seelos, C. and Mair, J. (2005), 'Social entrepreneurship: Creating new business models to serve the poor', *Business Horizons*, vol. 48, no. 3: 241–246.

Segars, A.H. and Kohut, G.F. (2001), 'Strategic communication through the World Wide Web: An empirical model of effectiveness in the CEO's letter to shareholders', *Journal of Management Studies*, vol. 38, no. 4: 535–556.

Segerlund, L. (2005), 'Corporate social responsibility and the role of NGOs in the advocacy of new forms for transnational corporations', unpublished licentiate thesis, Stockholm: University of Stockholm.

Selsky, J.W., and Parker, B. (2005), 'Cross–sector partnerships to address social issues: Challenges to theory and practice', *Journal of Management*, vol. 31, no. 6: 849–873.

Selznick, P. (1949), *TVA and the grass roots. A study of politics and organization*, Berkely: University of California Press.

Sen, A. (1987), *On ethics and economics*, Oxford: Basil Blackwell.

Sen, S. and Bhattacharya, C.B. (2001), 'Does doing good always lead to doing better? Consumer reactions to corporate social responsibility', *Journal of Marketing Research*, vol. 38, no. 2: 225–243.

Sethi, S.P. (1972), 'The corporation and the church, institutional conflict and social responsibility', *California Management Review*, vol. 15, no. 1: 63–74.

Sethi, S.P. (1975), 'Dimensions of corporate social responsibility', *California Management Review*, vol. 17, no. 3: 58–64.

Sethi, S.P. (2003), 'Globalization and the good corporation: A need for proactive co–existence', *Journal of Business Ethics*, vol. 43, no. 1–2: 21–32.

Sims, R.R. and Brinkmann, J. (2003), 'Enron ethics (or: Culture matters more than codes)', *Journal of Business Ethics*, vol. 45, no. 3: 243–256.

Sinding, K. (2000), 'Environmental management beyond the boundaries of the firm: Definitions and constraints', *Business Strategy and the Environment*, vol. 9, no. 2: 79–91.

Sjöström, E. (2004), *Investment stewardship. Actors and methods for socially and environmentally responsible investments*, Copenhagen: The Nordic Partnership, in collaboration with the Stockholm School of Economics.

Skulstad, A.S. (2002), *Established and emerging business genres*, Kristiansand: Høyskoleforlaget.

Smith, N.C. (2003), 'Corporate social responsibility: Whether or how?' *California Management Review*, vol. 45, no. 4: 52–76.

Smith, W., Wokutch, R., Harrington, K. and Dennis, B. (2001), 'An examination of the influence of diversity and stakeholder role on corporate social orientation', *Business & Society*, vol. 40, no. 3: 266–294.

Sobczak, A. (2003), 'Codes of conduct in subcontracting networks: A labour law perspective', *Journal of Business Ethics*, vol. 44, no. 2: 225–234.

Solli, R., Demediuk, P. and Sims, R. (2005), 'The Namesake: On Best Value and Other Reformmarks', in B. Czarniawska and G. Sevón (eds), *Global ideas. How ideas, objects and practices travel in the global economy*, Malmö: Liber AB, 30–46.

Stanton, P.A. and Stanton, J. (2002), 'Corporate annual reports: Research perspectives used', *Accounting, Auditing and Accountability Journal*, vol. 15, no. 4: 478–500.

Steger, U. (2000), 'Environmental management systems: Empirical evidence and further perspectives', *European Management Journal*, vol. 18, no. 1: 23–37.

Stinchcombe, A.L. (1965), 'Social structure and organizations', in J.G. March (ed), *Handbook of organizations*, Chicago: Rand–McNally, 142–193.

Strang, D. and Meyer, J.W. (1993), 'Institutional conditions for diffusion', *Theory and Society*, vol. 22, no. 4: 487–511.

Stubbs, M. (1996), *Text and corpus analysis. Computer–assisted studies of language and culture*, Oxford: Blackwell.

Stubbs, M. (2002), *Words and phrases. Corpus studies of lexical semantics*, Oxford: Blackwell.

Sturdivant, F. and Ginter, J. (1977), 'Corporate social responsiveness: Management attitudes and economic performance', *California Management Review*, vol. 19, no. 3: 30–39.

Sturdivant, F., Ginter, J. and Sawyer, A. (1985), 'Managers' conservatism and corporate performance', *Strategic Management Journal*, vol. 6, no. 1: 17–38.

Suchman, M.C. (1995), 'Managing legitimacy. Strategic and institutional approaches', *Academy of Management Review*, vol. 20, no. 3: 571–610.

Suddaby, R. and Greenwood, R. (2001), 'Colonizing knowledge: Commodification as dynamic of jurisdictional expansion in professional service firms', *Human Relations*, vol. 54, no. 7: 933–953.

Suddaby, R. and Greenwood, R. (2005), 'Rhetorical strategies of legitimacy', *Administrative Science Quarterly*, vol. 50, no. 1: 35–67.

Swales, J.M. (1990), *Genre analysis: English in academic and research settings*, Cambridge: Cambridge University Press.

Swales, J.M. (2004), *Research genres: Explorations and applications*, Cambridge: Cambridge University Press.

Sydserff, R. and Weetman, P. (1999), 'A texture index for evaluating accounting narratives', *Accounting, Auditing & Accountability Journal*, vol. 12, no. 4: 459–488.

Tainio, R., Huolman, M., Pulkinen, M., Ali–Yrkkö, J. and Ylä–Anttila, P. (2003), 'Global investors meet local managers: Shareholder value in the Finnish context', in M.–L. Djelic and S. Quack (eds), *Globalization and Institutions: Redefining the Rules of the Economic Game*, Cheltenham: Edward Elgar, 37–56.

Taylor, F.W. (1929), *The principles of scientific management*, New York: Harper Row.

Testhuset Marknad Opinion (TEMO) (1990), 'Survey on general awareness of Ideas for Life', conducted on behalf of Skandia in November–December, 1990, FS–9048.

Thomas, J. (1997), 'Discourse in the marketplace: The making of meaning in annual reports', *Journal of Business Communication*, vol. 34, no. 1: 47–66.

Tienari, J., Vaara, E. and Ainamo, A. (2002), 'The emergence and legitimization of business journalism in Finland', paper presented at the 6th European Business History Congress, Helsinki, 22–24 August.

Tierney, W. (2003), 'Undaunted courage: Life history and the postmodern challenge', in N. Denzin and Y. Lincoln (eds), *Strategies of qualitative inquiry*, Thousand Oaks: Sage, 509–536.

Tilt, C.A. (2001), 'The content and disclosure of Australian corporate environmental policies', *Accounting, Auditing & Accountability Journal*, vol. 14, no. 2: 190–212.

Tinker, T. and Neimark, M. (1987), 'The role of annual reports in gender and class contradictions at General–Motors, 1917–1976', *Accounting, Organizations and Society*, vol. 12, no. 1: 71–88.

Tirole, J. (2001), 'Corporate governance', *Econometrica*, vol. 69, no. 1: 1–36.

Trompenaars, F. and Hampden–Turner, C. (1997), *Riding the waves of culture: Understanding cultural diversity in business*, London: Nicholas Brealey.

Tsang, E.W.K. (1998), 'A longitudinal study of corporate social reporting in Singapore. The case of the banking, food and beverages and hotel industries', *Accounting, Auditing & Accountability Journal*, vol. 11, no. 5: 624–635.

Tschopp, D.J. (2005), 'Corporate social responsibility: A comparison between the United States and the European Union', *Corporate Social Responsibility and Environmental Management*, vol. 12, no. 1: 55–59.

Tsui, A. and Milkovich, G. (1987), 'Personnel department activities: Constituency perspectives and preferences', *Personnel Psychology*, vol. 40, no. 3: 519–537.

Tuffrey, M. (1995), *Employees and the community*, London: PRIMA Europe.

Tuffrey, M. (1998), *Valuing employee community involvement*, London: The Corporate Citizenship Company.

Turban, D. and Greening, D. (1997), 'Corporate social performance and organizational attractiveness to prospective employees', *Academy of Management Journal*, vol. 40, no. 3: 658–672.

Ullman, A. (1985) 'Data in search of a theory: A critical examination of the relationships among social performance, social disclosure and economic performance', *Academy of Management Review*, vol. 10, no. 3: 540–557.

United Nations (UN) (2000), *UN Global Compact. A code of conduct for large companies*, New York: United Nations Secretary–General.

United Nations Conference on Trade and Development (UNCTAD) (1999), 'The social responsibility of transnational corporations', New York: United Nations.

Useem, M. (1998), 'Corporate leadership in a globalizing equity market', *Academy of Management Executive*, vol. 12, no. 4: 43–59.

Utting, P. (2000), Business responsibility for sustainable development, UNRISD Occasional Paper no. 2, Geneva: UN Research Institute for Social Development, <http://www.unrisd.org/80256B3C005BCCF9/(httpAuxPages)/1CA8A49E3513DE1C80256B610059BA0D/$file/utting.pdf>, accessed 24 August, 2006.

van Marrewijk, M. (2003), 'Concepts and definitions of CSR and corporate sustainability: Between agency and communion', *Journal of Business Ethics,* vol. 44, no. 2: 95–105.

van Oosterhout, J. and Heugens, P.P.M.A.R. (2007), 'Much ado about nothing. A conceptual critique of CSR', in A. Crane, A. McWilliams, D. Matten, J. Moon and D. Siegel (eds), *Oxford handbook of corporate social responsibility*, Oxford: Oxford University Press: in press.

Van Sell, M., Brief, A. and Schuler, R. (1981), 'Role conflict and role ambiguity: integration of the literature and directions for future research', *Human Relations*, vol. 34, no. 1: 43–71.

Ventresca, M.J. and Mohr, J.W. (2002), 'Archival research methods', in J.A.C. Baum (ed), *The Blackwell companion to organizations*, London: Blackwell Business, 805–828.

Vogel, D. (2005), *The market for virtue. The potential and limits of corporate social responsibility*, Washington (DC): Brookings Institution Press.

Votaw, D. (1973), 'Genius becomes rare', in D. Votaw and S.P. Sethi (eds), *The corporate dilemma. Traditional values versus contemporary problems*, Englewood Cliffs: Prentice Hall, 11–45.

Votaw, D. and Sethi, S. (1969), 'Do we need a new corporate response to a changing social environment?', *California Management Review*, vol. 12, no.1: 3–31.

Waddell, S. (2002), 'The Global Reporting Initiative: Building a corporate reporting strategy globally', Boston: Global Action Network Net.

Waddock, S. (2003), 'Myths and realities of social investing', *Organization & Environment*, vol. 16, no. 3: 369–380.

Waddock, S. (2004), 'Creating corporate accountability: Foundational principles to make corporate citizenship real', *Journal of Business Ethics*, vol. 50, no. 4: 313–327.

Waddock, S.A. and Graves, S.B. (1997), 'The corporate social performance–financial performance link', *Strategic Management Journal*, vol. 18, no. 4: 303–319.

Waddock, S.A. and Smith, N. (2000a), 'Corporate responsibility audits: Doing well by going good', *Sloan Management Review*, vol. 41, no. 2: 75–83.

Waddock, S.A. and Smith, N. (2000b), 'Relationships: The real challenge of corporate global citizenship', *Business and Society Review*, vol. 105, no. 1: 47–62.

Walgenbach, P. and Beck, N. (2002), 'The institutionalization of management approach in Germany' in K. Sahlin–Andersson and L. Engwall (eds), *The expansion of management knowledge: Carriers, flows and sources*, Stanford: Stanford University Press, 145–174.

Wated, G. and Sanchez, J.I. (2005), 'The effects of attitudes, subjective norms, attributions, and individualism–collectivism on managers' responses to bribery in organizations: Evidence from a developing nation', *Journal of Business Ethics*, vol. 61, no. 2: 111–127.

Weaver, G.P. (2001), 'Ethics programs in global businesses: Culture's role in managing ethics', *Journal of Business Ethics*, vol. 30, no. 1: 3–15.

Weick, K.E. (1976), 'Educational organizations as loosely coupled systems', *Administrative Science Quarterly*, vol. 21, no. 1: 1–19.

Werre, M. (2003), 'Implementing corporate responsibility. The Chiquita case', *Journal of Business Ethics*, vol. 44, no. 2–3: 247–260.

Westphal, J.D., Gulati, R. and Shortell, S.M. (1997), 'Customization or conformity? An institutional and network perspective on the content and consequences of TQM adoption', *Administrative Science Quarterly*, vol. 42, no. 2: 366–394.

Wettstein, F. and Waddock, S. (2005), 'Voluntary or mandatory: That is (not) the question: Linking corporate citizenship to human rights obligations for business', *Zeitschrift für Wirtschafts- und Unternehmensethik*, vol. 6, no. 3: 304–320.

Whetten, D.A., Rands, G. and Godfrey, P. (2002), 'What are the responsibilities of business to society?' in A. Pettigrew, H. Thomas and R. Whittington (eds), *Handbook of strategy and management*, London: Sage, 373–408.

Whitehouse, L. (2006), 'Corporate social responsibility: Views from the frontline', *Journal of Business Ethics*, vol. 63, no. 4: 279–296.

Whiteley, A. (1995), *Managing change: A core values approach*, Melbourne: Macmillan.

Whiteley, A. (2004), 'Grounded research: A modified grounded theory for the business setting', *Qualitative Research*, vol. 4, no. 3: 27–46.

Whitley, R. (1999), *Divergent capitalisms*, Oxford: Oxford University Press.

Wilden, A. (1987), *The rules are no game*, London: Routledge.

Williams, R. (1983), *Keywords. A vocabulary of culture and society*, New York: Oxford University Press.

Windsor, D. (2001), 'Corporate citizenship: Evolution and interpretation', in J. Andriof and M. McIntosh (eds), *Perspectives on corporate citizenship*, Sheffield: Greenleaf, 39–52.

Wodak, R. and Busch, B. (2004), 'Approaches to media texts', in J.D.H. Downing, D. McQuail, P. Schlesinger and E. Wartella (eds), *The Sage handbook of media studies*, Thousand Oaks: Sage, 105–123.

Wokutch, R.E. (1998), 'The evolution of social issues in management', *Business & Society*, vol. 37, no. 1: 113–125

Wokutch, R.E. (1990), 'Corporate social responsibility Japanese style', *Academy of Management Executive*, vol. 4, no. 2: 56–74.

Wood, D.J. (1991), 'Corporate social performance revisited', *Academy of Management Review*, vol. 16, no. 4: 691–718.

Wood, E. (2004a), 'Making sense of corporate volunteering: An exploration of the experience and impact of corporate volunteering on employees and their work roles', unpublished doctoral dissertation, Perth: Curtin University of Technology.

Wood, E. (2004b), '"What does this mean for me?" Has anyone thought how corporate citizenship impacts on the corporate citizen?', paper presented at the 20th EGOS Colloquium, Ljubljana, Slovenia, 1–3 July.

Wright, C. (2002), 'Promoting demand, gaining legitimacy and broadening expertise: The evolution of consultancy–clients relationship in Australia', in M. Kipping and L. Engwall (eds), *Management consulting: Emergence and dynamics of a knowledge industry*, Oxford: Oxford University Press, 184–202.

Yin, R.K. (2003), *Case study research. Design and methods* (third edition), Thousand Oaks: Sage.

Yuthas, K., Rogers, R. and Dillard, J.F. (2002), 'Communicative action and corporate annual reports', *Journal of Business Ethics*, vol. 41, no. 1–2: 141–157.

Zadek, S. (1998), 'Balancing performance, ethics, and accountability', *Journal of Business Ethics*, vol. 17, no. 13: 1421–1441.

Zadek, S. (2001), *The civil corporation: The new economy of corporate citizenship*, London: Earthscan Publications.

Zadek, S. (2004), 'The path to corporate responsibility', *Harvard Business Review*, vol. 82, no. 12: 125–132.

Zajac, E.J. (1990), 'CEO selection, succession, compensation and firm performance: A theoretical integration and empirical analysis', *Strategic Management Journal*, vol. 11, no. 3: 217–230.

Zbaracki, M.J. (1998), 'The rhetoric and reality of Total Quality Management', *Administrative Science Quarterly*, vol. 43, no. 3: 602–636.

Zucker, L.G. (1987), 'Institutional theories of organizations', *Annual Review of Sociology*, vol. 13: 443–464.

Zutshi, A. and Sohal, A. (2004), 'Environmental management system adoption by Australasian organisations. Part 1: Reasons, benefits and impediments', *Technovation*, vol. 24, no. 4: 335–357.

Index

AA1000 29, 80, 159-161, 165
Abrahamson, Eric 5, 15, 17, 18, 35, 36, 95, 139, 153, 188
accountability 26, 165, 182-184, 189
AccountAbility 161, 165
accounting 9, 36, 38, 39, 54, 56, 118, 149, 152, 154-156, 158, 160-162, 176, 185, 189, 193, 194, 197-200, 220
accounting system 194, 198, 199, 218
acquisition 59, 127, 128, 130, 134, 140, 183
action orientation 118, 119, 123, 124
action research 190
adaptation 96, 155-157, 160, 171, 216
agency (organization) 80, 118, 151, 152, 171, 175, 177-185, 191, 218
Agency Theory, agency/agent 95, 113-115, 123, 137, 176, 184
altruism, altruistic 99, 118, 120-124
American/US 9, 20-22, 29, 113, 129, 131, 137, 154, 168, 172, 180, 183, 206, 208, 210, 211, 218
Amnesty International 10
Anglo-Saxon 154, 167, 168, 170, 171, 174, 182, 184, 185
annual report 6, 53-60, 62, 65, 68, 70-72, 97, 171, 178, 205, 207, 208
Arese 171-173, 175, 177, 180, 182, 185, 186
Argyris, Chris 137, 140, 141, 143, 212
Audit / auditing 53, 84, 132, 133, 149, 154-156, 158, 160-162, 165, 179, 180, 199, 216-220, 223
award 22

banking, banking industry 36, 106, 176
Bansal, Pratima 81, 84-86
benefits 4, 7, 77-80, 82, 84-90, 121, 123, 207, 210, 215
Best Value 96
board 56, 59, 65, 97, 103, 171, 174, 179, 191, 194
Body Shop 26, 44
Bowen, Harold R. 4, 112, 187, 208, 209

British / Great Britain 15, 19-22, 29, 152, 161, 165, 183, 206, 213
Brunsson, Nils 140, 153, 184, 220
Brundtland Commission 39
business
　case 3, 42, 44, 45, 51, 77, 79, 80, 89, 104, 149, 152, 185
　ethics 1, 3, 11, 22, 24, 38, 39, 129, 134, 136, 137, 214
　in society 24, 26, 29
　practice 21, 77, 79, 137, 218
　press 3, 6, 15-18, 20, 29, 30, 169, 173, 206
　school 21, 35, 131, 173

Canada, Canadian 6, 56-61, 63-70, 130, 205, 207, 213
capitalism 5, 22, 55, 133, 137, 184, 208, 218
Carroll, Archie B. 1, 3, 4, 17, 33, 77, 112, 122, 152, 187
Callon, Michel 150, 218
capabilities 134
case-study 58, 77, 97, 127, 135, 185, 212
CEO 27, 37, 53-59, 62, 65, 66, 68, 70, 72, 97-101, 103, 106, 107, 111, 112, 120, 169, 172-174, 178, 182, 216
certification 84, 149, 150, 152, 155, 156, 165, 183, 188
CFP – Corporate Financial Performance, *see also performance* 77, 78
Christian Aid 4, 10
citizenship 116, 118, 121
civil society 1, 33, 44, 97, 210
code of conduct 1, 22, 42, 65, 78, 90, 134, 180, 212, 213, 224
Collective Agreement 129
commercialization 33, 34, 36, 38, 44, 48-51, 207
communist, system 143
community, communities 3, 10-12, 17, 21, 23, 27, 29, 30, 33, 34, 36, 39, 42, 48-50, 71, 77, 81, 86, 93, 95, 104,

115, 116, 120, 121, 123, 125, 131, 138, 151, 154, 168, 170, 180, 182, 186, 188, 191, 193, 206, 208, 209, 213, 215
company-solicited rating 175, 177-180, 182-183
competitive(ness) 3, 11, 21, 27, 28, 66, 79, 82, 86, 102, 108, 131, 133, 144, 174, 180
consultant 5, 6, 15, 27, 30, 33-51, 131, 149, 152, 153, 161, 190, 205-208, 221
consulting 36, 37, 39, 48, 149, 150, 152, 156, 161, 165, 168, 207
consumer, consumerism 15, 59, 60, 68, 69, 82, 85, 115, 159, 165, 168, 180, 212, 224
content analysis 19, 20, 54, 70, 118
context, contextual 4-7, 9, 17, 21, 22, 29, 34, 39, 54-58, 64, 66, 71-73, 78-80, 90, 95-97, 106-108, 112, 118, 128, 134, 138, 139, 141, 143, 149, 152, 153, 155, 156, 158, 162, 167-171, 181, 183-185, 205, 207, 208, 211-213, 216-218, 220-224
context, institutional 9, 112, 128, 138, 139, 143, 149, 158169, 171, 211-213, 217, 218
controllability 201
convergence 167
cooperation 39, 129, 151, 160, 163, 164, 181, 192, 198
Core Ratings 152, 173
corporation 1, 10-12, 17, 23, 24, 26, 30, 33, 34, 36, 37, 39, 40, 42-46, 49-51, 58, 59, 62, 68, 93, 94, 101, 103-105, 107, 108, 112, 115, 121, 122, 127-130, 132-138, 140, 141, 143-145, 152, 154, 161, 165, 168, 173, 177, 180, 207-210, 214-216
corporate
  citizen, citizenship 1, 3, 12, 21, 39, 40, 104, 111-113, 115-119, 121-125, 207, 213, 221
  governance 26, 41, 167-171, 175, 180, 183-185, 210
  responsibility, see also CSR 4, 10, 93, 97, 122
  social orientation 115
  social performance, see CSP

values 144
volunteering, see volunteering 111, 115-125, 213, 215
website 212
corpus 20, 22, 56, 57, 62, 64, 169
corruption 132, 136
cost and benefits 7, 77-79, 80, 85 88-90, 215
criticism 4, 25, 43, 82, 98
CSP – Corporate Social Performance 3, 46, 77, 78, 115, 136, 149-155, 168, 169, 183, 223, 224
CSR – Corporate Social Responsibility
  definitions 10, 168
  industry 149-151, 153-159, 161, 163-165, 213, 217, 218
  Europe 10
  market 149, 164, 185
Clegg, Stuart R. 114
Crowther, David 2, 209, 221
culture, cultural 16, 19, 55, 71-73, 96, 102, 103, 108, 113, 124, 127-129, 134-136, 138, 140-144, 154, 156, 161, 161, 190-193, 195-199, 208, 211, 213-215, 218, 219, 222
Czarniawska, Barbara 7, 17, 18, 35, 93-96, 107, 108, 141, 214

Davis, Keith 4 209-211
democratic practice 128
Denmark, Danish 79, 80, 82, 129
deregulation 9, 210
dialogue 11, 12, 42, 128, 132, 162, 186, 224
diffusion 6, 7, 17, 64, 71, 95, 109, 127-129, 133, 135, 136, 144, 153, 169, 171, 173, 181, 185, 289, 207
DiMaggio, Paul J. 17, 94, 95, 127, 128, 136, 153, 167, 188, 200
disclosure (rating ~/ information ~) 8, 21, 55, 168, 170, 175, 177-179, 182, 184
disembedded 95, 106-108
diversity 2, 9, 40, 41, 79, 104, 138, 139, 159, 160, 174, 223
Djelic, Marie-Laure 171, 185, 211
DJSI – Dow Jones Sustainability Index 86, 102, 125, 151
Drucker, Peter F. 112, 209
Dutch 11, 56-59, 62, 64-66, 68, 70, 205, 207
Donaldson, Thomas 184

EC – European Commission 11, 22, 40, 57, 78, 93, 133, 139, 188
eco-labeling 79-90
edited 6, 95, 128, 133, 139, 141, 215
Elkington, John 3
employee(s) 1, 7, 11-12, 18-ff., 41, 43, 59, 65-ff., 80-ff., 90, 97, 99, 102-ff., 111-ff., 132-136, 168, 170, 173-ff., 186, 206, 214-ff., 223-224
Elsbach, Kimberly D. 158, 220
EMS – environmental management systems 80, 82, 84, 87, 89, 90
England, English 57, 64, 65, 96, 130, 179
Engwall, Lars 7, 15, 18, 34-36, 94, 131, 168
Enron 25, 26, 28, 30, 44, 135, 137-138, 155
environment 6, 11, 23-24, 33, 35, 40-42, 53, 63, 65-ff., 80-ff., 93, 95, 104-ff., 127, 135, 139, 156, 158, 163, 175, 180, 192, 214, 216
    business 42, 45, 95
environmental
    accounting 152, 161
    audit 161
    impact 11, 77, 81, 101
    issue 11, 21, 23, 38-39, 46, 62, 65-66, 101-104, 107-108, 210
    management system, *see EMS*
    label 79-ff.
    performance 1, 65, 78, 81, 102
    report 66, 70, 101-108, 152, 156
    standard 4, 80, 85
espoused theory 133, 142-ff., 212
ethics 22, 27, 62-ff., 134-ff., 179-ff.
    business, corporate 1, 3, 11, 21-ff., 38-39, 129, 136-ff., 207, 214
ethical 6, 10, 22-ff., 42, 44, 54, 65, 103, 112, 127, 134-ff., 153, 184, 188, 193, 197-ff., 207, 216
Europe 9, 15, 23, 68, 71, 80, 96, 129, 144, 169, 187, 209, 211
EU – European Union 1, 22, 58, 68, 96, 102, 189
EU Flower 80
European 9, 19, 21, 23, 27, 29, 37, 64, 68, 96, 129, 152, 171, 172, 183, 185, 212
European Commission, *see EC*
European Union, *see EU*
EP – European Parliament 80

excellence 64
expatriate managers 135, 141-ff.

Fairclough, Norman 71
fashion 15, 34-36, 48, 95-97, 105, 107-109, 139, 188, 214
Ferone, Geneviève 152, 171-174, 176-178, 180-184
finance, financial 3, 8, 10, 11, 23, 26, 30, 33, 43, 51, 53-56, 59, 60, 62, 65, 66, 77, 78, 85, 86, 88-90, 93, 96, 97, 100, 101, 103, 104, 108, 117, 133, 136, 149
Financial Times 6, 15, 16, 18-31, 34, 205, 206, 208
Fombrun, Charles J. 81, 82
Frederick, William 112, 113
French (language) 57, 64
France / French 8, 130, 151, 152, 154, 167-174, 176-179, 181-185, 218
free market 4, 25, 162
Freeman, R. Edward xi, 3, 90, 124, 181, 184
Friedman, Milton 2-4, 33, 77, 187, 209, 211

genre 17, 19, 56, 59, 73
Global Compact 4, 12, 22, 39, 40, 80, 132, 139, 160, 164, 213
globalization 6, 9, 12, 22, 24, 53, 55, 67, 71, 77, 128, 130, 133, 167, 171, 206, 208, 210, 211, 218, 221
governance 11, 23, 158, 162, 170, 173, 174, 178, 183, 184, 186, 187
government 1, 3, 5-7, 10, 15, 21-25, 39, 40, 43, 69, 81, 82, 85, 97, 99, 103, 118, 132, 139, 159, 165, 174, 175, 191, 192, 209-211, 219
Greenwood, Royston 15, 17, 18, 20, 34-36, 51, 220
GRI – Global Reporting Initiative 1, 29, 71, 151, 152, 159, 160, 162, 164, 168

Halliday, M.A.K. 56
Heald, M. 208
Hemingway and MacLagan framework of corporate responsibility 121-124
history 28, 97, 124, 129, 130, 134, 138, 205, 206, 208, 215
Hofstede, Geert 127, 134, 135, 214

human resource 133, 158, 175, 180, 186, 197
human rights 4, 10, 23, 26, 132, 164, 175, 180, 182, 186
hypocrisy 4, 140, 141, 144, 153, 184, 220, 223

ideas 5, 6, 9, 17, 21, 24, 25, 27-29, 34-36, 38-41, 45, 46, 48-51, 53, 72, 93-96, 98, 102, 104, 105, 107, 108, 127-129, 131, 132, 137, 140-144, 149, 154, 167-169, 171, 173, 178, 180, 181, 183-186, 188, 195, 207, 209, 215, 217
Ideas for Life 93-95, 97-109, 213, 214
ideology, ideological 1, 44, 47, 50, 51, 127, 129, 132, 137, 138, 141-144, 214, 220
import 136
independence 44, 59, 103, 114, 150, 157, 159, 163-165, 169, 173, 174, 177, 179, 182, 184, 212, 221, 222
individual-level perspective on CSR 112
innovation 81, 85, 156, 157, 163, 168, 209, 210
    modular 154, 157, 161
institutional
    investors 171, 176, 177, 182, 184, 185
    theory 7, 8, 15, 35, 95, 128, 136, 138, 139, 144, 213
institutionalization 18, 20, 35, 72, 149, 150, 157-159, 163, 164, 177, 217
instrumental 4, 6, 9, 139, 159, 173, 181, 182, 184, 199, 200, 211, 224
insurance 8, 81, 93, 94, 96-102, 105, 106, 109, 152, 170, 213
interoperability 156, 157, 161, 217
internet 30, 37, 48
investor-solicited rating 172, 175-177, 180, 182-184
ISO – International Standards Organization 11, 149, 160, 162, 165
ISO 14001 79, 80, 82, 84, 90, 156
ISO 26000 159, 160, 162, 165
isomorphism 109, 127, 136, 137

Jensen, Michael 2, 77, 184

Kotler, Philip 34, 112

knowledge 7, 18, 36, 48, 79, 94, 99, 102, 108, 114, 122, 128, 129, 132, 134, 136, 137, 140-144, 150, 152, 157, 159-161, 163, 190, 193, 214
    dynamics 151, 154, 164
    management 94, 102, 108, 216

labeling schemes 78, 84, 85, 87, 213
language 5, 35, 44, 45, 54, 56, 57, 64, 65, 68, 70, 112, 114, 153, 165, 189, 221
language study/studies 54
leadership 134, 157, 160, 210
learning 8, 41, 128, 136, 137, 140-142, 144, 151, 153, 155, 157, 160-165, 180, 182, 183, 186
legislation 56, 81, 87
legitimacy 4, 6, 17, 18, 30, 35, 45, 50, 55, 71, 72, 86, 101, 103, 104, 128, 138, 139, 144, 149-151, 153, 157-164, 171, 197, 200, 207, 211, 214, 217, 218, 220, 221, 224
    social 5, 191, 216
legitimization 35, 96, 171
letter from the CEO / CEO letters 53/57, 59, 61, 62, 65, 66, 68, 70, 72
director's report 61, 62, 72
Levitt, Theodore 4, 209
lexicology, lexicological 6, 53, 54, 56, 58, 70-72

Mahon, John 78, 86, 152
Maignan, Isabelle 34, 71, 93, 212
management / managerial
    as cultural phenomenon 113
    decision 115, 117, 206
    fashion 15, 34, 95, 96, 105, 107-109, 139, 214
    ideas 17, 18, 30, 33-37, 39, 41, 42, 48-51, 94, 95, 128, 131, 144, 215
    hierarchy 118, 120
    models 6, 16, 121
    principles 127, 131, 132, 134, 214
    recipes 131, 137
    trend 15-18, 29, 30, 36, 94-96, 105-107, 214
    skills 86
    system 80-82, 84, 149, 153-156, 165, 186, 197
    tools 153

manager / managerial employee 5, 10, 18, 23, 24, 26, 28, 35, 36, 42, 55, 82, 85, 90, 95, 111-117, 122-125, 127, 129-132, 134-144, 151-153, 155-157, 172, 175, 177, 178, 181, 184, 187, 189, 191, 198, 206, 209, 210, 212, 214, 215, 216, 220, 222, 225
   non-managerial employee 7, 111, 113, 115-125, 215
   as mouthpiece of corporate experience 111
managerial focus of CSR literature 111, 118
Margolis, J.D. 3, 15, 33, 78, 93, 152, 176, 181, 185
marketing 21, 34, 44, 46, 56, 93, 115, 118, 121, 167, 185
Matten, Dirk 34, 206, 208, 212, 224
McWilliams, Abigail 59, 152, 215, 222
meaning 4, 5, 15-23, 25-31, 34, 40, 41, 44, 46, 51, 56, 57, 62, 64, 77, 78, 95, 107, 124, 129, 137, 138, 141, 186, 198, 205, 206, 211, 218, 221-223
measurement 5, 7, 8, 89, 90, 114, 140, 150-153, 155, 205, 215-219
media 6, 15, 17-19, 29, 30, 34, 35, 43, 57, 59, 60, 98, 103, 172, 181, 182, 191
merger 59, 127, 128, 130, 131, 134, 140, 182, 183
Meyer, John W. 17, 34-36, 95, 137, 139, 153, 188, 200, 220
Micheletti, Michele 15, 34
Moon, Jeremy 1, 2, 34, 127, 206, 208, 212
Morgan, Gareth 113, 114, 189
MOSES project 189-191, 193-198
multinational corporation, firm, *see also transnational corporation* 7, 25-27, 93, 96, 118, 127-129, 137, 139, 140, 145, 179, 187, 213-215

national business system 167, 168, 185, 213, 218
neo–institutional theory, s*ee institutional theory*
Netherlands 6, 56-61, 63, 65-70, 130, 176
network 38, 127, 131, 142, 173, 176
NPM – new public management 5, 17, 35, 189
NGO – non-governmental organization 3-5, 15, 22, 24, 34, 37, 39, 43, 44, 50, 69, 79, 81, 82, 93, 97, 99, 159, 162, 165, 175, 183, 210, 211, 219, 224
Notat, Nicole 173, 174, 178-181, 183, 184, 186
non-canonical 138, 143, 144
NPO – non-profit organization 187-189, 199-201, 218, 219
normative 17, 48, 50, 51, 55, 72, 95, 133, 134, 137, 158, 180-183, 224, 225
Norway 127, 129-131, 133

passion 102, 118, 120, 124
performance 23, 64, 65, 78, 86, 114, 116, 117, 133, 139, 140, 151, 153, 154, 156, 161, 165, 168, 171, 175, 176, 180, 181, 184, 186, 220-222
   corporate (financial), *see also CFP* 51, 55, 101, 108, 113, 115, 116, 215
   corporate social, *see CSP*
   environmental 1, 65, 78, 81, 102, 151, 156, 168, 186
   (corporate) financial, *see also CFP* 3, 33, 65, 78, 86, 89, 90, 93, 103, 115, 133, 136, 151, 152, 170, 173, 181, 184, 224
   non-financial 8
   social 1, 8, 12, 65, 78, 81, 86, 151, 156, 168, 186
   work 117
philanthropy (corporate) 39, 115, 116
Porter, Michael E. 77, 79, 85, 86, 216
post-modern 58, 114
Power, Michael 153, 155, 189, 199, 201, 218, 219, 220
power 1, 12, 25, 84, 113-115, 128, 138, 142, 157, 162, 209
   corporate 4, 11, 26, 43, 209, 210
   distance 135
   management 113, 114
   NGO 44
   social 209-211
price 11, 84, 86, 87, 88, 139, 154, 175
   premium 87-88
   stock, share 82, 100, 180, 186
Pro-Bono 98
public 1, 3, 8, 20-ff., 59, 65, 77, 82-ff., 160, 164, 188, 189, 191, 197, 210-212
   affairs 98, 103-104
   new public management, *see NPM*

opinion 17, 45, 98-99, 181-182
relations 36, 102, 115, 118, 169, 198
sector 9
Preston, L.E. 55, 184
Powell, W.W. 17, 18, 19, 35-36, 94-95, 114, 127, 128, 136, 153, 188, 200

quality 5, 11, 12, 64, 86, 104, 128, 131, 139, 152, 155, 176, 186, 189, 195, 216, 220, 222
circles 16, 18, 35, 131
(total) quality management, *see TQM*
rating 8, 115, 149-ff., 167-ff., 216, 223
agency 8-9, 151-ff., 167-ff., 217
recipe 50, 131, 133, 137, 139
organizational 128, 137, 144, 215
report
annual, *see annual report*
CSR, environmental, social, sustainability 29, 49, 66, 70, 77, 101-ff., 171, 175, 205, 219
reporting 1, 8, 22, 23, 48, 93, 150
CSR, environmental, non-financial, social 8, 9, 21, 42, 54, 59, 65-66, 84, 150-ff., 190, 205, 207, 211-212, 218
system 78, 152, 155, 205, 213, 216-ff.
standard 8, 72, 217, 219
reputation 5, 23, 43, 86, 118, 139, 176, 188, 200
corporate 18, 26-27, 115
damage 43
rhetoric 8, 15, 20, 24-ff., 30, 35, 49-ff., 108, 112, 123-125, 151, 162, 207, 211, 221
strategies 28, 34-35, 38, 42-ff., 207, 220
risk 23, 25-28, 43-44, 59, 86, 114, 140, 151, 161, 163, 178, 180-182, 186, 199, 206, 213, 223
analysis 42, 180
management 26-28, 98-ff., 214
role theory 7, 116
Rowan, B. 95, 137, 153, 188, 200, 220

Sahlin-Andersson, Kerstin 7, 15, 17, 18, 34, 35, 36, 94, 95-96, 107, 128, 168
scandal 25, 27, 28, 103, 220
corporate 39, 103
Enron 26, 28, 44, 137
post-scandal credibility 220

Scandinavia, Scandinavian 80, 129, 143, 144, 214
way of conducting business, Model 128, 133
Scott, W. Richard 128, 137, 139
Seattle 22
self-regulation 3-4, 10, 55, 58, 210
Sethi, S. Pakrash 111, 112, 113, 187
semantic field 57, 62, 64-ff., 70
shareholder 3, 11, 24, 25, 26, 55, 64-ff., 77, 137, 168-ff., 184, 186, 211, 225
model 170
value 2, 3, 78, 180, 185, 206, 209, 225
wealth 77
Siegel, Donald S. 59, 152, 215, 222
Sigma Project (Sustainability Integrated Guidelines for Management) 159-162, 165
Skandia 8, 60, 93-ff., 213, 214
SME – small- and medium-sized enterprise 78, 80, 84, 89
social capital 183
SRI – Socially Responsible Investment 149, 171-ff., 176-ff., 184
stakeholder 2-3, 7, 8, 11, 23, 24, 30, 44, 54, 55, 58, 62, 64-65, 68-ff., 79, 82-ff., 111, 124, 152, 158-ff., 180-181, 184, 192-ff., 212-ff., 218-ff.
claim, demand, expectation 3, 8, 43, 50, 79, 84, 154, 158, 183, 216
management 3, 42, 159, 181, 183, 219, 224
pressure 7, 212-213
model, theory, view 90, 169-170, 184, 218
standardization 41, 46, 57, 154, 157-ff., 216-218
Stubbs, Michael 56, 57, 71
subsidiary 7, 104, 127-ff., 140-ff., 174, 178, 179, 209, 214-215
Suchman, Mark 149, 151, 153, 158, 162, 212
Suddaby, Roy 15, 17, 18, 20, 34-ff., 51, 220
SustainAbility 152
sustainability 3, 6, 11, 22-ff., 33, 38-ff., 45, 62, 63, 66, 86, 101-ff., 125, 151, 162, 164, 177
report, reporting 66, 151, 152, 161, 162, 164-ff., 175

sustainable 11, 12, 22-ff., 66, 151, 161, 186
  development 10, 12, 94, 101-ff., 158, 164, 167, 171-ff., 183-ff., 214
Swan Label 80
Sweden 6, 34, 37-ff., 48, 56-ff., 96-ff., 129, 207, 213
Swedish 8, 33, 37, 39-ff., 54, 56-ff., 64-ff., 93, 96-ff., 205, 207, 208
Swedish (language) 57

Taylor, Frederic 113, 114, 253
technical 136, 139, 159, 160, 176, 199
  feasibility 217-218
  system 150-151, 153-156, 163
  requirements 16
technology 85
  cleaner 84
text 5, 15, 17-ff., 23, 26-ff., 54-ff., 56-ff., 95
  analysis 18, 20, 27, 30, 61
theorization 17
TQM – Total Quality Management 5, 16, 35, 81, 131, 139, 143, 156
trade union 6, 128, 162, 171, 174, 179, 209
transfer of knowledge 114, 134, 136
transfer of values 130, 136
translation 7, 9, 18, 93-ff., 102, 105-ff., 131, 167, 205, 217
TNC – transnational corporation, *see also multinational corporation* 7, 10, 12, 23, 24, 29
transparency 1, 11, 26, 161, 173, 178, 183-184, 219, 224
trend 2, 17, 59, 62, 65, 70, 72, 93-ff., 97, 104-ff., 137, 171, 205, 216-217
  managerial, management, *see management trend* 15-ff., 29-30, 36, 96, 105-107, 214
trust 26, 98, 104, 132, 139, 143, 153, 158, 219

UN – United Nations 1, 4, 10, 12, 22, 29, 39, 40, 57, 71, 132, 139, 162, 164, 168, 181
UNCED – United Nations Conference on Environment and Development 39

UNCTAD – United Nations Conference on Trade and Development 12, 254
UNEP – United Nations Environment Programme 164
UN Global Compact, *see Global Compact*
UN Human Development Index 58
USA – United States of America 9, 21, 58, 64, 68, 71, 102, 131, 135, 137, 173, 176, 206, 208, 209, 211, 212

value 3, 7, 19, 21-ff., 40-ff., 49, 77, 85, 102-ff., 113, 118-ff., 186, 187, 191, 195-ff., 211, 217
  brand 82, 86
  chain 154
  creation 11, 170, 180, 185
  instrumental 4, 159
  shareholder, *see shareholder value*
values 21, 55-56, 62-ff., 65, 95, 112-ff., 122-ff., 127-ff., 158, 168, 182-ff., 193, 199, 214, 224
Vigeo 152, 169, 171-ff., 218
Vogel, David 3, 19, 77, 79, 89, 149, 168, 176, 185, 215
Volunteering 118, 120, 121, 123
  corporate 111, 115-117, 118-121, 122, 124, 213, 215
  non-managerial perspective on 118

Waddock, Sandra A. 3, 33, 34, 77, 111, 133, 222
Walsh, J.P 3, 15, 33, 78, 93, 152, 176, 181, 185
WCED – World Commission on Environment and Development 39
WBCSD – World Business Council for Sustainable Development 12, 101
Welfare 3, 26, 77, 96, 192, 209, 210, 212, 214
  state 58, 209-210
Wokutch, Richard E. 112, 212
WTO – World Trade Organization 22

Zadek, Simon 1, 34, 93, 108, 188